Lecture Notes in Computer Science 10835

Commenced Publication in 1973
Founding and Former Series Editors:
Gerhard Goos, Juris Hartmanis, and Jan van Leeuwen

Editorial Board

More information about this series at http://www.springer.com/series/7407

Peter Korošec · Nouredine Melab
El-Ghazali Talbi (Eds.)

Bioinspired Optimization Methods and Their Applications

8th International Conference, BIOMA 2018
Paris, France, May 16–18, 2018
Proceedings

 Springer

Editors
Peter Korošec
Computer Systems Department
Jožef Stefan Institute
Ljubljana
Slovenia

El-Ghazali Talbi
University of Lille
Lille
France

Nouredine Melab
University of Lille
Lille
France

ISSN 0302-9743   ISSN 1611-3349   (electronic)
Lecture Notes in Computer Science
ISBN 978-3-319-91640-8   ISBN 978-3-319-91641-5   (eBook)
https://doi.org/10.1007/978-3-319-91641-5

Library of Congress Control Number: 2018942348

LNCS Sublibrary: SL1 – Theoretical Computer Science and General Issues

Printed on acid-free paper

This Springer imprint is published by the registered company Springer International Publishing AG
part of Springer Nature
The registered company address is: Gewerbestrasse 11, 6330 Cham, Switzerland

Preface

BIOMA is one of the major scientific events focusing on the progress of the area of bioinspired optimization methods and their applications. As in the seven previous editions, BIOMA 2018 provided an opportunity to the international research community in bioinspired optimization to discuss recent research results and to develop new ideas and collaborations in a friendly and relaxed atmosphere. But this year, BIOMA was organized for the first time outside Slovenia, namely, in Paris, France. This event was part of the SYNERGY project that has received funding from the European Union's Horizon 2020 research and innovation program under grant agreement no. 692286.

BIOMA 2018 welcomed talks that cover various aspects of bioinspired optimization research such as new algorithmic developments, high-impact applications, new research challenges, theoretical contributions, implementation issues, and experimental studies. BIOMA 2018 strived for a high-quality program that was complemented by several invited talks and special sessions.

The call for papers resulted in a total of 69 submissions including 53 long papers and 16 short papers. Each submitted long paper was assigned to three members of the Program Committee for review, with short papers assigned to two reviewers. Based on the review process, 27 long papers were accepted for presentation and inclusion in the LNCS proceedings. In addition, eight short papers were accepted as posters. The long papers made up a strong program which was completed by three keynotes from Prof. Yaochu Jin (University of Surrey, UK), Prof. Swagatam Das (Indian Statistical Institute, Kolkata, India) and Prof. Celso C. Ribeiro (Universidade Federal Fluminense, Brazil). The accepted papers are from 18 countries: Algeria, Brazil, Canada, Chile, Czech Republic, Finland, France, Germany, India, Japan, Mexico, Portugal, Slovenia, Spain, Switzerland, Turkey, Uruguay, and USA.

We would like to thank all the contributors for the success of the BIOMA 2018 conference, in particular the members of the Program Committee for their careful review of the papers and useful feedback to the authors. Our special thanks go to the three keynote speakers, the members of the Organizing Committee, and the publicity chairs.

May 2018
Peter Korošec
Nouredine Melab
El-Ghazali Talbi

Organization

BIOMA 2018 was organized by the University of Lille, France, and the Jožef Stefan Institute, Slovenia.

Conference Chair

El-Ghazali Talbi   University of Lille, France

Program Chairs

Peter Korošec   Jožef Stefan Institute, Slovenia
Nouredine Melab   University of Lille, France

Publicity Chairs

Grégoire Danoy (Europe)   University of Luxembourg, Luxembourg
Hatem Masri (Middle East)   University of Bahrain, Sakhir, Bahrain
Sergio Nesmachnow   Universidad de la República, Uruguay
  (Latin America)
Méziane Aider (Africa)   USTHB, Algiers, Algeria

Social Networks

Jernej Zupančič   Jožef Stefan Institute, Slovenia

Organizing Committee

Rachid Ellaia   METAH Society, Morocco
Amir Nakib   University of Paris-Est, France
Omar Abdelkafi   University of Lille, France
Oumayma Bahri   University of Lille, France
Sohrab Faramarzi Oghani   Inria Lille, France
Jan Gmys   University of Mons, Belgium

Program Committee

Omar Abdelkafi   University of Lille, France
Mathieu Balesdent   ONERA, France
Ahcène Bendjoudi   CERIST, Algeria
Maria J. Blesa   Universitat Politécnica de Catalunya - BarcelonaTech,
                                    Spain

Contents

XII   Contents

Optimization of Home Care Visits Schedule by Genetic Algorithm

Filipe Alves[1](✉), Ana I. Pereira[1,2], Adília Fernandes[3], and Paulo Leitão[1]

[1] Research Centre in Digitalization and Intelligent Robotics (CeDRI),
Instituto Politécnico de Bragança, Campus de Santa Apolónia,
5300-253 Bragança, Portugal
{filipealves,apereira,pleitao}@ipb.pt
[2] Algoritmi R&D Centre, University of Minho, Braga, Portugal
[3] Instituto Politécnico de Bragança, Campus de Santa Apolónia,
5300-253 Bragança, Portugal
adilia@ipb.pt

Abstract. Currently, it has been verified that population is increasingly aged and it is necessary to perform home services. These services include home care visits to patients with impossibility of travel to healthcare centers, where the health professionals perform the medical treatments. Usually, this home care services are performed by nurses that need transportation for this purpose. Therefore, it is necessary to make a schedule of these home care visits that, usually, is made manually by the healthcare center. This work aims to carry out an automatic schedule of home care visits of the healthcare Center of Bragança, Portugal, in order to reduce the travel costs and optimize the time spent on trips. The Genetic Algorithm was used to solve this problem. In this paper it is presented the schedule of home care visits for three days of the healthcare center.

Keywords: Optimization · Schedule · Home care · Genetic algorithm

1 Introduction

Home Health Care (HHC) is increasingly important for the current society [1]. In Portugal, for example, there is a high number of older people that need support on theirs homes, so the home health care services are very important on these cases. For many of these people it is impossible to travel to hospitals, healthcare centers, laboratories, among other health services, due to many reasons, for example, their limited mobility, the high distance of health local, or even their homes are in isolated areas without public transportation. Thus, the Home care services are performed by the National Health System since it is economically advantageous to keep people at home instead of providing them a hospital bed [2]. So, these elderly/sick people need to perform the necessary treatments in their homes, so the health professionals need to travel to patients' residences to perform all the requested treatments [3].

© Springer International Publishing AG, part of Springer Nature 2018
P. Korošec et al. (Eds.): BIOMA 2018, LNCS 10835, pp. 1–12, 2018.
https://doi.org/10.1007/978-3-319-91641-5_1

To solve this issue, it is necessary to analyze the support needed for home care services to better perform the management of these services. According to studies already carried out, optimization strategies contributes to improve the Home Health Care services in many different ways [4–6]. Some reviews highlight a large number of papers from the Operational Research community and their main subject is the optimization of the daily planning of health care services. Recently, Nickel et al. [2] propose a heuristic to address the medium-term and short-term planning problem. In the literature, the routing problem is largely tackled as a "Travelling Salesman Problem (TSP)" approach for designing the caregiver's route using MILP [7] and/or heuristic [8] approaches for a static, deterministic problem. In this context, the Portuguese public health system includes two types of units: Hospitals and Healthcare Centers. The Healthcare Centers are closer to the population since they follow up their patients, continuously, and the home care services are performed by nurses teams of these units. The aim of this work consists in solving a common problem of Healthcare Centers: produce a daily vehicles schedule of a Healthcare Center where the health professionals (nurses) spent the minimum time to perform all home care visits (considering the travel and treatment patient time).

The paper is organized as follows: Sect. 2 gives a global framework, the description of the real problem and its formulation, and presents the real data collected. The Sect. 3 presents the Genetic Algorithm, the global method chosen to solve the problem. The numerical results are presented in the Sect. 4. Finally, the last scheduling presents the conclusions and future work.

2   Global Framework and Problem Definition

In this context, the global architecture of the HHC system must integrate computational support. Thus, the problem was solved sequentially using the architecture presented in Fig. 1.

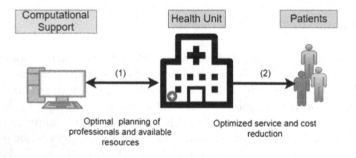

Fig. 1. Developed architecture

The first step (1), allows to connect the computational support with the informations from Health Unit, in particularly, the list of patients, human and physical resources, among other data, allow to obtain the planning of routes for a certain day of work, that is, the optimal route, instead the manual scheduling.

The second step (2) places the optimized routes into action, allowing the reduction of time spent and reduction of costs for the service.

The Healthcare Centers have a set of vehicles that are used to perform home care visits by the nurses. The Healthcare Center of Bragança (HCB) has, at maximum, five vehicles to perform home care visits for each day. Currently, the vehicles schedule of the HCB is done manually. So, the aim of this work is to produce a vehicles schedule in order to obtain the minimum total spent time to perform all home care visits by the nurses of HCB.

To solve this problem, and considering the information given by HCB, it was considered:

- 15 min for the trip, in the same city or locality, to visit different patients.
- The trips duration between the different locations is known.
- The list and the duration of the treatments are known for each patient (defined and given by Health National Unit).
- The number of patients that need home care, and assigned to a working day, is known in advance and does not change during that day.
- Patient's care activities cannot be performed at the same time or overlap.
- All trips begin and end up at the Healthcare Center.

2.1 Problem Formulation

Taking into account all the above information for a working day, it was also considered the following parameters for a given day: NP represents the total number of patients that need of home care and NC is the total number of vehicles used for home care visits. Other general information is needed to obtain the final formulation, such us:

- The locations of all patients.
- The time matrix that presents the travel time needed between different locations.
- Vehicles that perform home care visits is known in advance.
- The vehicle characteristics (in the same vehicle, the maximum number of travel persons is seven, hence can transport more than one team).
- Each vehicle carries nurses responsible for certain activities. Therefore, there is no interchangeability among caregivers for care activities.
- In general, each patient will be visited by a specific nurse. In some specific cases, a set of patients can be visited by the same nurse (explained later).

Consider the vector $\mathbf{x} = (p_1, ..., p_{NP}, c_1, ..., c_{NP})$ where the patient p_i will be visited by the vehicle c_i, for $i = 1, ..., NP$, and $\mathbf{x} \in \{1, \cdots, NP\}^{NP} \times \{1, \cdots, NC\}^{NP}$.

For a given $\mathbf{x}$ it is possible to define the vehicles schedule and the function $S^l(\mathbf{x})$, $l = 1, .., NC$, that represents the total time needed to perform all visits of the vehicle l, considering the vector $\mathbf{x}$. The objective function is defined as

$$f(\mathbf{x}) = \max_{l=1,...,NC} S^l(\mathbf{x}) \tag{1}$$

which represents the maximum time spent by all vehicles to perform all the visits. Then the constrained optimization problem will be defined as

$$\min f(\mathbf{x}) \tag{2}$$

where $\mathbf{x} = (p_1, ..., p_{NP}, c_1, ..., c_{NP})$ with $p_i \in \{1, ..., NP\}$ and $c_j \in \{1, ..., NC\}$; all the patients need to be treated $\cup_{i=1}^{P} p_i = \{1, ..., NP\}$ and the number of nurses in each vehicle trip is less or equal to seven.

To solve the minimization problem presented previously, Genetic Algorithm (GA) was used and it is presented in Sect. 3.

2.2   Real Data

The Healthcare Center of Bragança provided three typical working days in April 2016. The data used were available by the Healthcare Center of Bragança (chosen by the institution and simulated a normal working day). In these days, the HCB had:

- On the day $1 - 4$ vehicles available to perform the home care visits, 31 patients who require home-based treatments from 12 different locations.
- On the day $2 - 5$ vehicles available to perform home care visits, 25 patients who require home-based treatments from 5 different locations.
- On the day $3 - 5$ vehicles available to home care visits, 22 patients who require home-based treatments from 9 different locations.

The home care services provided by the nurses, can be classified into five different treatments (or home care visits) presented in Table 1. This information was provided by HCB, where the number of treatment was assigned depending on the type of treatment, described in Table 1.

Analyzing the Table 1, it is verified that the treatments are different and have different times between them. Each of these treatments will be considered for each patient according to the needs (information provided by the Health Center). It becomes necessary to know all the locations of all the patients for the vehicles scheduling.

Table 2 presents all patients locations for the three days (and the corresponding abbreviation) and the spent time between two locations (in minutes). As it was stated before, it was assigned 15 min to travel at the same location.

The values presented in Table 2 are based on the data provided by the HCB. As mentioned previously, it is also necessary to know the treatments list of the patients for the three days in study.

Table 1. Full characterization of the different treatments provided by the nurses

Treatment	Description	Characterization	Time (min)
1	Curative	Treatments, for example, pressure ulcer, venous ulcer, surgical wounds, traumatic wounds, ligaments, remove suture material, burns, evaluation and dressing of wound dressings	30
2	Surveillance and rehabilitation	Evaluation, implementation and patient monitoring	60
3	Curative and surveillance	Wound treatment, watch over bandage, frequency and tension monitoring, teach and instruct the patient of the complications and pathologies	75
4	Surveillance	Assess risk of falls, self-care, patient behaviors and still the providers knowledge. Monitor, height, tension and heart rate. Patients dietary and medical regimen	60
5	General	Evaluate, support and teach about mourning	60

Table 2. Data about travel times between different locations (in minutes)

	A	Bg	B	C	Cl	E	G	M	Ml	Mo	O	P	Pi	Rl	Rb	Rd	S	Sm	Sd	Sp
Alfaião (A)	15	24	16	28	35	25	16	22	21	18	20	29	25	21	26	18	24	15	30	32
Bragada (Bg)	24	15	22	33	30	31	27	34	31	16	30	26	15	32	15	19	15	20	16	17
Bragança (B)	16	22	15	25	33	17	16	16	18	16	17	29	23	18	25	15	23	15	29	31
Carrazedo (C)	28	33	25	15	44	24	31	39	39	26	38	39	32	35	33	23	34	24	37	42
Coelhoso (Cl)	35	30	33	44	15	42	38	44	29	19	19	17	17	43	31	29	29	30	36	21
Espinhosela (E)	25	31	17	24	42	15	24	18	34	25	33	37	32	26	34	24	32	25	37	40
Gimonde (G)	16	27	16	31	38	24	15	20	18	21	22	32	29	19	29	21	27	17	33	35
Meixedo (M)	22	34	16	39	44	18	20	15	31	27	29	40	35	17	37	27	34	23	39	42
Milhão (Ml)	21	31	18	39	29	34	18	31	15	23	15	36	31	27	33	27	31	21	36	39
Mós (Mo)	18	16	16	26	19	25	21	27	23	15	24	15	16	26	15	16	19	15	18	21
Outeiro (O)	20	30	17	38	19	33	22	29	15	24	15	27	31	27	32	26	30	20	36	38
Parada (P)	29	26	29	39	17	37	32	40	36	15	27	15	19	38	27	25	25	36	31	23
Pinela (Pi)	25	15	23	32	17	32	29	35	31	16	31	19	15	34	15	20	16	21	21	19
Rabal (Rl)	31	32	18	35	43	26	19	17	27	26	27	38	34	15	34	24	32	22	38	40
Rebordaínhos (Rb)	26	15	25	33	31	34	29	37	33	15	32	27	15	34	15	22	16	20	19	20
Rebordãos (Rd)	18	19	15	23	29	24	21	27	27	16	26	25	20	24	22	15	20	15	25	28
Salsas (S)	24	15	23	34	29	32	27	34	31	19	30	25	16	32	16	20	15	20	15	15
Samil (Sm)	15	20	15	24	30	25	17	23	21	15	20	36	21	22	20	15	20	15	26	28
Sendas (Sd)	30	16	29	37	36	37	33	39	36	18	36	31	21	38	19	25	15	26	15	17
Serapicos (Sp)	32	17	31	42	21	40	35	42	39	21	38	23	19	40	20	28	15	28	17	15

The list of treatments for each patient on days 1, 2 and 3, is:

- Day 1: the patients 1, 2, 3, 4, 8, 9, 10, 11, 12, 13, 14, 17, 19, 22, 23 and 24 need treatment 1, the patients 5, 6 and 7 need treatment 2, the patient 15 and 20 requires treatment 3, the patients 16, 21, 25, 26, 27, 28, 29, 30 and 31 need treatment 4 and the patient 18 requires treatment 5. There are some patients that have the same nurse. It is the case of patient 11 and 13; patient 4 and 22; patient 17 and 23; and patient 1 and 12.
- Day 2: the patients 3, 16, 17, 21, 22, 23, 24 and 25 need treatment 1, the patients 2, 8, 9 and 11 need treatment 2, the patients 4, 5, 10, 12, 13, 14, 15 and 18 need treatment 3, the patients 1, 19 and 20 requires treatment 4 and the patients 6 and 7 need treatment 5. In this day there are two pairs of patients that have the same nurse, that is the case of patient 3 and 16; and patient 21 and 25.
- Day 3: the patients 1, 2, 3, 6, 7, 8, 9, 17, 21 and 22 need treatment 1, the patients 4 and 5 requires treatment 2, the patients 13 and 14 need treatment 3, the patients 11, 12, 15, 16, 18, 19 and 20 need treatment 4 and the patient 10 requires treatment 5. The patients 16 and 18 must be visit by the same nurse.

Based on all the presented data, the main objective is to obtain the vehicles schedule, in order to minimize the total spent time needed to perform the trips, the treatments and return to the starting point, HCB.

3   Genetic Algorithm

Initially proposed by Holland [9], GA inspired by the natural biological evolution, uses a population of individuals to apply genetic procedures: crossover between two different individuals or/and mutation in one individual.

The values of the control parameters used in GA were adjusted to a suitable experience of the problem, i.e. it was considered a population size (Ps) and concerning the probability of the procedures (crossover and mutation), 50% rate was selected. Is expected that the following population (next generation) of individuals has a better capability. The algorithm repeats the crossover and mutation procedures in new populations until the desired diversity of solutions is performed [10,11].

The method applied in this work is summarized by the following Algorithm.

Algorithm 1. Genetic Algorithm

1: Generates a randomly population of individuals, $\mathcal{P}^0$, with dimension N_{pop}. Set $k = 0$.
2: **while** stopping criterion is not met **do**
3:      Set $k = k + 1$.
4:      $\mathcal{P}' =$ Apply crossover procedure in population $\mathcal{P}^k$.
5:      $\mathcal{P}'' =$ Apply mutation procedure in population $\mathcal{P}^k$.
6:      $\mathcal{P}^{k+1} = N_{pop}$ best individuals of $\{\mathcal{P}^k \cup \mathcal{P}' \cup \mathcal{P}''\}$.
7: **end while**

Details related to the algorithm implementation can be seen in [12]. The iterative procedure terminates after a maximum number of iterations (NI) or after a maximum number of function evaluations (NFE).

4 Numerical Results

The HCB also provides us the vehicles schedule, performed manually, that is, without any mathematical model or subject to computational mechanisms. Thus, for the days 1, 2 and 3, respectively, will be presented in the Tables 3, 4 and 5.

It was presented the real vehicles schedule used in the reference working days to compare the improvement. Each patient is visited by one nurse. In some specific situations there are a set of patients that will be visit for the same nurse

Table 3. HCB schedule for day 1

Vehicles scheduling in the health unit					
Vehicles					
1	HCB - B	P(1) - T.1	B - P	P(2) - T.1	P - B	P(3) - T.1
	P(4) - T.1	P(5) - T.2	B - Rb	P(6) - T.2	Lunch	Rb - B
	P(7) - T.2	B - M	P(22) - T.1	M - B	P(12) - T.1	P(24) - T.1
	B - Bg	P(25) - T.4	Bg - HCB			
2	HCB - C	P(8) - T.1	C - E	P(9) - T.1	E - B	P(10) - T.1
	B - Rd	P(11) - T.1	Rd - B	P(13) - T.1	B - S	P(14) - T.1
	S - HCB	Lunch				
3	HCB - B	P(15) - T.3	B - Sp	P(16) - T.4	Sp - P	P(17) - T.1
	P - B	P(18) - T.5	Lunch	B - O	P(19) - T.1	O - B
	P(20) - T.3	P(21) - T.4	P(23) - T.1	B - HCB		
4	HCB - B	P(26) - T.4	P(27) - T.4	P(28) - T.4	P(29) - T.4	Lunch
	B - MI	P(30) - T.4	P(31) - T.4	MI - HCB		

Table 4. HCB schedule for day 2

Vehicles scheduling in the health unit					
Vehicles					
1	HCB - B	P(1) - T.4	P(8) - T.2	P(19) - T.4	B - HCB	Lunch
2	HCB - B	P(2) - T.3	B - Rd	P(4) - T.3	Rd - G	P(5) - T.3
	Lunch	G - B	P(6) - T.5	P(7) - T.5	B - HCB	
3	HCB - CI	P(9) - T.2	P(10) - T.3	P(11) - T.2	P(12) - T.3	Lunch
	P(13) - T.3	P(14) - T.3	P(15) - T.3	CI - HCB		
4	HCB - B	P(16) - T.1	P(17) - T.1	P(18) - T.3	P(20) - T.4	B - G
	P(23) - T.1	Lunch	G - B	P(3) - T.1	B - HCB	
5	HCB - RI	P(21) - T.1	RI - B	P(22) - T.1	P(24) - T.1	B - Rd
	P(25) - T.1	Rd - HCB	Lunch			

Table 5. HCB shedule for day 3

Vehicles scheduling in the health unit						
Vehicles						
1	HCB - B	P(1) - T.1	P(2) - T.1	P(3) - T.1	P(19) - T.4	P(20) - T.4
	B - HCB	Lunch				
2	HCB - E	P(4) - T.2	E - B	P(5) - T.2	P(6) - T.1	P(7) - T.1
	B - Rd	P(8) - T.1	Rd - HCB	Lunch		
3	HCB - P	P(9) - T.1	P - Rd	P(10) - T.5	Rd - A	P(11) - T.4
	P(12) - T.4	A - HCB	Lunch			
4	HCB - B	P(13) - T.3	B - Sm	P(14) - T.3	Sm - B	P(15) - T.4
	P(16) - T.4	Lunch	B - Sd	P(18) - T.4	Sd - HCB	
5	HCB - Sd	P(17) - T.1	Sd - Mo	P(21) - T.1	Mo - MI	P(22) - T.1
	MI - HCB	Lunch				

(as was described previously). It is also possible to conclude that the maximum spent time by the vehicles was 694, 651 and 448 min for each day (without the lunchtime), respectively, as show Tables 3, 4 and 5.

Regarding the identification of patients and treatments, P(1) - T.1 represents Patient 1 who needs Treatment 1. For example, the schedule of the vehicle 1 for day 3 will be: begin the trip in HCB to Bragança to execute the home care visit of Patients 1, 2, 3, all with treatment 1, and then, still in the same locality, visits patient 19 and 20 (both need treatment 4). Finished, return to HCB for lunch.

For the computational results it was used the Matlab Software, version 2015a, running in a computer with a processor Intel (R) Core (TM) i5 2.40 GHz CPU with 4.0 GB of memory RAM.

In this work, the Genetic Algorithm (GA) was used to produce the vehicles schedule with the minimum spent time (not considering the lunchtime). For the population size, it was considered $Ps = 30$ individuals, the maximum number of function evaluation was fixed at $NFE = 5000$ and the maximum number of iterations as $NI = 100$.

Since GA is a stochastic method, it was performed 100 runs to solve the problem. Table 6 presents the GA overall performance, such as: the best solution obtained in all runs (f^*_{min}), the solution average (f^*_{avg}), and finally, the average time to solve the optimization problem (Time$_{avg}$) in seconds.

Table 6. Summary of GA results

	f^*_{min}	f^*_{avg}	Time$_{avg}$
Day 1	545	573	24
Day 2	498	510	20
Day 3	333	333	15

Table 7. Optimal vehicles schedules using GA for day 1

Vehicles Schedule using GA

Vehicles						
1	HCB - B	P(10) - T.1	P(12) - T.1	P(1) - T.1	P(15) - T.3	B - Rb
	P(6) - T.2	Lunch	Rb - P	P(2) - T.1	P - B	P(29) - T.4
	P(26) - T.4	B - HCB				
2	HCB - B	P(21) - T.4	P(5) - T.2	B - P	P(17) - T.1	P - B
	P(23) - T.1	P(3) - T.1	Lunch	B - MI	P(31) - T.4	MI - E
	P(9) - T.1	E - C	P(8) - T.1	C -HCB		
3	HCB - B	P(28) - T.4	P(20) - T.3	B - M	P(22) - T.1	M - B
	P(4) - T.1	P(27) - T.4	Lunch	B - Bg	P(25) - T.4	Bg - B
	P(18) - T.5	B - HCB				
4	HCB - MI	P(30) - T.4	MI - B	P(7) - T.2	B - Sp	P(16) - T.4
	Sp - B	P(24) - T.1	Lunch	B - Rd	P(11) - T.1	Rd - B
	P(13) - T.1	B - S	P(14) - T.1	S - O	P(19) - T.1	O - HCB

Analyzing the numerical results presented in the previous table, it is possible to verify that the total time found by GA for the different days, is less than the times planned manually. The first solution with the shortest total time was chosen as the final result. The average of the solutions is slightly higher in the first two days and the same on the third day, that is, optimized planning has almost always been found. In each run was always found solutions. Finally, the average time to solve the problem was always less than 24 s, i.e. very fast.

Consequently, the GA obtains the vehicles schedule for each working day. The Table 7 presents the vehicle schedule obtained by the algorithm for day 1. It is possible to conclude that the maximum spent time is 545 min.

In our problem only the effective time spent with the home care visits is considered by the Healthcare Center, excluding lunchtime. The same happens for the remaining computational results.

For the day 2, it was obtained the vehicles schedule presented in Table 8, that has 498 min to perform all the home care visits.

Finally, for the day 3 was collected a vehicles schedule with a maximum time spent by vehicles of 333 min, as it is possible to see in Table 9.

In order to conclude and for a better perception of the illustrated results, it will be presented the following example of home visits made by vehicle 1 on day 3. Thus, the vehicle 1 starts the route at the Healthcare Center (HCB) to Parada, provides care to Patient 9 (Treatment 1), then travels of Parada to Bragança, to provide care to Patient 19 (Treatment 4). After travel to Alfaião, takes care of Patient 11 (Treatment 4) and then travels again to Sendas to provide care to Patient 17 (Treatment 1). Finally, returns of Sendas to the point of origin (HCB) to end the home visits and have the lunchtime.

Table 10 presents a comparison of the maximum time spent by each vehicle, using GA, and the time provided by the HCB.

Table 8. Optimal vehicles schedules using GA for day 2

Vehicles schedule using GA						
Vehicles						
1	HCB - CI	P(14) - T.3	P(11) - T.2	P(15) - T.3	CI - B	P(19) - T.4
	Lunch	P(17) - T.1	B - HCB			
2	HCB - B	P(1) - T.4	P(7) - T.5	P(20) - T.4	B - CI	P(12) - T.3
	CI - HCB	Lunch				
3	HCB - G	P(5) - T.3	G - B	P(24) - T.1	B - CI	P(10) - T.3
	CI - B	P(6) - T.5	Lunch	B - CI	P(13) - T.3	CI - HCB
4	HCB - B	P(8) - T.2	P(3) - T.1	P(16) - T.1	B - Rd	P(4) - T.3
	Rd - B	P(18) - T.3	B - HCB	Lunch		
5	HCB - RI	P(21) - T.1	RI - Rd	P(25) - T.1	Rd - B	P(2) - T.3
	B - CI	P(9) - T.2	CI - G	P(23) - T.1	Lunch	G - B
	P(22) - T.1	B - HCB				

Table 9. Optimal vehicles schedules using GA for day 3

Vehicles schedule using GA						
Vehicles						
1	HCB - P	P(9) - T.1	P - B	P(19) - T.4	B - A	P(11) - T.4
	A - Sd	P(17) - T.1	Sd - HCB	Lunch		
2	HCB - B	P(20) - T.4	B - Rd	P(10) - T.5	Rd - A	P(12) - T.4
	A - B	P(6) - T.1	P(7) - T.1	B - HCB	Lunch	
3	HCB - B	P(2) - T.1	B - Rd	P(8) - T.1	Rd - B	P(1) - T.1
	B - MI	P(22) - T.1	MI - B	P(13) - T.3	B - HCB	Lunch
4	HCB - Mo	P(21) - T.1	Mo - E	P(4) - T.2	E - Sm	P(14) - T.3
	Sm - B	P(5) - T.2	B - HCB	Lunch		
5	HCB - B	P(15) - T.4	B - Sd	P(18) - T.4	Sd - B	P(16) - T.4
	P(3) - T.1	B - HCB	Lunch			

Table 10. Maximum time spent (minutes) by each vehicle on home care visits

	Vehicles		
	Day 1	Day 2	Day 3
HCB	694	651	448
GA	545	498	333

Comparing the results with the vehicles schedule provided by the HCB it is possible to conclude that the GA obtained vehicles schedule with a reduction (approximately 30%) of the maximum spent time to perform all the home visits.

The numerical results show more than an optimal solution, needing a few seconds for find them. GA, had 100% of successful rate since they found a feasible solution in all runs. While the manual process takes a long time, since they are complex cases and without optimization tests, it is possible to verify that the average time to solve the problem is quickly and allows several solutions.

5   Conclusions and Future Work

The home care visits are usually planned manually and without any computer support in HCB, this implies that the solution obtained may not be the best one, in addition to the process being complex and taking a higher time consuming. So, in an attempt to optimize the process, it is necessary to use strategies to minimize the maximum time spent by each vehicle on home care routes, without, however, worsening the quality of the provided services and, always, looking for the best schedules organization. In this paper, the scheduling problem of HCB was solved successfully using GA method, needing few seconds to find the problem solution.

This approach represents a gain for all entities involved, as health professionals and patients.

For future work, it is possible to reformulate the problem and take into account the multi-objective approach to minimize the total time spent by all vehicles. Another approach may be the use of multi-agent for real-time simulation.

Acknowledgements. The authors thank IICB, Bragança, Portugal. This work has been supported by COMPETE: POCI-01-0145-FEDER-007043 and FCT - Fundação para a Ciência e Tecnologia, Portugal, within the Project Scope: UID/CEC/00319/2013.

References

1. Benzarti, E., Sahin, E., Dallery, Y.: Operations management applied to home care services: analysis of the districting problem. Decis. Support Syst. **55**(2), 587–598 (2013)
2. Nickel, S., Schröder, M., Steeg, J.: Mid-term and short-term planning support for home health care services. Eur. J. Oper. Res. **219**(3), 574–587 (2012)
3. Rest, K.D., Hirsch, P.: Supporting urban home health care in daily business and times of disasters. IFAC-PapersOnLine **48**(3), 686–691 (2015)
4. Liu, R., Xie, X., Augusto, V., Rodriguez, C.: Heuristic algorithms for a vehicle routing problem with simultaneous delivery and pickup and time windows in home health care. Eur. J. Oper. Res. **230**(3), 475–486 (2013)
5. Rasmussen, M.S., Justesen, T., Dohn, A., Larsen, J.: The home care crew scheduling problem: preference-based visit clustering and temporal dependencies. Eur. J. Oper. Res. **219**(3), 598–610 (2012)
6. Sahin, E., Matta, A.: A contribution to operations management-related issues and models for home care structures. Int. J. Logistics Res. Appl. **18**(4), 355–385 (2015)
7. Kergosien, Y., Lenté, C., Billaut, J.C.: Home health care problem: an extended multiple traveling salesman problem. In: Proceedings of the 4th Multidisciplinary International Scheduling Conference: Theory and Applications, pp. 85–92 (2009)

8. Redjem, R., Marcon, E.: Operations management in the home care services: a heuristic for the caregivers routing problem. Flex. Serv. Manuf. J. **28**(1–2), 280–303 (2016)
9. Holland, J.H.: Adaptation in Natural and Artificial Systems: An Introductory Analysis with Applications to Biology, Control, and Artificial Intelligence. MIT press, Cambridge (1992)
10. Ghaheri, A., Shoar, S., Naderan, M., Hoseini, S.S.: The applications of genetic algorithms in medicine. Oman Med. J. **30**(6), 406 (2015)
11. Kumar, M., Husian, M., Upreti, N., Gupta, D.: Genetic algorithm: review and application. Int. J. Inf. Technol. Knowl. Manag. **2**(2), 451–454 (2010)
12. Bento, D., Pinho, D., Pereira, A.I., Lima, R.: Genetic algorithm and particle swarm optimization combined with Powell method. In: AIP Conference Proceedings, vol. 1558, pp. 578–581 (2013)

New Techniques for Inferring L-systems Using Genetic Algorithm

Jason Bernard$^{(\boxtimes)}$ and Ian McQuillan

Department of Computer Science, University of Saskatchewan, Saskatoon, Canada
jason.bernard@usask.ca, mcquillan@cs.usask.ca

Abstract. Lindenmayer systems (L-systems) are a formal grammar system that iteratively rewrites all symbols of a string, in parallel. When visualized with a graphical interpretation, the images have been particularly successful as a concise method for simulating plants. Creating L-systems to simulate a given plant manually by experts is limited by the availability of experts and time. This paper introduces the Plant Model Inference Tool (PMIT) that infers deterministic context-free L-systems from an initial sequence of strings generated by the system using a genetic algorithm. PMIT is able to infer more complex systems than existing approaches. Indeed, while existing approaches can infer D0L-Systems where the sum of production successors is 20, PMIT can infer those where the sum is 140. This was validated using a testbed of 28 known D0L-system models, in addition to models created artificially by bootstrapping larger models.

Keywords: L-systems · Inductive inference · Genetic algorithm
Plant modeling

1 Introduction

Lindenmayer systems (L-systems), introduced in [1], are a formal grammar system that produces self-similar patterns that appear frequently in nature, and especially in plants [2]. L-systems produce strings that get rewritten over time in parallel. Certain symbols can be interpreted as instructions to create sequential images, which can be visually simulated by software such as the "virtual laboratory" (vlab) [3]. Such simulations are useful as they can incorporate different geometries [2], environmental factors [4], and mechanistic controls [5], and are therefore of use to simulate and understand plants. L-systems often consist of small textual descriptions that require little storage compared to real imagery. Certainly also, they can produce a simulation extremely quickly with low cost computers in comparison to actually growing a plant.

An L-system is denoted by a tuple $G = (V, \omega, P)$, which consists of an alphabet V (a finite set of allowed symbols), an axiom ω that is a word over V, and

---

This research was supported in part by a grant from the Plant Phenotyping and Imaging Research Centre.

P. Korošec et al. (Eds.): BIOMA 2018, LNCS 10835, pp. 13–25, 2018.
https://doi.org/10.1007/978-3-319-91641-5_2

a finite set of productions, or rewriting rules, P. A deterministic context-free L-system or a D0L-system, has exactly one rule for each symbol in V of the form $A \rightarrow x$, where $A \in V$ (the predecessor) and x is a word over V (the successor, denoted by $succ(A)$). Words get rewritten according to a derivation relation, $\Rightarrow$, whereby $A_1 \cdots A_n \Rightarrow x_1 \cdots x_n$, where $A_i \in V, x_i$ is a word, and $A_i \rightarrow x_i$ is in P, for each i, $1 \leq i \leq n$. Normally, one is concerned with derivations starting at the axiom, $\omega \Rightarrow \omega_1 \Rightarrow \omega_2 \Rightarrow \cdots \Rightarrow \omega_n$. The sequence $(\omega_1, \ldots, \omega_n)$ is known as the developmental sequence of length n.

One common alphabet for visualization is the turtle graphics alphabet [2], so-called as it is imagined that each word generated contains a sequence of instructions that causes a turtle to draw an image with a pen attached. The turtle has a state consisting of a position on a (usually) 3D grid and an angle, and the common symbols that cause the turtle to change states and draw are: F (move forward with pen down), f (move forward with pen up), $+$ (turn left), $-$ (turn right), $[$ (start a branch), $]$ (end a branch), $\&$ (pitch up), $\wedge$ (pitch down), $\backslash$(roll left), $/$ (roll right), $|$ (turn around 180°). For branching models, $[$ causes the state to be pushed on a stack and $]$ causes the state to be popped and the turtle switches to it. It is assumed that the right hand side of rewriting rules have parantheses that are properly nested. Additional symbols are added to the alphabet, such as A and B, to represent the underlying growth mechanics. The "Fractal Plant" L-system is inferred commonly [6,7] and so is shown here as an example: $G = (\{X, F\}, X, \{X \rightarrow F[+X]F[-X] + X, F \rightarrow FF\})$. After 7 generations, "Fractal Plant" can produce the image in Fig. 1 after 7 generations. More realistic 3D models may be produced with extensions of D0L-systems.

Fig. 1. Fractal plant after 7 generations [2].

A difficult challenge is to determine an L-system that can accurately simulate a plant. In practice, this often involves manual measurements over time, scientific knowledge, and is done by experts [8]. Although this approach has been successful, it does have notable drawbacks. Producing a system manually requires an expert that are in limited supply, and it does not scale to producing arbitrarily many models. Furthermore, the more complex plant models require a priori knowledge of the underlying mechanics of the plant, which are difficult and time consuming to acquire. To address this, semi-automated (used as an aide for the expert) [9,10], and fully automated approaches [6,7], have been introduced to find an L-system that matches observed data. This approach has the potential to scale to constructing thousands of models, and also has the potential to expose biomechanics rather than requiring its knowledge beforehand.

The ultimate goal of this research is to automatically determine a model from a sequence of plant images over time. An intermediate step is to infer the model from a sequence of strings used to draw the images. This is known as the inductive inference problem, defined as follows. Given a sequence of strings $\alpha = (\omega_1, \ldots, \omega_n)$, find a D0L-system, or if it exists, $G = (V, \omega, P)$ such that $\omega = \omega_0 \Rightarrow \omega_1 \Rightarrow \cdots \Rightarrow \omega_n$ where α is the developmental sequence of length n.

This paper introduces the Plant Model Inference Tool (PMIT) that aims to be a fully automated approach to inductive inference of L-systems. Towards that goal, PMIT uses a genetic algorithm (GA) to search for an L-system to match the words produced. This paper presents a different encoding scheme than previous approaches, and shows that it is more effective for inferring D0L-systems. Additionally, some logical rules based on necessary conditions are used as heuristics to shrink the solution space. Between these two techniques, it is determined that PMIT is able to infer L-systems where the sum of the production successors is approximately 140 symbols in length; whereas, other approaches are limited to about 20 symbols. Moreover, the testbed used to test PMIT is significantly larger than previous approaches. Indeed, 28 previously developed D0L-systems are used, and for these systems that PMIT properly inferred, it did so in an average of 17.762 s. Furthermore, additional (in some sense "artificial") models are created by combining the existing models where the combined length of the successors is longer than 140 symbols (which PMIT does not solve), and then randomly removing "F" symbols until it can solve them. This work can be seen as a step towards the goal of 3D scanning a plant over time, converting the images into strings that describe how to draw them, then inferring the L-system from the sequence of strings.

The remainder of this paper is structured as follows. Section 2 describes some existing automated approaches for inferring L-systems. Section 3 describes the logical rules used to shrink the solution space, and Sect. 4 discusses the genetic algorithm. Section 5 will discuss the methodology used to evaluate PMIT and the results. Finally, Sect. 6 concludes the work and discusses future directions. Some details are omitted due to space constraints, but appear online [11].

2   Background

This section briefly describes some notation used throughout the paper, contains a brief description of genetic algorithms since they are used as the search mechanism here, then describes some existing approaches to L-system inference.

An alphabet is a finite set of symbols. Given an alphabet V, a word over V is any sequence of letters written $a_1 a_2 \cdots a_n$, $a_i \in V, 1 \leq i \leq n$. The set of all words over V is denoted by V^*. Given a word $x \in V^*$, $|x|$ is the length of x, and $|x|_A$ is the number of A's in x, where $A \in V$. Given two words $x, y \in V^*$, then x is a substring of y if $y = uxv$, for some $u, v \in V^*$ and in this case y is said to be a superstring of x. Also, x is a prefix of y if $y = xv$ for some $v \in V^*$, and x is a suffix of y if $y = ux$ for some $u \in V^*$.

The GA is an optimization algorithm, based on evolutionary principles, used to efficiently search N-dimensional (usually) bounded spaces [12]. In evolutionary biology, increasingly fit offspring are created over successive generations by intermixing the genes of parents. An encoding scheme is applied to convert a problem into a virtual genome consisting of N genes. Each gene is either a binary, integer, or real value and represents, in a problem specific way, an element of the solution to the problem. One common type of encoding is a real mapped encoding, where the genes have a real value from 0 and 1 and different ranges within are mapped contextually [12]. This encoding works best when the options at each step of the problem are unknown or dependent on prior choices.

The GA functions by first creating an initial population (P) of random solutions. Each member of the population is assessed using a problem specific fitness function. Then the GA, controlled by certain parameters, performs a selection, crossover, mutation, and survival step until a termination condition is reached. In the selection step, a set of pairs of genomes are selected from the population with odds in proportion to their fitness, i.e. preferring more fit genomes. During the crossover step, for each selected pair, a random selection of genes are copied between the two; thereby, producing two offspring. Each gene has a chance of being swapped equal to the control parameter *crossover weight*. The mutation step takes each offspring and randomly changes zero or more genes to a random value with each gene having a chance of being mutated equal to the *mutation weight*. Then each offspring is evaluated using the fitness function. The offspring are placed into the population and genomes are culled until the population is of size P again. Usually, the most fit members are kept (elite survival). The termination condition may be based on such criteria as finding a solution with sufficient fitness, or hitting a pre-determined maximum number of generations.

Various approaches to L-system inference were surveyed in [13]. There are several different broad approaches towards the problem: building by hand [2,8], algebraic approaches [6,14], using logical rules [6], and search approaches [7]. Since PMIT is a hybrid approach incorporating a search algorithm, GA, together with logical rules to reduce intractability by shrinking the search space, this section will examine some existing logic-based and search-based approaches.

Inductive inference has been studied theoretically (without implementation) by several authors [13], e.g. Doucet [14]. He devised a method that uses solutions to Diophantine equations to, in many cases, find a D0L-system that starts by generating the input strings. A similar approach was implemented with a tool called LGIN [6] that infers L-systems from a single observed string ω. They devise a set of equations that relate the number of each symbol observed in ω to the linear combination of the production values in the growth matrix.

LGIN is limited to two symbol alphabets, which is still described as "immensely complicated" [6], and was evaluated on six variants of "Fractal Plant" [2] and had a peak execution time of four seconds.

Runqiang et al. [7] propose to infer an L-system from an image using a GA. Each gene is encoded to represent a symbol in each successor. The fitness function matches the candidate system to the observed data using image processing. Their approach is limited to an alphabet size of 2 and a maximum total length of all successors of 14. Their approach is 100% successful for a variant of "Fractal Plant" [2] with $|V| = 1$, and has a 66% success rate for a variant of "Fractal Plant" [2] with $|V| = 2$. Although they do not list timings, their GA converged after a maximum of 97 generations, which suggests a short runtime.

3   PMIT Methodology for Logically Deducing Facts About Successors

In this section, the methodology that is used by PMIT to reduce the size of the solution space with heuristics—all of which are based on necessary conditions for D0L-systems—will be described. Indeed, the success and efficiency of a search algorithm is generally tied to the size of the solution space. As all these conditions are mathematically true, this guarantees that a correct solution is in the remaining search space (if there is a D0L-system that can generate the input). In PMIT, logical rules are used to reduce the dimensional bounds in two contexts. The first context is to determine a lower bound ℓ and upper bound u on the number of each symbol B produced by each symbol A for each $A, B \in V$, henceforth called growth of B by A. Thus, two programming variables $(A, B)_{min}$ and $(A, B)_{max}$ are created that change such that $(A, B)_{min} \leq |succ(A)|_B \leq (A, B)_{max}$. A second context is a separate lower ℓ and upper bound u on the length of each successor for each $A \in V$. Then, two programming variables A_{min} and A_{max} are used such that $A_{min} \leq |succ(A)| \leq A_{max}$ and their values improve as the program runs. The bounds on growth and on lengths depend on each other, so all the rules are run in a loop until the bounds stop improving.

For this paper, it is assumed that if a turtle graphic symbol has an identity production (e.g. $+ \rightarrow +$), then this is known in advance. Typically, these symbols do have identity productions. There are some instances where "F" may not, (some variants of "Fractal Plant" [2]). In such a case, "F" is treated as a non-turtle graphics symbol for the purposes of inferring the L-system. Also, all successors are assumed to be non-empty, which are commonly used in practice when developing models [2]. This implies that A_{min} is initialized to 1 for each $A \in V$. For each turtle symbol $T \in V$, $T_{min} = T_{max} = 1$, $(T, T)_{min} = (T, T)_{max} = 1$ and $(T, A)_{min} = (T, A)_{max} = 0$ for every $A \in V, A \neq T$.

3.1   Deducing Growth

Consider input $\alpha = (\omega_0, \ldots, \omega_n)$, $\omega_i \in V^*$, $0 \leq i \leq n$ with alphabet V. Deduction of growth in PMIT is based on two mechanisms; the first being the determination of so-called *successor fragments*, of which there are four types.

- A word ω is an A-subword fragment if ω must be a subword of $succ(A)$.
- A word ω is an A-prefix fragment if ω must be a prefix of $succ(A)$.
- A word ω is an A-suffix fragment if ω must be a suffix of $succ(A)$.
- A word ω is an A-superstring fragment if ω must be a superstring of $succ(A)$.

As PMIT runs, it can determine additional successor fragments, which can help to deduce growth. Certain prefix and suffix fragments can be found for the first and last symbols in each input word by the following process. Consider two words such that $\omega_1 \Rightarrow \omega_2$. It is possible to scan ω_1 from left to right until the first non-turtle graphics symbol is scanned (say, A, where the word scanned is αA). Then, in ω_2, PMIT skips over the graphical symbols in α (since each symbol in α has a known identity production), and the next A_{min} symbols, β, (the current value of the lower bound for $|succ(A)|$) must be an A-prefix fragment. Furthermore, since branching symbols must be paired and balanced within a successor, if a [symbol is met, the prefix fragment must also contain all symbols until a matching] symbol is met. Similarly, an A-superstring fragment can be found by skipping α symbols, then taking the next A_{max} symbols from ω_2 (the upper bound on $|succ(A)|$). If a superstring fragment contains a [symbol without the matching] symbol, then it is reduced to the symbol before the unmatched [symbol. Then, lower and upper bounds on the growth of B by A ($(A, B)_{min}$ and $(A, B)_{max}$) for each $B \in V$ can be found by counting the number of B symbols in any prefix and superstring fragments respectively and changing them if the bounds are improved. For a suffix fragment, the process is identical except from right to left starting at the end of ω_1. An example of this process appears in [11].

The second mechanism for deduction of growth is based on calculating the number of times each symbol $A \in V$ appears in word ω_i above the number implied from ω_{i-1} together with the current values of each lower bound $(B, A)_{min}$, for each $B \in V$. Formally, a programming variable for the *accounted for growth* of a symbol $A \in V$ for $1 \le i \le n$, denoted as $G_{acc}(i, A)$ is:

$$G_{acc}(i, A) := \sum_{B \in V} (|\omega_{i-1}|_B \cdot (B, A)_{min}). \tag{1}$$

The *unaccounted for growth* for a symbol A, denoted as $G_{ua}(i, A)$, is computed as $G_{ua}(i, A) := |\omega_i|_A - G_{acc}(i, A)$.

Then, $(B, A)_{max}$ is set (if it can be reduced) under the assumption that all unaccounted for A symbols are produced by B symbols. Furthermore, $(B, A)_{max}$ is set to be the lowest such value computed for any word from 1 to n, where B occurs, as any of the n words can be used to improve the maximum. And, $|succ(B)|_A$ must be less than or equal to $(B, A)_{min}$ plus the additional unaccounted for growth of A divided by the number of B symbols (if there is at least one; also the floor function is used since $|succ(B)|_A$ is a positive integer) in the previous word, as computed by

$$(B, A)_{max} := \min_{\substack{1 \le i \le n, \\ |\omega_{i-1}|_B > 0}} \left((B, A)_{min} + \left\lfloor \frac{G_{ua}(i, A)}{|\omega_{i-1}|_B} \right\rfloor \right). \tag{2}$$

An example is presented in [11].

Once $(B, A)_{max}$ has been determined for every $A, B \in V$, the observed words are re-processed to compute possibly improved values for $(B, A)_{min}$. Indeed for each (B, A), if $x := \sum_{\substack{C \in V \\ C \ne B}} (C, A)_{max}$, and $x < |\omega_i|_A$, then this means that $|succ(B)|_A$ must be at least $\left\lceil \frac{|\omega_i|_A - x}{|\omega_{i-1}|_B} \right\rceil$, and then $(B, A)_{min}$ can be set to this value if its bound is improved. For example, if ω_{i-1} has 2 A's and 1 B, and ω_i has 10 A's, and $(A, A)_{max} = 4$, then at most two A's produce eight A's, thus one B produces at least two A's (10 total minus 8 produced at most by A), and $(B, A)_{min}$ can be set to 2.

3.2 Deducing Successor Length

The deduction of A_{min} and A_{max} are found from two logical rules, one involving the sum of the minimum and maximum growth over all variables, and one by exploiting a technical mathematical property. The first rule simply states that A_{min} is at least the sum of $(A, B)_{min}$ for every $B \in V$ and similarly A_{max} is at most the sum of $(A, B)_{max}$ for every $B \in V$. The second rule is trickier but often improves the bounds for A_{max} and A_{min} for $A \in V$. This takes place in steps. First, the maximum number of symbols that can be produced by A in ω_i is computed by: $x := |\omega_i| - \sum_{B \in V, B \neq A}(B_{min} \cdot |\omega_{i-1}|_B)$. If $|\omega_{i-1}|_A > 0$, let:

$$A^i_{max} := \left\lfloor \frac{x}{|\omega_{i-1}|_A} \right\rfloor \tag{3}$$

if its value is improved. It follows that A_{max} can be set to $\min_{\substack{1 \leq i \leq n, \\ |\omega_{i-1}|_A > 0}} A^i_{max}$, if its value is improved. Next, now that these A^i_{max} values have been calculated, it is sometimes possible to further improve the A_{max} and A_{min} values. Let $Y^i \in V$, $1 \leq i \leq n$ be such that Y^i occurs the least frequently in ω_{i-1} with at least one copy. The current value of Y^i_{max} will be examined as computed by Eq. 3; note $Y^1, \ldots, Y^n$ can be different. Let $V^i_{max} := Y^i_{max} + \sum_{\substack{B \in V, \\ B \neq Y^i}} B_{min}$. Then, V^i_{max} can allow refinement of the upper bound for each successor, as A_{max} may be improved by assuming all other symbols produce their minimum and subtracting from V^i_{max}. Mathematically this is expressed as:

$$A_{max} := V^i_{max} - \sum_{\substack{B \in V, \\ B \neq A}} B_{min} \tag{4}$$

for $1 \leq i \leq n$, if A occurs in ω_{i-1}, and if the new value is smaller, which has the effect of the minimum over all i, $1 \leq i \leq n$. Although it is not immediately obvious that this formula is an upper bound on $|succ(A)|$, a mathematical proof has been completed (omitted due to space constraints), and appears in [11] along with an example of its use. Thus, A_{max} can be set in this fashion. Similarly, A_{min} can be set by taking Y^i that occurs most frequently.

4 Encoding for the L-system Inference Problem

In this section, the GA and encoding used by PMIT is described and contrasted with previous approaches.

The efficient search of a GA is controlled, in part, by the settings of the control parameters: population size, crossover weight, and mutation weight. The process of finding the optimal control parameter settings is called *hyperparameter search*. It was found via Random Search (details on methodology used in [11]) that the optimal parameter settings were 100 for population size, 0.85 crossover weight, and 0.10 for mutation weight. These parameters are henceforth used.

The fitness function for PMIT compares the symbols in the observed data to the symbols in the words produced by the candidate solution position by position. An error is counted if the symbols do not match or if the candidate solution is too long or short. The base fitness is the number of errors divided by total number of symbols. If the candidate solution produces more than double the number of symbols expected, it is not evaluated and assigned an extremely high fitness so that it will not pass the survival step. Since errors early on in the input words $\omega_0, \ldots, \omega_n$ will cause errors later, a word ω_i, is only assessed if there are no errors for each preceding word, and 1.0 is added to F for each unevaluated word. This encourages the GA to find solutions that incrementally match more of the observed words. PMIT is also evaluated using brute force, which is guaranteed to find the most fit solution and it was found that the solution found by the GA matches that found by brute force, showing that this fitness function is effective at finding an optimal solution.

PMIT uses three termination conditions to determine when to stop running. First, PMIT stops if a solution is found with a fitness of 0.0 as such a solution perfectly describes the observed data. Second, PMIT stops after 4 h of execution if no solution has been found. Third, PMIT stops when the population has converged and can no longer find better solutions. This is done by recording the current generation whenever a new best solution is found as Gen_{best}. If after an additional Gen_{best} generations, no better solutions are found, then PMIT terminates. To prevent PMIT from terminating early due to random chance, PMIT must perform at least 1,000 generations for the third condition only. This third condition is added to prevent the GA from becoming a random search post-convergence and finding an L-system by chance skewing the results.

The encoding scheme used most commonly in literature (e.g., [7,10]) is to have a gene represent each possible symbol in a successor. The number of genes for the approaches in literature varies due the specific method they use to decode the genome into an L-system, although they are approximately the total length of all successors combined. With this approach, each gene represents a variable from V (encoded as an integer from 1 to $|V|$). However, in some approaches (and PMIT) the decoding step needs to account for the possibility that a particular symbol in a successor *does not exist* (represented by $\oslash$). When the possibility of an $\oslash$ exists, such genes have a range from 1 to $|V| + 1$. As an example, assume $V = \{A, B\}$ and $A_{min} = 2, A_{max} = 3, B_{min} = 1, B_{max} = 3$. For A, it is certain to have at least two symbols in the successor and the third may or may not exist. So, the first three genes represent the symbols in $succ(A)$, where the first two genes have each possible values from $\{A, B\}$ and the third gene has $\{A, B, \oslash\}$.

Next the improvements made to the genomic structure defined by the basic encoding scheme will be described. Although they are discussed separately for ease of comprehension, all the improvements are used together.

PMIT uses the bounds and successor fragments to create a genomic structure. For example, if $V = \{A, B\}$, $A_{min} = 1$, and $A_{max} = 3$, then $succ(A)$ can be expressed as the genomic structure of $\{A, B\}, \{A, B, \oslash\}, \{A, B, \oslash\}$. If there is an A-prefix of B, then the genomic structure can change to $\{B\}, \{A, B, \oslash\}, \{A, B, \oslash\}$ since the first symbol in $succ(A)$ is B, essentially eliminating the need for the first gene. This is similar for an A-suffix. The second improvement to the basic encoding scheme further reduces the solution space by eliminating impossible solutions. When building the successor, PMIT first places the symbols known to be in $succ(A)$. For each successor, $\sum_{A,B \in V}(A,B)_{min}$ genes are created with a real value range between 0 and 1. Since these symbols must exist, the mapping selects an unused position within the successor. After these symbols are placed, if any additional symbols are needed up to the value of A_{max}, then PMIT selects the remainder allowing the option of using $\oslash$, ensuring that $(A,B)_{max}$ is not violated for any $A, B \in V$; i.e. the bounds computed by the heuristics shown in Sect. 3 ensure that the candidate solutions are always valid, and the genes' values are dynamically interpreted to ensure that the bounds are not violated. Further details and examples are in [11].

Lastly, it was determined that since new non-graphical symbols can only be produced by non-graphical symbols, it is possible to, at first, ignore the graphical symbols over a smaller alphabet V_{im}. Then, one can search for the successors over V_{im}^*, which is a simpler problem. For example, if $A \rightarrow F[+F]B$ and $B \rightarrow F[-F]A$, then with $V_{im} = \{A, B\}$ it is only necessary to find $A \rightarrow B$ and $B \rightarrow A$. Each graphical symbol can be added in one at a time. In the example above, the second step might add + to V_{im} and find $A \rightarrow +B$ and $B \rightarrow A$. Solving these smaller problems is more efficient as the individual search spaces are smaller and when summed are smaller than the solution space when trying to find the full successor in one step. Additional details, including the use of successor fragments to further simplify the number of genes needed, are omitted and appear in [11].

5   Data, Evaluation, and Results

To evaluate PMIT's ability to infer D0L-systems, ten fractals, six plant-like fractal variants inferred by LGIN [2,6], and twelve other biological models were selected from the vlab online repository [3]. The biological models consist of ten algaes, apple twig with blossoms, and a "Fibonacci Bush". The dataset compares favourably to similar studies where only some variants of one or two models are considered [6,7]. The data set is also of greater complexity by considering models with alphabets from between 2 to 31 symbols compared to two symbol alphabets [6,7]. However, there remain gaps both in terms of successor lengths and alphabet size. Hence, additional L-systems are created by bootstrapping; that is, by combining successors from multiple L-systems to create new "fake" systems with every combination of alphabet size from 3 to 25 in increments of 2 and longest successor length from 5 to 25 in increments of 5. To get successors of the proper length some "F" symbols were trimmed from longer successors. These are called *generated L-systems*.

Two metrics are used to measure success. *Success rate* (SR) is the percentage of times PMIT can find any L-system that describes the observed data. *Mean time to solve* (MTTS) is the time taken to solve the models (measured using a single core of an Intel 4770 @ 3.4 GHz with 12 GB of RAM on Windows 10). PMIT stops execution at 4 h (14400 s) calling the search a failure, as more than this time is not practical relative to other tools in the literature.

5.1 Results

Three programs were evaluated. The first is PMIT (implemented in C++ using Windows 10), the second is a restriction of PMIT that uses a brute force algorithm without the GA or logical rules, and the existing program LGIN. No comparison is made to the work by Runqiang et al. [7] as LGIN is strictly better; indeed, LGIN is the best approach that could be found in literature making it the best algorithm to which PMIT can be compared. The comparison between brute force and GA shows the effects of using GA on MTTS. Results are shown in Table 1. No SR is shown for LGIN as it is not explicitly stated; however, it is implied to be 100% [6] for all rows where a time is

Table 1. Results for PMIT, Brute Force, and LGIN [6], on existing L-system models.

Model	PMIT			Brute force		LGIN [6]
	SR	MTTS (s)	Infer growth	SR	MTTS (s)	MTTS (s)
Algae [2]	100%	0.001	n/a	100%	0.001	-
Cantor Dust [2]	100%	0.001	n/a	100%	0.001	-
Dragon Curve [2]	100%	0.909	n/a	100%	4.181	-
E-Curve [2]	0%	14400	Yes	0%	14400	-
Fractal Plant v1 [2,6]	100%	33.680	n/a	100%	163.498	2.834
Fractal Plant v2 [2,6]	100%	0.021	n/a	100%	5.019	0.078
Fractal Plant v3 [2,6]	100%	0.023	n/a	100%	5.290	0.120
Fractal Plant v4 [2,6]	100%	0.042	n/a	100%	6.571	0.414
Fractal Plant v5 [2,6]	100%	34.952	n/a	100%	171.003	0.406
Fractal Plant v6 [2,6]	100%	31.107	n/a	100%	174.976	0.397
Gosper Curve [2]	100%	71.354	n/a	100%	921.911	-
Koch Curve [2]	100%	0.003	n/a	100%	0.023	-
Peano [2]	0%	14400	Yes	0%	14400	-
Pythagoras Tree [2]	100%	0.041	n/a	100%	2.894	-
Sierpenski Triangle v1 [2]	100%	2.628	n/a	100%	267.629	-
Sierpenski Triangle v2 [2]	100%	0.086	n/a	100%	128.043	-
Aphanocladia [3]	0%	54.044	Yes	0%	14400	-
Dipterosiphonia v1 [3]	0%	14400	No	0%	14400	-
Dipterosiphonia v2 [3]	0%	14400	Yes	0%	14400	-
Ditira Reptans [3]	100%	73.821	n/a	100%	6856.943	-
Ditira Zonaricola [3]	0%	74.006	Yes	0%	14400	-
Herpopteros [3]	0%	81.530	Yes	0%	14400	-
Herposiphonia [3]	0%	298.114	Yes	0%	14400	-
Metamorphe [3]	0%	14400	Yes	0%	14400	-
Pterocladellium [3]	0%	14400	No	0%	14400	-
Tenuissimum [3]	0%	14400	No	0%	14400	-
Apple Twig [3]	0%	14400	No	0%	14400	-
Fibonacci Bush [3]	0%	14400	Yes	0%	14400	-

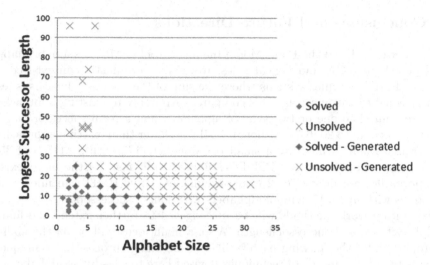

Fig. 2. L-systems solved with 100% SR by alphabet size and longest successor length.

written. The variants used by LGIN [2,6] are the six Fractal Plants. In general, PMIT is fairly successful at solving the fractals, the "Fractal Plant" variants, and also *Ditria reptans*. The success rates are all either 0% or 100%, indicating that a problem is either solved or not. It was observed that PMIT was able to solve many other models excluding the F and f symbols, as indicated in the "Infer Growth" column. For example, PMIT inferred for *Aphanocladia* that $A \rightarrow BA$, $B \rightarrow U[-C]UU[+/C/]U$; however, it was not able to then infer $C \rightarrow FFfFFfFFfFF[-F^4]fFFfFF[+F^3]fFFfFF[-FF]fFFf$. This is interesting as the growth mechanisms might be more complicated for a human to infer than the lines represented by the F and f symbols. Therefore, PMIT is a useful aide to human experts even when it cannot infer the complete L-system.

For the generated models, Fig. 2 gives one point for every L-system (generated or not) tested with PMIT. A model is considered *solved* if there is a 100% success rate and *unsolved* otherwise. It is evident that the figure shows a region described by alphabet size and longest successor length that PMIT can reliably solve. PMIT can infer L-systems with $|V| = 17$, if the successors are short (5) and can infer fairly long successors (25) when $|V| = 3$. Computing the *sum of successor words* $\sum_{A \in V} |succ(A)|$, then PMIT is able to infer L-systems where such a sum is less than 140, which compares favorably to approaches in literature where the sum is at most 20. Overall, in terms of MTTS, PMIT is generally slower than LGIN [6] for $|V| = 2$ although is still practically fast for these L-systems (less than 35 s); however, PMIT can reliably infer L-systems with larger alphabet sizes and successor lengths and still does so with an average of 17.762 s. Finally, the brute force algorithm required a MTTS of 621.998 s. Hence, the logical rules and the GA provide considerable improvement.

6   Conclusions and Future Directions

This paper introduced the Plant Model Inference Tool (PMIT) as a hybrid app-roach, combining GA and logical rules, to infer deterministic context-free L-systems. PMIT can infer systems where the sum of the successor lengths is less than or equal to 140 symbols. This compares favourably to existing approaches that are limited to one or two symbol alphabets, and a total successor length less than or equal to 20 [6,7]. Although PMIT is slower than existing approaches for "Fractal Plant" which has a small (2) alphabet [6,7] with a MTTS of 35 s or less compared to 2 s or less, PMIT is still practically fast. Furthermore, exist-ing approaches are limited to 2 symbol alphabets while PMIT can infer some L-systems with up to 17 symbol alphabets with longer successors.

For future work, methods will be investigated to further extend the limits of alphabet size and successor length. Also, a main focus will be on the ability to properly infer the drawing pattern likely using image processing techniques, perhaps taking advantage of techniques devised here to sub-divide alphabets.

References

1. Lindenmayer, A.: Mathematical models for cellular interaction in development, parts I and II. J. Theor. Biol. **18**, 280–315 (1968)
2. Prusinkiewicz, P., Lindenmayer, A.: The Algorithmic Beauty of Plants. Springer, New York (1990). https://doi.org/10.1007/978-1-4613-8476-2
3. University of Calgary: Algorithmic Botany
4. Allen, M.T., Prusinkiewicz, P., DeJong, T.M.: Using L-systems for modeling source-sink interactions, architecture and physiology of growing trees: the L-PEACH model. New Phytol. **166**(3), 869–880 (2005)
5. Prusinkiewicz, P., Crawford, S., Smith, R., Ljung, K., Bennet, T., Ongaro, V., Leyser, O.: Control of bud activation by an auxin transport switch. Proc. Nat. Acad. Sci. **106**(41), 17431–17436 (2009)
6. Nakano, R., Yamada, N.: Number theory-based induction of deterministic context-free L-system grammar. In: International Conference on Knowledge Discovery and Information Retrieval, pp. 194–199. SCITEPRESS (2010)
7. Runqiang, B., Chen, P., Burrage, K., Hanan, J., Room, P., Belward, J.: Derivation of L-system models from measurements of biological branching structures using genetic algorithms. In: Hendtlass, T., Ali, M. (eds.) IEA/AIE 2002. LNCS (LNAI), vol. 2358, pp. 514–524. Springer, Heidelberg (2002). https://doi.org/10.1007/3-540-48035-8_50
8. Prusinkiewicz, P., Mündermann, L., Karwowski, R., Lane, B.: The use of posi-tional information in the modeling of plants. In: Proceedings of the 28th Annual Conference on Computer Graphics and Interactive Techniques, pp. 289–300. ACM (2001)
9. Jacob, C.: Genetic L-system programming: breeding and evolving artificial flowers with Mathematica. In: Proceedings of the First International Mathematica Sym-posium, pp. 215–222 (1995)
10. Mock, K.J.: Wildwood: the evolution of L-system plants for virtual environments. In: Proceedings of the 1998 IEEE World Congress on Computational Intelligence, pp. 476–480. IEEE (1998)

11. Bernard, J., McQuillan, I.: New techniques for inferring L-systems using genetic algorithm (2017). https://arxiv.org/abs/1712.00180
12. Back, T.: Evolutionary Algorithms in Theory and Practice: Evolution Strategies, Evolutionary Programming, Genetic Algorithms. Oxford University Press, Oxford (1996)
13. Ben-Naoum, F.: A survey on L-system inference. INFOCOMP J. Comput. Sci. **8**(3), 29–39 (2009)
14. Doucet, P.G.: The syntactic inference problem for DOL-sequences. In: Rozenberg, G., Salomaa, A. (eds.) L Systems. LNCS, vol. 15, pp. 146–161. Springer, Heidelberg (1974). https://doi.org/10.1007/3-540-06867-8_12

An Adaptive Metaheuristic
for Unconstrained Multimodal
Numerical Optimization

Helder Pereira Borges[1], Omar Andres Carmona Cortes[1(✉)],
and Dario Vieira[2]

[1] Instituto Federal do Maranhão (IFMA), São Luis, MA, Brazil
{helder,omar}@ifma.edu.br
[2] Engineering School of Information and Digital Technologies (EFREI),
Villejuif, France
dario@efrei.fr

Abstract. The purpose of this paper is to show an adaptive meta-heuristic based on GA, DE, and PSO. The choice of which one will be used is made based on a probability that is uniform at the beginning of the execution, and it is updated as the algorithm evolves. That algorithm producing better results tend to present higher probabilities of being selected. The metaheuristic has been tested in four multimodal benchmark functions for 1000, 2000, and 3000 iterations, managing to reach better results than the canonical GA, DE, and PSO. A comparison between our adaptive metaheuristic and an adaptive GA has shown that our approach presents better outcomes, which was proved by a t-test, as well.

Keywords: Metaheuristics · Genetic Algorithms
Differential Evolution · Particle swarm optimization · Adaptive
Multimodal

1 Introduction

Different metaheuristics present unique exploration and exploitation capabilities, *i.e.*, they possess different forms of exploring and exploiting the search space. Thus, what works for solving a specific problem might be not good for tackling another one. Moreover, each problem can demand a particular set of parameters for each algorithm.

In this context, adaptive algorithms have appeared trying to solve as many problems as possible with no changes. Mostly approaches deal with adaptation in terms of operators or parameters. When dealing with operators, the adaptation tries to identify which operator is more suitable to the problem, while in parameters, the algorithm attempts to discover the best value. Both situations happen during the execution of the algorithm, *i.e.*, on-the-fly. For example, in [1], a

© Springer International Publishing AG, part of Springer Nature 2018
P. Korošec et al. (Eds.): BIOMA 2018, LNCS 10835, pp. 26–37, 2018.
https://doi.org/10.1007/978-3-319-91641-5_3

Genetic Algorithm choses between four crossover and three mutations operators as the metaheuristic solves multimodal benchmarks functions. Then, the authors evolve the algorithm to a self-adaptive one in [2], in which the parameters are encoded into the genes of each solution.

In fact, there are many works dealing with adaptive algorithms such as [3–8], etc. However, works that deal with different metaheuristics at the same time are rare. For instance, [9] came up with an algorithm that executes a GA and a PSO simultaneously; then they share information between their populations. The main drawback of this algorithm is the performance because both metaheuristics must execute at the same time. Costa's work [10] came up with the idea of upgrading the population in the SPEA2 (Strength Pareto Evolutionary Algorithm) using GA, DE and PSO by applying a stochastic approach, in which as the algorithm executes if a metaheuristic creates a population which dominates the previous one, then the probability of being chosen increases.

In this context, this paper is organized as follows: Sect. 2 illustrates the pseudo code and how the canonical algorithms GA, DE, and PSO work; Sect. 3 introduces our adaptive approach and how the algorithm chooses which metaheuristic to use in execution time; Sect. 4 shows how the experiments were set and explains the results; finally, Sect. 5 presents the conclusion and future work.

2 Metaheuristics

2.1 Genetic Algorithms

In 1962, Holland [11] proposed an adaptive system that will become the Genetic Algorithm as we know it. The pseudo code of a Genetic Algorithm is shown in Algorithm 1. Firstly, the GA creates a random set of candidate solutions. For each one, the algorithm calculates its fitness that expresses the quality of a solution. Then, individuals are chosen to form a temporary population using a selection mechanism. The temporary population undergoes genetic operators (crossover and mutation) to generate the new population. Finally, the new population is evaluated. If the algorithm is elitist and the previous population contains the best chromosome, this solution replaces the worst individual in the new one; otherwise, the old population is entirely replaced by the new one. The whole process is repeated while the stop criterion is not reached.

Algorithm 1. Genetic Algorithm

Population ← generateInitialPopulation();
fitness ← Eval(Population)
while stop Criteria not reached **do**
    TempPopulation ← Selection(Population);
    TempPopulation ← Crossover(TempPopulation);
    Population ← Mutation(TempPopulation);
    fitness ← Eval(Population)
end while

2.2 Particle Swarm Optimization

The particle swarm optimization was proposed by Kennedy and Eberhart [12] in 1995. The algorithm consists of particles that are placed into a search space, and move themselves combining its own history position and the current global optimal solution. A particle position is represented in the search space as $S_i^D = (s_i^1, s_i^2, \ldots, s_i^D)$ and it is updated based on its velocity $V_i^D = (v_i^1, v_i^2, \ldots, v_i^D)$, in which D represents the problem dimension. The new position is computed by Eqs. 1 and 2, where w represents the inertia weight, c_l and c_2 are acceleration constants, r_l and r_2 are random number in the range $[0, 1]$, p_i^d is the best position reached by the particle p, and g^d is a vector storing the global optima of the swarm so far.

$$v_i^d = w \times v_i^d + c_1 r_1 \times (p_i^d - x_i^d) + c_2 r_2 \times (g^d - x_i^d) \tag{1}$$

$$s_i^d = s_i^d + v_i^d \tag{2}$$

The Algorithm 2 outlines how PSO works. Initially, the swarm is created at random, in which each particle has to be within the domain $[a_i^d, b_i^d]$. Then, particles are evaluated to initialize the P matrix and the g^d vector, which are the best experience of each particle and the best solution that has been found so far, respectively. Thereafter, the velocity and the position of a particle are updated within a loop that obeys some stop criterion. In the pseudo code presented in the Algorithm 2, the stop criterion is a certain number of iterations.

Algorithm 2. PSO Pseudo Code

```
S ← InitSwarm();
fitness ← Eval(S);
g ← best(fitness);
P ← S;
while stop Criterion not reached do
    V = w * V + c₁r1 × (P − X) + c₂r2 × (g − X);
    S = S + V;
    fitness ← Eval(S);
    if best(fitness) is best than g then
        g ← best(fitness);
    end if
    if fitness(s) is best than p then
        p ← fitness(s);
    end if
end while
```

2.3 Differential Evolution

Differential Evolution (DE) is a metaheuristic developed by Storn and Price [13] in 1995. It works similarly to a Genetic Algorithm; however, using different operators. The Algorithm 3 presents its pseudo code. The DE algorithm starts initializing a random population along with its evaluation. Then, the mutation process selects three random individuals creating the vector v, which is also called vector of differences, where F is a constant chosen by the programmer. Afterward, a new individual is created using a gene from v if a random number is less than CR (*Crossover Rate*); otherwise, the gene comes from pop_{ij}. Finally, if the new individual is better than that one in the current population, the new one replaces it.

Algorithm 3. DE Pseudo Code

```
pop ← InitPopulation();
fitness ← Eval(pop);
while stop Criterion not reached do
    Select 3 individuals randomly: indiv₁, indiv₂, indiv₃;
    vⱼ ← indiv₃ + F × (indiv₁ − indiv₂);
    if (rand() ¡ CR) then
        new_indivⱼ ← vⱼ
    else
        new_indivⱼ ← popᵢⱼ
    end if
    if fitness(new_indiv) best than fitness(popᵢ) then
        popᵢ ← new_indiv;
    end if
end while
```

---

3 The Adaptive Metaheuristic

The adaptive metaheuristic was inspired in Carvalho's work [1], in which the authors use a similar process for choosing the proper genetic operators. The Algorithm 4 presents the pseudo code of our approach. Basically, the adaptive metaheuristic selects which one to use at execution time. All three algorithms start with a uniform distribution, *i.e.*, all of them have the same probability of being selected. Then, if the chosen algorithm improves the current solution then its probability of being selected increases by 1% while the other probabilities decrease by 0.5%; otherwise, the probability decreases, while the other ones increase with the same rate.

Also, the adaptation process can be done as many time as the programmer wants. In this work, we tested the adaptation done on each, 25, 50, 100 and 125 iterations. On each iteration means that the adaptation, *i.e.*, the algorithm is chosen on each iteration; on each 25, the adaptation is done in all iterations multiple of 25, and so on. For example, if the algorithm runs using 1000 iterations, will be performed 40 adaptation on each 25, 20 adaptation on each 50, and so on.

Algorithm 4. Adaptive Metaheuristic

    Population ← Init_Population();
    fitness ← eval(Population)
    while Number of Generations not reached **do**
        Select Metaheuristic()
        Use Metaheuristic(Population, fitness)
        if (Metaheuristic improves solution) **then**
            Prob_Metaheuristic++;
        else
            Prob_Metaheuristic- -;
        end if
        Population ← NewPopulation;
    end while

---

4 Computational Experiments

4.1 Experiment Setup

All experiments were conducted on an Intel Xeon X5650 2.67 GHz, 24 GB RAM, 500 GB Hard Disk on Ubuntu 16.04.2 LTS. In terms of parameters, all algorithms used a population of 50 individuals, 30 genes, and 50 trials. The number of trials were chosen based on the central limit theorem that allow us to use parametric tests. The algorithms were implemented in Java 7 using Eclipse Oxygen. Also, the following configurations were used on each kind of algorithm:

- GA: Probability of Crossover = 0.7; Probability of Mutation = 0.02; Selection method = Tournament; Tournament Size = 7; Crossover = Simple; Elitism = TRUE.
- PSO: $c_1 = 2.33; c_2 = 2.47$; linear inertia weight ($W_{max} = 0.9, W_{min} = 0.4$); Topology = Star (Fully Connected).
- DE: Crossover Rate = 0.6; $F = 0.815$; DE/Rand/1.
- Adaptive: Probability increasing = 1%; Probability decreasing = 0.5%; Iterations for adapting = 1, 25, 50, 100, and 125.

4.2 Benchmark Functions

In this work, we used four multimodal (several local optima) benchmark functions as presented in Table 1, which are minimization functions very common

Table 1. Benchmark functions

Code	Name	Function	Domain	Min.
ROS	Rosenbrock	$f_1(x) = \sum_{i=1}^{n-1}[100(x_{i+1} - x_i^2)^2 + (x_{i-1})^2]$	$[-5, 10]$	0
RAS	Rastringin	$f_2(x) = 10n + \sum_{i=1}^{n}[x_i^2 - 10\cos(2\pi x_i)]$	$[-5.12, 5.12]$	0
SCW	Schwefel	$f_3(x) = -\sum_{i=1}^{n} x_i * \sin\sqrt{|x_i|}$	$[-500, 500]$	-12569.49
GRI	Griewank	$f_4(x) = \sum_{i=1}^{n}(\frac{x(i)^2}{4000}) - \prod_{i=1}^{n}(\frac{x(i)}{\sqrt{i}}) + 1;$	$[-600, 600]$	0

for testing metaheuristic. In this context, minimize a function $f(x), x \in \mathbf{R}^n$ is to discover a vector x with dimension n in which the value of $f(x)$ is minimum. In the referred table we can see what the domain of each gene and its optimum value are.

The Rosenbrock function is commonly considered as unimodal. Nonetheless, the Generalized Rosenbrock ($f_1(x)$) is multimodal in dimensions higher than three [14].

4.3   Results for 1000, 2000 and 3000 Iterations

Table 2 presents the result (best, mean, worst and standard deviation) of each canonical algorithm optimizing each benchmark function. Whereas Table 3 shows the results of the adaptive metaheuristic on each type of adaptation. Both tables are considering 1000 iterations. As we can see, the best results were presented by the adaptive algorithms performing the adaptation on every 100 and 125 iterations. On the other hand, the canonical PSO shows better outcomes in the mean and worst results for ROS function; and, GA reached best mean and worst for SCW. However, the Adaptive gives better outcomes for RAS, SCW and GRI functions. Regarding the worsts, the GA shows the best worst result for RAS, SCW, and GRI. Nevertheless, the important thing here is that the best solutions are reached by our adaptive metaheuristic.

Tables 4 and 5 show the results after 2000 iterations for the canonical algorithms and the adaptive metaheuristic, respectively. Again the best results were

Table 2. Results for 1000 iterations - canonical

	Best	Mean	Worst	Std. Dev.
	GA			
ROS	29.732	105.830	175.230	45.658
RAS	0.256	0.843	**2.265**	0.421
SCW	−12568.247	**−12563.990**	**−12556.364**	3.308
GRI	0.612	0.984	**1.042**	0.077
	DE			
ROS	358.122	706.918	1505.896	234.446
RAS	137.588	160.048	179.952	10.394
SCW	−9330.961	−8612.050	−8091.159	288.092
GRI	1.029	1.061	1.095	0.018
	PSO			
ROS	28.551	**32.881**	**50.051**	4.924
RAS	0.088	19.328	61.822	16.761
SCW	−11306.211	−9155.361	−6479.682	1010.047
GRI	0.200	0.886	1.241	0.240

Table 3. Results for 1000 iterations - adaptive

	Best	Media	Worst	Std. Dev.
1 iteration				
ROS	32.547	133.657	204.346	42.589
RAS	0.188	**1.799**	3.948	1.067
SCW	−12568.710	−12560.413	−12534.404	7.355
GRI	0.267	0.893	1.049	0.194
25 iteration				
ROS	27.989	64.011	155.244	42.440
RAS	0.073	2.465	9.119	2.042
SCW	−12568.104	−12552.624	−12481.255	16.161
GRI	0.022	0.800	1.101	0.338
50 iteration				
ROS	27.534	49.323	157.457	38.451
RAS	0.258	3.951	15.306	3.430
SCW	−12569.344	−12560.870	−12517.038	11.205
GRI	0.071	0.764	1.192	0.318
100 iteration				
ROS	**26.362**	60.773	626.600	101.926
RAS	0.028	6.585	119.175	19.864
SCW	−12569.381	−12318.744	−8529.903	884.435
GRI	**0.006**	0.758	1.100	0.337
125 iteration				
ROS	26.945	55.341	218.926	45.152
RAS	**0.018**	8.177	176.832	29.462
SCW	**−12569.472**	−12294.613	−8428.805	881.318
GRI	0.041	**0.701**	1.120	0.403

Table 4. Results for 2000 iterations - canonical

	Best	Mean	Worst	Std. Dev.
GA				
ROS	6.470	79.330	151.804	45.048
RAS	0.030	**0.181**	**0.659**	0.125
SCW	−12569.150	−12568.279	**−12567.027**	0.548
GRI	0.276	0.690	1.009	0.181
DE				
ROS	31.279	89.137	207.356	48.936
RAS	95.899	129.277	154.292	11.721
SCW	−11743.363	−10256.110	−9176.490	746.605
GRI	0.002	**0.083**	0.200	0.062
PSO				
ROS	28.077	28.972	**30.422**	0.462
RAS	0.262	9.119	37.369	9.076
SCW	−11251.846	−9286.336	−7917.191	890.262
GRI	0.008	0.527	0.991	0.302

Table 5. Results for 2000 iterations - adaptive

	Best	Mean	Worst	Std. Dev.
1 iteration				
ROS	10.991	80.763	149.699	51.184
RAS	0.040	0.282	0.938	0.212
SCW	−12569.233	−12568.156	−12565.010	0.909
GRI	0.054	0.451	1.000	0.260
25 iteration				
ROS	**0.378**	39.603	134.218	34.498
RAS	0.004	0.261	2.103	0.425
SCW	−12569.213	−12567.382	−12560.399	1.812
GRI	0.013	0.137	**0.485**	0.131
50 iteration				
ROS	5.221	28.030	78.754	9.638
RAS	**0.001**	0.225	2.049	0.391
SCW	−12569.476	**−12568.625**	−12560.359	1.684
GRI	0.001	0.085	0.532	0.125
100 iteration				
ROS	1.636	27.517	74.411	9.349
RAS	0.002	0.190	1.277	0.285
SCW	−12569.485	−12567.591	−12560.978	2.381
GRI	**0.000**	0.115	0.966	0.207
125 iteration				
ROS	1.962	**26.640**	33.528	4.699
RAS	**0.001**	0.504	7.167	1.240
SCW	**−12569.486**	−12568.512	−12560.069	1.826
GRI	**0.000**	0.141	0.934	0.262

obtained by the adaptive metaheuristic. However, the canonical GA tended to reach the best results in terms of *mean* and *worst* in the Schwefel function, while PSO reached similar results in the Rosenbrock function.

Tables 6 and 7 present the outcomes after 3000 iterations for the canonical algorithms and the adaptive metaheuristic, respectively. In this experiment, we can notice that almost all results are better in the adaptive metaheuristic, excepting for Griewank function in which the DE presented the best result in *best* and *mean* columns.

Table 6. Results for 3000 iterations - canonical

	Best	Mean	Worst	Std. Dev.
	GA			
ROS	3.723	69.786	137.587	47.010
RAS	0.018	0.073	0.166	0.038
SCW	−12569.361	−12568.958	−12568.017	0.304
GRI	0.114	0.488	0.942	0.227
	DE			
ROS	25.537	27.366	51.774	4.368
RAS	88.416	116.684	134.385	9.051
SCW	−12444.607	−11851.003	−9850.102	511.812
GRI	**0.000**	**0.000**	0.002	0.001
	PSO			
ROS	26.566	28.543	29.442	0.462
RAS	0.004	5.257	28.130	7.292
SCW	−11138.709	−8869.721	−6479.683	1049.671
GRI	0.002	0.217	0.630	0.169

Table 7. Results for 3000 iterations - adaptive

	Best	Mean	Worst	Std. Dev.
	1 iteration			
ROS	10.149	76.380	150.567	51.695
RAS	0.011	0.112	0.387	0.098
SCW	−12569.457	−12568.978	−12567.635	0.430
GRI	0.014	0.193	0.776	0.151
	25 iteration			
ROS	0.413	35.954	134.695	33.232
RAS	0.001	**0.035**	**0.136**	0.032
SCW	−12569.388	−12568.692	−12566.106	0.743
GRI	**0.000**	0.033	0.159	0.039
	50 iteration			
ROS	**0.027**	25.111	27.082	4.409
RAS	**0.000**	0.073	1.993	0.335
SCW	−12569.486	−12569.228	−12566.700	0.538
GRI	**0.000**	0.020	0.132	0.033
	100 iteration			
ROS	0.082	**23.085**	**26.617**	7.149
RAS	**0.000**	0.059	0.949	0.181
SCW	**−12569.487**	**−12569.296**	−12567.423	0.460
GRI	**0.000**	0.023	0.253	0.053
	125 iteration			
ROS	0.378	23.154	28.790	8.095
RAS	**0.000**	0.061	0.894	0.168
SCW	**−12569.487**	−12569.289	−12567.281	0.441
GRI	**0.000**	0.015	0.199	0.037

4.4   Comparison Against an Adaptive GA

In this comparison, two characteristics have been changed. In the first one, the Schwefel function changed to $f_3(x) = 418d - \sum_{i=1}^{n} x_i * \sin\sqrt{|x_i|}$, in which d is the dimension of the function that in our case is 30. In the second one, the population size has been increased to 100. Table 8 shows the results for 1000 and 2000 iteration using the Adaptive GA [1], which stochastically chooses between four crossover and three mutation operators in execution time.

Table 9 presents the results of our approach considering the adaptation on "each 100" iterations. As we can observe, the adaptive metaheuristic presents better results compared to the adaptive GA.

Table 8. Results for the adaptive GA

	Best	Mean	Worst	Std. Dev.
Adaptive GA - 1000 iterations				
ROS	41.837	248.705	1072.296	169.331
RAS	12.757	43.533	2176.657	19.680
SCW	1.807	3999.956	1371.780	1046.521
GRI	0.586	0.956	47.799	0.136
Adaptive GA - 2000 iterations				
ROS	18.396	130.863	6543.140	902.405
RAS	4.7851	31.1575	73.7288	18.4707
SCW	0.329	1349.220	4118.256	1381.812
GRI	0.155	0.573	1.389	0.241

Table 9. Results for the adaptive metaheuristic using 1000 and 2000 iterations

	Best	Mean	Worst	Std. Dev.
1000 iteration				
Adaptation 100 iterations				
ROS	18.506	33.126	134.860	18.076
RAS	0.006	9.561	159.507	26.413
SCW	0.054	16.316	444.853	63.163
GRI	0.017	0.621	1.081	0.385
2000 iteration				
Adaptation 100 iteration				
ROS	0.525	25.401	29.152	5.080
RAS	0.000	0.063	0.690	0.113
SCW	0.001	5.915	280.429	39.618
GRI	0.000	0.072	0.500	0.124

Table 10. T-test: adpative metaheuristic vs adaptive GA

	Adaptive GA		Adaptive MH		
	Mean	Std. Dev.	Mean	Std. Dev.	t
1000 iteration					
ROS	248.705	169.331	33.126	18.076	**8.951**
RAS	43.533	19.68	9.561	26.413	**7.293**
SCW	3999.956	1046.521	16.316	63.163	**26.867**
GRI	0.956	0.136	0.621	0.385	**5.801**
2000 iteration					
ROS	130.863	902.405	25.401	5.08	0.826
RAS	31.1575	18.4707	0.063	0.113	**11.904**
SCW	1349.22	1381.812	5.915	39.618	**6.871**
GRI	0.573	0.241	0.072	0.124	**13.071**

A bicaudal-based t-test considering $\alpha = 0.05$ and a hypothesis test (H_0) that there are no differences between means, is presented in Table 10. Thus, if t is within $[-2.009, 2.009]$, we accept H_0, otherwise we reject it. As we can see, we rejected H_0 in almost all cases. Therefore, the differences are meaningful in the majority of the benchmark functions. In other words, the Adaptive metaheuristic presents the best results compared to the adaptive GA. Even though the difference between the adaptive GA and the adaptive metaheuristic is not meaningful in Rosenbrock function after 2000 iterations, the mean of the metaheuristic algorithm is smaller as well as the standard deviation, demonstrating that the adaptive metaheuristic is much more stable than the adaptive GA.

5   Conclusions

In this paper, we presented a stochastic adaptive metaheuristic based on GA, DE, and PSO. Experiments using 1000, 2000, and 3000 iterations have shown that our approach tends to present the best results with some variations in the means and in the worsts; however, those differences tend to disappear in favor of our approach as we increase the number of iterations. A comparison against an adaptive GA showed that the adaptive metaheuristic reached much better outcomes.

Future work includes: use a self-adaptive approach on all parameters of our method; parallelization of the adaptive metaheuristic using a General Purpose Graphical Unit Processing (GP-GPU); and to use fuzzy logic to select which algorithm to execute in a particular iteration.

References

1. Carvalho, E., Cortes, O.A.C., Costa, J.P., Rau-Chaplin, A.: A stochastic adaptive genetic algorithm for solving unconstrained multimodal numerical problems. In: IEEE Conference on Evolving and Adaptive Intelligent Systems (EAIS), pp. 130–137, May 2016

2. Carvalho, E., Cortes, O.A.C., Costa, J.P., Vieira, D.: A parallel adaptive genetic algorithm for unconstrained multimodal numerical optimization. In: Simpósio Brasileiro de Automação Inteligente (SBAI), October 2017

3. Qin, A.K., Tang, K., Pan, H., Xia, S.: Self-adaptive differential evolution with local search chains for real-parameter single-objective optimization. In: 2014 IEEE Congress on Evolutionary Computation (CEC), pp. 467–474, July 2014

4. Agrawal, S., Silakari, S., Agrawal, J.: Adaptive particle swarm optimizer with varying acceleration coefficients for finding the most stable conformer of small molecules. Mol. Inform. 34(11–12), 725–735 (2015)

5. Fan, Q., Yan, X.: Self-adaptive differential evolution algorithm with zoning evolution of control parameters and adaptive mutation strategies. IEEE Trans. Cybern. 46(1), 219–232 (2016)

6. Tambouratzis, G.: Modifying the velocity in adaptive PSO to improve optimisation performance. In: 2017 Ninth International Conference on Advanced Computational Intelligence (ICACI), pp. 149–156, February 2017

7. Toriyama, N., Ono, K., Orito, Y.: Adaptive GA-based AR-hidden Markov model for time series forecasting. In: 2017 IEEE Congress on Evolutionary Computation (CEC), pp. 665–672, June 2017

8. Zhang, X., Zhang, X., Wang, L.: Antenna design by an adaptive variable differential artificial bee colony algorithm. IEEE Trans. Magn. PP(99), 1–4 (2017)

9. Kusetogullari, H., Yavariabdi, A.: Self-adaptive hybrid PSO-GA method for change detection under varying contrast conditions in satellite images. In: 2016 SAI Computing Conference (SAI), pp. 361–368, July 2016

10. Costa, J.P.A., Cortes, O.A.C., Jnior, E.C.: An adaptive algorithm for updating populations on (SPEA2). In: Simpósio Brasileiro de Automação Inteligente (SBAI), July 2017

11. Holland, J.H.: Outline for a logical theory of adaptive systems. J. ACM 9(3), 297–314 (1962)

12. Kennedy, J., Eberhart, R.C.: Particle swarm optimization. In: Proceedings of the 1995 IEEE International Conference on Neural Networks, vol. 4, Perth, Australia, pp. 1942–1948. IEEE Service Center, Piscataway (1995)

13. Storn, R., Price, K.: Differential evolution - a simple and efficient adaptive scheme for global optimization over continuous spaces (1995)

14. al-Rifaie, M.M., Aber, A.: Dispersive flies optimisation and medical imaging. In: Fidanova, S. (ed.) Recent Advances in Computational Optimization. SCI, vol. 610, pp. 183–203. Springer, Cham (2016). https://doi.org/10.1007/978-3-319-21133-6_11

Scrum Task Allocation Based on Particle Swarm Optimization

Lucija Brezočnik(✉)(iD), Iztok Fister Jr.(iD), and Vili Podgorelec(iD)

Institute of Informatics, Faculty of Electrical Engineering and Computer Science,
University of Maribor, Koroška cesta 46, 2000 Maribor, Slovenia
lucija.brezocnik@um.si

Abstract. In this paper, we present a novel algorithm called STAPSO, which comprises Scrum task allocation and the Particle Swarm Optimization algorithm. The proposed algorithm aims to address one of the most significant problems in the agile software development, i.e., iteration planning. The actuality of the topic is not questionable, since nowadays, agile software development plays a vital role in most of the organizations around the world. Despite many agile software development methodologies, we include the proposed algorithm in Scrum Sprint planning, as it is the most widely used methodology. The proposed algorithm was also tested on a real-world dataset, and the experiment shows promising results.

Keywords: Agile software development
Particle Swarm Optimization · Scrum · Software engineering
Task allocation

1 Introduction

The idea of the iterative and agile development is all but new [1]. Ongoing changing priorities, desire to accelerate product delivery, the increase of productivity, improvement of project visibility, and enhancing software quality [2] are the top five reasons for adopting agile. Furthermore, in the report from Gartner Inc. [3], which is the world's leading research and advisory company, it is evident that the traditional project and development methods, e.g., waterfall, are evermore unsuitable [4,5]. Consequently, we can state that agile software development is, nowadays, not a competitive advantage anymore, but rather the need for the organizations to survive on the market.

Regardless of the chosen agile method, e.g., Scrum, Kanban, Scrumban, XP (extreme programming), and Lean, monitoring of its performance must be carried out. Success in agile projects is most often measured by velocity in 67%, followed by the iteration burndown (51%), release burndown (38%), planned vs. actual stories per iteration (37%), and Burn-up chart (34%) [2]. However, a prerequisite for a successful monitoring of the progress is undoubtedly precise

P. Korošec et al. (Eds.): BIOMA 2018, LNCS 10835, pp. 38–49, 2018.
https://doi.org/10.1007/978-3-319-91641-5_4

iteration planning. The latter is not only the number one employed agile technique in the organizations [2], but also one of the hardest tasks, as is evident from many scientific papers [6,7] and interviews conducted with different CIOs (Chief Information Officers). Also, each task defined in a given iteration must be estimated precisely. The estimation can be conducted with various techniques [2,8], e.g., number sizing (1, 2, ..., 10), Fibonacci sequence (1, 2, 3, 5, 8, ...), and T-shirt sizes (XS, S, M, L, XL, XXL or XXXL). However, we must not forget about dependencies between tasks which result in the implementation order.

Thus, from an apparently simple problem arises a considerable optimization problem that is dealt with daily in organizations all around the world. When dealing with numerous dependencies and tasks, solving a problem by hand becomes very hard. On the contrary, we propose a systematical solution that is based on nature-inspired algorithms. Nature-inspired algorithms are a modern tool for solving hard continuous and discrete problems. They draw inspiration for solving such problems from nature. Until recently, more than 100 nature-inspired algorithms have been proposed in the literature [9], where Particle Swarm Optimization (PSO) [10] is one of the oldest and well-established nature-inspired algorithms. Many studies have proved theoretically and practically that PSO is a very simple, as well as efficient algorithm [11,12] appropriate even for real-world applications [13].

In this paper, we show the modifications of the basic PSO algorithm that is applied to the problem of Scrum task allocation. The new algorithm, called STAPSO, is developed, implemented, and tested on a real dataset.

We believe that this is the first work that deals with the problem of Scrum task allocation in the optimization domain. Altogether, the purpose of this paper is to:

- represent Scrum task allocation as an optimization problem,
- propose the Particle Swarm Optimization algorithm for solving Scrum task allocation, or simply STAPSO, and
- test the proposed algorithm on a real dataset.

The structure of this paper is as follows: Sect. 2 outlines the fundamentals of Scrum, while Sect. 3 describes the fundamentals of the PSO algorithm, together with STAPSO algorithm. Section 4 presents the design of the experiment, along with the results in Sect. 5. The paper concludes with a summary of the performed work and future challenges.

2 Scrum

Scrum is the most used agile methodology, with 58% share of the market [2] and is by definition "a framework for developing, delivering, and sustaining complex products" [14,15]. It consists of three primary roles, i.e. the Scrum Master, the Product Owner, and the Development Team. In the organizations, the Scrum Master is responsible for Scrum promotion and offers support regarding Scrum theory, values, and practices. Product Owner is a focal role since it is connected with the development team and the stakeholders. Two of his/her primary goals are to maximize the value of the product, and definition of the user stories from the product backlog. The remaining role, i.e., the Development Team, is liable for product increment delivery at the end of each Sprint. The Development Team is cross-functional and self-organizing, meaning that the people in it have all the skills required to deliver the product successfully.

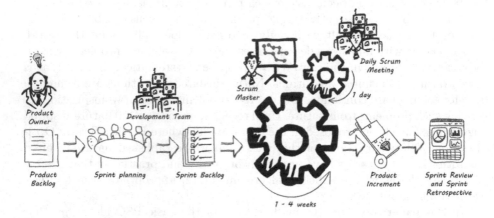

Fig. 1. The Scrum framework.

In Scrum, the process starts with the Product Owners' definition of the product backlog, which is a prioritized list of user stories (see Fig. 1). Afterwards, Sprint Planning starts. At this meeting, the team decides which user stories from the Product Backlog will be carried out in the upcoming Sprint (because the Product Backlog is prioritized, they pull user stories from the top of the list). The newly created document is called a Sprint Backlog and contains an in-depth description of the chosen user stories. After that, everything is ready for the beginning of the Sprint, that usually lasts between one and four weeks. Each day of the Sprint starts with a brief daily Scrum (short stand-up meeting) at which the Development Team exchanges opinions regarding the previous day and highlights possible problems. At the end of each Sprint, Sprint Review and Sprint Retrospective are carried out by the Development Team and the Product Owner, with the intention to find the potential for improvement.

For the calculation of the optimal line, it is necessary to determine the duration of the Sprint first (n_days). For example, if we decide on the two week long Sprints, the Development Team actually has ten working days, assuming Saturday and Sunday are free days. After that, based on tasks from the Sprint Backlog, the total estimated effort (t_effort) is obtained as their sum. Optimum per day (opt_d) can now be calculated by Eq. 1.

$$opt\_d = \frac{t\_effort}{n\_days} \tag{1}$$

Ideal or optimal line (*Oline*) is derived from linear function $f(x) = ax + b$ and is presented by Eq. 2, where x denotes the specific day of the Sprint.

$$Oline = -\frac{t\_effort}{n\_days} * x + t\_effort \tag{2}$$

Current line (*Cline*) is calculated by Eq. 3, where *Edone* denotes the summarized effort of the tasks per given day.

$$Cline = Oline(x) - (Oline(x - 1) - Edone) \tag{3}$$

3   Particle Swarm Optimization for Scrum Task Allocation

In this Section, the proposed algorithm called STAPSO is described in detail. Since the algorithm is based on the PSO, its explanation is divided into two Subsections. Subsect. 3.1 depicts the fundamentals of the PSO, and Subsect. 3.2 presents the proposed algorithm in detail.

3.1   Fundamentals of PSO

The PSO algorithm [10] preserves a population of solutions, where each solution is represented as a real-valued vector $\mathbf{x} = (x_{i,1}, \ldots, q_{i,D})^T$ for $i = 1, \ldots, Np$ and $j = 1, \ldots, D$, and the parameter Np denotes the population size, and the parameter D dimension of the problem. This algorithm explores the new solutions by moving the particles throughout the search space in the direction of the current best solution. In addition to the current population $\mathbf{x}_i^{(t)}$ for $i = 1, \ldots, Np$, also the local best solutions $\mathbf{p}_i^{(t)}$ for $i = 1, \ldots, Np$ are preserved, denoting the best i-th solution found. Finally, the best solution in the population $\mathbf{g}^{(t)}$ is determined in each generation. The new particle position is generated according to Eq. (4):

$$\begin{aligned}
\mathbf{v}_i^{(t+1)} &= \mathbf{v}_i^{(t)} + C_1 U(0,1)(\mathbf{p}_i^{(t)} - \mathbf{x}_i^{(t)}) + C_2 U(0,1)(\mathbf{g}^{(t)} - \mathbf{x}_i^{(t)}), \\
\mathbf{x}_i^{(t+1)} &= \mathbf{x}_i^{(t)} + \mathbf{v}_i^{(t+1)},
\end{aligned} \tag{4}$$

where $U(0,1)$ denotes a random value in interval $[0,1]$, and C_1 and C_2 are learning factors. Algorithm 1 depicts the original PSO algorithm.

Interestingly, many surveys have recently revealed that the PSO algorithm was used in numerous real-world applications [13,16]. However, the presence of the PSO algorithm in the software engineering research area is still in the minority.

In the next Subsection, the proposed STAPSO algorithm is presented for the Scrum task allocation problem.

Algorithm 1. Pseudocode of the basic PSO algorithm

Input: PSO population of particles $\mathbf{x_i} = (x_{i1}, \ldots, x_{iD})^T$ for $i = 1 \ldots Np$, MAX_FEs.
Output: The best solution $\mathbf{x}_{best}$ and its corresponding value $f_{min} = \min(f(\mathbf{x}))$.
 1: init_particles;
 2: $eval = 0$;
 3: **while** termination_condition_not_meet **do**
 4:   **for** $i = 1$ to Np **do**
 5:     $f_i = $ evaluate_the_new_solution($\mathbf{x}_i$);
 6:     $eval = eval + 1$;
 7:     **if** $f_i \leq pBest_i$ **then**
 8:       $\mathbf{p}_i = \mathbf{x}_i$; $pBest_i = f_i$; // save the local best solution
 9:     **end if**
10:     **if** $f_i \leq f_{min}$ **then**
11:       $\mathbf{x}_{best} = \mathbf{x}_i$; $f_{min} = f_i$; // save the global best solution
12:     **end if**
13:     $\mathbf{x}_i = $ generate_new_solution($\mathbf{x}_i$);
14:   **end for**
15: **end while**

3.2 STAPSO Algorithm

The following Section depicts the process of a Scrum task allocation problem using the STAPSO algorithm. For this problem, the following three modifications were applied to the basic PSO algorithm:

- representation of individuals,
- design of fitness function, and
- constraint handling.

Representation of Individuals. Candidate solutions in the basic PSO algorithm are represented as real-valued vectors $\mathbf{x}$, whilst a Scrum task allocation problem demands an integer vector $\mathbf{y}$ symbolizing the effort of a particular task. For that reason, mapping between representation of solutions in real-valued search space to the solution in a problem space is needed. In a STAPSO, this mapping is conducted in a similar manner as it was done for the problem of sport training sessions' planning [17]. A candidate solution in the proposed STAPSO algorithm is also represented, using the real-valued vector $\mathbf{x}_i = \{x_i0, \ldots, x_in\}^T$ for $i = 1 \ldots n$ with elements $x_{ij} \in [0, 1]$. In order to obtain effort values for fitness function calculation, firstly the permutation of task effort $\pi_i = \{\pi_{i1}, \ldots, \pi_{in}\}$ is mapped from the vector $\mathbf{x}_i$ such that the following relation is valid:

$$x_{i\pi_{i0}} < x_{i\pi_{i1}} < \ldots < x_{i\pi_{in}}. \tag{5}$$

Vector $y_i = \{y_{i0}, \ldots, y_{in}\}^T$ is determined from task description, Table 1. Table 2 presents an example of mapping the candidate solution $\mathbf{x}_i$ via permutation of task effort π_i to the final task allocation.

Table 1. Task description table (example)

Task_ID	Effort
0	3
1	2
2	4
3	3
4	5

Table 2. Candidate solution mapping

	Dimension j				
Elements i	0	1	2	3	4
Candidate solution $\mathbf{x}_i$	0.70	0.42	0.21	0.94	0.52
Permutation π_i	3	1	0	4	2
Task allocation $\mathbf{y}_i$	3	2	3	5	4

Fitness Function. Fitness function is calculated according to Eq. 6 as follows:

$$f(x) = \mid \sum_{j=0}^{n\_days} (calculated\ effort\_per\_day_j) \mid \qquad (6)$$

where n_days denotes the number of days, and $calculated\ effort\_per\_day$ is calculated effort for every day according to the constraint:

$$\forall d \in \{1, 2, \ldots, n\_days\}, \forall t \in \{1, 2, \ldots, n\_tasks(d)\},$$

$$\sum_{i=1}^{t} effort(i) \leq opt\_d \qquad (7)$$

where the variables d and t denote the current day of the Sprint, and the number of tasks per day, respectively. Final effort per day is then calculated as the sum of the tasks' efforts, that should not exceed the value of the opt_d (Eq. 1).

Constraint Handling. As discussed in previous Sections, there is sometimes a particular order (dependency) of some tasks. In other words, it means that one task must be completed before the beginning of another task. Most candidate solutions that are obtained according to mapping in Table 2 are unfeasible, i.e., they violate the dependency conditions. In our case, unfeasible solutions are penalized. Algorithm 2 presents our solution for handling constraints, where the function $is\_violated()$ checks if the dependency condition is violated. If the dependency condition is violated, the algorithm assigns a very high penalty [18] value to this particle. Despite many constraint handling methods, our penalization method behaves very well on the current problem. For that reason, we have not tested the behavior of any other constraint handling methods yet [19].

Algorithm 2. Constraint handling in STAPSO

1: $violations = 0$;
2: $fitness = f(x)$;{calculated by Eq. 6}
3: **for** $i = 1$ to Num_{Rules} **do**
4:    **if** $is\_violated()$ **then**
5:        $violations = violations + 1$;
6:    **end if**
7: **end for**
8: **if** $violations > 0$ **then**
9:    $fitness = violations * 1000$;
10: **end if**
---

4   Experiment

The experimental approach was used in order to show the power of the STAPSO algorithm. Thus, Subsect. 4.1 comprises parameter settings of the algorithm and the computer environment, and Subsect. 4.2 presents test data, along with the constraints on Scrum tasks that were used in this study.

4.1   Setup

Experiments were conducted on an Intel XEON Z240 computer. STAPSO is implemented in the Python programming language without using any special software libraries. The algorithm ran on a Linux Ubuntu 16.04 operating system. After the extensive parameter tuning, the following parameter settings were used based on their best performance:

- population size Np: 75,
- dimension of the problem D: 60,
- number of function evaluations per run $MAX\_FEs = 30000$,
- total runs: 25,
- cognitive component $C_1 = 2.0$,
- social component $C_2 = 2.0$,
- velocity: $[-4, 4]$,
- number of days: 10,
- number of Sprint: 1.

4.2   Test Data and Constraints

Table 4 presents test data that were used in this study. Test data for such experiments is very hard to get due to the company policy of confidential data. Thus, the source of test data is an internal project that was conducted within our laboratory. In Table 4, $Task\_ID$ denotes the identification number of a particular task, while $Effort$ symbolizes the effort of this task. In this study, the following constraints were considered:

$$\Psi = \{(T7, T3), (T6, T22), (T4, T58), (T33, T31)\}.$$

Thereby, Ψ denotes the implementation order of the tasks, i.e., task $T7$ must be implemented before task $T3$, task $T6$ must be implemented before task $T22$, etc. In the context of the algorithm, this means that all of the possible solutions must obey all of the given constraints and provide legitimate task allocation also considering Eqs. 2 and 3.

5   Results

In the total of 25 runs, an optimal solution was found 20 times (i.e. success rate: 80%), meaning that no tasks were left behind for the next Sprint. In three cases (12%), the algorithm did not allocate one task with the estimated effort of 1, and in two cases (8%), the algorithm did not allocate one task estimated with the effort of 2. We want to highlight that all constraints presented in Subsect. 4.2 were satisfied in all runs. On average, an optimal solution was found after 5533 function evaluations.

Table 3 comprises an in-depth description of one optimal solution. The latter presents the sequence of tasks' implementation for one Sprint, which is described with the Task IDs (column 2) and belonging tasks' effort (column 3). Per each day, the number of tasks and remaining effort is recorded, respectively.

Table 3. Example of task allocation from Table 4 (optimal solution)

Day	Tasks allocated	Tasks' effort	Number of tasks	Effort remaining
1	4, 12, 15, 17, 21, 32, 42	5, 3, 1, 1, 1, 2, 2	7	0
2	43, 27, 49, 48, 58, 33	3, 3, 3, 1, 1, 4	6	0
3	51, 7, 50, 5	1, 5, 4, 5	4	0
4	24, 26, 45, 35, 57, 54, 25	2, 1, 2, 2, 4, 2, 2	7	0
5	18, 10, 29, 16	2, 5, 3, 5	4	0
6	6, 22, 8, 53, 31	5, 4, 3, 1, 2	5	0
7	28, 44, 19, 0, 30, 3	4, 2, 1, 2, 4, 2	6	0
8	1, 14, 20, 37, 40, 52, 23, 38	2, 2, 2, 1, 1, 3, 3, 1	8	0
9	56, 34, 41, 11, 2, 9, 13	2, 3, 1, 2, 1, 3, 3	7	0
10	36, 39, 46, 47, 55, 59	3, 2, 4, 2, 2, 2	6	0
$\sum$	**60**	**150**	**60**	**0**

Figures 2 and 3 present the same proposed solution of the STAPSO algorithm, where two tasks with the estimated effort of 1 were not allocated. A non-optimal solution was chosen deliberately for easier explanation of the results and deviations. Figure 2 presents the solution in the form of the burndown chart, and Fig. 3 shows allocated tasks per day of the Sprint.

In Scrum, a burndown chart is one of the most frequently used graphs to present the current state of the work of the project [2, 20]. On the abscissa axis

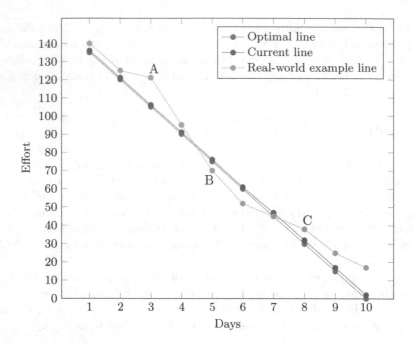

Fig. 2. Burndown chart of non-optimal solution (chosen deliberately for easier explanation of the results) (Color figure online)

(Fig. 2), days of the Sprint are displayed, and on the ordinate axis, the remaining effort of the Sprint. The preparation of such a graph is carried out in several stages. Firstly, the optimal line is drawn. The optimal line is calculated with Eq. 2 and shows an ideal or optimal course of the implementation of the tasks. In Fig. 2, this line is colored with red. As stated before, all tasks are estimated with effort (see Table 4) and with their fulfillment, we can monitor remaining effort in a Sprint. If we look at the first day of the Sprint in Fig. 2, we can see that ideal effort completed per day is 15 (calculated with Eq. 1). Thus, the Development Team should, on their first day, complete tasks with the sum of the effort of at least 15. As we can see from Fig. 3, algorithm STAPSO for the first day allocated 5 tasks with the estimated effort sum of 14, meaning that, after the first day, the Development Team is one effort behind the optimal line (see blue line). In a real-world scenario, we can witness lines that are similar to the green line. From the latter, it is evident that the Development Team was behind the optimal line for the first four days, and on day 3 (point A) they fulfilled tasks with the effort sum of only 4. However, after the third day, the fulfillment of tasks went very quickly, so in two days they caught up and were in front of the optimal line on day five (point B). Point C shows that the progress has stopped on day 8 (they were behind the optimal line again), and they stayed behind it until the end of the Sprint.

In Fig. 3 the days of the Sprint show the allocated tasks given by the STAPSO algorithm. As we have said in the description of Fig. 2, the optimal effort sum

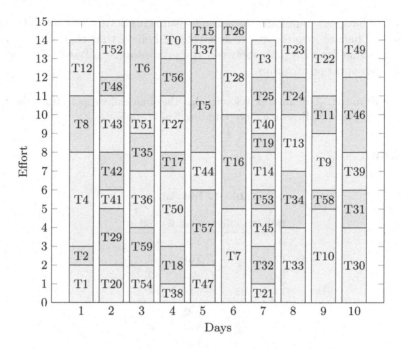

Fig. 3. Task allocation of non-optimal solution (chosen deliberately for easier explanation of the results)

per day is 15 (maximum value of the ordinate axis). This sum is also the value that the algorithm is trying to achieve per day. If we look at the results, on the first day the STAPSO algorithm allocated five tasks, i.e., $T1$, $T2$, $T4$, $T8$, and $T12$ (see Table 4), with the sum of effort of 14. On the second day, a sum of effort of 15 is fulfilled with the tasks $T20$, $T29$, $T41$, $T42$, $T43$, $T48$, and $T52$, etc. This kind of graph is beneficial for the Development Team and the Product Owner, since they have allocated tasks from the beginning of the Sprint.

6 Conclusion

A novel algorithm STAPSO was implemented and tested successfully on a real dataset. It offers a solution to the global problem of task allocation in the agile software development. The STAPSO algorithm can be applied to all of the known estimation techniques, e.g. number sizing, Fibonacci sequence, and T-shirt planning. Furthermore, it can be included in companies regardless of their size and maturity degree.

In the design of the algorithm, there is still significant room for improvement. In the future, we intend to study the impact of various constraint handling methods and variants of PSO on the behavior of the STAPSO algorithm. Hybridization of STAPSO with any other well-established algorithms, e.g., Differential Evolution is also a sparkling way for future research.

Since we have not found any similar algorithms for Scrum task allocation that are based on nature-inspired algorithms yet, we believe that this study could be a stepping stone for more links between the vibrant agile software development research area and optimization.

Acknowledgment. The authors acknowledge the financial support from the Slovenian Research Agency (Research Core Funding No. P2-0057).

Test Data

Table 4. Test data

Task_ID	Effort	Task_ID	Effort
T0	2	T30	4
T1	2	T31	2
T2	1	T32	2
T3	2	T33	4
T4	5	T34	3
T5	5	T35	2
T6	5	T36	3
T7	5	T37	1
T8	3	T38	1
T9	3	T39	2
T10	5	T40	1
T11	2	T41	1
T12	3	T42	2
T13	3	T43	3
T14	2	T44	2
T15	1	T45	2
T16	5	T46	4
T17	1	T47	2
T18	2	T48	1
T19	1	T49	3
T20	2	T50	4
T21	1	T51	1
T22	4	T52	3
T23	3	T53	1
T24	2	T54	2
T25	2	T55	2
T26	1	T56	2
T27	3	T57	4
T28	4	T58	1
T29	3	T59	2

References

1. Takeuchi, H., Nonaka, I.: The new new product development game. Harv. Bus. Rev. **64**, 137–146 (1986)
2. VersionOne: VersionOne 11th Annual State of Agile Report (2017)
3. Kyte, A., Norton, D., Wilson, N.: Ten things the CIO needs to know about agile development. Technical report. Gartner, Inc. (2014)
4. Gandomani, T.J., Nafchi, M.Z.: Agile transition and adoption human-related challenges and issues: a grounded theory approach. Comput. Hum. Behav. **62**, 257–266 (2016)
5. Chen, R.R., Ravichandar, R., Proctor, D.: Managing the transition to the new agile business and product development model: lessons from cisco systems. Bus. Horiz. **59**(6), 635–644 (2016)
6. Heikkilä, V.T., Paasivaara, M., Rautiainen, K., Lassenius, C., Toivola, T., Järvinen, J.: Operational release planning in large-scale scrum with multiple stakeholders – a longitudinal case study at f-secure corporation. Inf. Softw. Technol. **57**, 116–140 (2015)
7. Barney, S., Ke Aurum, A., Wohlin, C.: A product management challenge: creating software product value through requirements selection. J. Syst. Architect. **54**, 576–593 (2008)
8. Usman, M., Mendes, E., Weidt, F., Britto, R.: Effort estimation in agile software development: a systematic literature review. In: Proceedings of the 10th International Conference on Predictive Models in Software Engineering, PROMISE 2014, NY, USA, pp. 82–91. ACM (2014)
9. Fister Jr., I., Yang, X.S., Fister, I., Brest, J., Fister, D.: A brief review of nature-inspired algorithms for optimization. Elcktrotehniški vestnik **80**(3), 116–122 (2013)
10. Kennedy, J., Eberhart, R.: Particle swarm optimization. In: Proceedings of the IEEE International Conference on Neural Networks, vol. 4, pp. 1942–1948. IEEE (1995)
11. Shi, Y., et al.: Particle swarm optimization: developments, applications and resources. In: Proceedings of the 2001 Congress on evolutionary computation, vol. 1, pp. 81–86. IEEE (2001)
12. Yang, X.S.: Nature-Inspired Metaheuristic Algorithms. Luniver Press, Bristol (2010)
13. Zhang, Y., Wang, S., Ji, G.: A comprehensive survey on particle swarm optimization algorithm and its applications. Math. Probl. Eng. **2015**, 38 p. (2015). https://doi.org/10.1155/2015/931256. Article no. 931256
14. Sutherland, J.V., Sutherland, J.J.: Scrum: The Art of Doing Twice the Work in Half the Time. Currency, Redfern (2014)
15. Schwaber, K., Sutherland, J.: The Scrum Guide™ (2017)
16. Pluhacek, M., Senkerik, R., Viktorin, A., Kadavy, T., Zelinka, I.: A review of real-world applications of particle swarm optimization algorithm. In: Duy, V., Dao, T., Zelinka, I., Kim, S., Phuong, T. (eds.) AETA 2017. LNCS, vol. 465, pp. 115–122. Springer, Cham (2018). https://doi.org/10.1007/978-3-319-69814-4_11
17. Fister, I., Rauter, S., Yang, X.S., Ljubič, K., Fister Jr., I.: Planning the sports training sessions with the bat algorithm. Neurocomputing **149**, 993–1002 (2015)
18. Coello, C.A.C.: Theoretical and numerical constraint-handling techniques used with evolutionary algorithms: a survey of the state of the art. Comput. Methods Appl. Mech. Eng. **191**(11), 1245–1287 (2002)
19. Mezura-Montes, E., Coello, C.A.C.: Constraint-handling in nature-inspired numerical optimization: past, present and future. Swarm Evol. Comput. **1**(4), 173–194 (2011)
20. Cooper, R.G., Sommer, A.F.: Agile-stage-gate: new idea-to-launch method for manufactured new products is faster, more responsive. Ind. Mark. Manag. **59**, 167–180 (2016)

Cooperative Model for Nature-Inspired Algorithms in Solving Real-World Optimization Problems

Petr Bujok[✉]

Department of Informatics and Computers, University of Ostrava,
30. dubna 22, 70200 Ostrava, Czech Republic
petr.bujok@osu.cz

Abstract. A cooperative model of eight popular nature-inspired algorithms (CoNI) is proposed and compared with the original algorithms on benchmark set CEC 2011 collection of 22 real-world optimization problems. The results of experiments demonstrate the superiority of CoNI variant in the most of the real-world problems although some of original nature-inspired algorithms perform rather poorly. Proposed CoNI shares the best position in 20 out of 22 problems and achieves the best results in 8 out 22 test problems. Further fundamental points for improvement of CoNI are in selection of topology, migration policy, and migration frequency.

Keywords: Global optimization · Nature-inspired algorithms
Real-world problems · Cooperative model

1 Introduction

Many researchers have developed tens of optimization algorithms based on systems from nature [1]. Beside these methods, another scientists propose existing good-performing methods enhanced by new features [2,3]. The goal of this paper is to reveal possibility of cooperation of nature-inspired algorithms in order to obtain more efficient optimization algorithm.

In our recent works [4,5], we have experimentally compared the performance of nature-inspired algorithms on the collection of real-world optimization problems. It was found that none of eight nature-inspired algorithms selected to the comparison is able to provide a similar results as three recently proposed adaptive DE variants. Furthermore, some of the nature-inspired methods even perform worse than the blind random search.

In this paper, we apply and study the results of cooperative model of well-known nature-inspired optimization algorithms. A practicality of the proposed model will be achieved on the real-world problems [6] with various dimensionality. The purpose of use of these problems is simple, we want to show the performance of compared algorithms on selected real problems to help scientists

© Springer International Publishing AG, part of Springer Nature 2018
P. Korošec et al. (Eds.): BIOMA 2018, LNCS 10835, pp. 50–61, 2018.
https://doi.org/10.1007/978-3-319-91641-5_5

in choice of the proper optimization method. A blind random search method was not selected for this experiment.

When a problem is solved in global optimization, there is an objective function $f(\boldsymbol{x})$, $\boldsymbol{x} = (x_1, x_2, \ldots, x_D) \in \mathbb{R}^D$ defined on the search domain Ω limited by lower and upper boundaries, i.e. $\Omega = \prod_{j=1}^{D} [a_j, \ b_j]$, $a_j < b_j$, $j = 1, 2, \ldots, D$. The global minimum point $\boldsymbol{x}^*$, which satisfies condition $f(\boldsymbol{x}^*) \leq f(\boldsymbol{x}), \forall \boldsymbol{x} \in \Omega$ is the solution of the problem.

The rest of the paper is organized as follows. Section 2 shows brief description of the nature-inspired algorithms selected for experimental comparison. A cooperation model of nature-inspired algorithms is described in Sect. 3. Experimental setting and methods applied to statistical assessment are described in Sect. 4. Experimental results on real-world optimization problems are presented in Sect. 5. Section 6 describes conclusion of the paper with some final remarks.

2 Selected Nature-Inspired Algorithms

The survey of bio-inspired algorithms has been presented recently in [1]. The book [7] along with mentioned survey were the main sources for the selection of nature-inspired algorithms for this experimental comparison. Based on these sources and previous studies [4,5], the list of alphabetically sorted eight nature-inspired methods with their descriptions follows.

The artificial bee colony algorithm (ABC) was proposed by Karaboga in [8]. This algorithm models the behavior of the bees consist of three groups - employed bees, onlookers bees, and scouts. The only input parameter *limit*, usually equal to the population size, controls a number of unsuccessful new 'food positions' (position in Ω) necessary to find a new random food position. An employed ith bee jth position is updated by $y(i, j) = P(i, j) + (P(i, j) - P(r, j)) \, U(-1, 1)$, where j is randomly selected index from $(1, D)$ of the position to be updated (D is the dimension of the problem), r is randomly selected bee different from current ith bee and $U(-1, 1)$ is a random number from the uniform distribution with parameters given in parentheses.

The bat algorithm (abbreviated Bat) simulates an echolocation behavior of real bats controlled by emission rate and loudness. The artificial representation of this phenomenon uses parameter setting that follows the original publication of Yang [9]. Maximal and minimal frequencies are set up $f_{\max} = 2$, $f_{\min} = 0$, respectively. A local-search *loudness* parameter is initialized $A_i = 1.2$ for each bat-individual and reduced if a new bat position is better than the old one using coefficient $\alpha = 0.9$. The *emission rate* parameter is initialized to each bat-individual $r_i = 0.1$ and increased by parameter $\gamma = 0.9$ in the case of a successful offspring.

The dispersive flies optimization algorithm (abbreviated DFO hereafter) was proposed in [10] by al Rifaie. The only control parameter called *disturbance threshold*, is set to value from the recommended range $1 \times 10^{-2} < dt < 1 \times 10^{-4}$, i.e. $dt = 1 \times 10^{-3}$.

The cuckoo search algorithm (denoted Cuckoo) was introduced by Yang in [11]. This algorithm was inspired by cuckoo birds 'nest-parasitism'. Probability of the cuckoo's eggs laid in a bird-host nest is set $pa = 0.25$ and the control parameter of Lévy flight random walk is set to $\lambda = 1.5$.

The firefly algorithm (called Firefly in follows) proposed by Yang in [7] models the 'light-behavior' of fireflies when attracted another fireflies. This artificial representation of fireflies model has several control parameters that are set to recommended values – randomization parameter $\alpha = 0.5$, *light absorption* coefficient $\gamma = 1$, and *attractiveness* is updated using its initial $\beta_0 = 1$ and minimal $\beta_{min} = 0.2$ values.

The only representative of the algorithms modeling the life of plants is Flower Pollination Algorithm for Global Optimization (denoted Flower hereafter) and was proposed by Yang in [12]. The goal of this approach is to model a process of transferring pollen grains between the flowers to their further reproduction. The main control parameter equals to probability of switching between global and local search is set to $p = 0.8$. A second parameter controlling Lévy distribution is set up $\lambda = 1.5$, as in the Cuckoo search algorithm.

The particle swarm optimization (PSO) originally proposed by Kenedy and Eberhart in 1995 belongs to very popular and ofen studied nature-inspired algorithms [13]. In this experiment, the basic variant of PSO with slightly enhanced of particles' velocities updated by the variation coefficient w and coefficient c is used. The variation control parameter w is set as a linear interpolation from maximal value $w_{max} = 1$ to $w_{min} = 0.3$, for each generation. Parameter controlling a local and a global part of the velocity update is set $c = 1.05$. A new velocity is computed by $v_{i,G+1} = w_{G+1}\, v_{i,G} + c\, U(0,1)\, (p_{best} - x_i) + c\, U(0,1)\, (g_{best} - x_i)$, where G denotes generation, $U(0,1)$ is random number generated from uniform distribution with parameters given in parentheses, x_i is current particle position, p_{best} is up-to-now best historical position of the current particle, and g_{best} is a position of the best particle in swarm history.

The self-organizing migrating algorithm (abbreviated SOMA) was proposed by Zelinka and Lampinen in 2000 as a model of a pack of predators [14]. SOMA has several control parameters and particle strategies that crucially influence the algorithm's efficiency. The best settings based on our preliminary experiments was taken for this experiment. Parameter controlling the (maximal) length of individual way toward to leader is set *PathLenght* $= 2$, the step size is set to *Step* $= 0.11$, and perturbation parameter is set *Prt* $= 0.1$. There are also several strategies of individual movement, the best performing strategy *all-to-one* as indicated in the preliminary experiments was applied to comparison on the CEC 2011 benchmark.

3   Cooperative Model of Nature-Inspired Algorithms

The main goal of this paper is to construct cooperative model of the aforementioned nature-inspired algorithms to achieve better efficiency. There are many possibilities how to employ selected k various algorithms to cooperation. We applied a modification of our well-performed recent cooperative model described in [15,16]. A comprehensive review of a control parameters settings in a distributed evolutionary algorithms is in [17,18]. The idea of the cooperative model is based on *migration model* with ring topology [16] and its pseudo-code is illustrated in Algorithm 1.

Algorithm 1. Cooperative Model of Nature-Inspired Algorithms
***

    initialize nature-inspired algorithms' populations P_i, $i = 1, 2, \ldots, k$
    evaluate individuals of all algorithms' populations
    while stopping condition not reached **do**
      for $i = 1, 2, \ldots, k$ **do**
        perform n_{gen} generations of ith algorithm's population
      end for
      construct a ring topology of randomly ordered algorithms' populations
      migrate selected individuals between populations by the unidirectional ring
    end while

Proposed cooperative model has beside selected ring topology several input parameters. At first, k populations of equal size N_p is initialized and developed by k various algorithms. Then, n_{gen} generations of all nature-inspired algorithms are performed independently and several individuals are selected to exchange with other populations. This exchange is called *migration* and preliminary experiment [15] shows that combination of the best and n_{ind} randomly selected individuals is a good choice. Migration is performed between couple of populations such that selected the best individual from the donor population replaces the worst individual in the acceptor population. Randomly selected n_{ind} individuals from the donor population replaces n_{ind} randomly selected individuals in the acceptor population except the best individual.

The couples of populations to migration are given by ring topology where each population has two neighbors - preceding and following. For higher level of randomness, order of algorithms' populations in ring topology is given randomly for each migration. The populations are not communicated with the same counterparts for higher level of diversity of individuals in overall CoNI algorithm. Selected $n_{ind} + 1$ individuals from the donor population (*preceding* in circle manner) replaces the selected individuals in acceptor population (*following* in circle manner).

A pseudo-parallel representation will be used to estimate efficiency of the proposed cooperative model. Physically, n_{gen} generations are performed subsequently for each algorithm on single-CPU PC (pseudo-parallelism). The quality of the proposed cooperative model is evaluated by function value and also by number of function evaluations. The name of the proposed cooperative model of nature-inspired algorithms is abbreviated as CoNI in following text.

4   Experimental Setting

The test suite of 22 real-world problems selected for CEC 2011 competition in Special Session on Real-Parameter Numerical Optimization [6] is used as a benchmark in the experimental comparison. The functions in the benchmark differ in the computational complexity and in the dimension of the search space which varies from $D = 1$ to $D = 240$.

For each algorithm and problem, 25 independent runs were carried out. The run of the algorithm stops if the prescribed number of function evaluations $MaxFES = 150000$ is reached. The partial results of the algorithms after reaching one third and two thirds of $MaxFES$ were also recorded for further analysis. The point in the terminal population with the smallest function value is the solution of the problem found in the run.

The population size $N = 90$ was used in all the nature-inspired algorithms and CEC 2011 problems. The number of nature-inspired algorithms cooperative in CoNI is $k = 8$, the population size of each cooperative algorithm is set equally to $N_p = 15$, number of generations before migration is $n_{gen} = 10$ and $n_{ind} = 4$ individuals are randomly selected for each of migration. The other control parameters are set up according to recommendation of authors in their original papers. All the algorithms are implemented in Matlab 2010a and all computations were carried out on a standard PC with Windows 7, Intel(R) Core(TM)i7-4790 CPU 3.6 GHz, 16 GB RAM.

5   Results

A Table 1 contains the basic characteristics of CoNI algorithm at final stage of the search ($FES = 150000$) and the results of the Kruskal-Wallis test including significance and multiple comparison based on Dunn's method. The detailed results of the original nature-inspired algorithms on CEC 2011 real-world problems used in this experiment are presented in previous works [4,5]. The median value for the problem (row) where CoNI algorithm achieves the best result out of all algorithms in comparison is printed bold.

Kruskal-Wallis non-parametric one-way ANOVA test was applied to each problem to obtain significant differences. It was found that the performance of the algorithms in comparison differs significantly, the null hypothesis on the same performance is rejected in all the problems at all dimensions with achieved significance level $p < 1 \times 10^{-5}$ and it means that algorithms' performance differs even in the similar medians.

The best performing algorithms significantly different from the followers and mutually with no significant differences are listed in the column "best" ordered ascending with respect to the median function value. The worst performing algorithms significantly different from their predecessors and mutually with no significant differences are listed in the column "worst" ordered from the worst performing algorithm. Based on these columns, it is not easy to assess the superiority or inferiority of the algorithms. In the case of the proposed CoNI, the first position (column *best*) is not occupied only for the problems $T11.3$ and $T11.4$.

Table 1. The basic characteristics of function values found by the cooperative model and results of Kruskal-Wallis multiple comparison

F	D	Min	Max	Med	Mean	Std	Best	Worst
T01	6	1.18E−06	14.779	8.41626	6.92583	5.98041	Cuckoo, CoNI	Bat, DFO
T02	30	−25.5936	−15.3846	**−22.0875**	−21.5095	3.13850	CoNI, ABC, SOMA	Bat, DFO
T03	1	1.15E−05	1.15E−05	1.15E−05	1.15E−05	5.19E−21	All	Firefly
T04	1	0	0	0	0	0	All	Firefly
T05	30	−35.7924	−31.4839	−34.1075	−33.5094	1.29947	ABC, CoNI	DFO, Bat
T06	30	−29.1627	−21.2696	−27.4277	−26.5641	2.58163	CoNI, SOMA	DFO, Bat, Firefly
T07	20	0.807308	1.3313	**1.04799**	1.0488101	1.54E−01	CoNI, SOMA, Cuckoo	DFO, Bat, Firefly
T08	7	220	220	220	220	0	All	Bat, Firefly, DFO
T09	126	13082.7	36124.4	19363.4	21467.9	6618.66	ABC, CoNI	Firefly
T10	12	−20.8443	−12.773	−19.2706	−18.8992	2.00284	Cuckoo, CoNI	Bat, Firefly, DFO
T11.1	120	62744.9	212805	71228.1	79231.1	28762.1	ABC, CoNI	DFO, Firefly
T11.2	240	1.10E+06	1.17E+06	**1.12E+06**	1.12E+06	17712.3	CoNI, ABC	Bat, Firefly, DFO
T11.3	6	15445.5	15453.4	15447.6	15448.2	2.11792	Flower	Bat, Firefly, DFO
T11.4	13	18485.2	19148.6	18820	18853.86	155.764	Flower	ABC, Bat, DFO
T11.5	15	32781.8	32984.7	32878	32872.0	51.1892	SOMA, CoNI, Flower	Bat, Firefly
T11.6	40	129038	137573	133039	133312	2570.42	Flower, CoNI, SOMA	Firefly, DFO
T11.7	140	1.92E+06	2.54E+06	**1.95E+06**	2.01E+06	139086	CoNI, Flower, SOMA	Firefly, DFO, Bat
T11.8	96	941250	1.02E+06	**946333**	951888	16253.6	CoNI, SOMA	Firefly, Bat
T11.9	96	1.00E+06	1.84E+06	1.43E+06	1.42E+06	176918	SOMA, CoNI, PSO	Firefly, Bat
T11.10	96	941689	1.14E+06	**945565**	962950	45817.2	CoNI, SOMA	Firefly, Bat
T12	26	12.4059	20.3057	**16.7507**	17.0220	1.96866	CoNI, SOMA	DFO, Bat
T13	22	11.5376	26.6287	21.4875	20.5451	3.78682	ABC, CoNI, SOMA	Bat, DFO

Comparing medians of these problems it is obvious that CoNI takes at least the third position out of nine algorithms.

For better overview of the comparison of the presented algorithms' performance, the number of first, second, third, and the last positions from Kruskal-Wallis test are computed and showed in Table 2. It is clear that CoNI is able to achieve the first position in 8 out of 22 real-world problems. In the remaining problems, CoNI occupies the second or the third position without significant difference between CoNI and the best performing counterpart (based on Kruskal-Wallis test). Further promising results provide ABC, Flower, SOMA, and Cuckoo. An interesting is significant win of Flower algorithm in $T11.3$ and $T11.4$ problems. The worst performing algorithms in whole experiment are Firefly and Bat algorithm followed by DFO. Necessary to note that Firefly algorithm performs substantially better when solving an artificial problems as CEC 2014 (see results in [5]).

Table 2. Number of significant wins, second, third, and the last positions of the algorithms

Position	ABC	Bat	Cuckoo	DFO	Firefly	Flower	PSO	SOMA	CoNI
1st	4	0	2	0	0	3	0	2	8
2nd	2	0	1	0	0	1	1	5	9
3rd	0	0	3	0	0	2	5	7	2
Last	1	8	0	5	8	0	0	0	0

In Table 3 the results of Friedman test are presented. This test was carried out on medians of minimal function values at three stages of the search, namely after $FES = 50000, 100000$, and 150000. The null hypothesis on equivalent efficiency of the algorithms was rejected at the all stages of the search, p-value achieved in Friedman test was less than 5×10^{-6}.

Table 3. Mean rank of Friedman test for all algorithms

Alg	1st stage	2nd stage	3rd stage	Avg
CoNI	2.8	2.2	2.1	2.3
SOMA	2.7	3.0	3.0	2.9
PSO	4.3	4.2	4.4	4.3
ABC	3.9	4.5	4.6	4.3
Cuckoo	4.7	4.3	4.0	4.3
Flower	4.6	4.4	4.3	4.4
DFO	7.0	6.9	7.1	7.0
Firefly	7.6	7.6	7.7	7.6
Bat	7.6	7.8	7.9	7.8

The mean ranks from Friedman test of the algorithms in three stages are also illustrated in Fig. 1. Moreover, the mean rank values for each algorithm of three stages are joined for better conclusions. Notice that better performing algorithm over all 22 test problems achieves smaller mean rank and vice versa. Based on these results (especially a graphical representation) three groups of compared algorithms with respect to performance are arisen. The worst performing triplet is formed by DFO, Firefly, and Bat algorithm. All these nature-inspired algorithms are often used by researchers to solve the real problems. The "middle-performing" group is formed by PSO, Flower, Cuckoo, and ABC algorithm where performance of ABC and PSO is gradually in the search process surprisingly decreased. Mean ranks of these algorithms are approximately equal to the average rank. Whilst performance of SOMA in the best couple is gradually decreased with increasing FES, CoNI with increasing function evaluations achieved less mean rank.

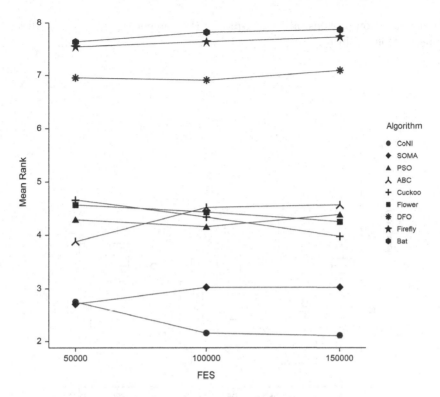

Fig. 1. Mean rank of Friedman test for all algorithms

Performance of new CoNI algorithm should be also compared with the performance of the winner of CEC 2011 competition, GA-MPC. Detailed results of this algorithm are provided in [19]. It is clear that CoNI is able to outperform GA-MPC in 5 problems, i.e. T04, T11.6-8, and T11.10 and in two problems (T03 and T08) both algorithms perform equally. In the remaining cases, the CEC 2011 winner performs better than cooperative model of nature-inspired algorithms.

Achieved results of this experimental study show that proposed cooperative model of nature-inspired algorithm is able to outperform the original algorithms and also partially the CEC 2011 winner. Further analysis of CoNI features should detect if some of the used nature-inspired algorithms performs better or worse. For this purpose, the number of successfully generated new individuals are computed for each of eight nature-inspired algorithms in CoNI. This characteristic denotes the number of newly generated individuals better than the old solution in accordance with the goal function. For better comparison, a percentage success of each (ith) used algorithm is computed as a proportion of its success (suc_i) from whole success (suc_{total}):

$$psuc_i = \frac{suc_i}{suc_{\text{total}}} \cdot 100, \qquad i = 1,\ 2, \ldots k \tag{1}$$

For better comprehensibility, box-plot of the percentage successes of all algorithms is depicted in Fig. 2.

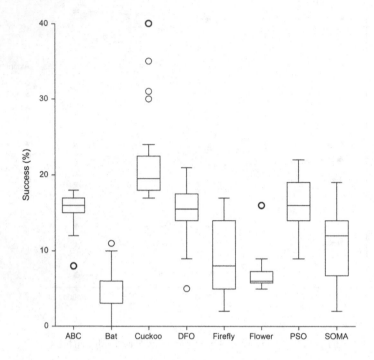

Fig. 2. Comparison of percentage successes (*psuc*) in CoNI algorithm

From the box-plot in Fig. 2, it is clear that the biggest proportion of successfully generated new-individuals provides Cuckoo algorithm with ABC and surprisingly DFO algorithm. This situation is caused by very simple reason. The worst individual of current algorithm in CoNI is replaced by the selected best individual (from another algorithm) and sometimes this new solution could be substantially better than current best solution (case of DFO). Then, some individuals of such algorithm will be more increased because of using of the new best solution. Thin boxes in the bottom of the plot for PSO and Flower suggest lower success-proportion in most of the real-world problems.

Except the percentage successes, the "name" of the nature-inspired algorithm employing the overall best solution of CoNI is stored in 17 stages of CEC 2011 problems. Because the lack of space, total number of "ownership" of the best solution in 17 stages of 22 test problems is computed: ABC (112), SOMA (79), Bat (70), Firefly (62), Cuckoo (34), Flower (11), PSO (3), and DFO (3). We can see that the most often algorithm providing the overall best solution of CoNI is ABC. This result is in contradiction with the mean rank of ABC algorithm (Fig. 1) and the success of this algorithm in CoNI (Fig. 2). The least counts of developed the best CoNI solution have DFO and PSO algorithms. When we consider presented results (Table 2 and Fig. 2), the performance of both these algorithms is rather less, especially for DFO variant. However, the percentage success of PSO algorithm in CoNI model belongs to better foursome. The phenomenon, when badly performing separately applied nature-inspired algorithm has high success in CoNI model is caused by big number of small improvements.

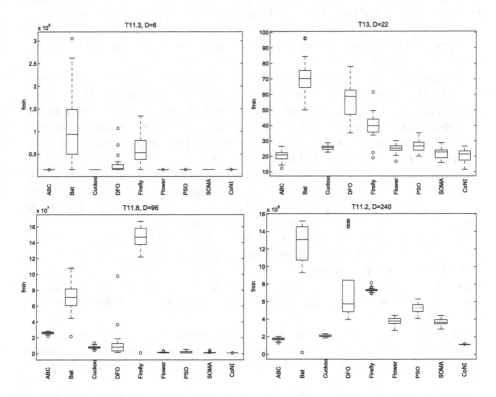

Fig. 3. Minimal function values from 25 runs in problems with various dimensionality

The various performance of nature-inspired algorithms is the main reason for using of the cooperative model because higher variability of partial solutions causes higher ability to produce more diverse individuals. The diversity of individuals is crucial feature of evolutionary algorithms in the search of the right solution of optimization problems.

The performance of CoNI algorithm in problems with various dimension level is depicted in Fig. 3. The $T11.3$ problem ($D = 6$) is solved successfully by most algorithms (boxes are flattened at the bottom of the figure). For higher dimensions (problems $T13$, $T11.8$), the better performance of CoNI is more obvious. Furthermore, for the problem with highest dimension, $T11.2$, ($D = 240$) CoNI achieves the best results among all algorithms in comparison.

6 Conclusion

In this paper the cooperation model of several algorithms based on well-known migration model is proposed to increase the efficiency of nature-inspired algorithms. The results of experimental comparison of eight popular nature-inspired algorithms with the cooperative model of these algorithms demonstrate clearly the superiority of the proposed CoNI algorithm. Good performance of CoNI is caused by exchange of the individuals between variously performing algorithms. A proper settings of the parameters of cooperative model promises better results in various real-world problems.

Although nature-inspired algorithms belong to very popular optimization methods, their efficiency is often poor as it is shown in results of [4,5]. When we consider a No-Free-Lunch theorem [20] – each algorithm is better performing in another kind of optimization tasks – cooperative model of nature-inspired algorithms is simple idea to achieve better results. The high performance of CoNI is caused by exchange the individuals of variously successful applied algorithms in various problems. Without the migration, the results are not better than the results of the best non-parallel nature-inspired algorithm. Proposed cooperative algorithm shares the best position in 20 out of 22 problems and achieves the best results (first position) in 8 out 22 test problems.

Comparison of CoNI with the winner of CEC 2011 real-world problems test suite – (GA-MPC [19]) shows that cooperative model is competitive in most of real problems. We believe that there exist possibilities of the improvements. Especially selection of proper topology, migration policy, and migration frequency are the fundamental points for improvement of the cooperative model [17,18].

The source code of newly proposed CoNI algorithm in Matlab is available at www1.osu.cz/~bujok/, the source code of some other state-of-the-art nature-inspired algorithms can be found on web site of MathWorks, www.mathworks. com.

References

1. Fister Jr., I., Yang, X.S., Fister, I., Brest, J., Fister, D.: A brief review of nature-inspired algorithms for optimization. Elektrotehniski vestnik **80**(3), 116–122 (2013)
2. Wang, H., Sun, H., Li, C., Rahnamayan, S., Pan, J.S.: Diversity enhanced particle swarm optimization with neighborhood search. Inf. Sci. **223**, 119–135 (2013)
3. Yang, M., Li, C., Cai, Z., Guan, J.: Differential evolution with auto-enhanced population diversity. IEEE Trans. Cybern. **45**(2), 302–315 (2015)
4. Bujok, P., Tvrdík, J., Poláková, R.: Nature-inspired algorithms in real-world optimization problems. MENDEL Soft Comput. J. **23**, 7–14 (2017)
5. Bujok, P., Tvrdík, J., Poláková, R.: Adaptive differential evolution vs. nature-inspired algorithms: an experimental comparison. In: 2017 IEEE Symposium Series on Computational Intelligence (IEEE SSCI), pp. 2604–2611 (2017)
6. Das, S., Suganthan, P.N.: Problem definitions and evaluation criteria for CEC 2011 competition on testing evolutionary algorithms on real world optimization problems. Technical report, Jadavpur University, India and Nanyang Technological University, Singapore (2010)

7. Yang, X.S.: Nature-Inspired Optimization Algorithms. Elsevier, New York (2014)
8. Karaboga, D.: An idea based on honey bee swarm for numerical optimization. Technical report-tr06, Erciyes University, Kayseri, Turkey (2005)
9. Yang, X.S.: A new metaheuristic bat-inspired algorithm. In: González, J.R., Pelta, D.A., Cruz, C., Terrazas, G., Krasnogor, N. (eds.) NICSO 2010. SCI, vol. 284, pp. 65–74. Springer, Heidelberg (2010). https://doi.org/10.1007/978-3-642-12538-6_6
10. al Rifaie, M.M.: Dispersive flies optimisation. In: Federated Conference on Computer Science and Information Systems, 2014. ACSIS-Annals of Computer Science and Information Systems, vol. 2, pp. 529–538 (2014)
11. Yang, X.S., Deb, S.: Cuckoo search via Lévy flights. In: 2009 World Congress on Nature Biologically Inspired Computing NaBIC, pp. 210–214 (2009)
12. Yang, X.-S.: Flower pollination algorithm for global optimization. In: Durand-Lose, J., Jonoska, N. (eds.) UCNC 2012. LNCS, vol. 7445, pp. 240–249. Springer, Heidelberg (2012). https://doi.org/10.1007/978-3-642-32894-7_27
13. Kennedy, J., Eberhart, R.: Particle swarm optimization. In: 1995 IEEE International Conference on Neural Networks Proceedings, vols. 1–6, pp. 1942–1948. IEEE, Neural Networks Council (1995)
14. Zelinka, I., Lampinen, J.: SOMA – self organizing migrating algorithm. In: Matousek, R. (ed.) MENDEL, 6th International Conference on Soft Computing, Brno, Czech Republic, pp. 177–187 (2000)
15. Bujok, P., Tvrdík, J.: Parallel migration model employing various adaptive variants of differential evolution. In: Rutkowski, L., Korytkowski, M., Scherer, R., Tadeusiewicz, R., Zadeh, L.A., Zurada, J.M. (eds.) EC/SIDE -2012. LNCS, vol. 7269, pp. 39–47. Springer, Heidelberg (2012). https://doi.org/10.1007/978-3-642-29353-5_5
16. Bujok, P.: Synchronous and asynchronous migration in adaptive differential evolution algorithms. Neural Netw. World 23(1), 17–30 (2013)
17. Laessig, J., Sudholt, D.: Design and analysis of migration in parallel evolutionary algorithms. Soft Comput. 17(7, SI), 1121–1144 (2013)
18. Gong, Y.J., Chen, W.N., Zhan, Z.H., Zhang, J., Li, Y., Zhang, Q., Li, J.J.: Distributed evolutionary algorithms and their models: a survey of the state-of-the-art. Appl. Soft Comput. 34, 286–300 (2015)
19. Elsayed, S.M., Sarker, R.A., Essam, D.L.: GA with a new multi-parent crossover for solving IEEE-CEC2011 competition problems. In: 2011 IEEE Congress on Evolutionary Computation (CEC), pp. 1034–1040. IEEE (2011)
20. Wolpert, D.H., Macready, W.G.: No free lunch theorems for optimization. IEEE Trans. Evol. Comput. 1, 67–82 (1997)

Collaborative Agent Teams (CAT): From the Paradigm to Implementation Guidelines

Marc-André Carle[1,2], Alain Martel[2], and Nicolas Zufferey[2,3(✉)]

[1] Département Opérations et Systèmes de Décisions, Université Laval,
Québec, Canada
marc-andre.carle@osd.ulaval.ca
[2] CIRRELT, Québec, Canada
alain.martel@cirrelt.ca
http://www.cirrelt.ca/
[3] Geneva School of Economics and Management, GSEM, University of Geneva,
Blvd du Pont-d'Arve 40, 1211 Geneva 4, Switzerland
n.zufferey@unige.ch

Abstract. We propose a general solution method framework based on a Collaborative Agent Teams (CAT) architecture to tackle large-scale mixed-integer optimization problems with complex structures. This framework introduces several conceptual improvements over previous agent teams' approaches. We discuss how to configure the three key components of a CAT solver for multidimensional optimization problems: the problem representation, the design of agents, and the information sharing mechanisms between agents. Implementation guidelines are also given.

Keywords: Multidimensional optimization · Asynchronous Teams

1 Introduction

Despite of the continuous improvements of the commercial/academic solvers and of the exact and solution methods, many optimization problems are so complex that finding good-quality solutions remains challenging. These problems are too large (in terms of size) and complex (in terms of structure) to be solved directly through classical solution methods (e.g., [1,2]). This paper extends the latter by generalizing and formulating the CAT (Collaborative Agent Teams) methodology for any optimization problem. We propose a general framework for CAT, an agent-based methodology based on the Asynchronous Teams (A-Teams) paradigm that is designed to tackle complex multi-dimensional optimization problems. We discuss how to design the three key components of a CAT solver: the problem representation; the design of the agents and their job description; the information sharing mechanisms between the agents.

"Decision problem" refers to a real-world issue requiring a solution as perceived by decision-makers. A decision problem can often be expressed qualitatively in terms of a choice between alternative options. An "optimization model"

© Springer International Publishing AG, part of Springer Nature 2018
P. Korošec et al. (Eds.): BIOMA 2018, LNCS 10835, pp. 62–74, 2018.
https://doi.org/10.1007/978-3-319-91641-5_6

refers to a mathematical system formulated to represent a view of a decision problem. It is specified in terms of a set of decision variables and parameters. It incorporates objective function(s) and a constraint set. "Optimization algorithm" and "solution method" refer to programmable procedures developed to generate high-quality solutions for a given optimization model. The Simplex and branch-and-bound methods, greedy heuristics and tabu search metaheuristics, are all examples of optimization algorithms, including simulation-optimization approaches [3]. A "heuristic" is a basic solution method that finds, in a reasonable amount of time, a "satisfying" solution to the considered optimization model. Optimality is generally not guaranteed. A "metaheuristic" (MH) is a higher-level methodology that guides underlying heuristics for solving the optimization problem. The term "solution" is used to designate a set of values for the decision variables that satisfy all the constraints of a given optimization model.

The paper is organized as follows. Section 2 presents a literature review of operations research approaches that contributed to design CAT. In Sect. 3, CAT and its components are presented. Section 4 concludes the paper.

2 Strategies to Tackle Complex Problems/Models

We describe here algorithmic strategies to solve complex decision problems and the optimization models used to represent them. We also position their relative strengths in achieving better performance or tackling more complex problems. A general description of relevant strategies is provided rather than a technical description of algorithms. Some strategies are not exclusive: they can be hybridized to tackle the most challenging problems (which opens the door for CAT).

2.1 Classical Approaches, Parallel Algorithms and Hybridization

Many optimization models are today "easy" to solve, even with the use of a solver (CPLEX/Gurobi) or with the help of filtering techniques to reduce the search space [4,5]. However, several optimization models are hard to solve using solvers, especially when the model is nonlinear/stochastic. Models with a single category of binary decision variables and few constraint types are often solved to near-optimality in a reasonable amount of time with MHs (e.g., the tabu search MH is efficient for the simple facility location model [6]). MHs can usually successfully tackle such problems even if they have nonlinear objective functions or constraints. Local-search MHs are efficient on these problems because it is straightforward to create a new solution by applying a local transformation on a given solution. When multiple types of integer, binary and continuous decision variables are present in the model, these approaches may not be effective.

Most state-of-the-art commercial solvers (CPLEX, Gurobi) use several processors at a time if possible. According to [7], parallelism [in MHs] allows for improved solution quality and reduction in the resolution time. Two strategies are especially relevant: (1) parallelization of the search: several copies of a given MH work in parallel, each having its own parameter settings and possibly exchanging solutions synchronously or asynchronously during the search process; (2) parallelization of some of the most computationally-intensive tasks of the search process (typically solution quality evaluation or neighborhood exploration).

Hybridization refers to the combination of different types of algorithms into one methodology [8]. The first main technique combines various MHs [9], hoping that one method's strengths compensate for the other method's weaknesses. Several hybridization strategies can be designed for any two given MHs, resulting in a larger number of potential solution methods. The second main hybridization technique combines MHs with exact methods [10]. These hybrid solution methods are often called matheuristics [11]. They effectively combine the ability of MHs to handle a large number of binary/integer decision variables, with the LP- (linear program) or MIP- (mixed integer program) based methods' ability to handle a large number of constraints and continuous decision variables.

2.2 Decomposition and Model-Based Strategies

Some methods use the optimization model's formulation to break it down into smaller/easier problems. Since the 1960s, decomposition-based solution methods (e.g., [12,13]) are effective at solving large optimization models that exhibit a specific model structure. The efficiency of these methods lies in clever reformulation of the optimization model and the availability of a sub-model that can be solved very fast. However, when the decomposed sub-models they yield are themselves difficult to solve, these methods may not perform well.

Multilevel techniques [14] are another family of methods making use of the model formulation. They start from the optimization model, then iteratively and recursively generate a smaller and smaller model by coarsening until a relatively small model is obtained, creating a hierarchy of optimization models [9]. A solution to the smallest model is found by some optimization algorithm. Then, the solution to this problem is successively transformed into a solution to the model of the next level until a solution to the original optimization model is found.

Recently, a number of progressive variable fixing solution methods have been proposed to solve complex models. The simplest method, the LP-rounding strategy [15], uses a solver to obtain the LP relaxation of the model. The values of integer and binary decision variables that are fractional in the LP relaxation are then rounded to obtain an integer-feasible solution. In [16], a sequence of linear relaxations of the original optimization model is solved, and as many binary and integer variables as possible are fixed at every iteration. These methods are effective to solve problems with a small number of binary and a large number of continuous decision variables.

2.3 Distributed Decision Making and Agent Optimization

Another strategy to cope with model complexity is to work at the decision problem level rather than directly on the optimization model. The decision problem can often be partitioned into various interconnected sub-problems under the responsibility of distinct organizational units. For each sub-problem, a sub-model is formulated and solved using an optimization algorithm. This approach has many advantages and is even more suited to decision problems involving multiple decision-makers. According to [17], "distributed decision making can be useful in order to better understand/manipulate a complex decision situation".

Multi-agent systems (MAS) and agent-based optimization algorithms have been used recently to model/analyze complex decision problems. MAS formalize complex decision problems as networks of simpler decision problems, each of these problems being tackled by a separate agent [17]. Depending on the degree of sophistication of the approach, the agent may use basic rules to make decisions, or formulate an optimization model which is then solved with an appropriate (exact or heuristic) optimization algorithm. An example of this approach is A-Teams [18], a cooperative MAS used for various problems (e.g. [1,19–21]).

2.4 Towards an Integrated Optimization Framework

Many approaches have integrated the above strategies to solve complex optimization models. Their strengths are often complementary: a MAS is indeed well suited to implement parallel and potentially hybrid optimization algorithms. A hybrid matheuristic can couple two algorithms working in parallel rather than sequentially. Despite these advantages, very few tools have been proposed to combine the strengths from all these strategies into one solution system. The five following elements should be present in an optimization framework designed for complex decision problems. (1) Draw inspiration from the decision problem and alternative optimization model formulations to design adapted solution methods, instead of one perspective. (2) Use partitioning strategies through organizational decomposition (at the problem level) or mathematical decomposition (at the model level), while working on each partition simultaneously in parallel. (3) Use the type of optimization algorithm that works best for each sub-model. (4) Share information/solutions between different optimization strategies. (5) Combine good solutions from sub-models into good solutions to the complete model. An optimization framework based on these characteristics is now proposed.

3 CAT as an Agent-Based Solution Method

CAT is a hybrid distributed agent-based solution method to solve complex decision problems and associated optimization models that cannot be efficiently addressed using classical MHs or mathematical decomposition methods. The approach builds on the A-Teams paradigm [18], and it relies on the foundations of Subsect. 2.4. We use the location-routing problem (LRP) [22] to illustrate the CAT concepts. It involves decisions on the number and location of distribution centers (DCs) in order to serve customers at minimum cost, and finding the best delivery schedules and vehicle routes to serve the customers. "An asynchronous team is a team of software agents that cooperate to solve a problem by dynamically evolving a shared population of solutions" [18]. Agents are autonomous: they incorporate their own representation of the problem, and rules to choose when to work, what to work on and when to stop working. The approach is well suited to implement multiple representations of a problem, such as advocated above. Previous work suggests that A-Teams can host a large variety of optimization algorithms. Whereas some applications [1] use simple heuristics and linear and integer programming, recent applications [20,21] employ MHs (e.g., tabu search). When facing complex optimization models, it makes sense to use the best tools for each (sub-)model. A MAS allows for that much flexibility.

3.1   Problem Solving Approach

The following steps are required to solve optimization problems with CAT: (1) identify different relevant points of view (dimensions) to examine the decision problem; (2) formulate optimization models and sub-models for these dimensional views; (3) design optimization algorithms to solve each sub-model; (4) design optimization algorithms to integrate solutions from sub-models into solutions of the complete optimization models. These steps are explained below.

Views and Sub-problems, Models and Sub-models. Complex decision problems can be analyzed from different views, that is, a filter/lens which emphasizes, reduces or reshapes some aspects of the decision problem to solve. It can reflect a stakeholder's perceptions. The integrated view refers to a holistic apprehension of the complete decision problem, that is, one that looks at all relevant facets from a centralized standpoint. Problem solving with CAT requires addressing the problem with an integrated view, and with alternative dimensional views. Dimensional views are rearrangements of the problem into systems of interrelated sub-problems. These sub-problems may cover only a subset of the objectives and decisions of the original problem and they may involve a reduction of some of its facets. Dimensional views are used to reduce the complexity of the problem by providing effective partitioning schemes. Dimensional views must be selected before optimization models can be formulated. A dimensional view may require the definition of several sub-problems. A sub-problem contains a portion of the decisions and context associated with the decision problem. The number of sub-problems used and the exact definition of each of them are critical issues. Useful sub-problems possess the following characteristics. First, they make sense from a business standpoint (i.e., they are easily understandable by a decision-maker). Second, the set of all the sub-problems associated with a dimensional view must constitute a valid representation of the complete decision problem. For the LRP, the following two dimensional views could be defined. First, a functional view is associated with the types of decisions (location, customer allocation to facilities, vehicle routing) associated with the decision problem. The problem can then be partitioned into a DC location sub-problem, a customer-to-DC allocation sub-problem, and a transportation or route design sub-problem. Second, the LRP has an inherent spatial dimension. Indeed, the customers served by a company may cover a large territory, and logistics decisions may be made on a national or sales region level instead of globally. In this context, the problem can be partitioned into several regional sub-problems. These dimensional views and the associated sub-problems are easily understandable by a decision-maker. Each regional sub-problem contains all decision types, and each functional sub-problem contains decisions for all regions. Thus, they both constitute a valid representation of the whole problem.

The integrated view leads to the formulation of a "complete" optimization model to represent the decision problem. This model is generally difficult to solve, but it will be used for various purposes. For each dimensional view, sub-models are formulated to represent sub-problems. These formulations are usually expressed in terms of partitions of complete model decision variable vectors and parameter matrices. They may also be based on alternative modeling formalisms: (e.g., a constraint programming sub-model can be defined even if the complete optimization model is a MIP). A sub-model is useful if it can be solved efficiently. It is usually the case if the sub-model: (1) corresponds to a generic class of decision models studied in depth in the literature (e.g., bin packing, facility location); (2) can be solved to optimality using generic LP-MIP solvers, or dynamic programming, or simple enumeration (explicit or implicit); (3) isolates a homogeneous group of binary/integer variables and their associated constraints.

Optimization Algorithms. Once the sub-models have been formulated, optimization algorithms must be designed to solve them. In CAT, optimization algorithms are implemented as a set of autonomous software agents. Solutions to sub-models are recorded and subsequently used to build complete solutions. The following guidelines are useful to select a solution method. (1) Develop greedy heuristics to construct feasible solutions for profit maximizing or cost minimizing sub-models. (2) When the sub-model has been studied in the literature, published solution methods can be integrated into CAT. (3) Purely linear sub-models can be solved using a LP-solver library. (4) Sub-models involving a homogeneous group of binary/integer variables can usually be solved effectively with a local search MH since it is rather straightforward to define a neighborhood in this context. In the LRP context, some of the sub-models formulated and the solution methods selected could be the following: a pure facility location sub-model solved with a MIP solver such as CPLEX; a location-allocation sub-model solved with a Lagrangean heuristic [23]; a vehicle routing sub-model solved with a tabu search MH [24]; a regional LRP sub-model solved with a tabu search [25].

Integration Sub-models. Integration refers to combining the solutions of the sub-models associated with one view into solutions to the full optimization model. It is done by exactly/heuristically solving an integration sub-model. Integration sub-models are restricted versions of the full optimization model obtained by fixing the value of several decision variables. The fixed values are provided by the solutions to the dimensional sub-models. By solving the integration sub-model, the optimal value of the non-fixed decision variables is found, and a solution to the complete model is produced. We refer to the set of decision variables to optimize in an integration sub-model as integration variables.

Integration variables not present in any dimensional sub-model are linking variables, and those present in various dimensional sub-models are overlapping variables.

Integration is also used as a search strategy. For a specific dimensional view, the choices of integration variables lead to different integration sub-models. When the dimensional sub-models solutions are mutually exclusive, the integration sub-model contains only linking variables, and optimizing these variables provides a feasible solution for the complete model. When the dimensional sub-models solutions are overlapping, a merging integration sub-model is obtained. Since it is unlikely that the overlapping variables have the same value in all partial solutions, the integration sub-model must find the optimal value of these variables. The search space created by a merging sub-model can be enhanced by including more than one partial solution from a given dimensional sub-model. This adds all the variables from that sub-model to the set of overlapping variables. If the resulting integration sub-model is difficult to solve, one can constrain the integration sub-model by fixing the values of the overlapping variables that are identical in all partial solutions or restricting the values of the overlapping variables to those found in the partial solutions, resulting in a smaller model.

Depending on the partial solutions chosen for integration, the resulting sub-model may be infeasible. When it occurs, an alternative integration sub-model that seeks to find a feasible solution while keeping most of the partial solutions' characteristics is used. In these sub-model's, the original objective function is replaced with the minimization of the number (or amplitude) of decision variable changes when compared with the values found in the sub-problems.

To conclude our LRP example, using the pure location sub-model and the vehicle routing sub-model solutions, one would formulate a merging integration sub-model as follows. The depot location decision variables are fixed using the solution to the pure min-cost location sub-model. Several vehicle routing sub-model solutions are also considered. The resulting integration sub-model selects a set of feasible routes among the routes provided by the vehicle routing sub-models. It is a capacitated set partitioning model for which many methods exist.

3.2   CAT System Structure

The structure of the CAT system incorporates a blackboard, utility agents and optimization agents. The blackboard acts as a memory and a hub for communications, and it is the repository of all solutions (to the complete optimization model and to all sub-models). Agents communicate solely through the blackboard. New complete or partial solutions are placed on the blackboard and existing solutions are retrieved when necessary. Utility agents provide functionalities required by all agents, such as building mathematical model files for solvers, formatting instance data, and compiling solution statistics. The optimization agents are the most important: (1) construction agents create new solutions from scratch; (2) improvement agents take existing solutions and try to improve them; (3) destruction agents remove unwanted solutions from the repository; (4) integration agents combine high-quality solutions from various dimensional sub-models into solutions to the complete optimization model. These agent roles are now defined.

3.3 Agent Jobs Descriptions

As pointed out by earlier works [20,26], a few key questions must be answered when designing a multi-agent optimization system. How many agents should be used? What should their role be? How should they decide when to act, what to act on, and how to act? For all their advantages, agent teams are complex to design and implement. Indeed, if the system uses several algorithms that are similar in nature (e.g., simulated annealing variants) on the same sub-model, it is likely that one of the optimization algorithms (usually the best) will be largely responsible for the team's performance. Also, on a computer with limited resources (memory or processor power), it is likely that adding agents will deteriorate performances. To avoid these pitfalls, it is advised in [18] to start with a small number of agents, and to add new agents with different skills as needed. According to the literature and to our experience in developing CAT systems, an agent team needs four important basic skills. (1) Quickly obtain feasible solutions to the complete optimization model. Although these may not be of high quality, they provide a basis for other agents to work upon. (2) Improve existing solutions. This can be done at the complete model level or agents can work on specific parts of the problem. (3) Remove unwanted or poor solutions from the population to control its size. (4) Efficiently combine features from solutions originating from different methods or dimensions. The nature of these skills is now discussed.

Construction Agents. Feasible solutions can be obtained quickly with simple heuristics (e.g., greedy or hill-climbing algorithms, or even randomly) for several classes of optimization models. Another option is to use generic LP/MIP heuristics (e.g., feasibility pump [27]). This approach tends to produce solutions that are very different from those obtained with greedy methods. The key goals at this task are speed and diversity, rather than solution quality. Using various methods usually results in a more diverse initial population of solutions, yielding a higher potential for improvement and collaboration, and reducing the need for specific diversification strategies. If the complete optimization model is difficult to solve but it is easy to find a feasible solution, one can generate solutions to the complete model then infer initial solutions for sub-models from these solutions, thus reducing the number of algorithms and agents needed for this role.

Improvement Agents. For complex decision problems, it is recommended to work on sub-models and not on the complete model. Since defining a neighborhood (or a set of neighborhoods covering the complete model's range of variables) may be challenging, local search is difficult to use. Evolutionary computing provides generic crossover operators, but solution encoding is complex and on highly constrained problems, developing effective repair functions may be problematic. To design a good set of improvement agents, the solution methods used to solve sub-models must be carefully selected. If the sub-model is a LP, existing LP-solvers can be used. If it has only one type of binary/integer variable (allowing for the construction of neighborhoods), a local search MH can be developed. If it is a variant of a well-known problem, the best available method can be implemented.

It may also be worthy to investigate alternative sub-model reformulations. Many strategies can tackle complex sub-models (e.g., an initial solution obtained with a simple heuristic may give a hot-start for a MIP-solver). Nowadays, commercial solvers incorporate several generic MIP heuristics [28]. When MHs are not efficient, generic MIP heuristics often are. In [29], a review of heuristics based on mathematical programming is provided. To ensure that the system continuously works on each sub-model (or, at least, looks for opportunities to work on it), a dedicated agent should be assigned to its solution. The creation of "super-agents" performing several tasks should be avoided. Such super-agents tend to use too much resource and require complex scheduling rules.

Destruction Agents. Solution destruction is as important as solution creation in agent-based optimization [18]. In some situations, the choice of solutions to destroy is obvious, such as when duplicates exist in the population. Aside from maintaining some control on the size of the population, destruction serves two purposes: removing poor quality solutions and maintaining diversity in terms of solution characteristics. At the beginning of the search, the solutions in the population are quite diverse. As improvement agents work, the solution quality of the best solutions in the population improves rapidly. At this stage, the destruction agent should focus on removing solutions that are of poor quality. A simple rule such as choosing a solution at random from those in the 4th quartile in terms of solution quality is appropriate. However, as the overall quality of solution improves, newly created solutions tend not to be competitive in terms of quality compared to those which have been improved by several agents. They should have a chance to be improved before they are discarded. Furthermore, as the population improves, working on the same solutions tends to accelerate convergence. As the search progresses, a destruction agent shifts its focus from removing poor solutions to either: (1) removing a random solution which has been improved at least $(I - 2)$ times and is in the bottom half in terms of performance, where I (parameter) is the number of improvements made on the solution that has been improved most frequently in the population; (2) finding the two most similar solutions in the population, and destroying the worst one; (3) finding the solution which has been used the most frequently to create new solutions among the solutions in the 4th quartile in terms quality, and destroying it. These rules can be encapsulated in destruction agents, and they work equally well on a population of complete solutions or on a population of partial solutions (solutions to a specific sub-problem). The metrics necessary to implement them are detailed in Subsect. 3.4. Alternatively, some solutions can be "protected" and be immune to deletion for a certain amount of time. These solutions may be the status quo or solutions provided by a decision-maker.

Integration Agents. Although the destruction agent works toward maintaining variety, additional diversification strategies may be needed. It is possible to add an agent whose sole objective is to provide the population with radically different solutions than those currently in the population. This agent should maintain a record of what has been proposed in the past, so it does not produce solutions similar to those already removed from the population due to poor solution quality. The integration of partial solutions from sub-models into complete solutions is a key component of an efficient agent team. At least one optimization algorithm should be provided for each integration sub-model. If two methods are available, they can both be used if they generate different high quality solutions. The number of agents to use depends on the relative speed at which the improvement agents generate new solutions to sub-models and the amount of computation effort required to solve the integration sub-models. Integration can be used in flexible ways. Integration of solutions to sub-models from different dimensional views can be desirable, as long as the resulting merging integration sub-models are not too difficult to solve. Solving these models often requires the design of specific heuristics or the use of a generic approach (see above). These heuristics are easily implemented using a MIP solver such as CPLEX or Gurobi. This approach is in line with scatter search and path-relinking MHs, and is an effective way of reaping the most benefits from using multiple dimensional views. As this type of integration is slightly different from the type of integration sub-models required to assemble complete solutions from partial solutions, these sub-models should be assigned to a different integration agent.

3.4   Decision Rules and Metrics: Solution Ancestry and Similarity

An agent needs formal rules to determine which solution to work on. A trivial option is to select a random solution from the population, but this does not give very good results. Obviously, an agent does not want to select a solution that it has recently worked on. A simple yet effective decision rule is that the agent waits that at least three others agents have improved the solution before attempting to work on it again. Some improvement agents such as local search MHs may want to push that rule a little further: since a local search explores thoroughly a restricted portion of the search space, an agent may want to select a solution that is significantly different from the one it just worked on. For more sophisticated decision rules, metrics can be computed as follows. Agents need an effective way to determine which solutions they recently worked on. In a cooperative context, this information should be accessible to all agents. A simple metric to achieve this objective is solution's ancestry. Simply put, a solution's ancestry is its genealogical tree. Each solution keeps track of the solutions used for its creation, or as a basis for its improvement, and the agents that worked on it. An improvement agent can then use this information to determine if it has worked on a solution recently, or on any of its parents. Tied to each solution is a list of agents that have worked on it, and whether this attempt at improving it succeeded. This list is sorted in reverse order. A similar mechanism is used to determine whether a solution has transmitted its characteristics to other solutions in the population. Anytime a solution is used to create a new solution or to alter an existing solution, its characteristics are propagated through the population. The new solution is linked to its parent solution(s) through an acyclic directed graph structure, so that it is easy to find all the parents or all offspring of a given solution. A propagation index is calculated for each solution, which is set to 0 when the solution is created. When a new solution s_0 is created, if it has one or more parent solutions, it parses its solutions digraph and updates the values of its parents' propagation index in a recursive manner.

There are occasions when an agent wishes to find similar, or very different, solutions in the population. A well-known metric to do this is the Hamming distance, which is the number of binary variables with different values in two solutions. Although it is useful in some contexts, that measure can be misleading for mixed-integer linear models. In most decision problems, some decisions have more importance than others. Often, a group of binary or integer variables is larger but of less significance. In the LRP, many more decision variables are associated with the vehicle routing decisions than the location decisions, despite the fact that location decisions have a more lasting impact on the quality of the solution. For this problem, two solutions could have the exact same depot locations but have a high Hamming distance, which would not reflect the importance of location decisions adequately. In order to obtain a more accurate distance metric, one can measure the percentage of variables of each type that have the same value. Different types of variables can even be weighted in order to account for their relative importance.

4   Conclusion

This paper gives a generic methodology and implementation guidelines to model and solve complex real-world decision problems. It shows how to look at decision problems from different point-of-views, and how to partition the problem as well as the associated optimization method into dimensional sub-models. We propose a general formulation of CAT, a new agent-based solution method designed to benefit from the complexity reductions resulting from the multi-dimensional views of the problem. CAT is scalable since its execution can easily be distributed over multiple computers. CAT is easily extendable by adding new agents or processing power as needed or by allowing some of the agents to work using more than one processor at a time.

References

1. Murthy, S., Akkiraju, R., Goodwin, R., Keskinocak, P., Rachlin, J., Wu, F.: Cooperative multiobjective decision support for the paper industry. Interfaces **29**(5), 5–30 (1999)
2. Carle, M.A., Martel, A., Zufferey, N.: The CAT metaheuristic for the solution of multi-period activity-based supply chain network design problems. Int. J. Prod. Econ. **139**(2), 664–677 (2012)
3. Silver, E., Zufferey, N.: Inventory control of an item with a probabilistic replenishment lead time and a known supplier shutdown period. Int. J. Prod. Res. **49**, 923–947 (2011)
4. Hertz, A., Schindl, D., Zufferey, N.: Lower bounding and tabu search procedures for the frequency assignment problem with polarization constraints. 4OR **3**(2), 139–161 (2005)

5. Zufferey, N.: Heuristiques pour les Problèmes de la Coloration des Sommets d'un Graphe et d'Affectation de Fréquences avec Polarités. Ph.D. thesis, École Polytechnique Fédérale de Lausanne (EPFL), Switzerland (2002)
6. Michel, L., Hentenryck, P.V.: A simple tabu search for warehouse location. Eur. J. Oper. Res. **157**, 576–591 (2004)
7. Melab, N., Talbi, E.G., Cahon, S., Alba, E., Luque, G.: Parallel metaheuristics: models and frameworks. Parallel Combinatorial Optimization, p. 330. Wiley, Hoboken (2006)
8. Talbi, E.G.: A taxonomy of hybrid metaheuristics. J. Heuristics **8**(5), 541–564 (2002)
9. Blum, C., Puchinger, J., Raidl, G., Roli, A.: Hybrid metaheuristics in combinatorial optimization: a survey. Appl. Soft Comput. **11**, 4135–4151 (2011)
10. Raidl, G.R., Puchinger, J.: Combining (Integer) linear programming techniques and metaheuristics for combinatorial optimization. In: Blum, C., Aguilera, M.J.B., Roli, A., Sampels, M. (eds.) Hybrid Metaheuristics. SCI, vol. 114, pp. 31–62. Springer, Heidelberg (2008). https://doi.org/10.1007/978-3-540-78295-7_2
11. Maniezzo, V., Stuetzle, T., Voß, S.: Matheuristics: Hybridizing Metaheuristics and Mathematical Programming. Springer, Heidelberg (2009). https://doi.org/10.1007/978-1-4419-1306-7
12. Dantzig, G.B., Wolfe, P.: Decomposition principle for linear programs. Oper. Res. **8**, 101–111 (1960)
13. Benders, J.F.: Partitioning procedures for solving mixed variables programming problem. Numer. Math. **4**, 238–252 (1962)
14. Walshaw, C.: Multilevel refinement for combinatorial optimization problems. Ann. Oper. Res. **131**, 325–372 (2004)
15. Melo, M., Nickel, S., da Gama, F.S.: An efficient heuristic approach for a multiperiod logistics network redesign problem. TOP **22**, 80–108 (2014)
16. Thanh, P., Péton, O., Bostel, N.: A linear relaxation-based heuristic approach for logistics network design. Comput. Ind. Eng. **59**, 964–975 (2010)
17. Schneeweiss, C.: Distributed Decision Making, 2nd edn. Springer, Heidlberg (2003). https://doi.org/10.1007/978-3-540-24724-1
18. Talukdar, S., Murthy, S., Akkiraju, R.: Asynchronous teams. In: Handbook of Metaheuristics. Kluwer Academic Publishers (2003)
19. Keskinocak, P., Wu, F., Goodwin, R., Murthy, S., Akkiraju, R., Kumaran, S.: Scheduling solutions for the paper industry. Oper. Res. **50**(2), 249–259 (2002)
20. Aydin, M., Fogarty, T.: Teams of autonomous agents for job-shop scheduling problems: an experimental study. J. Intell. Manuf. **15**, 455–462 (2004)
21. Ratajczak-Ropel, E.: Experimental evaluation of the A-team solving instances of the RCPSP/max problem. In: Jędrzejowicz, P., Nguyen, N.T., Howlet, R.J., Jain, L.C. (eds.) KES-AMSTA 2010. LNCS (LNAI), vol. 6071, pp. 210–219. Springer, Heidelberg (2010). https://doi.org/10.1007/978-3-642-13541-5_22
22. Nagy, G., Salhi, S.: Location-routing: issues, models and methods. Eur. J. Oper. Res. **177**, 649–672 (2007)
23. Beasley, J.E.: Lagrangean heuristics for location problems. Eur. J. Oper. Res. **65**, 383–399 (1993)
24. Cordeau, J.F., Laporte, G.: Tabu search heuristics for the vehicle routing problem. In: Sharda, R., Voß, S., Rego, C., Alidaee, B. (eds.) Metaheuristic Optimization via Memory and Evolution: Tabu Search and Scatter Search, pp. 145–163. Springer, Heidelberg (2005). https://doi.org/10.1007/0-387-23667-8_6
25. Wu, T.H., Low, C., Bai, J.W.: Heuristic solutions to multi-depot location-routing problems. Comput. Oper. Res. **29**, 1393–1415 (2002)

26. Zufferey, N.: Optimization by ant algorithms: possible roles for an individual ant. Optim. Lett. **6**(5), 963–973 (2012)
27. Achterberg, T., Berthold, T.: Improving the feasibility pump. Discrete Optim. **4**, 77–86 (2007)
28. Danna, E., Rothberg, E., Pape, C.L.: Exploring relaxation induced neighborhoods to improve MIP solutions. Math. Program. Ser. A **102**, 71–90 (2005)
29. Ball, M.: Heuristics based on mathematical programming. Surv. Oper. Res. Manag. Sci. **16**, 21–38 (2011)

A Bio-inspired Approach
for Collaborative Exploration with Mobile
Battery Recharging in Swarm Robotics

Maria Carrillo[1], Ian Gallardo[1], Javier Del Ser[1,2,3(✉)], Eneko Osaba[2],
Javier Sanchez-Cubillo[2], Miren Nekane Bilbao[1], Akemi Gálvez[4,5],
and Andrés Iglesias[4,5]

[1] University of the Basque Country (UPV/EHU), Bilbao, Spain
[2] TECNALIA, Derio, Spain
javier.delser@tecnalia.com
[3] Basque Center for Applied Mathematics (BCAM), Bilbao, Spain
[4] Universidad de Cantabria, Santander, Spain
[5] Toho University, Funabashi, Japan

Abstract. Swarm Robotics are widely conceived as the development of new computationally efficient tools and techniques aimed at easing and enhancing the coordination of multiple robots towards collaboratively accomplishing a certain mission or task. Among the different criteria under which the performance of Swarm Robotics can be gauged, energy efficiency and battery lifetime have played a major role in the literature. However, technological advances favoring power transfer among robots have unleashed new paradigms related to the optimization of the battery consumption considering it as a resource shared by the entire swarm. This work focuses on this context by elaborating on a routing problem for collaborative exploration in Swarm Robotics, where a subset of robots is equipped with battery recharging functionalities. Formulated as a bi-objective optimization problem, the quality of routes is measured in terms of the Pareto trade-off between the predicted area explored by robots and the risk of battery outage in the swarm. To efficiently balance these conflicting two objectives, a bio-inspired evolutionary solver is adopted and put to practice over a realistic experimental setup implemented in the VREP simulation framework. Obtained results elucidate the practicability of the proposed scheme, and suggest future research leveraging power transfer capabilities over the swarm.

Keywords: Swarm robotics · Battery recharging · Routing · NSGAII

1 Introduction

Robotics have evolved dramatically over the years to feature unprecedented levels of intelligence, resulting in an ever-growing number of scenarios benefiting from their widespread application to accomplish complex missions, e.g. structural

© Springer International Publishing AG, part of Springer Nature 2018
P. Korošec et al. (Eds.): BIOMA 2018, LNCS 10835, pp. 75–87, 2018.
https://doi.org/10.1007/978-3-319-91641-5_7

health monitoring, oil and gas industry, manufacturing, disaster management, precision agriculture and logistics, among many others. Providing robots with smart sensing, communication and organization functionalities allows them to capture information, operate, reason and infer knowledge from the environment in a collaborative manner. Research aimed at enhancing such functionalities by embracing elements from Artificial Intelligence and Distributed Computing has coined the so-called Swarm Robotics concept, which refers to the deployment of a set of robots that collaborate with each other so as to collectively perform a mission in a computationally efficient fashion [1,2].

In general, Swarm Robotics may rely on several key technologies to attain higher levels of autonomy, optimized operation and self-organization. Unfortunately, it is often the limited battery lifetime of robots not only what restricts most the autonomy of the swarm, but also what puts at risk the feasibility of complex missions where robots operate without any human intervention, as in e.g. the exploration of collapsed infrastructures after a massive disaster [3] or the structural assessment of undersea drilling equipment [4]. Despite notable advances in energy efficient robot mechanics, the battery capacity poses severe operational constraints to Swarm Robotics, to the point of jeopardizing their potential use in complex endeavors.

To overcome this issue, many research efforts have been devoted towards augmenting the power capacity of robot batteries, either by proposing new materials and chemical components or by deriving new mechanical improvements that extend further their lifetime by virtue of a lower power consumption [5]. For this same purpose, the community has also focused its attention towards the consideration of the aggregate battery power of the entire robotic swam as a whole, an unique resource whose management is to be optimized globally over all robots rather than locally. This approach grounds on advances in wireless/mobile robotic charging [6] and the deployment of mobile charging stations in the swarm [7], which can be exploited as a resource to actively locate and replenish the battery of other robots. This research topic has been very active in this regard, as evinced by the short literature review provided in what follows.

1.1   Related Work

A remarkable amount of interesting studies has been published in the last decade focused in power charging and battery consumption of swarm robots. Haek et al. discussed in [8] the importance of swarm robustness, defining this concept as the ability of the robotic swarm to perform a complex task avoiding the total drainage of their batteries. In this work authors present a solution to allow robots to robustly achieve their assigned tasks, which mainly consists of the use of power stations or power banks. In [9], a collective energy distribution system is proposed for a dust cleaning swarm of robots. Authors of this study explore the concept of *trophallaxis*, previously introduced in [10], which refers to individual robots donating an amount of their own energy reserve to other robots of the swarm. This same concept of altruistic behavior is explored in [11], materializing the idea in a specific robot architecture called CISSBot. Apart from battery charging, sharing and consumption, several additional features are also considered and studied in this contribution, such as a collision-free proximity motion control. Additional research on this topic can be found in [12].

Another interesting approach to energy consumption is the one recently proposed in [13], where an Energy-Aware Particle Swarm Optimization (EAPSO) bioinspired solver is designed to optimize the movement strategy of aerial microrobots. Interestingly, the optimization process considers the energy levels of the robots for their efficient movement. Although authors do not propose any charging mechanism, the designed method renders a considerable reduction of the total energy consumption, making the robotic swarm more reliable and robust. Another bioinspired scheme sensitive to the consumed energy is the Honey Bee inspired swarm in [14], which improves the energy efficiency and is proven to be effective for foraging environments, such as the collection of crops of materials.

Also interesting to mention is the preliminary research presented by [15], in which an immune system response is studied for the development of energy sharing strategies. In that case, the granuloma formation is explored, which is a process in which undesired components are removed by immune systems. This behavioral concept is mapped to the components of a Swarm Robotics system, enhancing the fault tolerance of the deployed robots. A further step was taken in [16], where another immune system mechanism is proposed based on the use of contact-less energy charging areas and their simulation-based comparison to other energy charging mechanisms. A similar technique was proposed in [17] to add self-healing capabilities to robotic swarms.

As stated in [18], an usual trend in the literature for dynamic energy charging of robots is based on the deployment of power banks or removable chargers. Despite being quite effective, this approach has its own disadvantages, such as the resulting weight increase of the robot equipment, often crucial in critical missions. With the intention of overcoming these issues, [18] describes initial research on the implementation of an energy-sharing scheme using a two-way communication mechanism. Finally, in [19] an energy-encrypted contact-less system is described for improving the charging performance and the energy transmission mechanism of swarm robots. To this end wireless power transfer is used, enabling robots to charge their batteries even in moving situations. Other contributions related to dynamic energy charging include [20], which elaborates on a novel tree-based schedule for mobile charger robots, which minimizes the travel distance without causing energy depletion; and [21], which presents a versatile mobile charging station capable of actively locating and replenishing the battery of inactive robots.

1.2   Contribution

Even though the literature has been profitable in what regards to Swarm Robotics with mobile battery recharging nodes, to the best of the authors' knowledge routing for exploration missions in Swarm Robotics has so far been addressed without considering such nodes as assets whose routes over the scenario at hand can be jointly optimized with those of exploring robots.

Furthermore, when dealing with overly complex scenarios to be explored, the total area sensed by exploring robots can be intuitively thought of as a conflicting objective with the remaining battery margin; in this sense, enforcing the swarm to explore the entire area spanned by the scenario could create a risk of any robot to run out of battery on site, and be left dead and unrecoverable. This work aims at addressing this research niche by modeling and solving a bi-objective routing problem for mobile swarm robotics considering the minimization of this risk as a second fitness metric that quantifies the quality of a generated route plan. The problem formulation also includes the search for optimal routing plans for mobile battery recharging nodes along with the routes of exploring robots. Both are solved efficiently by means of a bi-objective bio-inspired solver driven by the aforementioned objectives. Results obtained from a realistic simulation framework implemented in VREP [22] are shown to be promising, with several future research lines stemming therefrom.

The rest of this paper is structured as follows: first, Sect. 2 formulates mathematically the optimization problem under study, including the conflicting objectives to be maximized. Next, Sect. 3 delves into the utilized bi-objective solver, followed by Sects. 4 and 5 detailing the simulation setup and discussing the obtained results, respectively. Section 6 concludes the paper.

2   Problem Statement

Following the schematic diagram depicted in Fig. 1, we assume a swarm $\mathcal{N}$ of $|\mathcal{N}| = N$ robots, with time-dependent positions $\{\mathbf{p}_n^{\Delta,t}\}_{n=1}^N \doteq \{(x_n^{\Delta,t}, y_n^{\Delta,t})\}_{n=1}^N$ (with t denoting time) over a square area $S^{\square} \doteq [X_{min}, X_{max}] \times [Y_{min}, Y_{max}]$. Each of such robots is equipped with sensors that allow them to explore an area $\{S_n^{\Delta,t}\}_{n=1}^N$ around its location at time t, e.g. if the area is circular with radius R_n^{Δ}, then $S_n = \{(x,y) \in S^{\square} : (x - x_n^{\Delta,t})^2 + (x - x_n^{\Delta,t})^2 \leq R_n^2\}$ (areas shaded in ■, ■ and ■ in Fig. 1). The total area $S^T(t)$ explored by the robotic swarm at time t' will be then given by

$$S^T(t') = \bigcup_{t=1}^{t'} \bigcup_{n=1}^{N} S_n^{\Delta,t}. \tag{1}$$

Another set of $M \leq N$ robots $\mathcal{M}$ with battery recharging capabilities is deployed in the same location jointly with $\mathcal{N}$, with coordinates $\{\mathbf{p}_m^{\odot,t}\}_{m=1}^M \doteq \{(x_m^{\odot,t}, y_m^{\odot,t})\}_{m=1}^M$. A robot $m \in \mathcal{M}$ will recharge the battery of a robot $n \in \mathcal{N}$ whenever (1) their distance $d_{m,n}^t$ falls below a certain threshold D_{max} (area in ■ in Fig. 1), i.e.

$$d_{m,n} = \sqrt{\left(x_m^{\odot,t} - x_n^{\Delta,t}\right)^2 + \left(y_m^{\odot,t} - y_n^{\Delta,t}\right)^2} \leq D_{max}, \tag{2}$$

and (2) the above condition holds for a minimum of T_{min} seconds, comprising the power plug coupling/uncoupling along with physical maneuvers to align connectors. If both conditions hold, energy is transferred from robot $m \in \mathcal{M}$

to $n \in \mathcal{N}$ at a rate of β units of energy per second (measured in e.g. Watts). Furthermore, the movement of the robot itself involves a battery consumption of γ units of power per unit of distance, so that in a certain time gap ΔT measured from time t the remaining amount of battery $B_n^{\Delta, t+\Delta T}$ in robot n can be mathematically expressed as

$$B_n^{\Delta, t+\Delta T} = \min\left\{[1 + I_D \cdot I_T \cdot \beta] \cdot B_n^{\Delta, t} - \gamma V_n^{\Delta} \Delta T, B_{max}\right\}, \tag{3}$$

where V_n^{Δ} denotes the cruise speed of the robot (in units of distance per unit of time), and I_D and I_T are binary indicator functions such that $I_D = 1$ if $d_{m,n}^{t'} \leq D_{max}$ $\forall t' \in [t, t + \Delta T]$, and $I_T = 1$ if $\Delta T \geq T_{min}$ (0 otherwise in both cases). In the above expression B_{max} stands for the nominal maximum battery load (in units of power) of the robot model, which without loss of generality is assumed to be equal throughout the entire robotic swarm.

With this definition in mind, the goal of the routing optimization problem is essentially the determination of an optimal set of routes composed by $N + M$ waypoints $\mathbf{W}^{\Delta, t, \looparrowright} \doteq \{\mathbf{w}_n^{\Delta, t, \looparrowright}\}_{n=1}^N = \{(x_n^{\Delta, t, \looparrowright}, y_n^{\Delta, t, \looparrowright})\}_{n=1}^N$ and $\mathbf{W}^{\odot, t, \looparrowright} \doteq \{\mathbf{w}_m^{\odot, t, \looparrowright}\}_{m=1}^M = \{(x_m^{\odot, t, \looparrowright}, y_m^{\odot, t, \looparrowright})\}_{m=1}^M$ for all robots in the swarm (both explorers and battery chargers). Here optimality of the set of discovered routes refers to the Pareto relationship between the explored area and a quantitative measure of the *risk of no return* taken when the entire swarm is commanded to follow a certain route. Intuitively, the more area the swarm explores, the more likely is the chance that any of the robots in the swarm lacks enough battery to return to the point $\{(x^{\Delta, 0}, y^{\Delta, 0})\}$ where robots had been initially located. This risk is crucial in many practical situation, e.g. disaster events where the topological characteristics of the facility to be explored remain unknown to the command center before and while the mission is performed by the robotic swarm.

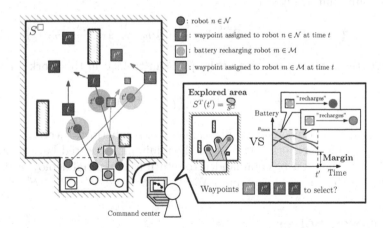

Fig. 1. Schematic diagram of the scenario tackled in this paper. (Color figure online)

Mathematically this risk can be modeled by accounting, over the whole robotic swarm, for battery margin $B_n^{\blacktriangle, t}$ expected to be left for every robot should it proceed and move to the assigned waypoint and return safely to $\{(x^{\Delta,0}, y^{\Delta,0})\}$. Assuming that the route optimization is performed at time t, the value of the battery margin $B_n^{\blacktriangle,t}$ for robot $n \in \mathcal{N}$ when commanded to go to waypoint $\mathbf{w}_n^{\Delta,t,\looparrowright} = (x_n^{\Delta,t,\looparrowright}, y_n^{\Delta,t,\looparrowright})$ can be estimated as

$$B_n^{\blacktriangle,t}(\mathbf{p}_n^{\Delta,t}, \mathbf{w}_n^{\Delta,t,\looparrowright}, \{\mathbf{p}_m^{\Delta,t}\}_{m=1}^M, \{\mathbf{w}_m^{\Delta,t}\}_{m=1}^M) = B_n^{\Delta,t} - B_n^{\Delta,t+\Delta T_{\mathbf{p},\mathbf{w}}+\Delta T_{\mathbf{w},\mathbf{p}_0}}, \quad (4)$$

where $\Delta T_{\mathbf{p},\mathbf{w}}$ and $\Delta T_{\mathbf{w},\mathbf{p}_0}$ are the times taken for robot $n \in \mathcal{N}$ to travel from its current point $\mathbf{p}_n^{\Delta,t}$ to the assigned waypoint $\mathbf{w}_n^{\Delta,t,\looparrowright}$ and therefrom to its initial position $\{(x^{\Delta,0}, y^{\Delta,0})\}$. This estimation is made by assuming that the robot goes straight without colliding with any object nor any other robot along its path. It should be remarked that as per (3), the battery expenditure reflected in $B_n^{\Delta,t+\Delta T_{\mathbf{p},\mathbf{w}}+\Delta T_{\mathbf{w},\mathbf{p}_0}}$ takes into account not only the power consumed by the robot dynamics (which depends on its speed V_n and the traversed distances), but also time periods along the path during which the relative position between battery recharging robots and robot $n \in \mathcal{N}$ fulfill conditions I_D and I_T required to recharge the battery of robot n on the move. The total duration of such recharging periods can be computed as $\sum_{(t_s,t_e)\in\mathcal{T}_n^{\Delta,t}}(t_e - t_s)$ over the set of periods $\mathcal{T}_n^{\Delta,t}$, defined as

$$\mathcal{T}_n^{\Delta,t} \doteq \{(t_s, t_e) \in [t, t + \Delta T_{\mathbf{p},\mathbf{w}} + \Delta T_{\mathbf{w},\mathbf{p}_0}] \text{ such that :}$$

$$(1) \ t_e > t_s; \ (2) \ \exists m \in \mathcal{M} : d_{mn}^{t'} \leq D_{max} \forall t' \in [t_s, t_e]; \text{ and } (3) \ t_e - t_s \geq T_{min}\}, \quad (5)$$

with $[t_s', t_e'] \cap [t_s'', t_e''] = \emptyset \ \forall (t_s', t_e'), (t_s'', t_e'') \in \mathcal{T}_n^{\Delta,t}$. Therefore, the swarm-wide battery margin $B^T(t)$ to be maximized at time t so as to keep the aforementioned risk to its minimum is given by

$$B^T(t) = \min_{n\in\mathcal{N}} \left\{ \max \left\{ 0, B_n^{\blacktriangle,t}(\mathbf{p}_n^{\Delta,t}, \mathbf{w}_n^{\Delta,t,\looparrowright}, \{\mathbf{p}_m^{\Delta,t}\}_{m=1}^M, \{\mathbf{w}_m^{\Delta,t}\}_{m=1}^M) \right\} \right\}, \quad (6)$$

from where the formal statement of the problem tackled in this work follows:

$$\underset{\mathbf{W}^{\odot,t,\looparrowright}, \mathbf{W}^{\Delta,t,\looparrowright}}{\text{maximize}} \left\{ S^T(t), B^T(t) \right\}, \quad (7a)$$

namely, as the simultaneous maximization of two conflicting objectives: the surface explored by the robotic swarm and the minimum expected battery margin over the robots should it be commanded to return to the initial deployment point after reaching the enforced waypoint. $\mathbf{W}^{\Delta,t,\looparrowright} \in S^{\square}$ and $\mathbf{W}^{\odot,t,\looparrowright} \in S^{\square}$.

3 Proposed Solver

In order to efficiently tackle the above problem, we propose to apply a centralized meta-heuristic solver capable of optimally balancing the two objective functions considered in its formulation. The optimizer relies on the renowned

Non-dominated Sorting Genetic Algorithm (NSGA-II, [23]), a bio-inspired approach that hinges on the concepts of non-dominance ranking and crowding distance to guide a multi-objective search over a set of potential candidate solutions (in this case, waypoints defining routes). In essence NSGA-II sorts a population of candidates according to (1) whether each solution within the population *dominates*, in terms of Pareto optimality, other solutions in the pool (yielding the so-called dominance rank of the Pareto front to which the solution at hand belongs); and (2) the closest distance from every individual to the rest of solutions (corr. crowding distance). By applying this dual selection procedure along with genetically inspired crossover and mutation operators (with probabilities P_c

---

Algorithm 1. NSGA-II solver applied to the problem under study.

Data: Number of exploration robots N; number of battery recharging robots M; dimensions of the scenario $X_{min}, X_{max}, Y_{min}, Y_{max}$; sensing radii $\{R_n\}_{n=1}^N$; maximum distance D_{max} and minimum time T_{min} for battery recharge; nominal robot speeds $\{V_n^\triangle\}_{n=1}^N$ and $\{V_m^\odot\}_{m=1}^M$; maximum battery capacity B_{max}; battery charging rate β; battery consumption rate γ; crossover and mutation probabilities P_c and P_m; population size P; maximum number of iterations $\mathbb{I}$; proportion of the minimum battery margin to the maximum battery capacity λ.

1 Deploy all robots on the initial location $(x^{\triangle,0}, y^{\triangle,0})$, and set waypoints $\mathbf{w}_n^{\triangle,t_{ini},\curvearrowright}$ and $\mathbf{w}_m^{\odot,t_{ini},\curvearrowright}$ equal to $(x^{\triangle,0}, y^{\triangle,0})$ $\forall n \in \mathcal{N}$ and $\forall m \in \mathcal{M}$

2 Set $t' = t_{ini}$ and $\mathcal{T} = \{t_{ini}\}$

3 **while** $B^T(t) \geq \lambda B_{max}$ **do**

4   **while** $\mathbf{p}_n^{\triangle,t} \neq \mathbf{w}_n^{\triangle,t',\curvearrowright}$ and $\mathbf{p}_m^{\odot,t} \neq \mathbf{w}_m^{\odot,t',\curvearrowright}$ $\forall n, m$ **do**

5   Let robots move to their assigned waypoints $\mathbf{w}_n^{\triangle,t_{ini},\curvearrowright}$ and $\mathbf{w}_m^{\odot,t_{ini},\curvearrowright}$

6   Update remaining battery $\{B_n^{\blacktriangle,t}\}_{n=1}^N$ as per (4) and (5)

7   **if** $t' = t_{ini}$ **then**

8   Initialize P individuals in the population uniformly at random from $\mathcal{S}^\square$

9   **else**

10   Retrieve the estimated Pareto from the previous run, introduce it in the population. and fill the remaining individuals randomly over $\mathcal{S}^\square$

11   **for** $it \leftarrow 1$ **to** $\mathbb{I}$ **do**

12   Select parents, recombine them (w.p. P_c) and mutate (w.p. P_m) the produced new offspring that represent a new set of P waypoints

13   Evaluate explored area and battery margin of offspring as per (1), (6)

14   Sort previous and new waypoints by rank and crowding distance

15   Discard the worst P individuals in the sorted, concatenated population

16   The estimated Pareto is given by the P individuals remaining in population

17   Select the set of waypoints in the estimated front that best suits the commanding policy (e.g. maintain a battery margin above 10%), and assign them to robots

18   Set $t' = t$, and $\mathcal{T} = \mathcal{T} + \{t\}$

19 All robots to initial position by $\mathbf{w}_n^{\triangle,t_{ini},\curvearrowright} = \mathbf{w}_m^{\odot,t_{ini},\curvearrowright} = (x^{\triangle,0}, y^{\triangle,0})$ $\forall n, m$

and P_m, respectively), the Pareto optimality of solutions contained in the population becomes improved iteration after iteration, to eventually yield a Pareto front estimation after a number of iterations of this search procedure.

An algorithmic description of the NSGA-II approach designed in this work is provided in Algorithm 1. Individuals are encoded directly as $N + M$ vectors $\mathbf{w}_i^p$ denoting the waypoints of all robots in the scenario, where $i \in \{1, \ldots, N, N + 1, \ldots, N + M\}$, $p \in \{1, \ldots, P\}$, P denoting the population size and $\mathbf{w}_i^p \in \mathcal{S}^\square$ $\forall i, p$. A uniform crossover operator and a Gaussian mutation with standard deviation σ have been selected as heuristic operators. The iterative application of these operators and the NSGA-II selection scheme outlined above is stopped after $\mathbb{I}$ iterations. It is important to remark at this point that the solver must be run incrementally at certain time instants, e.g. the solver is not run constantly along time but rather triggered at time ticks embedded in the set $\mathcal{T} \in \mathbb{R}[t_{ini}, t_{end}]$, where t_{ini} is the time at which the robotic swarm is first deployed and t_{end} is the time at which the battery margin $B^T(t_{end})$ in the estimated Pareto front falls below a fraction λ of the maximum battery capacity B_{max}. For the sake of simplicity, the NSGA-II solver will be executed once all robots have reached their commanded waypoints $\mathbf{W}^{\triangle, t, \curvearrowright}$ and $\mathbf{W}^{\odot, t, \curvearrowright}$ optimized previously, which yields the time instants contained in $\mathcal{T}$. To match this incremental nature of the proposed optimization schedule, the population of individuals is accordingly initialized by including the best front found in the previous NSGA-II execution, randomly setting the remaining individuals until filling the population.

4   Simulation Setup

In order to assess the performance of the proposed bi-objective routing approach, a simulation setup has been constructed by resorting to VREP, a renowned software platform that permits to realistically model and perform experimental studies with swarms of robots. In order to extract valuable insights, we have kept the dimensions of the experimental scenario reduced to $N = 5$ exploring robots and a single battery recharging node ($M = 1$) deployed on a 10×10 m^2 square area. The maximum distance and minimum time to recharge batteries are set to $D_{max} = 1$ m and $T_{min} = 3$ s, respectively. Robots with six mechanical legs (also referred to as *hexapods*) and diameter size equal to 0.5 m are utilized, with speeds equal to $V_n^\triangle = 3.5$ cm/s $\forall n \in \mathcal{N}$ and $V_m^\odot = 2.6$ cm/s. Battery recharging is done at a rate of 1% per second with respect to the nominal maximum capacity B_{max} of exploring robots, whereas the recharging node is equipped with a total battery capacity equal to $10 \cdot B_{max}$. The battery depletion rate is fixed to $\gamma = 1.5\%$ of B_{max} per linear meter. As for the parameters of the NSGA-II solver, crossover and mutation rates are set to $P_c = 1$ and $P_m = 0.1$, with a population size of $P = 20$ individuals and $\mathbb{I} = 100$ iterations per run. The decision making criterion adopted to select a route among the estimated Pareto fronts was based on selecting the route whose associated battery margin is closest to 20% of B_{max}. If no route with margin greater than this threshold, the robot swarm is enforced to return to the origin position. Figure 2 illustrates, from two different perspectives, the scenario generated in VREP and simulated to yield the results discussed in the next section[1].

5   Results and Discussion

The discussion on the results obtained by the proposed scheme starts with Fig. 3, which illustrates the set of estimated Pareto fronts along time under different assumptions. Specifically, every plot in this figure contains a three-dimensional cloud of points – each representing a given route plan (set of waypoints) – which results from the aggregation of all fronts estimated in simulation time for a single experiment. A total of 10 executions of the NSGA-II solver have sufficed for illustrating the main benefit of our proposed routing scheme: by incorporating battery recharging functionalities, the autonomy of the entire robotic swarm is enhanced, so that a larger area can be explored for a given decision making criterion imposed on the minimum admissible battery margin for the robots to return back and safe to the base.

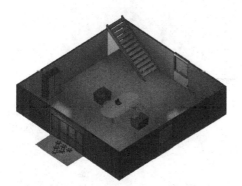 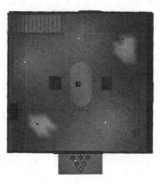

Fig. 2. Visual representation of the simulated setup yielding the results later discussed in the manuscript; (left) isometric view; (right) top-down view. The robot dynamics are provided by the VREP framework, whereas the NSGA-II routing approach has been implemented in Python and communicates with VREP via remote API functions.

To this end two different cases are assessed, depending on the exploration radii assumed for the sensing robots: (1) $R_n = 0.9$ m, which should a priori render minimum gains due to a more efficient area exploration; and (2) $R_n = 0.5$ m, smaller sensing radii for which the incorporation of battery recharging functionalities in the swarm should provide higher gains. Indeed, this intuition is confirmed by the results in the plots: as evinced by the plot on the left (higher exploration radii), almost no exploration gain is obtained by including battery recharging

---

[1] Videos showing how robots move over this scenario can be found at:
  https://youtu.be/r31teMtWRF0 and https://youtu.be/zewRVZQpvP8.

functionalities (■) when compared to a unassisted robot swarm (■). However, when reducing the sensing radius, robots must traverse longer distances in order to explore the entire scenario, which leads to higher battery consumption levels that could be compensated efficiently by including a battery recharging node. This is precisely what the plot on the right in Fig. 3 reveals: when inspecting the evolution of the maximum battery margin in the fronts computed along time, it is straightforward to note that the margin of the unassisted swarm (■) decreases much faster than that of its assisted counterpart (■), falling below the minimum admissible threshold (20%) imposed by the mission commander. As a result, the entire swarm is commanded to return to the base once 61% of the scenario has been explored. By including the mobile recharging node, the battery margin degrades smoothly along time, and is maintained above the threshold to explore a higher area percentage (ca. 80%) even for more conservative policies. For instance, should it have been set to 60% the unassisted swarm would have explored less than 50% of the area; in the assisted case robots would have been operative for a longer time, attaining explored area ratios close to 80%.

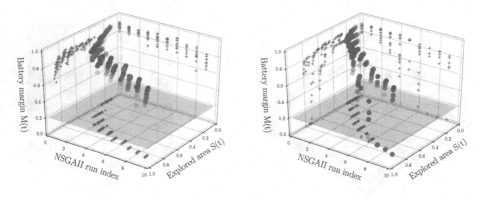

Fig. 3. Three-dimensional plot showing the Pareto trade-off between battery margin and explored area estimated by the NSGA-II solver as the simulation evolves (represented by the NSGA-II run index). The left plot corresponds to the case when $R_n = 0.9\,\text{m}$, whereas the right plot depicts the case when $R_n = 0.5\,\text{m}$, in both cases $\forall n \in \{1, \ldots, 5\}$. Also are included in the plots the two-dimensional projections of the point cloud along every axis, so that the progression of the maximum achievable value of each metric. The plane shaded in gray indicates the minimum admissible battery margin imposed by the mission commander (20%). (Color figure online)

Besides the evidence provided by the above plots, further insights can be extracted by taking a closer look at the trajectories traced by the robots in the swarm for both cases. One should expect that for high values of the sensing radii R_n, nodes should feature relatively less dynamic mobility patterns over the scenario than those corresponding to lower values of this parameter. The plots in Fig. 4 go in line with this expected behavior. In particular mobility traces of the robotic swarm are shown for the assisted robotic swarm with $R_n = 0.5\,\text{m}$

(left) and $R_n = 0.9\,\mathrm{m}$ (right). It can be noted that the former case features rectilinear trajectories composed by long segments, whereas in the latter all robots in the swarm describe topologically tangled traces, and few cases reach the boundaries of the scenario. In summary, the sensing radii plays a crucial role in the behavior of the swarm and ultimately, in the attainable performance gain from the introduction of mobile recharging nodes in the swarm.

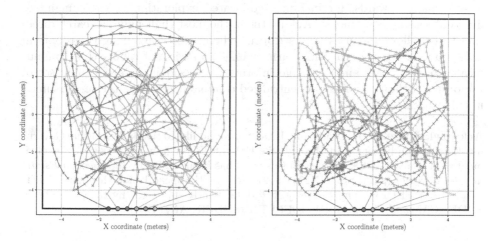

Fig. 4. Trajectories followed by the robots in the swarm for $R_n = 0.5\,\mathrm{m}$ (left) and $R_n = 0.9\,\mathrm{m}$ (right). A visual inspection permits to infer that lower values of the sensing radius make all trajectories be shorter and more complex as a result of a lower overlapping between the sensing areas of robots in the swarm. On the contrary, when the sensing radius increases robots describe cleaner, rectilinear trajectories.

6   Concluding Remarks

In this paper, a routing problem for collaborative exploration in Swarm Robotics has been presented. An analysis of the recent literature supports that one of the main issues in these systems is the energy consumption and reliability of the swarm, which jeopardizes the performance of complex missions and tasks. This identified issue is what lies behind the rationale for this research work: to include a subset of robots in the swarm endowed with battery charging capabilities. The challenge resides in how to properly route the robots in the scenario considering the existence of such nomadic battery recharging nodes, which has been formulated as a bi-objective optimization problem where a Pareto equilibrium must be met between the explored area and the risk of battery outage. In order to solve efficiently this problem, a bio-inspired approach has been designed based on the well-known NSGA-II solver. A realistic experimental setup comprising the VREP robotic simulation framework has been constructed so as to shed light on how the proposed solver performs in practice. The obtained results have proven empirically the practicality and inherent utility of the proposed routing scheme, which provides the commander of the mission with more valuable information for decision making than traditional schemes based on a single fitness function.

Several lines of research related to this work have been planned for the near future, e.g. the inclusion of other bioinspired multi-objective heuristic engines (e.g. SMPSO, MOEA/D) and their comparison to each other in terms of multi-objective indicators. Another research path that will be prospected will gravitate on relaxing and extending the assumptions and constraints defining the considered scenario towards, for instance, co-located exploration tasks (demanding different sensing equipment). Among them, the most challenging research direction to be followed focuses on distributing the intelligence among the robots in order to realize a *true* robotic swarm, namely, a swarm of robots that communicate to each other and exchange information, deciding on an optimal set of waypoints without requiring a centralized command center as the one assumed in this work.

Acknowledgments. E. Osaba and J. Del Ser would like to thank the Basque Government for its funding support through the EMAITEK program. Likewise, the involvement of A. Galvez and A. Iglesias in this work has been funded by the *Agencia Estatal de Investigación* (grant no. TIN2017-89275-R), the European Union through FEDER Funds (AEI/FEDER), and the project #JU12, jointly supported by the public body SODERCAN and European Funds FEDER (SODERCAN/FEDER).

References

1. Beni, G.: From swarm intelligence to swarm robotics. In: International Workshop on Swarm Robotics, pp. 1–9 (2004)
2. Brambilla, M., Ferrante, E., Birattari, M., Dorigo, M.: Swarm robotics: a review from the swarm engineering perspective. Swarm Intell. **7**(1), 1–41 (2013)
3. Miranda, K., Molinaro, A., Razafindralambo, T.: A survey on rapidly deployable solutions for post-disaster networks. IEEE Commun. Mag. **54**(4), 117–123 (2016)
4. Bogue, R., Bogue, R.: Underwater robots: a review of technologies and applications. Ind. Robot: Int. J. **42**(3), 186–191 (2015)
5. Mei, Y., Lu, Y.H., Hu, Y.C., Lee, C.G.: Energy-efficient motion planning for mobile robots. In: IEEE International Conference on Robotics and Automation (ICRA 2004), vol. 5, pp. 4344–4349 (2004)
6. Johnson, J., Stoops, M., Schwartz, B., Masters, N., Hasan, S.: Techniques for mobile device charging using robotic devices, 15 November 2016. US Patent 9,492,922
7. Couture-Beil, A., Vaughan, R.T.: Adaptive mobile charging stations for multi-robot systems. In: IEEE/RSJ International Conference on Intelligent Robots and Systems, pp. 1363–1368 (2009)
8. Haek, M., Ismail, A.R., Basalib, A., Makarim, N.: Exploring energy charging problem in swarm robotic systems using foraging simulation. Jurnal Teknologi **76**(1), 239–244 (2015)
9. Melhuish, C., Kubo, M.: Collective energy distribution: maintaining the energy balance in distributed autonomous robots using trophallaxis. Distrib. Auton. Robot. Syst. **6**, 275–284 (2007)

10. Schmickl, T., Crailsheim, K.: Trophallaxis among swarm-robots: a biologically inspired strategy for swarm robotics. In: IEEE/RAS-EMBS International Conference on Biomedical Robotics and Biomechatronics, pp. 377–382 (2006)
11. Schioler, H., Ngo, T.D.: Trophallaxis in robotic swarms-beyond energy autonomy. In: IEEE International Conference on Control, Automation, Robotics and Vision, pp. 1526–1533 (2008)
12. Schmickl, T., Crailsheim, K.: Trophallaxis within a robotic swarm: bio-inspired communication among robots in a swarm. Auton. Robots 25(1), 171–188 (2008)
13. Mostaghim, S., Steup, C., Witt, F.: Energy aware particle swarm optimization as search mechanism for aerial micro-robots. In: IEEE Symposium Series on Computational Intelligence, pp. 1–7 (2016)
14. Lee, J.H., Ahn, C.W., An, J.: A honey bee swarm-inspired cooperation algorithm for foraging swarm robots: an empirical analysis. In: IEEE/ASME International Conference on Advanced Intelligent Mechatronics, pp. 489–493 (2013)
15. Al Haek, M., Ismail, A.R., Nordin, A., Sulaiman, S., Lau, H.: Modelling immune systems responses for the development of energy sharing strategies for swarm robotic systems. In: International Conference on Computational Science and Technology, pp. 1–6 (2014)
16. Al Haek, M., Ismail, A.R.: Simulating the immune inspired energy charging mechanism for swarm robotic systems. J. Theor. Appl. Inf. Technol. 95(20), 5473–5483 (2017)
17. Timmis, J., Ismail, A.R., Bjerknes, J.D., Winfield, A.F.: An immune-inspired swarm aggregation algorithm for self-healing swarm robotic systems. Biosystems 146, 60–76 (2016)
18. Ismail, A.R., Desia, R., Zuhri, M.F.R.: The initial investigation of the design and energy sharing algorithm using two-ways communication mechanism for swarm robotic systems. In: Phon-Amnuaisuk, S., Au, T.W. (eds.) Computational Intelligence in Information Systems. AISC, vol. 331, pp. 61–71. Springer, Cham (2015). https://doi.org/10.1007/978-3-319-13153-5_7
19. Wang, J., Liang, Z., Zhang, Z.: Energy-encrypted contactless charging for swarm robots. In: International Magnetics Conference, p. 1 (2017)
20. He, L., Cheng, P., Gu, Y., Pan, J., Zhu, T., Liu, C.: Mobile-to-mobile energy replenishment in mission-critical robotic sensor networks. In: IEEE INFOCOM, pp. 1195–1203 (2014)
21. Arvin, F., Samsudin, K., Ramli, A.R.: Swarm robots long term autonomy using moveable charger. In: International Conference on Future Computer and Communication, pp. 127–130 (2009)
22. Rohmer, E., Singh, S.P., Freese, M.: V-REP: a versatile and scalable robot simulation framework. In: IEEE/RSJ International Conference on Intelligent Robots and Systems (IROS), pp. 1321–1326 (2013)
23. Deb, K., Pratap, A., Agarwal, S., Meyarivan, T.: A fast and elitist multiobjective genetic algorithm: NSGA-II. IEEE Trans. Evol. Comput. 6(2), 182–197 (2002)

Constructive Metaheuristics for the Set Covering Problem

Broderick Crawford[1(✉)], Ricardo Soto[1], Gino Astorga[1,2], and José García[1,3]

[1] Pontificia Universidad Católica de Valparaíso, Valparaíso, Chile
{broderick.crawford,ricardo.soto}@pucv.cl
[2] Universidad de Valparaíso, Valparaíso, Chile
gino.astorga@uv.cl
[3] Centro de Investigación y Desarrollo Telefónica, Santiago, Chile
joseantonio.garcia@telefonica.com

Abstract. Different criteria exist for the classification of the meta-heuristics. One important classification is: improvement metaheuristics and constructive. On the one hand improvement metaheuristics, begins with an initial solution and iteratively improves the quality of the solution using neighborhood search. On the other hand, constructive meta-heuristics, are those in which a solution is built from the beginning, finding in each iteration a local optimum. In this article, we to compare two constructive metaheuristics, Ant Colony Optimization and Intelligent Water Drops, by solving a classical NP-hard problem, such like the Set Covering Problem, which has many practical applications, including line balancing production, service installation and crew scheduling in railway, among others. The results reveal that Ant Colony Optimization has a better behavior than Intelligent Water Drops in relation to the problem considered.

Keywords: Intelligent Water Drops · Set Covering Problem
Constructive metaheuristic

1 Introduction

The Set Covering Problem (SCP) is a NP-hard problem [10], which consists into find a subset of columns in a zero-one matrix such that they cover all the rows of the matrix at a minimum cost. Some of its applications includes line balancing production, emergency services location, crew scheduling in mass-transit companies, logical analysis of numerical data, metallurgical production, vehicle routing and treatment of boolean expressions.

Given the complex nature of the SCP and the huge size of real datasets, the problem has been studied and solved by several metaheuristics, such like genetic algorithms [3], simulated annealing [4], indirect genetic algorithms [1], ant colony optimization [11], cat swarm optimization [5], cuckoo search [13] and a meta optimization [7], among others.

© Springer International Publishing AG, part of Springer Nature 2018
P. Korošec et al. (Eds.): BIOMA 2018, LNCS 10835, pp. 88–99, 2018.
https://doi.org/10.1007/978-3-319-91641-5_8

Constructive metaheuristics for the SCP includes Ant Colony Optimization and Meta-RaPS. The aim of this article is to study the performance of the Ant Colony Optimization (ACO) and Intelligent Water Drops (IWD) algorithms applied to the SCP. These constructive metaheuristics were introduced by: [8] to solve the Traveling Salesman Problem (TSP), based on the behavior of ant colonies and [12] to solve the Multiobjective Knapsack Problem (MKP) and it is based on the behavior of natural water drops flowing in the beds of rivers, carrying soil and moving between different branches to reach their destination; the interesting on this is that the path constructed to the destination tends to be optimal, despite the obstacles in the environment.

This article is organized as follows: In Sect. 2 we describe the SCP, in Sect. 3 we present the ACO algorithm, in Sect. 4 we present the IWD algorithm, in Sect. 5 we describe the results obtained for several SCP instances and finally in Sect. 6, we present the conclusions and future work.

In the construction phase of the solution a degree of randomness must be incorporated, with the aim of avoiding that the same solution is built in each iteration. Each iteration ends when the solution is found, therefore in this type of metaheuristics is avoided the problem of the infeasibility.

2   Set Covering Problem

The SCP consists into find a subset of columns in a zero-one matrix such that they can cover all the rows of that matrix at a minimum cost.

The SCP can be defined as:

$$Minimize \quad Z = \sum_{j=1}^{n} c_j x_j \tag{1}$$

Subject to

$$\sum_{j=1}^{n} a_{ij} x_j \geq 1 \quad \forall i \in I \tag{2}$$

$$x_j \in \{0, 1\} \quad \forall j \in J \tag{3}$$

Let $A = (a_{ij})$ be a $m \times n$ binary matrix with $I = \{1, \ldots, m\}$ and $J = \{1, \ldots, n\}$ being the row and column sets respectively. We say that a column j can cover a row i if $a_{ij} = 1$. The cost of selecting the column j is represented by c_j, a non-negative value, and x_j is a decision variable to indicate if the column j is selected ($x_j = 1$) or not ($x_j = 0$).

One of the many practical applications of this problem is the location of fire stations. Lets consider a city divided in a finite number of areas which need to locate and build fire stations. Each one of this areas need to be covered by at least one station, but a single fire station can only bring coverage to its own area and the adjacent ones; also, the problem requires that the number of stations to build needs to be the minimum.

Being the SCP a NP-hard class problem, one of the many difficulties that benchmarks arise is regarding their size and the computational cost associated. To solve this, many authors have proposed to simplify (or "pre-process") the problem before apply any exact method or metaheuristic. By doing this, we are dealing with problems that are equivalent to original but smaller in terms of rows and columns. We introduce a preprocessing phase before run the metaheuristic; the goal of this phase is to reduce the size of instances and improve the performance of the algorithm. In this article, we use two methods that have proven to be more effective: Column Domination and Column Inclusion, presented in [2, 9] respectively.

3   Ant Colony Optimization

Ant Colony Optimization Algorithm (ACO) it was inspired by the behavior of ant colonies in the search for their food, was proposed by [8], is a probabilistic technique that allows to find the shortest path in a graph. In the nature, the ants leave a chemical signal called pheromone, in the path through which pass. The pheromone has an important role in the survival of the ants allowing to find the shortest way to its power supply.

An ant exploratory moves in random searching for food, depositing pheromone in its path which is followed by more ants which reach the source of food found. When transiting more ants by this path, the amount of pheromone will be increased reinforcing the path. If there are two paths to the same food source, the shortest path will be the busiest because of its amount of pheromone, considering that in the longest path the pheromone will disappear because it is volatile. The behavior of the ants is shown in the Fig. 1.

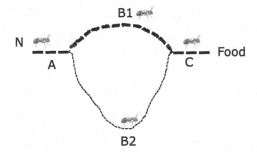

Fig. 1. Path of the ants to its source of food.

The main idea, is to model an optimization problem as the search for the lowest cost route in a graph by a colony of artificial ants. The ACO algorithms are essentially constructive, that is to say, for each iteration all the ants build a solution depositing pheromone, according to the quality of the solution, allowing to guide to the rest of the ants of the colony.

The ACO Algorithm can be applied directly to the SCP. The columns are chosen as the solution components and have associated a cost and a pheromone trail. Constraints say that each column can be visited by an ant once and only once and that a final solution has to cover all rows.

A walk of an ant over the graph representation corresponds to the iterative addition of columns to the partial solution obtained so far. Each ant starts with an empty solution and adds columns until a cover is completed. A pheromone trail τ_j and a heuristic information η_j are associated to each eligible column j. A column to be added is chosen with a probability that depends of pheromone trail and the heuristic information. The probability function is given by the equation Eq. 5:

$$p_j^k(t) = \frac{\tau_j \eta_j^{\beta}}{\sum\limits_{l \in N^k} \tau_l [\eta_l]^{\beta}} \quad \text{if } j \in N^k \tag{4}$$

where N^k is the feasible neighborhood of the ant k. The β parameter controls how important is η in the probabilistic decision. τ_j is the pheromone and η_j is the heuristic information.

In this work we use a dynamic heuristic information η_j that depends on the partial solution of an ant. We defined as $\eta_j = \frac{e_j}{c_j}$, where e_j is the so called cover value, that is, the number of additional rows covered when adding column j to the current partial solution, and c_j is the cost of column j. An ant ends the solution construction when all rows are covered.

An important step in ACO Algorithm is the pheromone update on the path. The pheromone trails are updated as given by the following equation:

$$\tau_j = p\,\tau_j + \omega_i, \ \forall j \in J \tag{5}$$

where $p \in J\ [0,1)$ is the pheromone persistence and $\omega_i > 0$ is the amount of pheromone put on column j.

The general pseudocode for the ACO is presented in Algorithm 1.

Algorithm 1. Ant Colony System

1: {Step 1: initialize parameters}
2: **while** not stop condition **do**
3:     {Step 2: All the ants in the colony generate a solution}
4:     **for** each ant in the nest **do**
5:         generate a new solution
6:     **end for**
7:     {Step 3: Update}
8:     update local optimal
9:     update pheromone trails
10: **end while**
11: {Step 4: Best solution}
12: return the best solution found

Step 1. Algorithm parameters are initialized.

Step 2. Once each ant generated a solution, the local optimal solution is updated if needed. Due to evaporation, all pheromone trails are decreased uniformly. The ants deposit some amount of pheromone on good solution to mark promising areas for next iterations.

Step 3. The algorithm ends when a certain stop condition is reached.

Step 4. The best solution found is returned.

The Set Covering Problem has been solved by the following variants of the algorithm: Ant Colony Optimization (ACO), Ant Colony System (ACS), Max-Min Ant System (MMA'S) and Hyper-Cube Framework for ACO [11].

4   Intelligent Water Drops Algorithm

The IWD algorithm is a population-based constructive metaheuristics proposed in [12] and designed to imitate the flow properties of natural water drops, which tend to describe an optimal path to their destination considering the distance and despite the constraints in the environment.

In the algorithm, the population is composed by N water drops (denoted by IWD^k, $k \in [1 \dots N]$) moving in a discrete environment, represented by a graph with N_c nodes in which the drops will move from one node to another.

Each drop has two main properties: the amount of soil it carries (denoted by $soil^k$) and the velocity (denoted by vel^k). Both properties can change how the drop flows in the environment.

In case of soil, it is expected that as iterations passes, the amount of soil carried by each drop will increase, making the drop bigger (Fig. 2A). Also the velocity in a water drop determines the amount of soil removed; the faster the water drop is, the bigger the amount of soil removed (Fig. 2B). However, the velocity of a water drop can increase or decrease according to the branch chosen in each iteration.

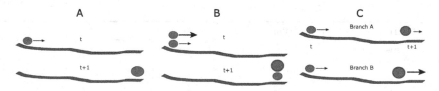

Fig. 2. Behavior of water drops in a river.

Choosing a branch (of the path) or another depends basically on how "desirable" -in terms of the amount of soil- the branch is; so, if the branch has a high amount of soil then that branch is more difficult to flow (more soil, less velocity) than another branch with a less amount (Fig. 2C). In the algorithm, this behavior is implemented by a probabilistic function of inverse of soil.

The IWD algorithm has been applied to several problems like: air robot path planning, smooth trajectory planning, vehicle routing problem, economic load dispatch problem, image processing, rough set feature selection, reservoir operation, code coverage, data aggregation in wireless sensor networks, multi-objective job shop scheduling, among others.

The general pseudocode for the IWD is presented in Algorithm 2.

Algorithm 2. Intelligent Water Drops

1: {Step 1: Static Parameters Initialization}
2: Initialize parameters N, $MAX\_ITERATION$, N_c.
3: Initialize soil parameters: a_s, b_s, c_s
4: Initialize velocity parameters: a_v, b_v, c_v
5: **for** $i = 1$ to $MAX\_ITERATION$ **do**
6:     {Step 2: Dynamic Parameter Initialization}
7:     **for** $k = 1$ to N **do**
8:         Initialize VC^k list as empty.
9:         Initialize $soil^k$ value as zero.
10:        Initialize vel^k value as $InitVel$.
11:    **end for**
12:    {Step 3: Create and Distribute Water Drops}
13:    **for** $k = 1$ to N **do**
14:        Create the kth water drop (IWD^k).
15:        Select randomly a node for IWD^k.
16:    **end for**
17:    {Step 4: Update Visited List of Water Drops}
18:    **for** $k = 1$ to N **do**
19:        Update VC^k.
20:    **end for**
21:    {Step 5: Complete Each Water Drop Solution}
22:    **for** $k = 1$ to N **do**
23:        Choose a path for IWD^k.
24:        Update velocity (vel^k).
25:        Compute the amount of soil ($\Delta soil$) to be carried by IWD^k
26:        Remove $\Delta soil$ from the path and add it to IWD^k
27:    **end for**
28:    {Step 6: Find the Best Solution from the Iteration}
29:    **for** $k = 1$ to N **do**
30:        Calculate $fitness^k$
31:    **end for**
32:    {Step 7: Update Paths of the Best Solution from Iteration}
33:    {Step 8: Update the Total Best Solution}
34: **end for**

Step 1. In this step we set the static parameters to run the IWD algorithm; all of these values will remain constant during execution and can only change between experiments.

The two properties of intelligent water drops -soil and velocity- also have parameters to set in this step; these parameters are constants required to update the soil and velocity values in each iteration. For soil, parameters are: a_s, b_s and c_s; for velocity, parameters are: a_v, b_v, c_v.

Step 2. Each water drop (denoted by IWD^k, $k \in [1 \ldots N]$) need to update certain values in each iteration: a list of nodes visited, the value for soil property and the value for velocity property.

In case of nodes, a list (denoted by VC^k) will be updated by adding the last node visited; in case of the first iteration, this list will be set to empty ($VC^k = \{\}$).

For soil and velocity, the first iteration will set arbitrarily these values to the static parameters of *InitSoil* and *InitVel* respectively.

Step 3. In this step the water drops are created and then distributed randomly along the nodes. At this point, we do not use any probability function yet.

Step 4. With all water drops distributed, we can update their list of visited nodes by adding the nodes from Step 4.

Step 5. This step will build a valid path to solution by moving the recently created water drops across nodes and updating their soil and velocity properties each time. All steps described here will be executed in a loop until reach a solution.

Step 5.1. Select the next node (called j) to be visited by water drop IWD^k. Considering a water drop at node i and with a visited list of VC^k, this step will look at all nodes that have not been visited yet and will select one of them according to a probability function based on the amount of soil present in the path to that next node (Eq. 6).

$$p_i^k(j) = \frac{f(soil(i,j))}{\sum_{\forall l \notin VC^k} f(soil(i,l))} \tag{6}$$

The function $f(soil(i,j))$ represents the inverse amount of soil in the path between nodes i and j respectively and uses a constant ε with the solely purpose to avoid zero division (Eq. 7).

$$f(soil(i,j)) = \frac{1}{\varepsilon + g(soil(i,j))} \tag{7}$$

The function $g(soil(i,j))$ is introduced to always get a positive value when calculating the amount of soil between nodes i and j respect to the amount of soil in the visited path (Eq. 8).

$$g(soil(i,j)) \begin{cases} soil(i,j) \ if \ \min\limits_{l \notin vc(IWD)} (soil(i,l)) \geq 0 \\ soil(i,j) - \min\limits_{l \notin vc(IWD))} (soil(i,l)) \ else \end{cases} \tag{8}$$

Step 5.2. Update velocity of the water drop. As long as the water drop moves between nodes i and j certain amount of soil will be carried by the drop, turning the drop bigger. To calculate this change, the algorithm will use a function based on the soil in the path between i and j (Eq. 9).

$$vel^k(t+1) = vel^k(t) + \frac{a_v}{b_v + c_v \cdot soil(i,j)} \tag{9}$$

Step 5.3. Update soil amount of the water drop. Depending on the velocity value of the water drop when moving between i and j, the amount of soil removed from environment $(soil(i,j))$ and carried by the drop for the next iteration $(soil^k(t + 1))$ will be different (Eqs. 10, 11 and 12). The more time it takes, the more soil the water drop will carry (Eq. 13).

$$soil(i,j) = (1 - \rho) \cdot soil(i,j) - \rho \cdot \Delta soil(i,j) \tag{10}$$

$$soil^k(t + 1) = soil^k(t) + \Delta soil(i,j) \tag{11}$$

$$\Delta soil(i,j) = \frac{a_s}{b_s + c_s \cdot time(i,j : vel^k(t + 1))} \tag{12}$$

$$time(i,j : vel^k(t + 1)) = \frac{HUD(i,j)}{vel^k(t + 1)} \tag{13}$$

The $HUD(i,j)$ is a local heuristic function proposed in [12] to measure the undesirability of the water drop to move from one node to another. In this article, we applied the same idea for SCP; the heuristic function applied considers the cost of moving to node j $(cost_j)$ and the number of constraints covered by the node (R_j); the function is presented in Eq. 14.

$$HUD(i,j) = \frac{cost_j}{R_j \notin VC^R} \tag{14}$$

Step 5.4. Remove soil from the path and add it to the water drop. In previous steps, we calculated the amount of soil removed from the path $(\Delta soil)$; now, the value of soil property for each water drop $(soil^k)$ needs to be updated.

Step 6. Once all water drops have completed their solutions, the algorithm requires to evaluate which one was the best in the current iteration (T^{IB}); to do this, we have to consider specifically the problem we are solving -SCP in this case- where the best solution is given by the one with the minimum cost associated. The equation that will compute this step is presented in Eq. 15.

$$T^{IB} = \arg\min q(IWD^k) \tag{15}$$

Step 7. The path traveled by the best water drop in the iteration (T_{IB}) will modify the environment for the future drops. In this step, the algorithm will update the amount of soil in the arcs of the graph that were traveled by T^{IB} in order to reflect the impact of this drop on them.

The soil update then, will be done based on Eq. 10 but considering the quality of the best solution found during the current iteration (T^{IB}). As better the solution is, then more soil will be removed. In the algorithm, this is calculated in terms of the soil present during the current iteration and the quality of the iteration-best solution (Eq. 16). The parameter ρ_{IWD} is a negative constant.

$$soil(i,j) = (1 - \rho_{IWD}) \cdot soil(i,j) +$$
$$\rho_{IWD} \cdot soil(i,j)^{IB} \cdot \frac{1}{q(T^{IB})} \tag{16}$$

Step 8. Finally, if the iteration-best solution is better than the global-best, then the global-best solution needs to be replaced with the new one (Eq. 17).

$$T^{TB} = \begin{cases} T^{IB} & \text{if } q(T^{TB}) > q(T^{IB}), \\ T^{TB} & \text{else} \end{cases} \tag{17}$$

5   Computational Results

The proposed IWD algorithm has been implemented in Java language in an Intel CORE i7 CPU, 8 GB of RAM, running Windows 7 Ultimate 64 bit.

5.1   Parameters

With the objective of finding a better behavior of the algorithm we consider different configurations for the static parameters based on the size of the families of instances. The values of each family is obtained when running the algorithm 10 times by varying the parameters: Number of intelligent water drops, Maximum number of iterations and initial soil value. The selected configuration is the one which corresponds to the solution with best RPD.

The parameters tuning for the IWD algorithm is detailed in Table 1 considering the different instances families.

Table 1. Tuning for static parameters in IWD.

Dataset	m	n	N	MAX $ITERATION$	$Initial$ $soil$	a_s	b_s	c_s	$Initial$ vel	a_v	b_v	c_v	ε	ρ
4	200	1000	250	300	1600	1000	0.01	1	3	10	0.01	1	0.01	0.95
5	200	2000	300	600	1600	1000	0.01	1	3	10	0.01	1	0.01	0.95
6	200	1000	250	600	1600	1000	0.01	1	3	10	0.01	1	0.01	0.95

The instances tested are from Beasley's OR Library. Details on instances are presented in Table 2.

Table 2. Set covering instances.

Instance set	No. of instances	m	n	Cost range	Density (%)	Optimal solution
4	10	200	1000	[1, 100]	2	Known
5	10	200	2000	[1, 100]	2	Known
6	5	200	1000	[1, 100]	5	Known

After performed experiments for the 3 families presented before, results can be seen at Table 3. This tables, presents the instance number, the optimum result known (Z_{opt}), the minimum result obtained by our experiments (Z_{min}), the average result obtained (Z_{avg}) and the relative percentage deviation (RPD) for IWD with Pre-Processing and IWD [6] techniques.

The RPD value quantifies the deviation of the objective value Z_{min} from the optimal known Z_{opt}. To calculate it, we use Eq. 18

$$RPD = \left(\frac{Z_{min} - Z_{opt}}{Z_{opt}} \right) \times 100 \tag{18}$$

Table 3. Computational results

Instance	Z_{opt}	Z_{min}	Z_{avg}	RPD_{ACO}	Z_{min}	Z_{avg}	$RPD_{IWD_{preprocess}}$	$Diff_{RPD}$
4, 1	429	443	449	0, 23	430	434	3, 26	92, 94
4, 2	512	560	579	0, 00	512	518	9, 38	100, 00
4, 3	516	546	561	0, 00	516	518	5, 81	100, 00
4, 4	494	536	554	0, 20	495	501	7, 84	97, 45
4, 5	512	552	592	0, 39	514	519	7, 81	95, 01
4, 6	560	614	263	2, 68	575	575	9, 64	72, 20
4, 7	430	456	478	0, 70	433	437	6, 05	88, 43
4, 8	492	536	568	0, 41	494	497	8, 94	95, 41
4, 9	641	706	721	0, 78	646	654	10, 14	92, 31
4, 10	514	586	596	0, 78	518	522	14, 01	94, 43
5, 1	253	277	301	0, 79	255	259	9, 49	91, 68
5, 2	302	334	357	1, 32	306	309	10, 60	87, 55
5, 3	226	245	264	2, 65	232	234	8, 41	68, 49
5, 4	242	263	291	0, 41	243	243	8, 68	95, 28
5, 5	211	232	254	0, 47	212	212	9, 95	95, 28
5, 6	213	234	250	0, 00	213	216	9, 86	100, 00
5, 7	293	325	351	1, 71	298	298	10, 92	84, 34
5, 8	288	316	344	0, 35	289	289	9, 72	96, 40
5, 9	279	325	355	0, 72	281	282	16, 49	95, 63
5, 10	265	291	302	1, 13	268	269	9, 81	88, 48
6, 1	138	156	181	2, 90	142	145	11, 54	74, 87
6, 2	146	184	194	4, 79	153	156	20, 65	76, 80
6, 3	145	172	189	0, 00	145	149	15, 70	100, 00
6, 4	131	152	181	2, 29	134	136	13, 82	83, 43
6, 5	161	188	198	0, 62	162	169	14, 36	95, 68

In accordance with the results showed in the Table 3 it is visualized that ACO was mejor in all the instances achieving 4 optimals, however also it is appreciated that the RPD of IWD is similar for all instances.

6   Conclusions and Future Work

This article presents the comparison of two constructive metaheuristics (IWD and ACO), solving a classic combinatorial problem as SCP which has been used for modeling problems of the industry. For this problem ACO had a better behavior than IWD, reaching 4 optimum for the instances used in contrast to IWD that did not reach any. We used the instances of the groups 4, 5, 6. For group 4, ACO obtained 2 optimum, 1 in group 5 and 1 in group 6. In order to improve the behavior of IWD, it incorporated a stage of preprocessing which helped to improve the response but without reaching a reach some optimal. Although the results of IWD have not been better than ACO, these are encouraging. In the same line, the future work proposed it is related to improve the tuning of parameters to improve the results. Also, another very interesting line is related to test the algorithm for the remaining instances from OR Library and other SCP libraries, such like the Unicost (available at OR-Library website), Italian railways, American airlines and the Euclidean benchmarks.

Acknowledgements. Broderick Crawford is supported by grant CONICYT/FONDECYT/REGULAR 1171243 and Ricardo Soto is supported by Grant CONICYT/FONDECYT/REGULAR/1160455, Gino Astorga is supported by Postgraduate Grant, Pontificia Universidad Catolica de Valparaíso, 2015 and José García is supported by INF-PUCV 2016. The authors are grateful for the support of the Project CORFO 14ENI2-26905 "Nueva Ingeniería para el 2030" - PUCV.

References

1. Aickelin, U.: An indirect genetic algorithm for set covering problems. J. Oper. Res. Soc. **53**, 1118–1126 (2002)
2. Beasley, J.: An algorithm for set covering problem. Eur. J. Oper. Res. **31**, 85–93 (1987)
3. Beasley, J.E., Chu, P.C.: A genetic algorithm for the set covering problem. Eur. J. Oper. Res. **94**, 392–404 (1996)
4. Brusco, M.J., Jacobs, L.W., Thompson, G.M.: A morphing procedure to supplement a simulated annealing heuristic for cost and coverage correlated set covering problems. Ann. Oper. Res. **86**, 611–627 (1999)
5. Crawford, B., Soto, R., Berríos, N., Johnson, F., Paredes, F., Castro, C., Norero, E.: A binary cat swarm optimization algorithm for the non-unicost set covering problem. In: Mathematical Problems in Engineering (2015)
6. Crawford, B., Soto, R., Córdova, J., Olguín, E.: A nature inspired intelligent water drop algorithm and its application for solving the set covering problem. In: Silhavy, R., Senkerik, R., Oplatkova, Z.K., Silhavy, P., Prokopova, Z. (eds.) Artificial Intelligence Perspectives in Intelligent Systems. AISC, vol. 464, pp. 437–447. Springer, Cham (2016). https://doi.org/10.1007/978-3-319-33625-1_39
7. Crawford, B., Soto, R., Monfroy, E., Astorga, G., García, J., Cortes, E.: A meta-optimization approach for covering problems in facility location. In: Figueroa-García, J.C., López-Santana, E.R., Villa-Ramírez, J.L., Ferro-Escobar, R. (eds.) WEA 2017. CCIS, vol. 742, pp. 565–578. Springer, Cham (2017). https://doi.org/10.1007/978-3-319-66963-2_50

8. Dorigo, M., Maniezzo, V., Colorni, A.: Ant system: optimization by a colony of cooperating agents. IEEE Trans. Syst. Man Cybern. Part B (Cybern.) **26**(1), 29–41 (1996)
9. Fisher, M., Kedia, P.: Optimal solution of set covering/partitioning problems using dual heuristics. Manag. Sci. **36**(6), 674–688 (1990)
10. Hartmanis, J.: Computers and intractability: a guide to the theory of np-completeness (Michael R. Garey and David S. Johnson). SIAM Rev. **24**(1), 90 (1982)
11. Lessing, L., Dumitrescu, I., Stützle, T.: A comparison between ACO algorithms for the set covering problem. In: Dorigo, M., Birattari, M., Blum, C., Gambardella, L.M., Mondada, F., Stützle, T. (eds.) ANTS 2004. LNCS, vol. 3172, pp. 1–12. Springer, Heidelberg (2004). https://doi.org/10.1007/978-3-540-28646-2_1
12. Shah-Hosseini, H.: Intelligent water drops algorithm: A new optimization method for solving the multiple knapsack problem. Int. J. Intell. Comput. Cybern. **1**(2), 193–212 (2008)
13. Soto, R., Crawford, B., Galleguillos, C., Barraza, J., Lizama, S., Muñoz, A., Vilches, J., Misra, S., Paredes, F.: Comparing cuckoo search, bee colony, firefly optimization, and electromagnetism-like algorithms for solving the set covering problem. In: Gervasi, O., Murgante, B., Misra, S., Gavrilova, M.L., Rocha, A.M.A.C., Torre, C., Taniar, D., Apduhan, B.O. (eds.) ICCSA 2015. LNCS, vol. 9155, pp. 187–202. Springer, Cham (2015). https://doi.org/10.1007/978-3-319-21404-7_14

Single and Multiobjective Evolutionary Algorithms for Clustering Biomedical Information with Unknown Number of Clusters

María Eugenia Curi[1], Lucía Carozzi[1], Renzo Massobrio[1],
Sergio Nesmachnow[1(✉)], Grégoire Danoy[2], Marek Ostaszewski[3],
and Pascal Bouvry[2]

[1] Universidad de la República, Montevideo, Uruguay
{maria.curi,lucia.carozzi,renzom,sergion}@fing.edu.uy
[2] FSTC/CSC-ILIAS, University of Luxembourg, Luxembourg City, Luxembourg
{gregoire.danoy,pascal.bouvry}@uni.lu
[3] LCSB, University of Luxembourg, Luxembourg City, Luxembourg
marek.ostaszewski@uni.lu

Abstract. This article presents single and multiobjective evolutionary approaches for solving the clustering problem with unknown number of clusters. Simple and ad-hoc operators are proposed, aiming to keep the evolutionary search as simple as possible in order to scale up for solving large instances. The experimental evaluation is performed considering a set of real problem instances, including a real-life problem of analyzing biomedical information in the Parkinson's disease map project. The main results demonstrate that the proposed evolutionary approaches are able to compute accurate trade-off solutions and efficiently handle the problem instance involving biomedical information.

Keywords: Clustering · Biomedical information · Multiobjective

1 Introduction

The clustering problem aims at grouping a set of elements in such a way that elements in the same group (*cluster*) are more similar to each other than to the elements in other clusters [1]. Similarity between elements is evaluated according to a predefined similarity metric to be maximized. Clustering is one of the most important unsupervised learning problems, which models many other problems dealing with finding a structure in a given set of data.

In particular, biomedical research demands dealing with a large number of concepts linked by complex relationships, which are often represented using large graphs. In order to process and understand these knowledge bases, researchers need reliable tools for visualizing and exploring large amounts of data conveniently. In order to get a deep understanding of such knowledge bases, concepts with similar characteristics need to be accurately grouped together.

© Springer International Publishing AG, part of Springer Nature 2018
P. Korošec et al. (Eds.): BIOMA 2018, LNCS 10835, pp. 100–112, 2018.
https://doi.org/10.1007/978-3-319-91641-5_9

Clustering is an NP-hard optimization problem [2] that has been thoroughly studied in the last 30 years [3]. Heuristics and metaheuristics [4] have been applied to solve the clustering problem efficiently. Among them, evolutionary algorithms (EAs) have proven to be accurate and powerful methods [5,6].

This article addresses two formulations of the clustering problem, a first one in which the number of clusters is known in advance, and a multiobjective variant which simultaneously maximizes the similarity between elements in the same cluster and minimizes the number of clusters. Three EAs are presented, two for the single objective and one for the multiobjective clustering problem. The proposed EAs are compared against several methods from the related literature. The evaluation focuses on a large problem instance from the Parkinson's disease map project [7], a research initiative that proposes building a knowledge repository to describe molecular mechanisms related to that condition [8]. The repository compiles literature-based information about Parkinson's disease and organizes the main concepts and contents in an easy to explore and freely accessible map, including experimental data, drug targets and other concepts.

The article is organized as follows. Section 2 presents the single and multiobjective clustering problem formulation and reviews related works on heuristics and metaheuristics applied to the clustering problem. The proposed EAs are described in Sect. 3 and the experimental evaluation is reported in Sect. 4. Finally, Sect. 5 presents the conclusions and the main lines for future work.

2   Clustering Problem and Related Work

This section defines the clustering problem in both its single and multiobjective variants and reviews related works.

2.1   Problem Formulation

Let us consider the following elements:

- The set $E = \{e_1, e_2, \ldots, e_n\}$ of elements to be grouped.
- The function $s : E \times E \to [0,1]$; $s(e_i, e_j)$ is the similarity between e_i and e_j. The following conditions hold: $\forall e_i, e_j, s(e_i, e_j) = s(e_j, e_i)$ and $s(e_i, e_i) = 1$.
- An integer $k > 0$, which indicates the number of clusters to consider for grouping elements (*only for the single-objective version of the problem*).

The clustering problem consists in assigning the elements in E to a set of groups (*clusters*) $G = \{G_1, \ldots, G_k\}$; $G_i = \{c_i\} \cup \{e_m/s(e_m, c_i) \leq s(e_m, c_j) \forall e_m \in E, c_j, c_i \in C, i \neq j\}$; $C \subseteq E, |C| = k$ is the set of centers of the groups. The following properties hold: a) *cluster index in* $[1, k]$) $\forall(i, j), i \neq j : 1 \leq i, j \leq k$, and b) *clusters are disjoint sets* $G_i \cap G_j = \emptyset$.

The goal of the single objective version of the problem is to maximize the *total similarity* metric (TS) defined in Eq. 1.

$$\max TS = \sum_{e_i \in E} \max_{c_i \in C} s(e_i, c_i) \tag{1}$$

In the multiobjective version of the problem, the goal is to simultaneously maximize the value of TS and minimize the number of clusters k.

2.2   Related Work

Many articles have presented heuristic and metaheuristic methods applied to the clustering problem. Early works considered the single objective version of the problem, based on minimizing the distance or maximizing similarity.

Das et al. [9] reviewed the application of metaheuristics for clustering problems. Trajectory-based metaheuristics offer limited problem solving capabilities, mainly due to scalability issues when solving large problem instances. Deng and Bard [10] applied GRASP for the Capacitated Clustering Problem, which proposes grouping elements in clusters, where each cluster has capacity constraints (minimum and maximum number of elements). GRASP was able to find optimal solutions for the problem instances with 30 and 40 nodes, and outperformed solutions found using CPLEX when using an execution time limit of one hour.

Early proposed EAs did not follow an explicit multiobjective approach. Sheng and Liu [6] compared k-medoids, local search, and Hybrid K-medoid Algorithm (HKA) over two datasets (517 elements/10 groups, and 2945 elements/30 groups). HKA obtained the best results on the largest problem instance and slightly better results for the small test problem. The EA by Cowgill et al. [11] optimized clustering metrics defined in terms of external cluster isolation and internal cluster homogeneity, improving over hierarchical clustering algorithms considering an internal criterion. Bandyopadhyay and Maulik [12] proposed an EA for clustering with a number of clusters not defined a priori, to analyze several clustering metrics.

Multiobjective EAs (MOEAs) for clustering have been presented in the book by Maulik et al. [13], most of them focused on optimizing two similarity metrics, thus studying different features of the data to analyze. The multiobjective approach by Ripon et al. [14] considered intracluster variation and intercluster distance, without assuming the number of clusters. The experimental analysis over problems with up to 3000 elements, nine classes, and two features, showed improved solutions over a custom NSGA-II. Handl and Knowles [15] proposed multiobjective clustering with automatic k determination (MOCK), considering objective functions based on compactness (deviation) and connectedness of clusters. These are conflicting objectives because the overall deviation improves when using more clusters, but the connectivity decreases. MOCK showed good behavior and scalability when compared with single-objective clustering algorithms. Korkmaz et al. [16] presented a Pareto-based MOEA to find a set of non-dominated clusters considering intracluster variation and the number of clusters. The experimental evaluation was performed over two small standard datasets (150 and 75 elements, with only two attributes), but no numerical results or multiobjective optimization analysis is reported.

Most of the previous works have proposed ad-hoc EAs to address the clustering problem and few of them have solved multiobjective variants. This article contributes with simple EAs and an explicit MOEA designed to scale properly for solving large problem instances, and we focus on a real-life instance considering biomedical information in the context of the Parkinson disease map project.

3   Evolutionary Algorithms for Clustering

This section describes in detail the single and multiobjective EAs proposed to tackle the clustering problem.

3.1   Single Objective EAs

Fitness Function. The fitness function computes the sum of similarities between each element and its most similar center, as presented in Sect. 2.1.

Solution Encoding. Two solution encodings are proposed and evaluated. Binary encoding: a solution is represented as a binary vector of length n (the number of elements to be grouped). Each position in the vector represents whether the corresponding element is a group center (1) or not (0). Integer encoding: each solution is a vector of k integers in $[1, N]$, representing the set of cluster centers. Numbers only appear once, as the k clusters must have different centers.

Crossover Operators. Two crossover operators were implemented for the binary encoding: Single Point Crossover (SPX) randomly selects a crossover position and exchanges the genes after the crossover point between both parents. Two-Point Crossover (2PX) randomly selects two crossover positions and exchanges the genes located between these two points.

For the integer encoding, three crossover operators were implemented: SPX, Generalized Cut and Splice (GenC&S), and Hybrid Crossover (SPX-GenC&S). GenC&S is a variant of Cut and Splice (C&S) [17] for the clustering problem, to preserve useful features of the information in both parents (Algorithm 1). GenC&S selects a random cutting point cp on one parent and a random integer $s \in [0, k]$. Two lists are created, sorted by similarity with the element on position cp in parent1: LP1 (elements on parent1) and LP2 (elements in parent2). The first s elements in LP1 are copied to offspring1 and the $k - s$ remaining elements are copied from LP2, if their similarity to elements already copied to offspring1 is smaller than the input parameter ε. If less than k centers are copied to offspring1, the solution is completed with randomly selected centers. SPX-GenC&S uses a single random number p instead of cp and s. Elements before p in parent1 are copied to offspring1 (like in SPX), and the $k - p$ remaining elements in offspring1 are copied from parent2, if their similarity to elements already copied to offspring1 is smaller than ε (like in GenC&S). If less than k centers are copied to offspring1, the solution is completed with randomly selected centers.

Mutation Operators. Five mutation operators were implemented. For binary encoding, Bit Flip Mutation changes encoded values by the opposite binary value; Add Mutation changes data points to centers; and Delete Mutation changes centers to data points. For integer encoding, One Gene Mutation changes

Algorithm 1. GenC&S crossover for the clustering problem (integer encoding)

1: **Input:** parent1, parent2, ε; **Output:** offspring1
2: $cp = \text{rand}(0,k)$
3: $s = \text{rand}(0,k)$
4: cp_element = parent1[cp]
5: offspring1.add(cp_element)
6: LP1 = sortAscending(parent1,cp_element)
7: LP2 = sortAscending(parent2,cp_element)
8: **for** $i = 0$ to $s - 1$ **do**   ▷ Copy the first s elements from LP1 to offspring1
9:    offspring1.add(LP1[i])
10: **end for**
11: **for** $j = 0$ to $k - s$ **do**   ▷ Copy the first $N - s$ elements from LP2 to offspring1
12:   **if** similarity(LP2[j],offspring1)$< \varepsilon$ **then**   ▷ not too close
13:      offspring1.add(LP2[j])   ▷ already in offspring1
14:   **end if**
15: **end for**
16: **while** offspring1.length() $< k$ **do**   ▷ Complete with random elements
17:   new_center = rand(0,N)
18:   offspring1.add(new_center)
19: **end while**

elements to another that is not included in the solution (randomly selected according to a uniform distribution in the set E) and Adapted One Gene Mutation changes an element in the encoding to the most similar element, found by applying the following search: all elements in the solution are processed, and the similarity to the element being mutated is evaluated. The best similarity value (γ) is stored and the new center is selected to have a similarity less than γ.

Corrective Function. Some evolutionary operators do not guarantee to preserve the number of centers in a solution. A simple corrective function is applied both for binary and integer encodings. For binary encoding, if the number of 1 s in the solution is not k, random centers are added or deleted until the solution becomes feasible. For integer encoding, if the same element appears more than once in the vector, each repeated element is replaced with another chosen randomly (uniform distribution) among elements that are not already centers.

Population Initialization. The individuals in the population are randomly generated following a uniform distribution in $\{0, 1\}$ (binary encoding) and a uniform distribution in the set of centers C (integer encoding). The initialization procedure generates feasible solutions by applying the corrective function to each individual in the initial population.

3.2   Multiobjective EA

A variant of NSGA-II [18] was implemented to solve the multiobjective variant of the clustering problem. Following an incremental approach, the encoding and evolutionary operators that achieved the best results in the comparative analysis of the single objective EA for the problem were used in the proposed NSGA-II: binary encoding, SPX, and Delete Mutation.

In the multiobjective problem, the solution with all genes set to 0 is not feasible, since it does not represent any grouping at all. To avoid this situation, the corrective function randomly adds a center to the solution. The initial population is randomly generated following a uniform distribution in $[0, 1]$ and the corrective function is applied to the generated individuals.

4   Experimental Evaluation

This section describes the evaluation of the proposed EAs for clustering.

4.1   Problem Instances

A total number of 13 problem instances were used to evaluate the proposed EAs. These instances correspond to clustering problems arising in different fields of study, including two instances that model the Parkinson's disease map:

- Instance #1 consists of hydrometric data from 46 basins in Uruguay [19].
- Instances #2 to #8 and #10 to #12 are from the Knowledge Extraction based on Evolutionary Learning dataset [20], a data repository for classification problems. These instances have between 80 and 846 elements each.
- Instances #9 and #13 contain data from the Parkinson's disease map, which visually represents all major molecular pathways involved in the Parkinson disease pathogenesis. Instance #9 has 801 elements. Instance #13 has 3056 elements and it is used to test the performance of the multiobjective approach on a large problem instance containing biomedical information.

4.2   Experimental Configuration and Methodology

Development and Execution Platform. The proposed EAs were developed using ECJ [21], an open source framework for evolutionary computation in Java. Experiments were performed on an Intel Core i5 @ 2.7 GHz and 8 GB of RAM.

Results Evaluation. The results computed by the proposed EAs are compared against clustering algorithms from the literature in terms of the objective function (total similarity) and in terms of the relative hypervolume (RHV) metric for the multiobjective variant of the clustering problem. RHV is the ratio between the volumes (in the objective functions space) covered by the computed Pareto front and the volume covered by the true Pareto front. The ideal value for RHV is 1. The true Pareto front—unknown for the problem instances studied—is approximated by the set of non-dominated solutions found in each execution.

The algorithms used in the comparison are:

- *k-medoids* [22], a classic partitional method related to *k*-means. Clusters are built to minimize the distance between points and the center of the corresponding cluster, according to a given distance metric.

– *Linkage*, an agglomerative hierarchical clustering technique based on building
   clusters by combining elements of previously defined clusters. A distance function evaluates a relevant similarity metric for the problem and different linkage
   implementations use different distance functions. The Matlab implementation
   of single linkage (nearest neighbor), which uses the smallest distance between
   objects in the two cluster, in the results comparison.
– *Local Search* [6], combining k-medoids and an exhaustive search performed
   for each cluster. Starting from a randomly selected set of centers, the set of
   p nearest neighbors is found for each center. A local search is performed over
   these sets to find a new center that minimizes the distance with all elements.
   The search ends when no center is changed in two consecutive iterations.
– *Greedy*, which builds clusters iteratively, taking a locally optimal decision in
   each step. Starting from a randomly selected center, in each step searches
   for the element with the lowest similarity with the solution already built.
   This element is included in the solution as a new center. All clusters are
   recomputed and the procedure is applied until building k clusters.
– *Hybrid EA*, combining an EA and the local search by Sheng and Liu [6]
   (Algorithm 2). The hybrid EA uses binary encoding, random initialization,
   tournament selection, Mix Subset Recombination, and Bit Flip Mutation.

Algorithm 2. Generic schema of the hybrid EA for the clustering problem

---

1: Initialize k centers randomly
2: **while** not stopping_criterion **do**
3:     [parent1, parent2] = TournamentSelection(P)
4:     **if** rand(0,1) > p_C **then**
5:         [offspring1, offspring2] = Mix Subset Recombination(parent1, parent2)
6:     **end if**
7:     [offspring1, offspring2] = Bit Flip Mutation(p_M)
8:     **if** rand(0,1) > p_{LS} **then**
9:         [offspring1, offspring2] = Local Search()
10:     **end if**
11: **end while**
12: **return** best solution found

Statistical Analysis. Thirty independent executions of each algorithm were performed over each problem instance to have statistical confidence. For each problem instance, the best and the average fitness value (for the single objective
problem) and the average multiobjective metrics (for the multiobjective problem) are reported. The Kolmogorov-Smirnov test is applied to each set of results
to assess if the values follow a normal distribution. After that, the non-parametric
Kruskal-Wallis test is applied to compare the results distributions obtained by
different algorithms. A confidence level of 95% is used for both statistical tests.

4.3   Single Objective Clustering Problem

Parameter Settings. The parameter values of each algorithm were configured based on preliminary experiments and suggestions from related works:

- *Single objective EAs*: population size (pop) = 100, crossover probability (p_C) = 0.75, mutation probability (p_M) = 0.01, tournament size = 2, and stopping criterion of 10000 generations.
- *k-medoids*: the algorithm stops when the cluster centers remain unchanged in consecutive iterations.
- *Local search*: size of the search neighborhood = 3 and the stopping criterion is the same as for k-medoids, as recommended by Sheng and Liu [6].
- *Hybrid EA*: pop = 30, p_C = 0.95, p_M = 0.02, p_{LS} = 0.2, neighborhood size = 3, tournament size = 2, and stopping criterion of 10000 generations.

Comparison of Evolutionary Operators. For the binary encoding, two crossovers and three mutations were proposed, generating six possible combinations: SPX and Bit Flip Mutation (*SPX-bit*), SPX and Add Mutation (*SPX-add*), SPX and Delete Mutation (*SPX-del*), 2PX and Bit Flip Mutation (*2PX-bit*), 2PX and Add Mutation (*2PX-add*), and 2PX and Delete Mutation (*2PX-del*). Experimental results showed that *SPX-del* performed better on small problem instances, outperforming the other combinations of evolutionary operators. On medium sized instances #5 and #6, *SPX-bit* computed the best results, while on large instances *2PX-del* achieved the best results. Therefore, the rest of the experimental analysis of the single objective EA using binary encoding focused on these three combinations of evolutionary operators.

For the integer encoding, three crossover operators and two mutations were presented, generating six possible combinations: SPX and One Gene Mutation (*SPX-One*), SPX and Adapted One Gene Mutation (*SPX-Adapt*), SPX-GenC&S Crossover and One Gene Mutation (*SPXGCS-One*), SPX-GenC&S Crossover and Adapted One Gene Mutation (*SPXGCS-Adapt*), GenC&S Crossover and One Gene Mutation (*GCS-One*), and GenC&S Crossover and Adapted One Gene Mutation (*GCS-Adapt*). Results showed that *SPX-One* computed the best results in 7 instances and *GCS-One* in 5 instances, both outperforming the other combinations. Therefore, the rest of the experimental analysis of the single objective EA using integer encoding focused on these two combinations.

Comparison of Solution Encodings. Table 1 reports the average similarity results computed on 30 independent executions of the proposed EA using binary and integer encoding and the evolutionary operators that achieved the best results in the previous analysis.

Results indicate that the binary encoded EA using *SPX-del* and *2PX-del* significantly outperformed the results computed using integer encoding and *SPX-bit*. There is no significant difference when using *SPX-del* and *2PX-del*, and for simplicity, the rest of the experimental evaluation was performed using *SPX-del*.

Table 1. Average similarity using different encodings and evolutionary operators.

#I	Integer encoding		Binary encoding		
	SPX-One	*GCS-One*	*SPX-bit*	*SPX-del*	*2PX-del*
#1	**18.66**	**18.66**	**18.66**	**18.66**	**18.66**
#2	**1.96**	**1.96**	**1.96**	**1.96**	**1.96**
#3	12.42	12.44	12.27	**12.46**	**12.46**
#4	16.43	16.41	15.93	**16.50**	**16.50**
#5	78.35	78.16	**78.61**	78.51	78.42
#6	116.18	116.39	**116.45**	115.69	115.34
#7	54.71	54.68	54.80	**54.98**	**54.98**
#8	63.27	63.30	61.10	63.42	**63.43**
#9	673.57	656.56	633.91	**675.20**	**675.20**
#10	37.77	36.49	35.88	**38.22**	**38.22**
#11	235.33	229.58	221.17	**236.11**	**236.11**
#12	32.89	32.08	31.20	**33.23**	**33.23**

Comparison Against Other Algorithms. The proposed EA with binary encoding, SPX, and delete mutation was compared against the baseline algorithms. Table 2 reports the average similarity computed over 30 independent executions of each algorithm for the 12 problem instances (the best results are marked in bold). The Kolmogorov-Smirnov test was performed on the results' distributions. In most cases, the test allowed rejecting–with 95% confidence–the null hypothesis that the results follow a normal distribution. Therefore, the Kruskal-Wallis test was used to compare the results' distributions computed by each EA (the p-value is

Table 2. Comparison of average similarity against other algorithms.

Instance	Greedy	Linkage	k-medoids	Local search	Hybrid	EA SPX-del	p-value K-W
#1	7.28	17.01	17.03	15.49	**18.66**	18.66	$<10^{-15}$
#2	1.12	1.65	1.95	1.70	**1.96**	1.96	$<10^{-15}$
#3	5.77	10.18	12.14	10.50	12.45	**12.46**	$<10^{-15}$
#4	7.41	14.04	16.00	13.23	16.22	**16.50**	$<10^{-15}$
#5	47.69	76.08	76.47	69.11	**78.62**	78.51	$<10^{-15}$
#6	83.61	109.68	116.30	108.86	**116.45**	115.69	$<10^{-15}$
#7	29.31	50.77	54.98	41.68	**54.98**	**54.98**	$<10^{-15}$
#8	31.81	62.25	62.51	52.99	63.24	**63.42**	$<10^{-15}$
#9	499.54	523.19	667.94	615.64	661.48	**675.20**	$<10^{-15}$
#10	22.90	30.61	37.09	32.94	36.73	**38.22**	$<10^{-15}$
#11	170.65	198.75	236.10	205.96	229.56	**236.11**	$<10^{-15}$
#12	22.80	27.02	32.85	28.56	33.10	**33.23**	$<10^{-15}$

reported in the last column). Kruskal-Wallis allows rejecting the null hypothesis that the results computed by all algorithms follow the same distribution.

The proposed EA outperformed all other algorithms, computing the best average results in 10 instances. Improvements were up to 9.5% over k-medoids and 156.2% over greedy. The proposed EA also improved over Linkage in up to 29.1% and over the local search on of 31.9%. Finally, the improvements against the hybrid algorithm are smaller. In the best case (instance #10) the proposed EA outperformed the hybrid EA in up to 4.0% (2.3% on average).

4.4   Multiobjective Clustering Problem

Parameters Setting. The parameters of the proposed MOEA were defined based on preliminary experiments: $pop = 100$, $p_C = 0.75$, $p_M = 0.01$, tournament of size 2, and a stopping criteria of 1000 generations.

Numerical Results. The best EA for the single objective clustering problem (i.e., using SPX and delete mutation) and k-medoids were used to compare the NSGA-II results. 30 independent executions of each algorithm were executed, changing the number of clusters for the single objective algorithms.

Figures 1 and 2 show sample Pareto fronts computed by the proposed MOEA and the best solutions computed by k-medoids and in 30 independent executions of the single objective EA using different numbers of clusters. These are representative results for the set of problem instances solved.

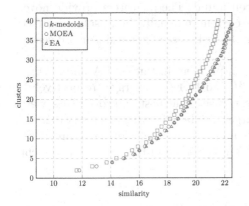
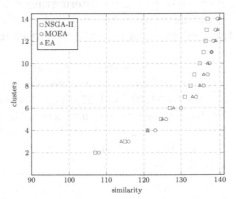

Fig. 1. Pareto fronts for instance #4   **Fig. 2.** Pareto fronts for instance #6

Results showed that for small number of clusters there is no significant difference in the solutions computed by EA and MOEA. Both evolutionary approaches improve over k-medoids. As the number of groups increases, the MOEA is able to found solutions with better similarity values than the single objective EA, and both significantly improves over the k-medoids results. In addition, the MOEA is able to obtain a Pareto front of solutions with different trade-off values in a single execution, while several executions (each one for a different number of clusters) are needed for the single objective EA and k-medoids. Therefore, the MOEA is useful for a decision-maker to be able to visualize several groupings with different trade-offs between the problem objectives and select the one that better captures the problem features. This is especially relevant in the case of biomedical information, where the number of clusters is particularly difficult to define a priori for a given dataset.

The RHV results over 30 independent executions, reported in Table 3, indicated that the proposed MOEA is robust and computes accurate Pareto fronts for the problem instances studied. The average RHV was 0.99, the maximum difference from the ideal RHV was 0.02 (instances #6 and #12), and the optimum value of 1.00 was achieved for three problem instances.

Table 3. RHV values obtained by the proposed algorithms.

MOEA		EA		k-medoids	
Average	Best	Average	Best	Average	Best
0.99	1.00	0.96	1.00	0.83	0.92

Regarding the problem instances from the Parkinson's disease map, the proposed EAs allowed to compute accurate configurations that provide different trade-offs between the problem objectives. Using the evolutionary approaches, several new possible clusterings have been found. These clusters provide novel promising information, different to the current manually built solutions (see the project website at http://wwwen.uni.lu/lcsb/research/parkinson_s_disease_map).

Overall, considering the complete set of problem instances, EA and MOEA were able to improve over k-medoids 15.8% and 14.1% in average (respectively), and up to 31.4% and 27.0% in the best case. The best improvements were obtained in the problem instances with larger number of elements, clearly demonstrating the good scalability behavior of the proposed evolutionary approaches. The best improvement of EA over MOEA was 8.7% and the best improvement of MOEA over EA was 4.4%.

5   Conclusions and Future Work

This article presented evolutionary algorithms applied to the clustering problem in its single and multiobjective variants, with unknown number of clusters. This is a very important problem in many research areas that involve dealing with large volumes of information to be categorized and grouped.

The proposed evolutionary algorithms were conceived to apply simple and ad-hoc operators, trying to keep the search as straightforward as possible in order to scale up for solving large instances of the clustering problem.

The experimental evaluation was performed considering a set of real problem instances, including one problem consisting of biomedical information in the context of the Parkinson disease map project. The main results from the experimental analysis indicate that the proposed evolutionary algorithms are able to compute accurate solutions for the problem instances studied. The evolutionary approaches outperform several algorithms of the related literature. In the single objective clustering problem, the proposed evolutionary algorithm is able to compute the best average result in 10 out of 12 problem instances. For the multiobjective clustering problem, the proposed evolutionary algorithm is able to compute accurate Pareto fronts, which offer decision-makers solutions with different trade-offs between the problem objectives.

The evolutionary approach is especially helpful for organizing biomedical information in the case of the Parkinson's disease map project. The proposed EAs are able to find accurate organizations for the data, which provide different trade-offs between the problem objectives and allow capturing different features of the information. The computed solutions provide new promising clustering patterns to be examined along the existing ones, manually built by experts.

The main lines of future work include extending the experimental analysis considering datasets from different fields of study. Additionally, a parallel model for EAs should be considered to both reduce execution times and handle bigger datasets. Finally, the possibility of combining the proposed evolutionary algorithms with visualization tools should be studied, in order to help researchers analyze the information in a more intuitive way.

References

1. Kaufman, L., Rousseeuw, P.: Finding Groups in Data: An Introduction to Cluster Analysis. Wiley, New York (1990)
2. Welch, W.: Algorithmic complexity: Three NP- hard problems in computational statistics. J. Stat. Comput. Simul. 15(1), 17–25 (1982)
3. Hastie, T., Tibshirani, R., Friedman, J.: The Elements of Statistical Learning. Springer, New York (2009). https://doi.org/10.1007/978-0-387-84858-7
4. Nesmachnow, S.: An overview of metaheuristics: accurate and efficient methods for optimisation. Int. J. Metaheuristics 3(4), 320–347 (2014)
5. Hruschka, E., Campello, R., Freitas, A., de Carvalho, A.: A survey of evolutionary algorithms for clustering. IEEE Trans. Syst. Man Cybern. Part C (Appl. Rev.) 39(2), 133–155 (2009)
6. Sheng, W., Liu, X.: A hybrid algorithm for k-medoid clustering of large data sets. In: IEEE Congress on Evolutionary Computation, pp. 77–82 (2004)
7. University of Luxembourg: Parkinson's disease map project http://wwwen.uni.lu/lcsb/research/parkinson_s_disease_map, November 2017
8. Fujita, K., et al.: Integrating pathways of Parkinson's disease in a molecular interaction map. Mol. Neurobiol. 49(1), 88–102 (2014)
9. Das, S., Abraham, A., Konar, A.: Metaheuristic Clustering. Studies in Computational Intelligence, vol. 178. Springer, Heidelberg (2009). https://doi.org/10.1007/978-3-540-93964-1

10. Deng, Y., Bard, J.: A reactive GRASP with path relinking for capacitated clustering. J. Heuristics **17**(2), 119–152 (2011)
11. Cowgill, M., Harvey, R., Watson, L.: A genetic algorithm approach to cluster analysis. Comput. Mathematics Appl. **37**(7), 99–108 (1999)
12. Bandyopadhyay, S., Maulik, U.: Nonparametric genetic clustering: comparison of validity indices. IEEE Trans. Syst. Man Cybern. Part C (Appl. Rev.) **31**(1), 120–125 (2001)
13. Maulik, U., Bandyopadhyay, S., Mukhopadhyay, A.: Multiobjective Genetic Algorithms for Clustering. Springer, Heidelberg (2011). https://doi.org/10.1007/978-3-642-16615-0
14. Ripon, K., Tsang, C.H., Kwong, S., Ip, M.K.: Multi-objective evolutionary clustering using variable-length real jumping genes genetic algorithm. In: 18th International Conference on Pattern Recognition, pp. 3609–3616 (2006)
15. Handl, J., Knowles, J.: An evolutionary approach to multiobjective clustering. IEEE Trans. Evol. Comput. **11**(1), 56–76 (2007)
16. Korkmaz, E., Du, J., Alhajj, R., Barker, K.: Combining advantages of new chromosome representation scheme and multi-objective genetic algorithms for better clustering. Intell. Data Anal. **10**(2), 163–182 (2006)
17. Deaven, D., Ho, K.: Molecular geometry optimization with a genetic algorithm. Phys. Rev. Lett. **75**, 288–291 (1995)
18. Deb, K.: Multi-Objective Optimization Using Evolutionary Algorithms. Wiley, Hoboken (2001)
19. Ministerio de Vivienda Ordenamiento Territorial y Medio Ambiente (Uruguay): Red de estaciones hidrométricas http://www.mvotma.gub.uy, November 2017
20. Alcalá, J., et al.: KEEL data-mining software tool: Data set repository, integration of algorithms and experimental analysis framework. J. Multiple-valued Logic Soft Comput. **17**(2–3), 255–287 (2010)
21. Luke, S., et al.: ECJ 23: A Java-based Evolutionary Computation Research System. https://cs.gmu.edu/eclab/projects/ecj. Accessed March 2017
22. Kaufman, L., Rousseeuw, P.: Clustering by means of medoids. In: Statistical Data Analysis Based on the L1-Norm and Related Methods (1987)

Evolutionary Algorithms for Scheduling of Crude Oil Preheating Process Under Linear Fouling

Dimbalita Deka$^{(\boxtimes)}$ and Dilip Datta[ID]

Department of Mechanical Engineering, Tezpur University, Tezpur 784 028, India
dimbalitadeka@gmail.com, ddatta@tezu.ernet.in, datta_dilip@rediffmail.com

Abstract. The crude oil preheating process in refineries is required to be scheduled in a way to minimize the processing cost involved with it, subject to the satisfaction of various process related constraints. The process forms a mixed-integer optimization problem as the scheduling of the processing units involves binary variables, while the discharges from the running units are real valued. The two parts of such problems are usually handled by two different algorithms, where the optimum scheduling obtained by one algorithm is fed to another algorithm for optimizing its discharge process. In the present work, formulating the crude oil preheating process under the effect of linear fouling as a mixed-integer nonlinear programming (MINLP) model, three binary-real coded evolutionary algorithms (EAs) are investigated in order to demonstrate that a single EA can successfully tackle its both binary and real parts. Further, the statistical analysis of the performances of the EAs are also presented through their application to a benchmark instance of the problem.

Keywords: Evolutionary algorithms · Optimization
Crude oil preheating process

1 Introduction

Evolutionary algorithms (EAs) are known to have the ability to find approximate solutions in reasonable time for such problems also, where classical optimization methods either become too expensive or even ineffective. EAs are usually independent of problem domains unlike classical optimization methods, which are restricted to specific classes of problems only. Hence, EAs have found applications in a wide range of real-life problems, including linear and nonlinear, convex and non-convex, continuous and discrete, and many more.

However, EAs still could not be generalized in case of many classes of discrete or mixed-discrete problems, but require the incorporation of some problem information for their effective performance. Unit scheduling of continuous flow process systems in industries is such a problem, which consists of two optimization sub-problems. The first part is the integer-valued scheduling of the

P. Korošec et al. (Eds.): BIOMA 2018, LNCS 10835, pp. 113–125, 2018.
https://doi.org/10.1007/978-3-319-91641-5_10

processing units, while the second part is concerned with the optimization of the discharge process based on the scheduling of the first part. Accordingly, the optimization of an industrial continuous flow process system essentially becomes a mixed-integer non-linear programming (MINLP) problem involving both integer variables to represent operational status of the units and real variables to represent the flows from the running units. Due to the complexities involved with such MINLP problems, two parts of a problem are often tackled separately through two different algorithms, where the first algorithm is employed to schedule the processing units over a time horizon and then the second algorithm optimizes the flow processes in the schedule of the first algorithm [1,2]. However, such an isolating system may suffer from the drawback of missing better solutions as the possibility of more promising solutions cannot be denied if both the parts of the problem were tackled interactively [3,4].

In view of above, three EAs are investigated here for handling an MINLP based two-step continuous flow process system by a single EA. The studied problem is the optimum scheduling of the crude oil preheating process arising in refineries, which is carried out through a crude preheat train (CPT) over a time horizon. The aim of preheating is to increase the crude oil temperature to a certain degree before its entry into a furnace, so that the energy (fuel) requirement in the furnace gets reduced. The CPT consists of a network of heat exchangers, commonly known as the heat exchanger network (HEN), to run a productive heat treatment process. The heat exchangers of HEN require periodic shutting down for the purpose of cleaning or other maintenance. This demands the effective scheduling of the HEN in order to get the optimum performance from the active units.

2   Literature Review

In the case of EAs, mixed-integer problems involving distinct real and integer valued parts are often solved by hybridizing two optimization techniques, allowing one technique to handle the integer part and another to handle the real part. As an example, Trivedi et al. [5] solved the mixed-integer unit commitment problem, where binary variables are evolved using a genetic algorithm (GA) and the continuous variables using a differential evolution (DE). Similar hybridization procedures are found in many other works, such as hybridization of GA and particle swarm optimization (PSO) [6,7], artificial bee colony (ABC) and GA [8], and DE and PSO [9].

Some works are also found where both integer and real parts of mixed-integer problems are handled by a single algorithm [3,4]. However, no such work on scheduling the crude oil preheating process in refineries could be found in specialized literature.

3   Problem Description and Formulation

The studied problem of crude oil preheating process in a CPT is adopted from Smaïli et al. [10], which is shown schematically in Fig. 1. In this problem, the

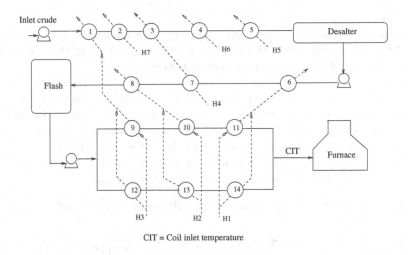

Fig. 1. Crude oil preheating process in a CPT [10].

raw crude oil passes through 14 heat exchangers (marked in Fig. 1 by 1 to 14), where it is preheated by 7 heating streams (marked in Fig. 1 by H1 to H7) prior to entering into the furnace. Heat exchangers 1–8 are connected in series; while the remaining 6 heat exchangers are arranged in two parallel lines, one containing heat exchangers 9–11 and the other connecting heat exchangers 12–14. The desalter and flash used in the processing line remove, respectively, any salt and vapour dissolved in the crude oil. The preheated crude oil is then burnt in the furnace at a higher temperature, after which it is distilled into different products.

During the preheating process of the crude oil, some impurities mixed with the crude oil get precipitated/deposited on the inner surfaces of the heat exchangers, which is called fouling. Such deposition forms a thick layer over time, which gradually reduces the performance of heat exchangers. In other words, the crude oil cannot be heated up to the possible level, which consequently increases the energy requirement in the furnace, thus increasing the energy cost. Further, the periodic cleaning of the heat exchangers for mitigating fouling is associated with cleaning cost. Hence, the process needs optimization for minimizing the total operational cost (i.e., the total of energy cost and cleaning cost) subject to some processing constraints.

Since the process is operated continuously over several years without any interruption, it can be considered that a cycle of a shorter time period is repeated in the entire time horizon. For the purpose of analysis, the cycle can further be divided equally into a certain number of time instants. At a time instant, a unit (heat exchanger) will remain either in full operation or partially/fully shutdown. In a shutting down instant, a unit may go through cleaning process also. Accordingly, the general optimization problem of a cycle of the process can be defined as follows:

– Determine
   1. Operational status of each unit at every time instant.
   2. Outlet temperature of the crude from the CPT at every time instant.
– To minimize total cost (cleaning cost plus energy cost).
– Subject to
   1. Limit on operational units in each series segment at every instant.
   2. Limit on operational units in each parallel segment at every instant.
   3. Limit on operational units in each heating line at every instant.
   4. Limit on crude oil temperature from the outlet of the CPT.
   5. Limit on cleaning instants of each unit in the entire time horizon.
   6. Limit on cleaning a unit at consecutive time instants.

The above optimization problem is formulated in Eqs. (1) and (2).

$$\text{Minimize} \quad f = C^{\text{cl}} \sum_{i=1}^{N} \sum_{t=1}^{T} \beta_{it} + C^{\text{ener}} F_N^{\text{f}} c_N^{\text{f}} \sum_{t=1}^{T} \left(\Theta^{\text{fmax}} - \Theta_{Nt}^{\text{f,out}} \right) \quad (1)$$

$$\text{Subject to} \quad g_1 \equiv \sum_{j=1}^{\text{nsu}_i} u_{\text{su}_{ij},t} \geqslant \text{su}_i^{\text{on}}; \qquad t = 1, 2, \cdots, T; \ i = 1, 2, \cdots, \text{ns}$$
$$(2a)$$

$$g_2 \equiv \sum_{k=1}^{\text{npsu}_{ij}} u_{\text{psu}_{ijk},t} \geqslant \text{psu}_{ij}^{\text{on}}; \qquad \begin{array}{l} t = 1, 2, \cdots, T; \ j = 1, 2, \cdots, \text{nps}_i \\ i = 1, 2, \cdots, \text{npl} \end{array}$$
$$(2b)$$

$$g_3 \equiv \sum_{j=1}^{\text{nhlu}_i} u_{\text{hlu}_{ij},t} \geqslant \text{hlu}_i^{\text{on}}; \qquad t = 1, 2, \cdots, T; \ i = 1, 2, \cdots, \text{nhl}$$
$$(2c)$$

$$g_4 \equiv \Theta_{Nt}^{\text{f,out}} \leqslant \Theta^{\text{fmax}}; \qquad t = 1, 2, \cdots, T \qquad (2d)$$

$$g_5 \equiv \sum_{t=1}^{T} v_{it} \geqslant 1; \qquad i = 1, 2, \cdots, N \qquad (2e)$$

$$g_6 \equiv (1 - u_{ip})(1 - u_{it}) \neq 0; \qquad p = \begin{cases} T; & \text{if } t = 1 \\ t - 1; & \text{otherwise.} \end{cases}$$
$$t = 1, 2, \cdots, T; \ i = 1, 2, \cdots, N$$
$$(2f)$$

The objective function, f, in Eq. (1) represents the total operational cost, where the two summing terms on the right side represent the cleaning cost and energy cost, respectively. The constraints, g_1–g_3, in Eqs. (2a)–(2c) represent, respectively, the minimum number of operational units in series segments, parallel segments, and heating medium flow lines; while the constraints, g_4–g_6, in Eqs. (2d)–(2f) ensure the specified temperature of the crude oil at the outlet of the CPT, cleaning of each unit at least once in the entire time horizon, and avoiding the cleaning of a unit at two consecutive time instants, respectively.

In Eqs. (1) and (2), N and T are respectively the total number of units (heat exchangers) and time instants in a production cycle, C^{cl} is the cleaning cost coefficient per cleaning instant for the ith unit at the tth time instant (in practice, C^{cl} may remain same in all units and time instants), C^{ener} is the energy cost coefficient per unit of energy requirement, F_N^{f} is the flow rate in the last unit (Nth unit), c_N^{f} is the specific heat transfer capacity of the crude oil in the last unit, $\Theta_{Nt}^{\mathrm{f,out}}$ is the crude outlet temperature from the last unit at the tth time instant, Θ^{fmax} is the temperature up to which the crude is to be heated in the furnace, ns is the number of series segments, nsu_i is the number of units in the ith series segment with su_{ij} as its jth unit and $\mathrm{su}_i^{\mathrm{on}}$ as the required minimum number of operational units, npl is the number of parallel segments, nps_i is the number of branches in the ith parallel segment with npsu_{ij} as the number of units in its jth branch and psu_{ijk} as the kth unit while $\mathrm{psu}_{ij}^{\mathrm{on}}$ as the required minimum number of operational units in that branch, nhl is the number of heating lines with nhlu_i as the number of units in the ith heating line and hlu_{ij} as the jth unit and $\mathrm{hlu}_i^{\mathrm{on}}$ as the required minimum number of operational units in that heating line.

The cleaning time (β_{it}), operational status (u_{it}) and cleaning status (v_{it}) of the units, as used in Eqs. (1) and (2), are expressed by Eq. (3), where $v_{it} = 1$ means that the ith unit will be cleaned at the tth time instant.

$$u_{it} = \begin{cases} 1; & \text{if the } i\text{th unit is fully in operation} \\ 0; & \text{if the } i\text{th unit is shutdown partially} \\ & t = 1, 2, \cdots, T; \ i = 1, 2, \cdots, N. \end{cases} \tag{3a}$$

$$v_{it} = \begin{cases} 0; & \text{if } u_{it} = 1 \\ \{0, 1\}; & \text{otherwise} \\ & t = 1, 2, \cdots, T; \ i = 1, 2, \cdots, N. \end{cases} \tag{3b}$$

$$\beta_{it} = \begin{cases} 0; & \text{if } v_{it} = 0 \\ \in [0, \alpha_{it}]; & \text{otherwise} \\ & t = 1, 2, \cdots, T; \ i = 1, 2, \cdots, N. \end{cases} \tag{3c}$$

For obtaining the crude oil outlet temperatures from the last unit at different time instants, $\Theta_{Nt}^{\mathrm{f,out}}$ used in Eqs. (1) and (2d), the same for different units are computed using Eq. (4a), where $t = 1, 2, \cdots, T$ and $i = 1, 2, \cdots, N$.

$$\Theta_{it}^{f,out} = \begin{cases} \Theta_{it}^{f,in}; & \text{if } u_{it} = 0 \\ \phi_{it}^{h}\Theta_{i}^{hinit}(1-\alpha_{it}) + \{\alpha_{it} + (1-\alpha_{it})\phi_{it}^{c}\}\Theta_{it}^{f,in}; & \text{otherwise.} \end{cases}$$

$$(4a)$$

$$\text{where,} \quad \Theta_{it}^{f,in} = \begin{cases} \Theta^{f,inlet}; & \text{if } i = 1 \\ \Theta_{i-1,t}^{f,out}; & i \in \{2-14; i \neq 6, 12\} \\ \Theta_{5,t}^{f,out} - \Theta^{desalter}; & \text{if } i = 6 \\ \Theta_{8,t}^{f,out}; & \text{if } i = 12 \end{cases} \quad (4b)$$

$$\phi_{it}^{h} = \frac{(1-x)C_{min}}{(1-xR_i)c_i^f} \quad (4c)$$

$$\phi_{it}^{c} = \frac{(1-xR_i)c_i^f - (1-x)C_{min}}{(1-xR_i)c^f} \quad (4d)$$

$$C_{min} = \min\{F_i^f c_i^f, F_i^h c_i^h\} \quad (4e)$$

$$x = \exp\left\{-\frac{h_{it}A_i}{C_{min}}(1-R_i)\right\} \quad (4f)$$

$$R_i = \frac{C_{min}}{C_{max}} \quad (4g)$$

$$\alpha_{it} = \begin{cases} 0; & \text{if } u_{it} = 1 \\ \in (0,1); & \text{otherwise} \\ & t = 1, 2, \cdots, T; \ i = 1, 2, \cdots, N. \end{cases} \quad (4h)$$

In Eq. (4), $\Theta_{it}^{f,out}$ is the crude outlet temperature from ith unit at tth time instant, $\Theta_{it}^{f,in}$ is the crude oil inlet temperature of ith unit at tth time instant, Θ_{i}^{hinit} is the initial temperature of heating medium of ith unit, α_{it} is the partial shutdown time during operation, $\Theta^{f,inlet}$ is the crude oil temperature at the inlet of the CPT, $\Theta^{desalter}$ is the temperature drop in desalter, C_{min} is the minimum heat capacity rate, C_{max} is the maximum heat capacity rate, F_i^f is the flow rate of crude oil of ith unit, c_i^f is the specific heat capacity of crude oil of ith unit, F_i^h is the flow rate of heating medium of ith unit, c_i^h is the specific heat capacity of heating medium of ith unit, h_{it} is the heat transfer co-efficient of ith unit at tth time instant and A_i is the area of ith unit.

The heat transfer co-coefficients for cleaning/shutdown sub-period (h_{it}^{cl}) and processing sub-period (h_{it}^{pr}) can be obtained from the linear fouling rates ($\dot{R}_t^f$), which are expressed by Eq. (5).

$$\dot{R}_{it}^{f,pr} = \dot{R}_{it}^{f,cl} = \dot{R}_t^f \quad (5a)$$

$$h_{it}^{cl} = \frac{h_{i,t-1}^{pr}}{1 + \{h_{i,t-1}^{pr}\dot{R}_{i,t-1}^{f,pr}(1-\alpha_{it})\Delta t\}} \quad (5b)$$

$$h_{it}^{pr} = \frac{h_{it}^{cl}}{1 + (h_{it}^{cl}\dot{R}_{i,t-1}^{f,cl}\beta_{it}\Delta t)} + (v_{it}h_{it}^{clean}) \quad (5c)$$

In Eq. (5), $\dot{R}_{it}^{\mathrm{f,pr}}$ is the fouling resistance under processing sub-period, $\dot{R}_{it}^{\mathrm{f,cl}}$ is the fouling resistance under cleaning sub-period and Δt is the duration of each time interval.

4 Evolutionary Algorithms (EAs) for Solving the Problem

The optimization problem studied in the present work seeks the scheduling of the crude oil preheating process in a CPT of N heat exchangers over T time instants, so as to minimize the total cost arising from the requirement of external energy for additional heating of the crude oil and periodic cleaning of the heat exchangers. The scheduling of the heat exchangers needs $2NT$ number of $\{0, 1\}$ binary variables (u_{it} and v_{it}; $i = 1, \ldots, N$ and $t = 1, \ldots, T$), while the crude preheating process requires NT number of real variables (α_{it}; $i = 1, \ldots, N$ and $t = 1, \ldots, T$). For solving the problem, three mixed-binary EAs are investigated here, which are genetic algorithm (GA), differential evolution (DE) and particle swarm optimization (PSO). In all the three EAs, an individual (solution representation) for the problem at hand consists of two one-dimensional arrays, the first one of size $2NT$ takes the $\{0, 1\}$ binary variables and the second one of size NT takes the real variables.

The investigated binary-real coded GA (brGA) is the one applied by Datta [3] to a problem of similar nature, namely the unit commitment problem arising in the area of power systems, which involves the scheduling of given power generating units and optimization of discharge from the operational units in a way to meet the hourly power demand at a minimum production cost subject to a series of system related fixed and dynamic constraints. In the brGA, the standard binary tournament selection operator, single-point crossover operator and swapping mutation operators are used for handling the $\{0, 1\}$ valued binary variables; while the binary tournament selection operator, simulated binary crossover (SBX) operator [11] and polynomial mutation operator [11] are used for handling the real variables of a problem.

Datta and Figueira [12] proposed a real-integer-discrete coded differential evolution (ridDE) algorithm for working with any type of variables (real, binary, integer, or discrete) without any conversion, which was also applied successfully to the unit commitment problem by Datta and Dutta [2]. The ridDE replaces the real valued mutation operator of the 'DE/rand/1/bin' variant of DE [13] by a binary valued mutation operator, which generates only $\{0, 1\}$ valued binary mutant elements with a mutation probability based on some basic properties of DE and such binary numbers. The ridDE is investigated here as another EA for solving the problem at hand.

Similar to the ridDE [12], Datta and Figueira [14] proposed a real-integer-discrete coded particle swarm optimization (ridPSO) algorithm for working with any type of variables (real, binary, integer, or discrete) without any conversion, whose application was demonstrated on various engineering design problems. The ridPSO defines particle vectors by $\{0, 1\}$ valued binary elements with a mutation probability, based on some basic properties of PSO and such binary numbers. The ridPSO is investigated here as the third EA for solving the crude oil preheating problem.

Since all the three EAs are stochastic in nature, there is no guarantee that the new individuals formed in a generation (iteration) will be better than those of the current individuals from where they were generated. Hence, in order to prevent the search from moving opposite to the optimum in worst cases, the elite individuals at every generation are preserved using the mechanism proposed by Deb et al. [15]. In this case, instead of forming the population for the next generation directly with the newly generated individuals, they are first combined with the existing individuals of the current population. Then the best 50% of them, based on their objective values, are taken as the population for the next generation.

5   Numerical Experimentation

The EAs stated in Sect. 4 are coded in the C programming language by incorporating the optimization problem formulated in Eqs. (1) and (2). Then the performances of the EAs are evaluated with the help of a case study.

5.1   Case Study

The investigated case study of crude oil preheating is taken from Smaïli et al. [10]. As shown in Fig. 1, the CPT in the case study consists of 14 number of shell and tube heat exchangers ($N = 14$) of the type of counter-current flow. The heat exchanger network (HEN) starts with two series segments (ns = 2); the first one contains units (heat exchangers) 1–5, followed by a desalter, and then the second series segment containing units 6–8. Fixing a flash after the second series segment, the remaining six units are then arranged in a parallel segment (npl = 1) having two branches; the first one contains units 9–11 and the second one contains units 12–14. At the end of the HEN, a furnace is placed for further heating of the crude oil, if required.

There are seven heating lines (nhl = 7) in the HEN, which are marked in Fig. 1 as H1–H7. The units (heat exchangers) covered by the heating lines are as follows—H1: (1, 9, 12), H2: (8, 10, 13), H3: (6, 11, 14), H4: (3, 7), H5: (2), H6: (4) and H7: (5).

The case study is subjected to some operational constraints in the form of minimum number of units to be made always fully operational. Each of the two series segments and the two branches of the parallel segment requires minimum of two of its units to be made fully operational. Some heating lines also have similar requirement, which are as follows—H1: 2, H2: 2, H3: 2 and H4: 1.

For solving the problem, a repeating production cycle of 3 years is considered, which is divided into 36 time instants ($T = 36$), i.e., each time instant is of a duration of one month. Except the cost coefficients, the problem related other input parameters are taken from Smaïli et al. [10] and given in Table 1 in terms of

Table 1. Design and fouling data for the case study (source: Smaïli et al. [10])

Unit	Θ_i^{hinit} (°C)	F_i^h (kg/s)	F_i^f (kg/s)	c_i^h (kJ/kgK)	c_i^f (kJ/kgK)	h_{it}^{clean} (W/m²K)	A_i (m²)	$\dot{R}_i^f \times 10^{-7}$ (m²K/J)
HE-1	194	19.1	95	2.8	1.92	0.5	56.6	0.6
HE-2	296	3.3	95	2.9	1.92	0.5	8.9	0.9
HE-3	197	55.8	95	2.6	1.92	0.5	208.3	0.6
HE-4	170	49.7	95	2.6	1.92	0.5	112.9	0.8
HE-5	237	49.7	95	2.6	1.92	0.5	121.6	0.8
HE-6	285	34.8	95	2.8	2.3	0.5	110.1	1.5
HE-7	205	55.8	95	2.6	2.3	0.5	67.2	1.1
HE-8	254	45.5	95	2.9	2.3	0.5	67.1	1.5
HE-9	249	9.5	46	2.8	2.4	0.5	91.0	1.6
HE-10	286	22.8	46	2.9	2.4	0.5	61.3	1.8
HE-11	334	17.4	46	2.8	2.4	0.5	55.6	1.9
HE-12	249	9.5	46	2.8	2.4	0.5	91.0	1.6
HE-13	286	22.8	46	2.9	2.4	0.5	61.3	1.8
HE-14	334	17.4	46	2.8	2.4	0.5	55.6	1.9

the notations used in the problem formulation in Eqs. (1)–(5). The cleaning cost coefficient (C^{cl}) and energy cost coefficient (C^{ener}) are taken from Tian et al. [16], which are 20000 $ per cleaning instant and 15.5 $ per MWh, respectively. Further, the initial temperature of the crude oil at any time instant is considered to be 26 °C ($\Theta_t^{\text{finit}} = 26$ °C), requiring it to be preheated up to 250 °C ($\Theta^{\text{fmax}} = 250$ °C) with a drop of 10 °C in the desalter ($\Theta^{\text{desalter}} = 10$ °C).

5.2 Experimental Setup

The considered EA related parameter values are given in Table 2, where a non-applicable value is marked by (−). Since the performance of a stochastic optimizer is likely to be influenced by the user-defined algorithmic parameter setting, instead of fixed values, some parameter values in Table 2 are made self-adaptive within given ranges with an attempt to reduce their influences on the performance of an EA. In this process, every time a random value for such a parameter is generated within its given range. Further, in order to analyze the statistical performance, 30 number of independent runs of each EA are performed with different sets of initial individuals (solutions).

5.3 Results and Discussion

With the above problem and algorithm related input information, each of the EAs are executed for 30 independent runs. For the purpose of illustration, the best schedule obtained by the brGA is given in Table 3, where '1' in the schedule means that the particular unit (heat exchanger) is in fully operation at the

Table 2. User-defined parameter values for the investigated EAs.

Parameter	brGA	ridDE	ridPSO
Population size	100	100	100
Maximum number of generations performed	7000	7000	7000
Crossover probability	90%	(0, 90%]	–
Distribution index for SBX operator	20	–	–
Mutation probability	(0, 1%]	–	–
Distribution index for polynomial mutation operator	35	–	–
Mutation probability (for binary variables only)	–	(0, 15%]	(0, 15%]
Scaling factor (for real variables only)	–	(0, 70%]	–
Inertia constant (for real variables only)	–	–	(0, 0.75]
Cognitive factor (for real variables only)	–	–	(0, 1.5]
Social factor (for real variables only)	–	–	(0, 2]
Number of runs	30	30	30

Table 3. The best schedule of the case study obtained by the brGA.

Time instant	Schedule	Number of operating units	Time instant	Schedule	Number of operating units
1	01111101111111	12	19	11111110111111	13
2	11111111111110	13	20	11111111111011	13
3	11111111111101	13	21	11110111011111	12
4	11101111011111	12	22	11111110110111	12
5	01111111110111	12	23	11111101111111	13
6	11111111111111	14	24	11111111111111	14
7	11011111101111	12	25	11111011011111	12
8	11111111101111	13	26	11111111111111	14
9	11110111011111	12	27	11111111011111	13
10	11111111101111	13	28	11111111111111	14
11	11111110011111	12	29	11111111111110	13
12	11111011101111	12	30	11110111111111	13
13	11011111101111	12	31	11111111101011	12
14	11101111111011	12	32	11101111111111	13
15	11111110111111	13	33	11111111110111	13
16	11111111101111	13	34	11111111111111	14
17	11111111111101	13	35	11111111111111	14
18	11110111101111	12	36	10111111101111	12

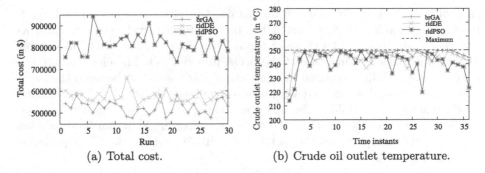

(a) Total cost.   (b) Crude oil outlet temperature.

Fig. 2. Total cost over 30 runs and crude outlet temperatures over different time instants of a random run.

corresponding time instant, while '0' means it was partially shutdown during which period the unit may go through cleaning also. The schedule shows that no two units are cleaned at two consecutive time instants and each unit is cleaned at least once in the entire production cycle.

Table 4. Statistical analysis of the overall cost over 30 independent runs of the EAs.

EA	Overall cost (in $)			
	Best	Worst	Mean	Standard deviation
brGA	477150	582772	526507	31555
ridDE	534629	662064	576553	26633
ridPSO	733464	912245	815510	46860

Table 5. The t-test values for the solutions of the EAs at a significance level of 5%.

EA	brGA-vs-ridDE	brGA-vs-ridPSO	ridDE-vs-ridPSO
t-value	−6.64	−28.02	−24.28

The overall costs, i.e., the values of the objective function expressed by Eq. (1), obtained from 30 runs of each of the EAs are visualized in Fig. 2(a), where it is observed that the lowest cost could be obtained by the brGA among the three EAs. Further, the obtained crude oil outlet temperatures from the heat exchanger network at different time instants of a random run are shown in Fig. 2(b), where the outlet temperatures obtained from the brGA are found to be almost close to the required maximum furnace temperature, while those obtained from the ridPSO are found to be the worst ones.

For further detail of the performances of the EAs, a statistical analysis of the overall costs (best, worst, mean, and standard deviation) over 30 independent runs of the EAs is performed and the obtained results are presented in Table 4. It is seen in Table 4 that the brGA has better objective values (best, worst as well as mean), followed by those of the ridDE. However, the ridDE has better standard deviation than those of the brGA and ridPSO. Therefore, finally the EAs are statistically compared by conducting pair-wise t-test between the mean objective value and standard deviation at a significance level of 5%. The obtained t values are given in Table 5, by marking a value with a '-ve' sign if the second EA in a pair is not better than the first one. Accordingly, it can be concluded that the brGA outperforms the ridDE and ridPSO, and the ridDE outperforms the ridPSO.

6   Conclusion

A typical crude oil preheating process arising in refineries is formulated as a constrained mixed-integer nonlinear programming (MINLP) problem for minimizing total of the cost of additional energy requirement and the cost for cleaning the heat exchangers of the process. It involves two separate optimization sub-problems, the integer valued scheduling of the heat exchangers and the real valued heating levels in the operational heat exchangers. Such problems are usually handled by two separate algorithms, one for the integer part and another for the real part. The potentiality of thee mixed-binary evolutionary algorithms (EAs), namely genetic algorithm (GA), differential evolution (DE) and particle swarm optimization (PSO), are investigated here for handling both the parts of the problem by a single EA. From statistical analysis of the results for a benchmark problem, the GA is found outperforming both the DE and PSO, followed by the DE outperforming the PSO.

References

1. Chandrasekaran, K., Simon, S.: Multi-objective unit commitment problem using Cuckoo search Lagrangian method. Int. J. Eng. Sci. Technol. **4**, 89–105 (2012)
2. Datta, D., Dutta, S.: A binary-real-coded differential evolution for unit commitment problem. Electr. Power Energy Syst. **42**, 517–524 (2012)
3. Datta, D.: Unit commitment problem with ramp rate constraint using a binary-real-coded genetic algorithm. Appl. Soft Comput. **13**, 3873–3883 (2013)
4. Deka, D., Datta, D.: Multi-objective optimization of the scheduling of a heat exchanger network under milk fouling. Knowl.-Based Syst. **121**, 71–82 (2017)
5. Trivedi, A., Srinivasan, D., Biswas, S., Reindl, T.: A genetic algorithm differential evolution based hybrid framework: case study on unit commitment scheduling problem. Inf. Sci. **354**, 275–300 (2016)
6. Juang, C.F.: A hybrid of genetic algorithm and particle swarm optimization for recurrent network design. IEEE Trans. Syst. Man Cybern.-Part B: Cybern. **34**(2), 997–1006 (2004)
7. Kuo, R.J., Syu, Y.J., Chen, Z.Y., Tien, F.C.: Integration of particle swarm optimization and genetic algorithm for dynamic clustering. Inf. Sci. **195**, 124–140 (2012)

8. Ozturk, C., Hancer, E., Karaboga, D.: A novel binary artificial bee colony algorithm based on genetic operators. Inf. Sci. **297**, 154–170 (2015)
9. Epitropakis, M.G., Plagianakos, V.P., Vrahatis, M.N.: Evolving cognitive and social experience in particle swarm optimization through differential evolution: a hybrid approach. Inf. Sci. **216**, 50–92 (2012)
10. Smaïli, F., Vassiliadis, V.S., Wilson, D.I.: Mitigation of fouling in refinery heat exchanger networks by optimal management of cleaning. Energy Fuels **15**, 1038–1056 (2001)
11. Deb, K.: Multi-Objective Optimization Using Evolutionary Algorithms. Wiley, Chichester (2001)
12. Datta, D., Figueira, J.R.: A real-integer-discrete-coded differential evolution. Appl. Soft Comput. **13**(9), 3884–3893 (2013)
13. Storn, R., Price, K.: Differential evolution - a simple and efficient heuristic for global optimization over continuous spaces. J. Glob. Optim. **11**, 341–354 (1997)
14. Datta, D., Figueira, J.R.: A real-integer-discrete-coded particle swarm optimization for design problems. Appl. Soft Comput. **11**(4), 3625–3633 (2011)
15. Deb, K., Agarwal, S., Pratap, A., Meyarivan, T.: A fast and elitist multi-objective genetic algorithm: NSGA-II. IEEE Trans. Evol. Comput. **6**(2), 182–197 (2002)
16. Tian, J., Wang, Y., Feng, X.: Simultaneous optimization of flow velocity and cleaning schedule for mitigating fouling in refinery heat exchanger networks. Energy **109**, 1118–1129 (2016)

Hybrid Weighted Barebones Exploiting Particle Swarm Optimization Algorithm for Time Series Representation

Antonio Manuel Durán-Rosal[(✉)], David Guijo-Rubio,
Pedro Antonio Gutiérrez, and César Hervás-Martínez

Department of Computer Science and Numerical Analysis,
University of Córdoba, Córdoba, Spain
i92duroa@uco.es

Abstract. The amount of data available in time series is recently increasing in an exponential way, making difficult time series preprocessing and analysis. This paper adapts different methods for time series representation, which are based on time series segmentation. Specifically, we consider a particle swarm optimization algorithm (PSO) and its barebones exploitation version (BBePSO). Moreover, a new variant of the BBePSO algorithm is proposed, which takes into account the positions of the particles throughout the generations, where those close in time are given more importance. This methodology is referred to as weighted BBePSO (WBBePSO). The solutions obtained by all the algorithms are finally hybridised with a local search algorithm, combining simple segmentation strategies (Top-Down and Bottom-Up). WBBePSO is tested in 13 time series and compared against the rest of algorithms, showing that it leads to the best results and obtains consistent representations.

Keywords: Time series representation · Segmentation
Barebones particle swarm optimization · Hybrid algorithms

1 Introduction

Nowadays, the exponential increase of time series and their big amount of data hamper their processing [1]. Time series data mining (TSDM) includes several tasks such as the reconstruction of missing values [2], clustering [3], classification [4], forecasting [5] or segmentation [6]. Different areas of application can significantly benefit from efficient TSDM algorithms, including climate [7] or finances [8], among others.

Time series segmentation consists in dividing the time series into consecutive parts or points, trying to satisfy different objectives. There are two points of view that time series segmentation is focused on. On the one hand, segmenting time series is used for discovering patterns in them. On the other hand, there is

P. Korošec et al. (Eds.): BIOMA 2018, LNCS 10835, pp. 126–137, 2018.
https://doi.org/10.1007/978-3-319-91641-5_11

another objective when segmenting time series, which tries to reduce the number of points of the time series (i.e. its dimensionality). With respect to this second objective, one of the main problems is the difficulty of processing and mining large time series, their dimensionality making them very difficult to analyse. Due to this fact, several algorithms have been proposed trying to simplify time series, which are also known as time series representation procedures. Keogh et al. [9] proposed different algorithms using piecewise linear approximations (PLA), which try to discover a set of points whose interpolations are the representation of the segments. Two PLA well-known algorithms are Top-Down and Bottom-Up, which iteratively reduce the error of the approximation. Other time series representation algorithms are the piecewise aggregate approximation (PAA) or the adaptative piecewise constant approximation (APCA) [10].

In this work, the contribution is focused on PLA segmentation algorithms, trying to find the set of points whose interpolations minimize the error of the resulting approximation. To do so, we propose a new variant of the barebones exploiting particle swarm optimization algorithm (BBePSO) [11], using the weighted average values of the visited positions of the particles and the best one from all the generations, instead of considering only the current ones. PSO is another evolutionary algorithm which simulates the behaviour of a set of particles when looking for food, and it has been applied to a lot of problems, such as routing vehicle [12], video tracking [13], etc. BBePSO has been proposed to improve the convergence of the standard BBPSO (which used a normal distribution to decide the movement of the particles), adding an exploiter component. In BBePSO, the algorithm converges using the current positions. In this paper, we show that the consideration of the past values in the evolution is important for the performance of the algorithm, and we propose a method in this direction, WBBePSO. This method takes the previous and the current positions into account, dynamically adapting the current positions by a weighted mean of the past values (giving more importance to those positions closer in time). This methodology modifies the mean and the standard deviation of the normal distribution considered in the standard BBePSO.

Evolutionary algorithms are able to find high-quality areas using populations of individuals. For this reason, they are robust heuristics which can solve different problems. However, their main drawback is their poor ability when finding the precise optimum in the areas they converge. The application of local searches in different parts of the evolutionary process is a way to prevent this problem. In this work, we combine the best solutions obtained by all the evolutionary methods (PSO, BBePSO and the proposed WBBePSO) with a local search combining Bottom-Up and Top-Down algorithms. In this sense, the resulting hybrid methods are referred to as HPSO, HBBePSO, and HWBBePSO, respectively.

This paper is organised in the following sections: Sect. 2 describes the problem of time series segmentation, Sect. 3 presents all the algorithms adapted to time series segmentation, Sect. 4 describes the datasets, the performed experiments and the discussion of the results (including a statistical validation) and Sect. 5 concludes the paper.

2   Time Series Segmentation Problem Definition

The main objective of this paper is to reduce the number of points of a given time series $Y = \{y_i\}_{i=1}^{N}$ in a set of L segments by cutting the values of the time series using $L - 1$ cut points ($t_1 < t_2 < \cdots < t_{L-1}$). The error approximation resulting from the linear interpolation between the cut points needs to be minimised with the aim of avoiding information loss. That is, the cut points $\mathbf{t}$ (arranged from the smallest to the largest) are extracted from all time indexes, obtaining the set of segments $\mathcal{S} = \{s_1, s_2, \ldots, s_L\}$, where $s_1 = \{y_1, \ldots, y_{t_1}\}$, $s_2 = \{y_{t_1}, \ldots, y_{t_2}\}, \ldots, s_L = \{y_{t_{L-1}}, \ldots, y_N\}$. As stated before, a linear interpolation each pair of consecutive cut points is considered. Note that the cut points belongs to two segments (the previous and the next one). The number of segments of the approximation is a value predefined by the user. In order to solve this problem, we apply swarm intelligence algorithms.

3   Algorithms and Their Adaptations

This section presents the details of PSO, BBePSO and WBBePSO, together with their specific adaptation for time series segmentation.

3.1   Particle Swarm Optimisation Algorithm (PSO) and Its Barebones Exploiting Version (BBePSO)

The particle swarm optimisation (PSO) [14] is another evolutionary-type algorithm which simulates the behaviour of a set of particles in a swarm when they are looking for food (i.e. birds or fish). The population of individuals corresponds with a set of K particles moving in a dimensional space of length D. Each particle k is represented by a position array of real values ($\mathbf{x}_k$), which represents a solution of the problem, and the velocity of the particle $\mathbf{v}_k$, which represents the strength and the direction of the movement of the particle. The quality of a particle is calculated by a fitness function (f). PSO also stores the best position found by the particle ($\mathbf{p}_k$) and the best position found by the entire swarm ($\mathbf{g}$). The evolution is based on a good compromise between local and global best positions, also known as cognitive and social components, respectively. In each iteration t, the PSO algorithm performs the following updates:

- Velocity update: the velocity $\mathbf{v}_k$ is updated in iteration t ($\mathbf{v}_k^t$) following the next expression.

$$\mathbf{v}_k^t = w \cdot \mathbf{v}_k^{t-1} + \rho_1^t \cdot C_1 \cdot \left(\mathbf{p}_k^{t-1} - \mathbf{x}_k^{t-1}\right) + \rho_2^t \cdot C_2 \cdot \left(\mathbf{g}^{t-1} - \mathbf{x}_k^{t-1}\right), \quad (1)$$

  where w is the inertia weight (a parameter used for velocity reduction, i.e., particles roaming), ρ_1^t, ρ_2^t are uniform random values obtained at iteration t, ρ_1, $\rho_2 \sim U(0,1)$, and C_1, C_2 are the acceleration constants.
- Position update: the position of a particle at iteration t ($\mathbf{x}_k^t$) is then updated using the expression:

$$\mathbf{x}_k^t = \mathbf{x}_k^{t-1} + \mathbf{v}_k^t. \quad (2)$$

– Best local and global position update: finally, the best local position at iteration t is:

$$\mathbf{p}_k^t = \begin{cases} \mathbf{p}_k^{t-1} & \text{if } f(\mathbf{x}_k^t) \geq f(\mathbf{p}_k^{t-1}), \\ \mathbf{x}_k^t & \text{if } f(\mathbf{x}_k^t) < f(\mathbf{p}_k^{t-1}), \end{cases} \tag{3}$$

for $k = 1, \ldots, K$, and the global best position is updated as:

$$\mathbf{g}^t = \arg\min_{\mathbf{x} \in \{\mathbf{g}, \mathbf{p}_1^t, \ldots \mathbf{p}_K^t\}} \{f(\mathbf{x})\}. \tag{4}$$

Note that we consider minimisation problems (the lower value of $f(\mathbf{x}_k)$, the higher quality of $\mathbf{x}_k$), which is the case of the problem to solve (minimisation of approximation error).

An improved version of PSO is the exploiting barebones PSO (BBePSO) [11]. This algorithm updates the position of the particles in the swarm without considering velocities. BBePSO replaces Eqs. 1 and 2 by:

$$x_{k,j}^t = \begin{cases} N\left(\frac{p_{k,j}^{t-1} + g_j^{t-1}}{2}, |p_{k,j}^{t-1} - g_j^{t-1}|\right) & \text{if } U(0,1) < 0.5, \\ p_{k,j}^{t-1} & \text{otherwise,} \end{cases} \tag{5}$$

where $N(\mu, \sigma)$ is a normal distribution with mean (μ) equal to the average value of the best global and local positions, and the standard deviation (σ) equal to the difference, in absolute terms, of their values. This expression represents a 0.5 probability that the j-th dimension of the particle k takes a random value from the previous normal distribution (exploration) or from the best personal position (exploitation). BBePSO outperforms other variants of PSO [11], and it is also better when the values of the velocities or the acceleration constants are difficult to estimate.

PSO and BBePSO for Time Series Segmentation: The particle representation corresponds to a real array ($\mathbf{x_i}$). The closest integer of each value represents a cut point, for instance, if $\mathbf{x_i} = \{2.56, 6.08, 9.10, 11.75\}$, its corresponding set of cut points in the time series is $\mathbf{t} = \{3, 6, 9, 12\}$. In this way, the length of the chromosome will be the same that the number of cut points $L - 1$. The initial population of PSO and BBePSO is formed by K particles with integer values without repetition (the values need to be unique). The standard procedures are used for updating velocities (in PSO), the particle positions and the best personal and global positions. However, after position update, the new particle has to satisfy two constraints:

– The values of the positions must be sorted, that is, $(x_{k,1} < x_{k,2} < x_{k,L-1})$. For this reason, if $x_{k,j} > x_{k,j+1}$, or $x_{k,j} < x_{k,j-1}$, the cut points of the chromosome are sorted in ascending order.
– Furthermore, the cut points need to be higher than 1 and lower than N. If this constraint is not satisfied, the algorithm rescales the values of the particle with:
$$\mathbf{x}_i^{t'} = \frac{\mathbf{x}_i^t - \min\{\mathbf{x}_i^t\}}{\max\{\mathbf{x}_i^t\} - \min\{\mathbf{x}_i^t\}}(\max\{\mathbf{x}_i^{t-1}\} - \min\{\mathbf{x}_i^{t-1}\}) + \min\{\mathbf{x}_i^{t-1}\}.$$

Finally, the algorithm is run until a number of evaluations is reached.

3.2   Weighted BBePSO (WBBePSO)

Our proposal is a new dynamic version of BBePSO. BBePSO updates the values of the positions taking into account the best personal and global positions. In this sense, the previous values are forgotten during the evolution when a particle is updated. In PSO, the velocities and the inertia weight w can be considered as a memory of the previous values, but this algorithm is poorer than BBePSO in finding solutions, given that it lacks an exploiter component. Keeping in mind the necessity of this memory and that more recent positions should be given more importance, we define a new Weighted BBePSO (WBBePSO), where the position update is made as follows:

$$x_{k,j}^t = \begin{cases} N\left(\frac{\bar{p}_{k,j}^{t-1} + \bar{p}_{g,j}^{t-1}}{2}, |\bar{p}_{k,j}^{t-1} - \bar{g}_j^{t-1}|\right) & \text{if } U(0,1) < 0.5, \\ p_{k,j}^{t-1} & \text{otherwise,} \end{cases} \tag{6}$$

where the best local position is updated as:

$$\bar{p}_{k,j}^t = \frac{\sum_{m=1}^t m p_{k,j}^m}{\sum_{m=1}^t m}, \tag{7}$$

and the best global one as:

$$\bar{g}_j^t = \frac{\sum_{m=1}^t m g_j^m}{\sum_{m=1}^t m}. \tag{8}$$

It is important to mention that the higher the value of m, the more importance is given to the solution, so that more recent particles have more influence in the update process.

WBBePSO for Time Series Segmentation: The adaptation of the algorithm to time series segmentation follows the same considerations than for PSO and BBePSO (a real encoding, rounding the values to time indices, and a procedure for ensuring the fulfilling of the constraints).

3.3   Common Elements for All the Algorithms

This section presents the elements which are common for PSO, BBePSO and the proposed WBBePSO, i.e. the fitness function and the local search procedure.

Fitness Function. As we mentioned before, the main objective is to reduce the number of points of the time series with the minimum information loss. For that, we minimise the approximation error, which is the difference between a real point of the time series and its corresponding approximation. The error of the i-th point in the k individual is:

$$e_i(\mathbf{x}_k) = (y_i - \hat{y}_i(\mathbf{x}_k)), \tag{9}$$

where y_i is the real value of the time series, and $\hat{y}_i$ is the approximation resulting of the interpolation coded in individual $\mathbf{x}_k$. The fitness function is defined as the root mean square error:

$$\text{RMSE}(\mathbf{x}_k) = f(\mathbf{x}_k) = \sqrt{\frac{1}{N} \sum_{i=1}^{N} e_i^2(\mathbf{x}_k)}. \tag{10}$$

Local Search. The best solution obtained by all evolutionary algorithms in the last generation (PSO, BBePSO, or WBBePSO) is hybridised with a local search [2] based on the combination of Bottom-Up and Top-Down segmentation procedures [9], resulting in hybrid algorithms (HPSO, HBBePSO, HWBBePSO). On the one hand, Bottom-Up is an iterative algorithm which starts considering each point of the time series as a cut point. In each iteration, it removes the cut point (merging two consecutive segments) that results in the minimum increase of approximation error. On the other hand, Top-Down is the opposite algorithm, starting by considering only one segment. Then, in each iteration, the algorithm recursively adds the cut point (splitting a segment) which results in the maximum decrease of error. The local search is based on removing a percentage of cut points with the Bottom-Up algorithm and adding the same percentage of points with Top-Down. For that, the stopping criteria of these algorithms is the number of segments to be merged or cut.

4   Experimentation

The time series used, the experiments performed and the discussion of the results are shown in this section.

4.1   Time Series

For the experiments, we use 13 time series collected from different fields. Table 1 summarises the following information of each time series: name, type, length, and source. Also, the time series are represented in Fig. 1.

4.2   Experimental Setting

We evaluate the performance of HWBBePSO against the rest of hybrid methods described in Sect. 3, and we analyse the existence of significant differences using statistical tests. For all the algorithms, we consider the same parameter configuration than in [18] (which has been proved to be effective for many different optimisation problems): the population size is $K = 200$, the maximum number of evaluations is 20,000, the inertia (w) is established to 0.72 and the acceleration constants (C_1, C_2) to 0.49. Finally, the percentages of reduction and hybridization are 2.5% and 40%, respectively. The percentage of reduction corresponds to the number of points of the approximation with respect to the original size, while the percentage of hybridisation represents the number of cut points which are removed and added in the local search. All the algorithms are run 30 times with different seeds, due to their stochastic nature.

Table 1. Time series used

Name	Type	Length	Source
Arrhytmia	Cardiology data	9000	PhysioBank ATM [15]
B41043	Wave height TS	7303	NDBC [16] (Puerto Rico)
B41044	Wave height TS	7303	NDBC [16] (Puerto Rico)
B46001	Wave height TS	8767	NDBC [16] (Alaska)
B46075	Wave height TS	7303	NDBC [16] (Alaska)
BBVA	Bank market rates	4174	(Spain)
DEUTSCHE	Bank market rates	4174	(Germany)
HandOutlines	Benchmark TS	8127	UCR repository [17]
IBEX	Stock prices TS	5730	https://es.finance.yahoo.com/
Mallat	Benchmark TS	8192	UCR repository [17]
SANPAOLO	Bank market rates	4174	(Italy)
Société Generalé	Bank market rates	4174	(France)
StarLight	Benchmark TS	8192	UCR repository [17]

Table 2. RMSE results and mean ranks ($\bar{R}_{RMSE}$) for all the algorithms

Algorithm	HPSO (Mean ± SD)	HBBePSO (Mean ± SD)	HWBBePSO (Mean ± SD)
Arrhytmia	*0.052 ± 0.002*	0.052 ± 0.002	**0.051 ± 0.001**
B41043	0.395 ± 0.006	*0.394 ± 0.006*	**0.389 ± 0.003**
B41044	0.392 ± 0.009	*0.391 ± 0.007*	**0.382 ± 0.004**
B46001	0.984 ± 0.008	*0.980 ± 0.007*	**0.975 ± 0.006**
B46075	1.046 ± 0.011	*1.040 ± 0.012*	**1.034 ± 0.009**
BBVA	*0.319 ± 0.008*	0.323 ± 0.009	**0.317 ± 0.008**
DEUTSCHE	1.926 ± 0.055	*1.915 ± 0.062*	**1.905 ± 0.076**
HandOutlines	**0.006 ± 0.000**	**0.006 ± 0.000**	**0.006 ± 0.000**
IBEX	*205.688 ± 3.894*	206.132 ± 3.954	**203.128 ± 4.085**
Mallat	*0.162 ± 0.007*	0.167 ± 0.007	**0.157 ± 0.009**
SANPAOLO	0.111 ± 0.003	*0.110 ± 0.002*	**0.109 ± 0.001**
SOGeneralé	2.154 ± 0.052	**2.127 ± 0.042**	*2.136 ± 0.031*
StarLightCurves	*0.024 ± 0.001*	*0.024 ± 0.001*	**0.023 ± 0.001**
$\bar{R}_{RMSE}$	2.62	2.23	1.15

The best method is shown in bold face and the second one in italics

4.3   Discussion

The approximation errors in RMSE are shown in Table 2, together with associated average ranks ($R = 1$ for the best method in each dataset and $R = 3$ for the worse one). For all the algorithms, the mean and the standard deviation (SD) of the 30 runs are presented (Mean ± SD). As can be seen, HWBBePSO outperforms the rest of algorithms with the best results in all datasets except in the case of Société Générale, where it is the second best. The second best method seems to be HBBePSO with better results than HPSO in several datasets (B41043 or DEUTSCHE among others). However, this algorithm (HPSO) obtains lower errors in other datasets, such as BBVA or Mallat.

Analysing the standard deviation of the results, HWBBePSO presents the lowest values in almost databases (8 out of 13 datasets, and the second one in other two) showing its effectiveness and that the evolution does not depend on the initialisation. From this analysis, it can be observed that the algorithm HWBBePSO balances the use of previously visited positions, giving more importance to the most recent ones. In this way, it is able to converge to high-quality areas, avoiding a premature convergence, and, moreover, when combined with the local search, the resulting hybrid algorithm finds an optimum solution in these areas.

To determine the statistical significance of the rank differences observed for each swarm intelligence algorithm in the different time series, we have carried out a non-parametric Friedman test [19] with the ranking of RMSE of the best models as the test variable (since a previous evaluation of the RMSE values resulted in rejecting the hypothesis of normality and equality of variances). The test shows that the effect of the algorithm used for dimensionality reduction is statistically significant at a significance level of 5%, as the confidence interval is $C_0 = (0, F_{0.05} = 3.40)$ and the F-distribution statistical value is $F^* = 16.16 \notin C_0$. Consequently, we reject the null-hypothesis stating that all the algorithms perform equally in mean ranking for RMSE.

Based on this rejection, the Holm post-hoc test is used to compare the three algorithms to each other. Holm test is a multiple comparison procedure that considers a control algorithm (CA), in this case HWBBePSO, and compares it with the remaining methods [20]. The test statistics for comparing the mean rank of the i-th and j-th algorithm using this procedure is:

$$z = \frac{\bar{R}_i - \bar{R}_j}{\sqrt{\frac{k(k+1)}{6N}}},$$ (11)

where k is the number of algorithms and N the number of datasets. The z value is used to find the corresponding probability from the table of normal distribution, which is then compared with an appropriate level of confidence α. Holm's test adjusts the value for α in order to compensate for multiple comparison.

The results of the Holm test for $\alpha = 0.05$ can be seen in Table 3, using the corresponding p and α^*_{Holm} values. From the results of this test, it can be

Table 3. Holm tests comparing HWBBePSO (CA) with the rest of methods: p-values and α^*_{Holm} with initial $\alpha = 0.05$

CA: HWBBePSO	HPSO	HBBePSO
p-value	$1.90 \times 10^{-4} (*)$	$6.04 \times 10^{-3} (*)$
α^*_{Holm}	0.025	0.050

(*): statistically significant differences were found for $\alpha = 0.05$

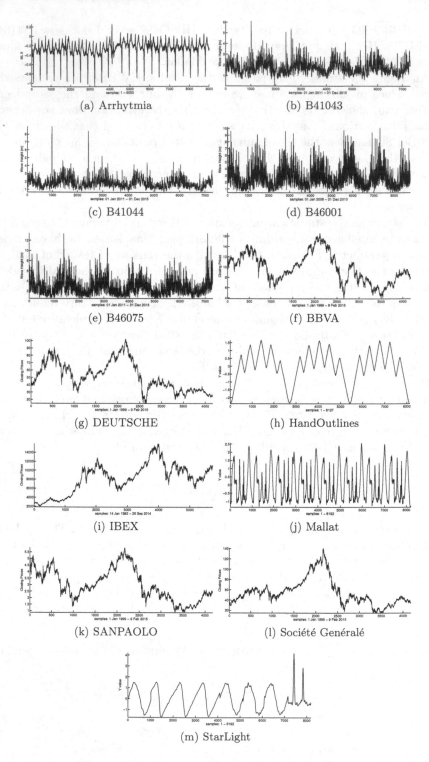

Fig. 1. Time series considered for the experiments.

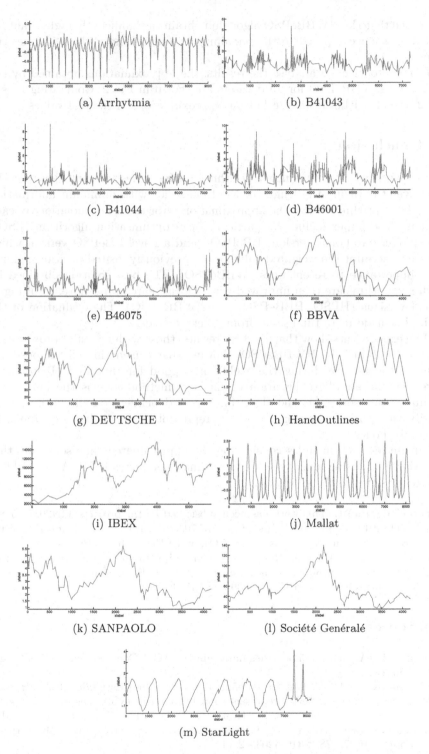

(a) Arrhytmia

(b) B41043

(c) B41044

(d) B46001

(e) B46075

(f) BBVA

(g) DEUTSCHE

(h) HandOutlines

(i) IBEX

(j) Mallat

(k) SANPAOLO

(l) Société Generalé

(m) StarLight

Fig. 2. Approximation time series of HWBBePSO.

concluded that the HWBBePSO algorithm obtains a significantly higher ranking of RMSE when compared to the remaining two algorithms, which justifies the proposal.

Finally, to visually analyse the results, the approximations obtained by the algorithms HWBBePSO for all datasets are shown in Fig. 2. Comparing Figs. 1 and 2, the algorithm results in faithful approximations of the real values.

5   Conclusions

In this paper, we propose a new algorithm for time series segmentation with the objective of reducing the length of the time series with minimum information loss. The algorithm reduces the approximation error using interpolations of each segment. The paper includes a particle swarm optimisation algorithm (PSO), its exploiter barebones version (BBePSO), and a novel BBePSO version which takes into account the weighted value of the previously visited positions, giving more importance to recent ones (WBBePSO). The best solution obtained by all the algorithms are then improved with a local search procedure, resulting in hybrid versions (HPSO, HBBePSO, and HWBBePSO). The evaluation of the method is made in 13 time series from different fields.

The experiments show that the best results, those with lowest approximation error, are obtained by HWBBePSO, showing that considering all the positions visited by a particle during the evolution is good for this kind of problems. Moreover, the standard deviation of the new methodology is the lowest one in almost time series, i.e. the algorithm is less dependent on the initialisation. Finally, the approximated time series are represented, they being very similar to the original ones.

Future research includes considering the approximated time series in other posterior tasks, using other types of approximations (instead of PLA) and adding more time series to the validation.

Acknowledgement. This work has been subsidized by the projects TIN2017-85887-C2-1-P, TIN2014-54583-C2-1-R and TIN2015-70308-REDT of the Spanish Ministry of Economy and Competitiveness (MINECO), and FEDER funds (FEDER EU). The research of Antonio M. Durán-Rosal and David Guijo-Rubio have been subsidized by the FPU Predoctoral Program of the Spanish Ministry of Education, Culture and Sport (MECD), grant references FPU14/03039 and FPU16/02128.

References

1. Esling, P., Agon, C.: Time-series data mining. ACM Comput. Surv. (CSUR) **45**, 12 (2012)
2. Durán-Rosal, A.M., Gutiérrez-Peña, P.A., Martínez-Estudillo, F.J., Hervás-Martínez, C.: Time Series representation by a novel hybrid segmentation algorithm. In: Martínez-Álvarez, F., Troncoso, A., Quintián, H., Corchado, E. (eds.) HAIS 2016. LNCS (LNAI), vol. 9648, pp. 163–173. Springer, Cham (2016). https://doi.org/10.1007/978-3-319-32034-2_14

3. Ferreira, L.N., Zhao, L.: Time series clustering via community detection in networks. Inf. Sci. **326**, 227–242 (2016)
4. Zhao, J., Itti, L.: Classifying time series using local descriptors with hybrid sampling. IEEE Trans. Knowl. Data Eng. **28**, 623–637 (2016)
5. Chen, M.Y., Chen, B.T.: A hybrid fuzzy time series model based on granular computing for stock price forecasting. Inf. Sci. **294**, 227–241 (2015)
6. Pérez-Ortiz, M., Durán-Rosal, A., Gutiérrez, P., Sánchez-Monedero, J., Nikolaou, A., Fernández-Navarro, F., Hervás-Martínez, C.: On the use of evolutionary time series analysis for segmenting paleoclimate data. Neurocomputing (2017)
7. Nikolaou, A., Gutiérrez, P.A., Durán, A., Dicaire, I., Fernández-Navarro, F., Hervás-Martínez, C.: Detection of early warning signals in paleoclimate data using a genetic time series segmentation algorithm. Clim. Dyn. **44**, 1919–1933 (2015)
8. Gong, X., Si, Y.W., Fong, S., Biuk-Aghai, R.P.: Financial time series pattern matching with extended UCR suite and support vector machine. Expert Syst. Appl. **55**, 284–296 (2016)
9. Keogh, E.J., Chu, S., Hart, D., Pazzani, M.: Segmenting time series: a survey and novel approach. In: Data Mining in Time Series Databases, pp. 1–22 (2004)
10. Chakrabarti, K., Keogh, E., Mehrotra, S., Pazzani, M.: Locally adaptive dimensionality reduction for indexing large time series databases. ACM Trans. Database Syst. (TODS) **27**, 188–228 (2002)
11. Kennedy, J.: Bare bones particle swarms. In: Proceedings of the Swarm Intelligence Symposium, SIS 2003, pp. 80–87. IEEE (2003)
12. Okulewicz, M.I., Mandziuk, J.: A particle swarm optimization hyper-heuristic for the dynamic vehicle routing problem. In: 7th BIOMA Conference, pp. 215–227 (2016)
13. Zhang, M., Xin, M., Yang, J.: Adaptive multi-cue based particle swarm optimization guided particle filter tracking in infrared videos. Neurocomputing **122**, 163–171 (2013). Advances in cognitive and ubiquitous computing
14. Kennedy, J., Eberhart, R.: Particle swarm optimization. In: 1995 Proceedings of the IEEE International Conference on Neural Networks, vol. 4, pp. 1942–1948 (1995)
15. Moody, G., Mark, R.: The impact of the MIT-BIH arrhythmia database. Eng. Med. Biol. Mag. **20**, 45–50 (2001)
16. National Buoy Data Center: National Oceanic and Atmospheric Administration of the USA (NOAA) (2015). http://www.ndbc.noaa.gov/
17. Chen, Y., Keogh, E., Hu, B., Begum, N., Bagnall, A., Mueen, A., Batista, G.: The UCR time series classification archive (2015). www.cs.ucr.edu/~eamonn/time_series_data/
18. Clerc, M., Kennedy, J.: The particle swarm-explosion, stability, and convergence in a multidimensional complex space. IEEE Trans. Evol. Comput. **6**, 58–73 (2002)
19. Friedman, M.: A comparison of alternative tests of significance for the problem of m rankings. Ann. Math. Stat. **11**, 86–92 (1940)
20. Demšar, J.: Statistical comparisons of classifiers over multiple data sets. J. Mach. Learn. Res. **7**, 1–30 (2006)

Data-Driven Preference-Based Deep Statistical Ranking for Comparing Multi-objective Optimization Algorithms

Tome Eftimov[1,2](✉), Peter Korošec[1,3], and Barbara Koroušić Seljak[1]

[1] Computer Systems Department, Jožef Stefan Institute,
Jamova cesta 39, 1000 Ljubljana, Slovenia
{tome.eftimov,peter.korosec,barbara.korousic}@ijs.si
[2] Jožef Stefan Postgraduate School, Jamova cesta 39, 1000 Ljubljana, Slovenia
[3] Faculty of Mathematics, Natural Sciences and Information Technologies,
University of Primorska, Glagoljaška ulica 8, 6000 Koper, Slovenia

Abstract. To find the strengths and weaknesses of a new multi-objective optimization algorithm, we need to compare its performance with the performances of the state-of-the-art algorithms. Such a comparison involves a selection of a performance metric, a set of benchmark problems, and a statistical test to ensure that the results are statistical significant. There are also studies in which instead of using one performance metric, a comparison is made using a set of performance metrics. All these studies assume that all involved performance metrics are equal. In this paper, we introduce a data-driven preference-based approach that is a combination of multiple criteria decision analysis with deep statistical rankings. The approach ranks the algorithms for each benchmark problem using the preference (the influence) of each performance metric that is estimated using its entropy. Experimental results show that this approach achieved similar rankings to a previously proposed method, which is based on the idea of the majority vote, where all performance metrics are assumed equal. However, as it will be shown, this approach can give different rankings because it is based not only on the idea of counting wins, but also includes information about the influence of each performance metric.

Keywords: Multiple criteria decision analysis
Multi-objective optimization · Quality indicators
Deep statistical ranking · Statistical comparison · Data-driven

1 Introduction

When working on a new optimization algorithm, a crucial task is to compare its performance with state-of-the-art algorithms [1]. In single-objective optimization, the performance of algorithms is analyzed using the best algorithmic solution. For example, in the case of minimization problems, the solution with the

P. Korošec et al. (Eds.): BIOMA 2018, LNCS 10835, pp. 138–150, 2018.
https://doi.org/10.1007/978-3-319-91641-5_12

lowest value is the best. However, in multi-objective optimization algorithms (MOAs), it is not clear what the quality of a solution means in the presence of several optimization criteria. This is because the result is an approximation of the *Pareto-optimal* front, called an approximation set, which can be analyzed according to different quality aspects related to properties of convergence and diversity e.g., the closeness to the optimal front, coverage of a wide range of diverse solutions [2]. Quality indicators can be used to evaluate the performance of MOAs. Each quality indicator maps an approximation set to a real number [3]. In comparative studies, algorithms are used to solve a number of benchmark problems followed by the application of quality indicators to assess their performance [1]. Meta-heuristics are non-deterministic techniques, meaning there is no guarantee that the result will be the same for every run. To test the quality of an algorithm, it is not enough to perform just one run, but many runs of the algorithm on the same problem are needed, from which conclusions can be drawn. Additionally, this data must be analyzed with some statistical tests to ensure that the results are significant.

The aim of this study is to compare the performance of MOAs using a data-driven preference-based approach with a set of quality indicators. In Sect. 2, an overview of the related works is presented. Section 3 introduces the data-driven preference-based methodology. In Sect. 4 the experimental study is presented, while Sect. 4.3 gives a discussion of the proposed methodology. The conclusions of the paper are presented in Sect. 5.

2   Related Work

Many studies that address the problem of how to compare approximation sets in a quantitative manner have been conducted. Riquelme et al. [3] presented a study of a large number of metrics for comparing the performance of different multi-objective optimization algorithms, and presented a review and an analysis of 54 multi-objective optimization metrics and a discussion about the advantages/disadvantages of the most cited metrics in order to give researchers sufficient information for choosing them. A lot of the presented metrics use quality indicators to evaluate the quality of the solutions. Additionally, after calculating the quality indicator of interest, the data must be analyzed using a statistical test to ensure that the results are significant [4,5]. In [6], Eftimov et al. presented a study on how to compare the performance of MOAs using quality indicators and a Deep Statistical Comparison (DSC) approach. They used the DSC approach because it gives more robust statistical results to compare MOAs regarding the data obtained for a single quality indicator. However, there are also studies that use more than one quality indicator to evaluate the performance of MOAs. In [7], Yen and He presented a double-elimination tournament using a quality indicator ensemble to rank MOAs. The tournament contains approximation sets obtained from MOAs for the same initial population and involves a series of binary tournament selections and in each one a quality indicator from an ensemble is randomly chosen for comparison. The result of the tournament is one winning approximation set, so the corresponding MOA is ranked one. Then the approximations sets that are generated by the winning MOA are removed and the remaining approximation sets will go through another double elimination tournament to identify the second best algorithm and so on. The results of the evaluation show that the method is performing more or less as a majority vote. The same idea was used by Ravber et al. [8], where instead of double elimination tournament, they used the chess rating system based on the Glicko-2 system [9]. The comparison between two approximation sets was made by a randomly selected quality indicator from the ensemble. In both approaches, the selection of the quality indicator that is used for a binary tournament is random and comes from a uniform distribution, such that all quality indicators in the ensemble are equal. Eftimov et al., also presented a comparative study of MOAs using an ensemble of quality indicators together with DSC [10]. This study used two ensemble combiners to rank and compare MOAs. Using one of them, each algorithm obtains a ranking for each problem, which is the average of its DSC rankings for each quality indicator for that problem. The other proposed ensemble is a hierarchical majority vote, which is a recursive approach where each algorithm is checked for the number of wins. In both scenarios, there is no preference between the quality indicators used in the comparison and all are assumed equal.

2.1 The Deep Statistical Ranking

Deep Statistical Comparison (DSC) is a recently proposed approach for making a statistical comparison of meta-heuristic stochastic optimization algorithms on a set of single-objective problems [4]. Its main contribution is its ranking scheme, which is based on the whole distribution instead of using just one statistic to describe the distribution, such as either the average or the median. A study on how to compare the performance of MOAs using quality indicators and DSC can be found in [6,10], where DSC gave more robust results compared to a standard statistical test recommended for making a statistical comparison.

2.2 The PROMETHEE

PROMETHEE methods are used in decision making to solve a decision problem in which a set of alternatives are evaluated according to a set of criteria that are often conflicting. Without loss of generality, we can assume that these criteria have to be minimized. For the method, an evaluation matrix is constructed, in which each alternative is estimated for each criteria. The method performs pairwise comparisons between all the alternatives for each criteria to provide either a complete or partial rankings of the alternatives. Four PROMETHEE methods exist, named as I, II, III, and IV. They can be used depending on the nature of the data that is involved in the comparison and the type of ranking that is preferred.

3 The Proposed Methodology

The proposed methodology consists of two steps. In the first, the DSC ranking scheme is used to obtain robust statistics regarding each quality indicator separately, which are combined in the second step using the PROMETHEE II method [11].

3.1   The PROMETHEE II

Let us assume that a comparison needs to be made between m algorithms (i.e., alternatives) regarding n quality indicators (i.e., criteria) for a single problem. Let $A = \{A_1, A_2, \ldots, A_m\}$ be the set of algorithms we want to compare regarding the set of quality indicators $Q = \{q_1, q_2, \ldots, q_n\}$. The decision matrix is a $m \times n$ matrix (see Table 1) that contains the DSC rankings obtained for the algorithms for each quality indicator separately.

Table 1. Decision matrix.

	q_1	q_2	$\cdots$	q_n
A_1	$q_1(A_1)$	$q_2(A_1)$	$\cdots$	$q_n(A_1)$
A_2	$q_1(A_2)$	$q_2(A_2)$	$\cdots$	$q_n(A_2)$
$\vdots$	$\vdots$	$\vdots$	$\vdots$	
A_m	$q_1(A_m)$	$q_2(A_m)$	$\cdots$	$q_n(A_m)$

The DSC ranking scheme always ranks the best algorithm as one, the second best as two, and so on. In our case, we are interested in minimizing the criteria since lower DSC ranking values are preferable. Before we start with the PROMETHEE, the decision matrix is transformed in such a way that the DSC rankings, which are in the same column, are transformed using a standard competition ranking scheme [10]. This should be done because for the DSC rankings it does not matter if rankings are 1.50, 3.00, and 1.50 or 1.00, 3.00, and 1.00. In both scenarios having 1.00 and 1.50 means that the algorithm is the best according to some quality indicator. Since the DSC ranking scheme can never give a 1.00, 3.00, and 1.00 when comparing three algorithms (since it follows the idea of fractional ranking), the DSC rankings for each quality indicator are transformed using the standard competition ranking scheme.

The appropriate method in our case is PROMETHEE II. It is based on pairwise comparisons that need to be made between all algorithms for each quality indicator. The differences between DSC rankings for each pair of algorithms according to a specified quality indicator are taken into consideration. For larger differences the decision maker might consider larger preferences. The preference function of a quality indicator for two algorithms is defined as the degree of preference of algorithm A_1 over algorithm A_2 as seen in the following equation:

$$P_j(A_1, A_2) = \begin{cases} p_j(d_j(A_1, A_2)), & \textit{if maximizing the quality indicator} \\ p_j(-d_j(A_1, A_2)), & \textit{if minimizing the quality indicator} \end{cases}, \quad (1)$$

where $d_j(A_1, A_2) = q_j(A_1) - q_j(A_2)$ is the difference between the DSC rankings of the algorithms for the quality indicator q_j and $p_j(\cdot)$ is a generalized preference function assigned to the quality indicator. There exist six types of generalized preference functions [11]. In our case, usual preference function is used for each quality indicator because of the importance of any differences between the rankings, which is presented in Eq. 2.

$$p(x) = \begin{cases} 0, & x \leq 0 \\ 1, & x > 0 \end{cases}, \tag{2}$$

After selecting the preference function for each quality indicator, the next step is to define the average preference index and outranking (preference and net) flows. The average preference index for each pair of algorithms gives information of global comparison between them using all quality indicators. The average preference index can be calculated as:

$$\pi(A_1, A_2) = \frac{1}{n} \sum_{j=1}^{n} w_j P_j(A_1, A_2), \tag{3}$$

where w_j represents the relative significance (weight) of the jth quality indicator. The higher the weight value of a given quality indicator the higher its relative significance. The selection of the weights is a crucial step in the PROMETHEE II method because it defines the priorities used by the decision-maker. In our case, we used the Shannon entropy weight method, which will be explained in the next subsection. For the average preference index, we need to point out that it is not a symmetric function, so $\pi(A_1, A_2) \neq \pi(A_2, A_1)$.

To rank the algorithms, the net flow for each algorithm needs to be calculated. It is the difference between the positive preference flow, $\phi(A_i^+)$, and the negative preference flow of the algorithm, $\phi(A_i^-)$. The positive preference flow gives information how a given algorithm is globally better than the other algorithms, while the negative preference flow gives the information about how a given algorithm is outranked by all the other algorithms. The positive and the negative preference flows are defined as:

$$\phi(A_i^+) = \frac{1}{(n-1)} \sum_{x \in A} \pi(A_i, x),$$

$$\phi(A_i^-) = \frac{1}{(n-1)} \sum_{x \in A} \pi(x, A_i). \tag{4}$$

The net flow of an algorithm is defined as:

$$\phi(A_i) = \phi(A_i^+) - \phi(A_i^-). \tag{5}$$

The PROMETHEE II method ranks the algorithms by ordering them according to decreasing values of net flows.

3.2 The Shannon Entropy Weighted Method

To find the quality indicator weights, we use the Shannon entropy weighted method [12]. For this reason, the decision matrix presented in Table 1 needs to be normalized. Because the smaller value is preferred, the matrix is normalized using the following equation:

$$q_j(A_i)' = \frac{\max_i(q_j(A_i)) - q_j(A_i)}{\max_i(q_j(A_i)) - \min_i(q_j(A_i))}, \tag{6}$$

where $q_j(A_i)'$ is the normalized value for $q_j(A_i)$.

The entropy for each quality indicator is defined as:

$$e_j = K \sum_{i=1}^{m} W\left(\frac{q_j(A_i)'}{D_j}\right), \tag{7}$$

where D_j is the sum of the jth quality indicator in all algorithms, $D_j = \sum_{i=1}^{m} q_j(A_i)'$, K is the normalized coefficient, $K = \frac{1}{(e^{0.5}-1)m}$, and W is a function defined as $W(x) = xe^{(1-x)} + (1-x)e^x - 1$.

The weight of each quality indicator used in Eq. 3 is calculated using the following equation:

$$w_j = \frac{\frac{1}{(n-E)}(1 - e_j)}{\sum_{j=1}^{n}\left[\frac{1}{(n-E)}(1 - e_j)\right]}, \tag{8}$$

where E is the sum of entropies, $E = \sum_{j=1}^{n} e_j$.

4 Results

4.1 Experimental Setup

The data from six algorithms is available from [13]. The algorithms are compared using 16 test problems. The number of objectives is set to four. More about the parameters of the test problems and the algorithms can be found in [13]. All test problems assume minimization of all objectives. Each algorithm was run for each problem 30 times. Before calculating the quality indicators, each approximated *Pareto* front was normalized. In our experiment quality indicators are hypervolume (q_1), epsilon indicator (q_2), r_2 indicator (q_3), and generational distance (q_4). All of them are unary indicators. Since we are introducing a methodology, we are not specifically dealing which quality indicators are used. The selection is up to user to make sure that relevant quality indicators are selected (e.g., if all quality indicators should be Pareto compliant, convergence, diversity, etc.). For calculating the hypervolume, the reference point $(1, \ldots, 1)$ is used, while for the other quality indicators, the reference set consists of all non-dominated solutions already known from all runs for each algorithm for a given problem. Because the DSC ranking scheme involves a statistical test for comparing distributions, a two-sample *Anderson-Darling (AD)* test is used and the significance level is set to 0.05. The benefits of using this test are presented in [14].

4.2 Experimental Results

In the experiment, three out of six algorithms are randomly selected. The algorithms are: $DEMO^{SP2}$, $DEMO^{NS-II}$, and NSGA-II. First, for each quality indicator, the DSC ranking scheme is used to compare the quality indicator data for a single problem. Further, the DSC rankings obtained for each quality indicator and each problem are transformed using the standard competition ranking scheme (see Table 2). The highest ranked algorithm for each problem and each quality indicator has the best performance.

Table 2. Transformed DSC rankings for each quality indicator of the algorithms, $A_1 = DEMO^{SP2}$, $A_2 = DEMO^{NS-II}$, and $A_3 = NSGA-II$.

Problem	Hypervolume			r_2			Epsilon			Generational distance		
	A_1	A_2	A_3	A_1	A_2	A_3	A_1	A_2	A_3	A_1	A_2	A_3
DTLZ1	2.00	1.00	3.00	1.00	2.00	3.00	1.00	2.00	3.00	1.00	2.00	3.00
DTLZ2	2.00	1.00	3.00	3.00	1.00	2.00	2.00	1.00	3.00	2.00	1.00	3.00
DTLZ3	1.00	1.00	3.00	2.00	1.00	3.00	1.00	1.00	3.00	1.00	1.00	3.00
DTLZ4	1.00	2.00	3.00	1.00	2.00	2.00	1.00	2.00	3.00	1.00	2.00	3.00
DTLZ5	2.00	2.00	1.00	1.00	1.00	3.00	1.00	1.00	1.00	1.00	3.00	2.00
DTLZ6	2.00	1.00	3.00	2.00	1.00	3.00	2.00	1.00	3.00	1.00	2.00	3.00
DTLZ7	2.00	1.00	3.00	2.00	1.00	3.00	2.00	1.00	3.00	2.00	1.00	3.00
WFG1	1.00	2.00	3.00	1.00	2.00	3.00	1.00	2.00	3.00	1.00	3.00	2.00
WFG2	1.00	2.00	3.00	1.00	2.00	2.00	1.00	2.00	2.00	1.00	3.00	1.00
WFG3	1.00	3.00	2.00	1.00	2.00	2.00	1.00	2.00	2.00	1.00	2.00	2.00
WFG4	1.00	2.00	3.00	2.00	1.00	2.00	2.00	1.00	3.00	3.00	2.00	1.00
WFG5	3.00	2.00	1.00	3.00	1.00	1.00	1.00	3.00	2.00	3.00	2.00	1.00
WFG6	1.00	2.00	3.00	2.00	1.00	3.00	1.00	2.00	2.00	3.00	1.00	1.00
WFG7	1.00	2.00	3.00	2.00	1.00	3.00	1.00	2.00	2.00	3.00	2.00	1.00
WFG8	1.00	2.00	2.00	1.00	2.00	3.00	1.00	2.00	2.00	1.00	3.00	2.00
WFG9	1.00	2.00	2.00	1.00	1.00	3.00	1.00	2.00	2.00	3.00	2.00	1.00

Before we find the complete ranking of the algorithms, the weights of each quality indicator are calculated for each single problem using the Shannon entropy weighted method. The weights for all problems are presented in Table 3.

Then, the PROMETHEE II method is used to rank the algorithms for each problem. If the original decision matrix is involved in the PROMETHEE II calculations, the preference function that is used is the one for minimizing the quality indicator, while if the normalized matrix is used, the preference function is the one used to maximize the quality indicator. In our case, we have a set of three algorithms $A = \{A_1, A_2, A_3\}$ that need to be compared according to a set of four quality indicators $Q = \{q_1, q_2, q_3, q_4\}$. The rankings obtained for PROMETHEE II method are presented on the left side of Table 4. They are

Table 3. Weights for each quality indicator.

Problem	q_1	q_2	q_3	q_4	Problem	q_1	q_2	q_3	q_4
DTLZ1	0.25	0.25	0.25	0.25	WFG2	0.14	0.37	0.37	0.12
DTLZ2	0.25	0.25	0.25	0.25	WFG3	0.13	0.29	0.29	0.29
DTLZ3	0.24	0.28	0.24	0.24	WFG4	0.18	0.46	0.18	0.18
DTLZ4	0.18	0.46	0.18	0.18	WFG5	0.26	0.22	0.26	0.26
DTLZ5	0.57	0.20	0.00	0.23	WFG6	0.19	0.19	0.47	0.15
DTLZ6	0.25	0.25	0.25	0.25	WFG7	0.18	0.18	0.46	0.18
DTLZ7	0.25	0.25	0.25	0.25	WFG8	0.36	0.14	0.36	0.14
WFG1	0.25	0.25	0.25	0.25	WFG9	0.37	0.12	0.37	0.14

further compared with the rankings obtained by the average ensemble with the DSC rankings (DSC ensemble I) [10], presented in the middle part of Table 4 and the hierarchical majority vote with the DSC rankings (DSC ensemble II) [10], presented on the right side of Table 4. From it, we can see that the rankings obtained using PROMETHEE II with DSC differ from the rankings obtained using the average ensemble with DSC or the hierarchical majority vote with DSC only in two bolded problems: DTLZ5 and WFG7.

Table 4. Ensemble combiner for the algorithms: $A_1 = \mathrm{DEMO}^{SP2}$, $A_2 = \mathrm{DEMO}^{NS-II}$, and $A_3 = \mathrm{NSGA\text{-}II}$.

Problem	PROMETHEE II			DSC ensemble I			DSC ensemble II		
	A_1	A_2	A_3	A_1	A_2	A_3	A_1	A_2	A_3
DTLZ1	1.00	2.00	3.00	1.00	2.00	3.00	1.00	2.00	3.00
DTLZ2	2.00	1.00	3.00	2.00	1.00	3.00	2.00	1.00	3.00
DTLZ3	2.00	1.00	3.00	2.00	1.00	3.00	2.00	1.00	3.00
DTLZ4	1.00	2.00	3.00	1.00	2.00	3.00	1.00	2.00	3.00
DTLZ5	**2.00**	**3.00**	**1.00**	**1.00**	**2.50**	**2.50**	**1.00**	**2.50**	**2.50**
DTLZ6	2.00	1.00	3.00	2.00	1.00	3.00	2.00	1.00	3.00
DTLZ7	2.00	1.00	3.00	2.00	1.00	3.00	2.00	1.00	3.00
WFG1	1.00	2.00	3.00	1.00	2.00	3.00	1.00	2.00	3.00
WFG2	1.00	3.00	2.00	1.00	3.00	2.00	1.00	3.00	2.00
WFG3	1.00	3.00	2.00	1.00	3.00	2.00	1.00	3.00	2.00
WFG4	2.00	1.00	3.00	2.00	1.00	3.00	2.00	1.00	3.00
WFG5	3.00	2.00	1.00	3.00	2.00	1.00	3.00	2.00	1.00
WFG6	1.00	2.00	3.00	2.00	1.00	3.00	2.00	1.00	3.00
WFG7	**1.00**	**2.00**	**3.00**	**1.50**	**1.50**	**3.00**	**1.00**	**2.00**	**3.00**
WFG8	1.00	2.50	2.50	1.00	2.50	2.50	1.00	2.50	2.50
WFG9	1.00	2.00	3.00	1.00	2.00	3.00	1.00	2.00	3.00

To see what happens on a single problem, let us focus on the DLTZ5 problem. The decision matrix and its normalization are presented at top of Table 5. The transformed DSC rankings for the r_2 indicator and the DLTZ5 problem are 1.00, 1.00, and 1.00. Further, there is a problem in the normalization process because the normalized rankings are indeterminate forms (i.e., 0/0) [15], so the weight or the relative significance of this quality indicator can not be calculated. However, according to this quality indicator and the obtained DSC rankings, the compared algorithms are the same and they are all winners. Let us suppose that the weight w_3 could be calculated in some way, then the part of the average preference index that is related to the q_3 indicator is a product of $w_3 P_3(A_{i_1}, A_{i_2})$, where $i_1, i_2 = 1, \ldots, m$ and $i_1 \neq i_2$. In this case, it will be zero and will not influence the average preference index, which is used for calculating the positive and negative flows. Because it can not provide any additional information, it is removed and the result will be the same as comparing the algorithms regarding the remaining quality indicators, which in our case are q_1, q_2, and q_4. By removing the r_3 indicator, the decision matrix and its normalization are presented at the bottom part of Table 5. The weights obtained using the Shannon entropy weighted method are 0.57, 0.20, and 0.23. The final rankings and the outranking flows are given on the left side od Table 6. On the right part of Table 6 the average preference indices that are used for calculating the positive and negative flows for DLTZ5 are presented.

Table 5. Decision matrices for DLTZ5.

Algorithm	Decision matrix				Normalized matrix			
	q_1	q_2	q_3	q_4	q_1	q_2	q_3	q_4
DEMO^{SP2}	2.00	1.00	1.00	1.00	0.00	1.00	0/0	1.00
DEMO^{NS-II}	2.00	1.00	1.00	3.00	0.00	1.00	0/0	0.00
NSGA-II	1.00	3.00	1.00	2.00	1.00	0.00	0/0	0.50
Algorithm	Decision matrix				Normalized matrix			
	q_1	q_2	q_3	q_4	q_1	q_2	q_3	q_4
DEMO^{SP2}	2.00	1.00	/	1.00	0.00	1.00	/	1.00
DEMO^{NS-II}	2.00	1.00	/	3.00	0.00	1.00	/	0.00
NSGA-II	1.00	3.00	/	2.00	1.00	0.00	/	0.50

Table 6. Outranking flows, PROMOTHEE II rankings, and average indices for DLTZ5.

Algorithm	ϕ^+	ϕ^-	ϕ	Ranking		$\pi(A_i, A_1)$	$\pi(A_i, A_2)$	$\pi(A_i, A_3)$
DEMO^{SP2}	0.11	0.10	0.01	2.00	$\pi(A_1, A_j)$	0.00	**0.08**	**0.14**
DEMO^{NS-II}	0.03	0.17	−0.14	3.00	$\pi(A_2, A_j)$	**0.00**	0.00	**0.06**
NSGA-II	0.23	0.10	0.13	1.00	$\pi(A_3, A_j)$	**0.19**	**0.27**	0.00

Using the decision matrix presented in Table 5, the rankings obtained using the average ensemble and the hierarchical majority vote are the same and are 1.00, 2.50, and 2.50. In the case of hierarchical majority vote, DEMO^{SP2} is ranked as first because it wins in three out of four quality indicators, while DEMO^{NS-II} and NSGA-II are ranked second (e.g., 2.5) because both are ranked first in the case of two quality indicators, then both are second in the case of one quality indicator and third in the case of one quality indicator. All quality indicators are assumed equal and the ranking is made by counting the number of wins. However, the obtained rankings using the data-driven preference-based approach are 2.00, 3.00, and 1.00, which are completely different from the other ensembles. From the left part of Table 6, we can see that NSGA-II has the highest positive flow. The question is why it is ranked first when DEMO^{SP2} has two wins. This happens because the quality indicators that are involved have a data-driven preference for each of them, which is obtained by the Shannon entropy weighted method. The quality indicators are ordered as q_1, q_4, q_2, (e.g, hypervolume, generational distance, and epsilon indicator), starting from the most significant one to the least significant one. The average preference indices between A_1 and A_3 that are used for calculating the positive and negative flows are:

$$\pi(A_1, A_3) = \frac{1}{3}\left[0.57 \cdot 0 + \mathbf{0.20 \cdot 1} + \mathbf{0.23 \cdot 1}\right] = 0.14$$

$$\pi(A_3, A_1) = \frac{1}{3}\left[\mathbf{0.57 \cdot 1} + 0.20 \cdot 0 + 0.23 \cdot 0\right] = 0.19 \tag{9}$$

Using the calculations presented in Eq. 9, we can see that the average preference index between NSGA-II and DEMO^{SP2} is 0.19 and it is a result of only one win regarding the quality indicator q_1, while the average preference index between DEMO^{SP2} and NSGA-II is 0.14 and it is smaller even though it is a result of two wins regarding q_2 and q_4. This happens because q_1 is the most significant and its weight is much more than the sum of the weights of q_2 and q_4. In our experiment, the proposed data-driven preference-based approach gives different rankings from the hierarchical majority vote only for DLTZ5. This happens because only on that problem the compared algorithms are the same regarding one of the used quality indicators, which is the r_3 indicator. However, if this happens for other single-problems, the rankings can also differ from the rankings obtained by a hierarchical majority vote.

Furthermore, the obtained rankings using PROMETHEE II with DSC can be used as input data for a multiple-problem scenario. The appropriate statistical test is the *Friedman test*. Using it, the obtained p-value is 0.00, so using a significance level 0.05, we can conclude that there is a statistical significant difference between the compared algorithms using a set of benchmark problems. When comparing MOAs, often more than three algorithms are involved in the comparison, or especially a new algorithm is compared with state-of-the-art algorithm as a multiple comparisons with a control algorithm. When the number of algorithms increases the DSC rankings can be affected when correcting the p-values to control the FWER. In such a scenario, it is better to use multiple *Wilcoxon tests*, one for each pairwise comparison and then combine the p-values to find the actual p-value for the scenario. More about this scenario and the DSC approach is presented in [4]. If we are interested in to compare them using a data-driven preference-based approach, we just need to use PROMETHEE II with DSC instead of the original DSC ranking scheme to find the rankings for each pairwise comparison on each problem.

4.3   Discussion

Comparing the performance of a new MOA with the performance of state-of-the-art MOAs is a crucial task in order to find its strengths and weaknesses. Different performance metrics can be used for evaluation and they are usually combined with statistical tests to ensure that the results are significant. Several previously proposed approaches are focused on comparing MOAs using a set of quality indicators. They follow the idea of ensemble learning, but all of them assume that all quality indicators are equal. The performance metric and the way how the algorithms will be compared also depend on the user preference or the concrete application. For example, in our previous work, we presented an average ensemble and a hierarchical majority vote based on counting wins according to different quality indicators, but in this paper we proposed a data-driven preference-based approach that is a combination of PROMETHEE II and DSC ranking scheme. According to the user preference all involved quality indicators are still equal, but the data-driven preference changes this by using its entropy. Organizing the DSC rankings for each quality indicator and each problem into a decision matrix, the Shannon entropy weighted method is used to find the relative significance of each quality indicator for each problem. The relative significance of each quality indicator is related to its entropy, which is the amount of information conveyed by it. The experimental results have shown that the preference-based approach performs more or less as a hierarchical majority vote. However, it can give different rankings, and the algorithm can overrank another one even if it has a lower number of wins, but it wins in most preferred quality indicator(s). Also, if there is a quality indicator for which all compared algorithms perform the same (they all win), it does not have an influence in the comparison and it can be removed from the set of quality indicators. Comparing the hierarchical majority vote and data-driven preference-based ranking, we can say that the hierarchical majority vote is more appropriate in cases where the performance is estimated by counting wins and loses such as in the case of dynamic multi-objective optimization, otherwise data-driven preference-based ranking can be used in cases when the influence of each quality indicator is required.

5   Conclusion

In this paper, we presented a data-driven preference-based approach for comparing MOAs using a set of quality indicators. The approach is a combination of PROMETHEE II, which is a method in MCDA, and a DSC ranking scheme, that gives more robust statistical results and is based on comparing distributions instead of using only one statistic to describe the data. We compared our method with previously proposed methods where all involved quality indicators are assumed equal. We have shown that our method performs similar to a hierarchical majority vote, but also can give different rankings regarding the influence of each quality indicator, which is its preference and is estimated according to its entropy.

Acknowledgments. This work was supported by the project from the Slovenian Research Agency (research core funding No. P2-0098) and from the European Union's Horizon 2020 research and innovation program under grant agreement No. 692286.

References

1. Durillo, J.J., Nebro, A.J., Alba, E.: The jMetal framework for multi-objective optimization: design and architecture. In: 2010 IEEE Congress on Evolutionary Computation (CEC), pp. 1–8. IEEE (2010)
2. Coello Coello, C.A., Lamont, G.B., Van Veldhuizen, D.A., et al.: Evolutionary Algorithms for Solving Multi-objective Problems, vol. 5. Springer, New York (2007). https://doi.org/10.1007/978-0-387-36797-2
3. Riquelme, N., Von Lücken, C., Baran, B.: Performance metrics in multi-objective optimization. In: Computing Conference (CLEI), 2015 Latin American, pp. 1–11. IEEE (2015)
4. Eftimov, T., Korošec, P., Seljak, B.K.: A novel approach to statistical comparison of meta-heuristic stochastic optimization algorithms using deep statistics. Inf. Sci. **417**, 186–215 (2017)
5. García, S., Molina, D., Lozano, M., Herrera, F.: A study on the use of nonparametric tests for analyzing the evolutionary algorithms behaviour: a case study on the CEC2005 special session on real parameter optimization. J. Heuristics **15**(6), 617–644 (2009)
6. Eftimov, T., Korošec, P., Korousić Seljak, B.: Deep statistical comparison applied on quality indicators to compare multi-objective stochastic optimization algorithms. In: Nicosia, G., Pardalos, P., Giuffrida, G., Umeton, R. (eds.) MOD 2017. LNCS, vol. 10710, pp. 76–87. Springer, Cham (2018). https://doi.org/10.1007/978-3-319-72926-8_7
7. Yen, G.G., He, Z.: Performance metric ensemble for multiobjective evolutionary algorithms. IEEE Trans. Evol. Compu. **18**(1), 131–144 (2014)
8. Ravber, M., Mernik, M., Črepinšek, M.: Ranking multi-objective evolutionary algorithms using a chess rating system with quality indicator ensemble. In: 2017 IEEE Congress on Evolutionary Computation (CEC), pp. 1503–1510. IEEE (2017)
9. Glickman, M.E.: Example of the Glicko-2 system. Boston University (2012)
10. Eftimov, T., Korošec, P., Seljak, B.K.: Comparing multi-objective optimization algorithms using an ensemle of quality indicators with deep statistical comparison approach. In: 2017 IEEE Symposium Series on Computational Intelligence (SSCI) Proceedings, pp. 2801–2809. IEEE (2017)
11. Brans, J.P., Vincke, P.: Note - a preference ranking organisation method: (the PROMETHEE method for multiple criteria decision-making). Manag. Sci. **31**(6), 647–656 (1985)

12. Boroushaki, S.: Entropy-based weights for multicriteria spatial decision-making. Yearb. Assoc. Pac. Coast Geogr. **79**, 168–187 (2017)
13. Tušar, T., Filipič, B.: Differential evolution versus genetic algorithms in multiobjective optimization. In: Obayashi, S., Deb, K., Poloni, C., Hiroyasu, T., Murata, T. (eds.) EMO 2007. LNCS, vol. 4403, pp. 257–271. Springer, Heidelberg (2007). https://doi.org/10.1007/978-3-540-70928-2_22
14. Eftimov, T., Korošec, P., Seljak, B.K.: The behaviour of deep statistical comparison approach for different criteria of comparing distributions. In: Proceedings of 9th International Joint Conference on Computational Intelligence. SCITEPRESS Digital Library (2017)
15. Gordon, S.P.: Visualizing and understanding l'hopital's rule. Int. J. Math. Educ. Sci. Technol. **48**(7), 1096–1105 (2017)

Construction of Heuristic for Protein Structure Optimization Using Deep Reinforcement Learning

Rok Hribar[1,2(✉)], Jurij Šilc[1], and Gregor Papa[1,2]

[1] Jožef Stefan Institute, Ljubljana, Slovenia
{rok.hribar,jurij.silc,gregor.papa}@ijs.si
[2] Jožef Stefan International Postgraduate School, Ljubljana, Slovenia

Abstract. Deep neural networks are constructed that are able to partially solve a protein structure optimization problem. The networks are trained using reinforcement learning approach so that free energy of predicted protein structure is minimized. Free energy of a protein structure is calculated using generalized three-dimensional AB off-lattice protein model. This methodology can be applied to other classes of optimization problems and represents a step toward automatic heuristic construction using deep neural networks. Trained networks can be used to construct better initial populations for optimization. It is shown that differential evolution applied to protein structure optimization problem converges to better solutions when initial population is constructed in this way.

Keywords: Protein folding · Heuristic · Deep learning
Differential evolution

1 Introduction

Prediction of protein structure from the sequence of its residues is a hard optimization problem. All proteins are endowed with a primary structure consisting of the chain of amino acids. Folding of this chain results into so-called 3D protein structure. The biological functional role of the protein is strictly dependent on the protein 3D structure. Knowledge of a proteins structure provides insight into how it can interact with other proteins, DNA/RNA, and small molecules. It are these interactions which define the proteins function and biological role in an organism. Thus, protein structure and structural feature prediction is a fundamental area of computational biology. Its importance is exacerbated by large amounts of sequence data coming from genomics projects and the fact that experimentally determining protein structures remains expensive and time consuming [1].

Over the last decades a lot of effort have been invested in reducing the computational cost of calculating the 3D structures of proteins. One way to decrease the computational cost is the introduction of approximate models for the calculation of protein's free energy which is minimal for appropriate 3D structure.

P. Korošec et al. (Eds.): BIOMA 2018, LNCS 10835, pp. 151–162, 2018.
https://doi.org/10.1007/978-3-319-91641-5_13

Because the computation of free energy is less costly, optimization that finds the right structure is also less costly to preform. Examples of such approximate models include models using a cubic lattice [2] and AB type models [3]. Another way to speed up the optimization process is to make optimization more efficient, so that less free energy evaluations are needed. This resulted in development of heuristics that are tailored specifically for this optimization problem. Since protein folding process is in nature guided only by the physical laws, optimization methods were devised that include principles from statistical physics. Heuristics from this category include annealing contour Monte Carlo [4] and conformational space annealing [5]. Another approach to developing a specialized optimization algorithm is to modify known metaheuristics such as artificial bee colony [6] or evolutionary algorithm [7].

A different approach to prediction of protein 3D structure is the use of machine learning. Here the prediction of 3D structure is based only on features directly calculated from the sequence of amino acids. There is no optimization performed during prediction. The structure is calculated simply by applying the model. Optimization is used only during the model training, when appropriate model is searched for. Currently, deep neural networks (DNNs) are the most widely used models for this problem. Properly trained DNNs are very successful at predicting protein's secondary structure ($\approx80\%$ accuracy) [8] and its disordered regions ($\approx90\%$ accuracy) [9]. However, full 3D structure prediction is much less accurate ($\approx20\%$ accuracy) [10]. DNN models are usually trained using supervised learning where experimentally acquired 3D structures of proteins are used as training examples. Advantage of this approach is that protein's free energy does not need to be calculated. But on the other hand, by using only experimental data one is limited to possibly insufficient amount of training examples to properly train DNN.

In this paper a different approach to DNN training is presented and used in which explicit training examples are not needed. Instead, the free energy of a protein is used to provide information about the quality of predicted solutions. This is possible because this problem can be interpreted as an optimization problem or a prediction problem. This allows the combination of both views to generate a new method for addressing the protein structure problem. In this regard such methodology can be applied to any optimization problem to generate DNNs able to predict a solution of an optimization problem. In other words, given a class of optimization problems one can construct a DNN that represents extremely fast heuristic specially designed for this class of optimization problems. This is a step toward automatic heuristic generation.

2   Deep Neural Network as an Optimization Algorithm

Optimization problems are often solved using approximate algorithms (heuristics) that are tailored for a specific class of problems. For example, there are specific heuristics that work well for vehicle routing [11], production scheduling [12], protein folding [13] and so on. Heuristics are especially useful if similar problems need to be solved over and over again. In such cases it is sensible to develop specialized optimization procedures which are optimized for that specific class of problems.

In this section a methodology is presented where DNNs are trained in a way that they are able to approximately solve an optimization problem that belongs to a given class of problems. Such class of optimization problems can be represented with a fitness function f with two inputs.

$$f : \mathcal{S}, \mathcal{X} \to \mathbb{R}$$
$$f_s(x) = \min. \tag{1}$$

Set $\mathcal{S}$ holds all possible optimization problems in the class, while set $\mathcal{X}$ holds all possible candidate solutions for that class of problems. For example, in case f represents a class of production scheduling problems, s encodes the orders that need to be fulfilled and x encodes the production schedule.

Given function f, it is possible to define a function g that takes a problem specification s as an input and returns the position x_s^{optimal} where function f_s has a global minimum.

$$g : \mathcal{S} \to \mathcal{X}$$
$$g(s) = \arg \min_{x \in \mathcal{X}} f_s(x) = x_s^{\text{optimal}} \tag{2}$$

In other words, $g(s)$ is a solution of optimization problem $f_s(x) = \min$. Calculation of function g is in general intractable. But it might be possible to find a model that approximates g to some degree. One aim of this paper is to find out whether a trained DNN is able to approximate g. It is important to note that the input and output of DNN are traditionally floating point numbers. Therefore, s and x should be encoded as vectors of floating point numbers. Even for discrete s and x it is usually possible to find such an encoding.

It is known that a neural network can approximate arbitrary function to an arbitrary precision [14]. So g can be approximated well using DNN, however it is unknown how large such a network should be and whether it is possible to find it using known training techniques. If DNN could be trained to approximate g, such DNN can preform partial optimization extremely quickly. While DNN training is known to be resource intensive, prediction is usually not.

Training DNN to approximate g is also an optimization problem, however optimization landscape of DNN training is not similar to f_s landscape. DNN parameters encode a strategy for predicting x_s^{optimal} from s, so optimization is not performed on a single problem encoded by s, but for all possible s at once. Also DNN optimization landscape has particular properties, like the fact that saddle points are exponentially more common compared to local minima [15]. Therefore, a suitable optimization method that takes those specific properties into account should be used for training them. Currently, stochastic gradient descent (SGD) is the prevalent and very successful approach to DNN training [16].

2.1 Supervised Learning Approach

DNN can be trained to approximate g using supervised learning. Let $\hat{g}(s)$ be the output of DNN when s is its input. In supervised learning pairs $(s_i, x_{s_i}^{\text{optimal}})$ are provided and DNN error is minimized using SGD so that

$$J = \sum_i \left\| \hat{g}(s_i) - x_{s_i}^{\text{optimal}} \right\| = \min. \tag{3}$$

Since x_s^{optimal} is in general unknown, its best approximation has to be used which results to nonideal DNN model. So $x_{s_i}^{\text{optimal}}$ need to acquired using external optimization algorithms. In order to prevent DNN overfitting it is necessary to provide a large amount of training examples, i.e. much more than the number of DNN parameters. Therefore, such approach is extremely resource intensive.

2.2 Reinforcement Learning Approach

Another approach to DNN training is reinforcement learning. In this case functions f_s are used to calculate the error of DNN. DNN is trained so that

$$E = \sum_i f_{s_i}(\hat{g}(s_i)) = \min. \tag{4}$$

In reinforcement learning terminology, E can be understood as a penalty that needs to be minimized. In this case $x_{s_i}^{\text{optimal}}$ are not needed and so no external optimization is required. The downside is that SGD can not be applied as simply as with supervised learning. Error function J from Eq. (3) can be easily differentiated with respect to DNN parameters using backpropagation. But penalty E from Eq. (4) also includes application of f_s. This makes the calculation of the gradient difficult and different methods have been introduced by deep reinforcement learning community to mend this problem.

In this paper an adapted version of deterministic policy gradient method [17] is used. This method uses a differentiable model called a critic that approximates function f from Eq. (4). The derivative of E can then be approximately calculated using the derivative of the critic by applying the chain rule. Our adaptation of this method is to not model f with a critic but instead use f directly. In order to calculate derivative of E in this scope, the derivative $\nabla_x f_s(x)$ is required.

Fortunately, derivation of f_s can also be preformed using backpropagation principles, i.e. applying chain rule coupled with dynamic programming. There are good libraries that can preform such automatic differentiation, for example theano, TensorFlow and CNTK. In this paper theano was used to write expressions for the calculation of E. These expressions are then transformed to a computational graph for calculation of E which can be used to build computational graph for gradient calculation ∇E using the chain rule. In this respect procedure is returned for analytical gradient calculation ∇E without any assistance from the user. Computational graphs for E and ∇E calculation can be compiled to C++, CUDA or OpenCL which brings multi processor support and can easily be accelerated on GPGPU or even FPGA [18]. Therefore, use of `theano` is beneficial even if just calculation of E is needed.

Therefore, by using `theano` DNN can be trained using SGD so that E from Eq. (4) is minimized. Great advantage of this approach is an unlimited amount of training examples s_i which can be drawn from desired distribution over s_i. This generation of training examples is extremely cheap compared to supervised learning approach where training examples need to be generated by optimization algorithm or acquired by experimental measurement.

3   Generalized Three-Dimensional AB Off-Lattice Protein Model

AB off-lattice model has been widely used to describe the protein secondary structure folding process for decades [3]. The off-lattice protein model was initially developed to consider 2D folding problems and was extended to deal with 3D scenarios where additional torsional energy contributions of each bond are taken into account [19]. According to the AB off-lattice model, the main driving forces that contribute to protein structure formulation are the hydrophilic and hydrophobic interactions.

The protein chain is modeled as a vector s where each component s_i specifies the hydrophilicity of amino acid at the site i. The distance of two neighboring amino acids is set to one ($d_{i,i+1} = 1$). Under this model free energy G is calculated as

$$G(u, d) = \frac{1}{4} \sum_{i=1}^{n-2} (1 - u_i \cdot u_{i+1}) + 4 \sum_{i=1}^{n-2} \sum_{j=i+2}^{n} \left(d_{ij}^{-12} - C(s_i, s_j) d_{ij}^{-6} \right), \quad (5)$$

where u_i is a vector from amino acid on site i to amino acid on site $i+1$ and d_{ij} is a distance between amino acids on site i and j (see Fig. 1). The interaction between two amino acids is specified by a function

$$C(s_i, s_j) = \frac{1}{8} \left(1 + s_i + s_j + 5 s_i s_j \right). \quad (6)$$

Structure of a protein of length n can be encoded using angles θ_i and φ_i that tell how vectors u_i are oriented in space (see Fig. 2). Therefore, a protein structure of length n is fully determined by

$$x = (\theta_2, \ldots, \theta_{n-1}, \varphi_3, \ldots, \varphi_{n-1}). \quad (7)$$

Use of this encoding reduces the dimensionality of search space and allows us to automatically fulfill the constraint $\|u_i\| = 1$. The values u_i and d_{ij} that are needed for free energy calculation can be calculated from x in the following way

$$u_i = (\cos \theta_i \sin \varphi_i, \sin \theta_i \sin \varphi_i, \cos \varphi_i) \quad (8)$$

$$r_{i+1} = r_i + u_i \quad (9)$$

$$d_{ij} = \|r_i - r_j\|. \quad (10)$$

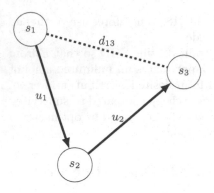
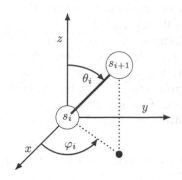

Fig. 1. Visualization of direction vectors u_i and distances d_{ij} on a protein with three amino acids.

Fig. 2. Visualization of angles θ_i and φ_i from Eq. (7) that determine the direction of vectors u_i.

The first two amino acids in a sequence are fixed to specific coordinates and the third one is constrained to xy-plane.

$$r_1 = (0,0,0) \tag{11}$$

$$r_2 = (1,0,0) \tag{12}$$

$$\varphi_2 = \frac{\pi}{2} \tag{13}$$

By this choice, rotational symmetry of the model is eliminated.

In protein structure optimization problem we want to find a structure of a protein that minimizes the free energy G. Therefore, given a protein defined with s, we want to find x that determines the structure of that protein. So the problem class is defined by a function

$$f_s(x) = G(u(x), d(x)) = \min. \tag{14}$$

Traditionally $s_i = \pm 1$, where hydrophobic amino acid has $s_i = -1$ and hydrophilic $s_i = 1$. In this regard quantity s_i tells how hydrophilic an amino acid is. However, this paper uses a generalization of this model where $s_i \in \mathbb{R}$. One reason for this choice is the fact that amino acids in nature are not hydrophilic to the same degree [20]. Some may attract or repel water more than others. Also hydrophilicity changes with temperature [21] which allows one to use this generalized model to study how protein structure changes with temperature. Use of generalized model is also beneficial with regard to DNN training because this brings a richer set of training examples and makes the training landscape smoother.

4   Experiments

In this section DNN training procedure using reinforcement learning is presented and how solutions predicted by DNNs were used as initial population of differential evolution (DE) algorithm. A variant of SGD called Adam [22] was used and gradient of E was used to guide the training. The calculation of ∇E was calculated using **theano** library.

$$E = \sum_{i=1}^{B} f_{s_i}(\hat{g}(s_i)) \tag{15}$$

In each step of Adam algorithm a batch of proteins s_i of random length was randomly selected. Distribution over length was uniform and over hydrophilicity a mixture of two Gaussians with mean at ± 1 and standard deviation 0.15. Based on the selected s_i calculation of E and ∇E was done by **theano**. The number of sampled proteins for E and ∇E calculation is called a batch size B. The training is more stochastic if B is low and becomes more deterministic if B is high. By experimenting with different batch sizes a good balance between speed and accuracy was found at $B = 512$.

Stated more informally, in each step, DNN tries to solve 512 random protein optimization problems and gets updated in direction that would improve its solving capabilities for those 512 proteins. Because DNN gets a different batch of random proteins in each step, it converges to a state that is able to solve all protein optimization problems equally well. Picking training batches randomly also ensures that DNN can not overfit since duplicates in the training data are extremely unlikely. Therefore, the training error of DNN is not a biased estimate of its accuracy and validation set is not needed.

A DNN structure was chosen that can take proteins with up to $n = 100$ amino acids. To allow prediction on smaller proteins zero padding was used. Example of small scale DNN is shown in Fig. 3. DNNs with different number of hidden layers was trained in order to quantify how DNN depth influences the accuracy. In all cases the width of hidden layers was chosen to be $2n = 200$. Rectified linear units were used as activation functions on hidden layers and tanh on the output layer to ensure that $\theta_i, \varphi_i \in [-\pi, \pi]$.

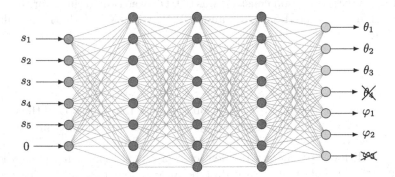

Fig. 3. Small scale example of how DNN receives the protein specification and how its output is interpreted. If a protein is shorter than DNN input layer, zero is placed on sites where there are no amino acids. In this case some angles from the output are discarded (crossed out outputs).

Before training, initial DNN weights need to be set. Initial weights were generated randomly using Glorot initialization [23]. However, if the magnitude of initial weights is to large, it can happen that initial DNN predicts very densely packed structures which causes a very large gradient due to d_{ij}^{-12} repulsive term in free energy. This causes an unstable gradient descent. Therefore, a prefactor w_i was added to initialization and DNN models with $w_1 = 0.1$ and $w_2 = 1.0$ was trained.

To avoid unstable gradient descent the predictions of initial DNN should be unfolded protein structures. This, however, produces another problem. The first summand in Eq. (5) forces proteins to be unfolded which means that unfolded structure is a local minimum that is common to all proteins. To avoid getting stuck in this common local minimum the first summand in Eq. (5) was simply not included in the calculation of free energy at the beginning of training. When DNN predicted structures began to fold, the previously ignored summand was gradually added during training. In the last stage of training the full version of free energy was used.

During DNN training it can happen that for some s_i in the batch DNN predicts a structure where two amino acids are very close to each other. A repulsive interaction causes the gradient ∇E to be very large for the entire batch. In the next step of gradient descent the DNN is thrown away from a possibly good region. Such events might be rare, but can severely disturb the progress of training. To mitigate the effect of such events, gradient norm clipping can be used. In other words, if the gradient length exceeds a given threshold, the gradient is clipped so that its length is equal to the threshold.

Solutions predicted by DNNs might be a good initial population for optimization. To test whether this is true protein structure optimization using DE was implemented. DE was shown to be the best known optimization method for this problem [7]. Specifications of implemented DE algorithm was taken from [7], but without parameter control. DE type was `best/1/bin`, population size was 100, mutation with dithering was employed with mutation constant taken between 0.1 and 1 and recombination constant was 0.9. DE was run 30 times for three proteins found in nature (1CB3, 1CRN and 2EWH) with random initial population and with initial population where 50% of candidates were predicted by DNNs.

5   Results

To measure how good a candidate solution is, we use free energy G of the protein. In case of comparing solutions gotten by DE, this is a sound measure from the point of view of statistical physics. That is, the protein is most likely to be in states with low free energy. In ideal case one could check if the solution is equivalent to the native structure, but because global minima of this protein model are unknown this is not possible. To evaluate the performance of DNN, training error is used. It is equivalent to validation error and defined as a mean of free energy values predicted by DNN for a batch of random proteins. The variance of this error measure is very low because the batch size $B = 512$ is large.

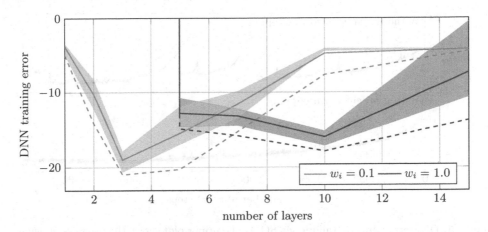

Fig. 4. Training error of DNNs with respect to the number of hidden layers for two different magnitudes of initial DNN weights. Full line is the mean error of models, shaded area shows the range of error for central 66% of the models and the dashed line is the error of the best model.

Table 1. Free energy calculated for three proteins found in nature by using structures predicted by DNN and by DE.

Protein	Length	Best DNN	Mean DE	Best DE
1CB3	13	−4.6235	−2.1513	−6.7700
1CRN	46	−42.765	−64.948	−79.906
2EWH	98	−65.163	−148.32	−170.47

The training error of DNNs depends of the number of layers. This dependence is usually monotonically decreasing [16], but for this problem this is not the case (see Fig. 4). This can be attributed to the sensitivity of training to selection of initial DNN weights. DNNs were initialized using random matrices. Therefore, the magnitude of DNN output is exponentially dependent of the number of layers. Since initial weights have small components ($\ll 1$), this means that initial DNNs with small number of layers predict very folded structures, while initial DNNs with high number of layers predict practically straight structures. Figure 4 shows that initial DNN predictions should not be very folded nor very straight. Best models are somewhere in between.

The most accurate DNN models have three layers. Given that DNNs are able to partially solve an optimization problem this is a surprisingly shallow DNN architecture. Free energy of structures predicted by DNNs and by DE is shown in Table 1. It was found that gradient norm clipping is very beneficial for DNN training. Figure 5 shows the progress of DNN training with and without the use of gradient norm clipping. Occurrence of very high gradients is rare, however they substantially alter the progress of DNN training.

Using structures predicted by DNN in initial population of DE was found to be beneficial. When using predicted initial population, DE converges to lower

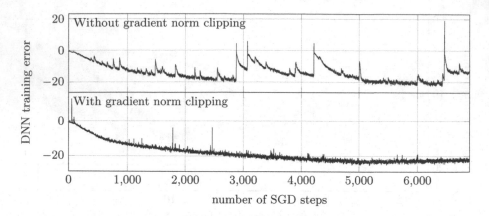

Fig. 5. DNN error during training via SGD. The upper plot shows the progress of usual SGD procedure, while the lower plot shows SGD progress when gradient norm has a predefined upper bound by using gradient norm clipping.

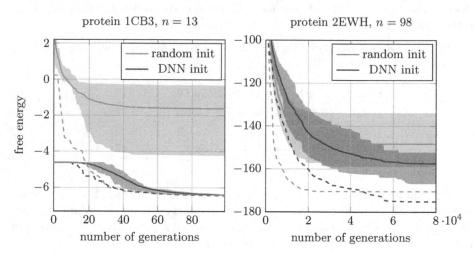

Fig. 6. Progress of 30 runs of DE by using a random initial population or initial population partially populated with solutions predicted by DNNs. Full line is the mean over all runs, shaded area shows the range of central 66% of runs and the dashed line shows the best run.

values of free energy (see Fig. 6). But the convergence is slightly less rapid for predicted population which could indicate that the population is actually more diverse. On the other hand, DE progresses are less dispersed among runs which means that less runs are needed to find a satisfactory solution. In case of 1CB3 protein the predicted structures are in fact so good that all DE runs converge to the best known solution in just 100 generations. For larger proteins the predicted solution are not as good, however the DE performs considerably better when using the predicted population.

6   Conclusion and Future Work

In this paper it is shown that deep neural networks can be trained to partially solve optimization problems belonging to a given class. The networks can be successfully trained using reinforcement learning method by knowing only the fitness function of the class of optimization problems. This is shown for the class of protein structure optimization problems. The predicted solutions were found to be good initial points for further optimization. Such trained networks can be used to acquire moderately good solutions of optimization problem when solution is needed very quickly. Therefore, the method is suitable for optimization problems that need to be solved repeatedly and is a step towards automatic heuristic construction.

For future work it should be possible to extend the method to combinatorial optimization problem where unified methodology should be further developed. The procedure of finding the best architecture of deep neural network could be more automated so that depth and width of the network is automatically found. The same goes for the training specification. Another opportunity for future work is to combine supervised learning approach with reinforcement learning approach so that the training is guided by both approaches simultaneously.

Acknowledgments. The authors acknowledge the financial support from the Slovenian Research Agency (research core funding No. P2-0098 and PR-07606) and from the European Union's Horizon 2020 research and innovation program under grant agreement No. 692286.

References

1. Cheng, J., Randall, A.Z., Sweredoski, M.J., Baldi, P.: SCRATCH: a protein structure and structural feature prediction server. Nucleic Acids Res. **33**(Suppl. 2), W72–W76 (2005)
2. Bošković, B., Brest, J.: Genetic algorithm with advanced mechanisms applied to the protein structure prediction in a hydrophobic-polar model and cubic lattice. Appl. Soft Comput. **45**, 61–70 (2016)
3. Stillinger, F.H., Head-Gordon, T., Hirshfeld, C.L.: Toy model for protein folding. Phys. Rev. E **48**(2), 1469 (1993)
4. Liang, F.: Annealing contour Monte Carlo algorithm for structure optimization in an off-lattice protein model. J. Chem. Phys. **120**(14), 6756–6763 (2004)
5. Kim, S.Y., Lee, S.B., Lee, J.: Structure optimization by conformational space annealing in an off-lattice protein model. Phys. Rev. E **72**(1), 011916 (2005)
6. Li, B., Lin, M., Liu, Q., Li, Y., Zhou, C.: Protein folding optimization based on 3D off-lattice model via an improved artificial bee colony algorithm. J. Mol. Model. **21**(10), 261 (2015)
7. Bošković, B., Brest, J.: Differential evolution for protein folding optimization based on a three-dimensional AB off-lattice model. J. Mol. Model. **22**(10), 252 (2016)
8. Pollastri, G., Przybylski, D., Rost, B., Baldi, P.: Improving the prediction of protein secondary structure in three and eight classes using recurrent neural networks and profiles. Proteins: Struct. Funct. Bioinf. **47**(2), 228–235 (2002)

9. Cheng, J., Sweredoski, M.J., Baldi, P.: Accurate prediction of protein disordered regions by mining protein structure data. Data Min. Knowl. Disc. **11**(3), 213–222 (2005)

10. Di Lena, P., Nagata, K., Baldi, P.: Deep architectures for protein contact map prediction. Bioinformatics **28**(19), 2449–2457 (2012)

11. Vidal, T., Crainic, T.G., Gendreau, M., Prins, C.: Heuristics for multi-attribute vehicle routing problems: a survey and synthesis. Eur. J. Oper. Res. **231**(1), 1–21 (2013)

12. Branke, J., Nguyen, S., Pickardt, C.W., Zhang, M.: Automated design of production scheduling heuristics: a review. IEEE Trans. Evol. Comput. **20**(1), 110–124 (2016)

13. Perez, A., MacCallum, J., Dill, K.A.: Using physics and heuristics in protein structure prediction. Biophys. J. **108**(2), 210a (2015)

14. Hornik, K.: Approximation capabilities of multilayer feedforward networks. Neural Netw. **4**(2), 251–257 (1991)

15. Dauphin, Y.N., Pascanu, R., Gulcehre, C., Cho, K., Ganguli, S., Bengio, Y.: Identifying and attacking the saddle point problem in high-dimensional non-convex optimization. In: Advances in Neural Information Processing Systems, pp. 2933–2941 (2014)

16. Goodfellow, I., Bengio, Y., Courville, A.: Deep Learning. MIT Press, Cambridge (2016). http://www.deeplearningbook.org

17. Silver, D., Lever, G., Heess, N., Degris, T., Wierstra, D., Riedmiller, M.: Deterministic policy gradient algorithms. In: ICML (2014)

18. Ling, A.C., Aydonat, U., O'Connell, S., Capalija, D., Chiu, G.R.: Creating high performance applications with Intel's FPGA OpenCL SDK. In: Proceedings of the 5th International Workshop on OpenCL. ACM (2017). Article No. 11

19. Bachmann, M., Arkın, H., Janke, W.: Multicanonical study of coarse-grained off-lattice models for folding heteropolymers. Phys. Rev. E **71**(3), 031906 (2005)

20. Parker, J., Guo, D., Hodges, R.: New hydrophilicity scale derived from high-performance liquid chromatography peptide retention data: correlation of predicted surface residues with antigenicity and X-ray-derived accessible sites. Biochemistry **25**(19), 5425–5432 (1986)

21. Wolfenden, R., Lewis, C.A., Yuan, Y., Carter, C.W.: Temperature dependence of amino acid hydrophobicities. Proc. Nat. Acad. Sci. **112**(24), 7484–7488 (2015)

22. Kingma, D., Ba, J.: Adam: a method for stochastic optimization. arXiv preprint arXiv:1412.6980 (2014)

23. Glorot, X., Bengio, Y.: Understanding the difficulty of training deep feedforward neural networks. In: Proceedings of the Thirteenth International Conference on Artificial Intelligence and Statistics, pp. 249–256 (2010)

Comparing Boundary Control Methods
for Firefly Algorithm

Tomas Kadavy[✉][iD], Michal Pluhacek[iD], Adam Viktorin[iD],
and Roman Senkerik[iD]

Tomas Bata University in Zlin, T. G. Masaryka 5555, Zlin, Czech Republic
{kadavy,pluhacek,aviktorin,senkerik}@utb.cz

Abstract. This paper compares four different methods for handling the roaming behavior of fireflies in the firefly algorithm. The problems of boundary constrained optimization forces the algorithm to actively keep the fireflies inside the feasible area of possible solutions. The recent CEC'17 benchmark suite is used for the performance comparison of the methods and the results are compared and tested for statistical significance.

Keywords: Firefly Algorithm · Boundary · Lévy flight

1 Introduction

Firefly Algorithm (FA) [1,2] is one of the modern and versatile optimization algorithms developed by Yang in 2008. Since then, the FA has proven its robust performance either on single objective [3] or many/multi-objective optimization problems [4]. Recently, many new modifications have been introduced to improve the results and overall quality of FA. Modifications like Lévy flights [5], or chaos-driven FA [6] show the large potential of this modern algorithm.

One of the tasks left to discuss lies in the question what to do if fireflies (or particles in general) try to violate defined boundaries by particular optimization problem. When optimizing the real problem, very often are optimized parameters limited. This is caused in many cases due to simple physical nature of the problem (for example length cannot be in negative numbers). The violation of particle could happen whenever a new position is evaluated thanks to the nature of the metaheuristic optimization algorithm. Select the most suitable border strategy is a difficult task as the numerous similar studies for PSO show [7,8].

Since there are no such studies for FA available in the literature, we have decided to perform and present this original experimental research. In this paper, three relatively common borders strategies (or rather methods) are implemented and compared on CEC'17 benchmark set [9]. Also, a new hypersphere border strategy [10], initially developed for PSO, is also tested and compared given its promising results on some test functions.

The paper is structured as follows. The FA and its Lévy flight modification are described in Sect. 2. The border strategies are in detail described in Sect. 3. The

P. Korošec et al. (Eds.): BIOMA 2018, LNCS 10835, pp. 163–173, 2018.
https://doi.org/10.1007/978-3-319-91641-5_14

experiment setup is detailed in Sect. 4. Section 5 contains statistical overviews of the results and performance comparisons obtained during the evaluation on benchmark set. Finally, the paper is concluded in Sect. 6.

2   Firefly Algorithm

This optimization nature-based algorithm was developed and introduced by Yang in 2008 [1]. The fundamental principle of this algorithm lies in simulating the mating behavior of fireflies at night when fireflies emit light to attract a suitable partner. The main idea of Firefly Algorithm (FA) is that the objective function value that is optimized is associated with the flashing light of these fireflies. The author for simplicity set a couple of rules to describe the algorithm itself:

- The brightness of each firefly is based on the objective function value.
- The attractiveness of a firefly is proportional to its brightness. This means that the less bright firefly is lured towards, the brighter firefly. The brightness depends on the environment or the medium in which fireflies are moving and decreases with the distance between each of them.
- All fireflies are sexless, and it means that each firefly can attract or be lured by any of the remaining ones.

The movement of one firefly towards another one is then defined by Eq. (1). Where $x_i^{'}$ is a new position of a firefly i, x_i is the current position of firefly i and x_j is a selected brighter firefly (with better objective function value). The α is a randomization parameter and $sign$ simply provides random direction -1 or 1.

$$x_i^{'} = x_i + \beta \cdot (x_j - x_i) + \alpha \cdot sign \tag{1}$$

The brightness I of a firefly is computed by the Eq. (2). This equation of brightness consists of three factors mentioned in the rules above. On the objective function value, the distance between two fireflies and the last factor is the absorption factor of a media in which fireflies are.

$$I = \frac{I_0}{1 + \gamma r^m} \tag{2}$$

Where I_o is the objective function value, the γ stands for the light absorption parameter of a media in which fireflies are and the m is another user-defined coefficient and it should be set $m \geq 1$. The variable r is the Euclidian distance (3) between the two compared fireflies.

$$r_{ij} = \sqrt{\sum_{k=1}^{d} (x_{i,k} - x_{j,k})^2} \tag{3}$$

Where r_{ij} is the Euclidian distance between fireflies x_i and x_j. The d is current dimension size of the optimized problem.

The attractiveness β (4) is proportional to brightness I as mentioned in rules above and so these equations are quite similar to each other. The β_0 is the initial attractiveness defined by the user, the γ is again the light absorption parameter and the r is once more the Euclidian distance. The m is also the same as in Eq. (2).

$$\beta = \frac{\beta_0}{1 + \gamma r^m} \tag{4}$$

One of the recent and quite commonly used modifications of FA lies in the introduction of Lévy flights [5, 11]. With this Lévy flights characteristic the new modification of FA is called Lévy-flight Firefly Algorithm (LFA). This modification only customizes the computation of the position of fireflies described originally in Eq. (1). The new modified version with Lévy flight is defined in (5).

$$x_i' = x_i + \beta \cdot (x_j - x_i) + \alpha \cdot sign \bigoplus Lévy \tag{5}$$

The Lévy stands for Lévy flight randomization together with λ being the randomization parameter as in the original equation. The product $\bigoplus$ means entrywise multiplications. The Lévy distribution is drawn as (6).

$$Lévy \sim u = t^{-\lambda} \tag{6}$$

Where parameter λ is another user-defined variable that controls the Lévy distribution described in [5] and it should be set in range $1 < \lambda \leq 3$. The pseudocode below shows the fundamentals of FA operations (Fig. 1).

```
1.  FA initialization
2.  while(terminal condition not met)
3.    for i = 1 to all fireflies
4.      for j = 1 to all fireflies
5.        if(Ij < Ii) then
6.          move xi to xj
7.          evaluate xi
8.        end if
9.      end for j
10.   end for i
11.   record the best firefly
12. end while
```

Fig. 1. FA pseudocode.

3   Border Strategies

Every time, when a single objective function optimization problem has defined a range where the best value is being found by the metaheuristic algorithm, one of the many difficult tasks could arise to an operator or a user. After each step of an algorithm, in this case after position update of a firefly, the new position should be checked if it lies in the appropriate range or boundaries (inside space of feasible solution). In case that the new position of the particle is outside this allowed region a certain correction has to be made. Several possible correction methods or strategies could do the trick. However, select the most appropriate is not an easy task since each of them could have a very different effect on the algorithm ability to achieve a good solution. For this paper, the few most common ones were selected and compared together to show how they could affect the FA on different benchmark functions.

3.1 Hard Borders

The particle (or in this case firefly) cannot cross the given boundaries in each dimension. This strategy is very simple to implement and is described as (7).

$$x_i' = \begin{cases} x_i = b^u, \; if \; x_i > b^u \\ x_i = b^l, \; if \; x_i < b^l \\ \quad x_i, \; otherwise \end{cases} \tag{7}$$

Where x_i is the position of i firefly before boundary check, the x_i' is a newly updated position after the boundary check and the b^u and b^l are the upper and lower boundary given to each dimension.

3.2 Random Position

If a firefly violates the boundary in any dimension, the new position for this firefly for a particular dimension is created between the lower and upper boundary (with a pseudo-random uniform distribution). Again this strategy is rather simple and very easy to implement.

3.3 Hypersphere

This strategy tries to simulate an endless hypersphere. To simplify this statement, an example is given. If a firefly violates upper boundary limit, it appears then in the search space but from the lower boundary. In other words, the upper boundary is neighboring the lower one in corresponding dimension and vice versa.

This strategy also brings one interesting and also an important feature. The firefly has now two options how to achieve a new position when flying towards another firefly. The new possible way is throughout the boundaries which are now passable. The modification of previous Eq. (5) is given in (8).

$$x_i' = x_i + \beta \cdot v_{ij} + \alpha \cdot sign \bigoplus Lévy \tag{8}$$

Where the v_{ij} is the vector of difference between particles i and j defined as (9).

$$v_{ij} = \begin{cases} \hat{v}_{ij}, if \; |\hat{v}_{ij}| \leq d \\ \hat{v}_{ij} \; mod \; (-d), if \; (|\hat{v}_{ij}| > d \wedge |\hat{v}_{ij}| > 0) \\ \hat{v}_{ij} \; mod \; (+d), if \; (|\hat{v}_{ij}| > d \wedge |\hat{v}_{ij}| \leq 0) \end{cases} \tag{9}$$

The $\hat{v}_{ij}$ and range d are computed by formulas (10) and (11), where b^u and b^l are again the upper boundary and lower boundary limits and x_i and x_j are the fireflies i and j.

$$\hat{v}_{ij} = x_j - x_i \tag{10}$$

$$d = \frac{|b^u - b^l|}{2} \tag{11}$$

3.4   Reflection

The reflection strategy [7] reflects the particle back to feasible space of solution if it tries to violate the defined borders. This strategy tries to emulate the reflection characteristic of for example a mirror. For violated dimension, the correction of a position of a particle is computed as (12). Where again the b^u and b^l are the upper boundary limit and lower boundary limit.

$$x_i' = \begin{cases} x_i' = b^u - (x_i - b^u), & if \ x_i > b^u \\ x_i' = b^l + (b^l - x_i), & if \ x_i < b^l \\ x_i, \ otherwise \end{cases} \tag{12}$$

4   Experimental Setup

The experiments were performed on a set of well-known benchmark functions CEC'17 which are detailly described in [9]. The tested dimensions were 10 and 30. The maximal number of function evaluation was set as $10\,000 \cdot dim$ (dimension size). The lower and upper boundary was as $b^l = -100$ and $b^u = 100$ according to CEC'17 definition. The number of fireflies was set to 40 for both dimension sizes. Every test function was repeated for 30 independent runs and the results were statistically evaluated. The benchmark itself includes 30 test functions in four categories: unimodal, multimodal, hybrid and composite types. The global minimum of each function is easy to determine as it is $100 \cdot f_i$ where i is an order of the particular test function.

The parameters of LFA were experimentally set as $\alpha = 0.2, \lambda = 1.5, \gamma = 0.01$, $\beta_0 = 0.5$, and $m = 1$.

5   Results

The results of performed experiments are given in this section. Firstly, the results overviews and comparisons are presented in Tables 1 and 2, which contain the simple statistic like mean, std. dev., min. and max. values. Further, examples of convergence behavior of the compared methods are given in Figs. 2, 3, 4 and 5.

Furthermore, we present the Friedman ranks with critical distance evaluated according to the Bonferroni Dunn post-hoc test for multiple comparisons. The visual outputs of multiple comparisons with rankings are given in Fig. 6. The dashed line represents the critical distance from the best boundary method (the

Table 1. Statistical results for dimension 10 (mean, std. dev., min., max.)

Function	Hard				Random				Hypersphere				Reflection			
	mean	std	min	max	mean	std	min	max	mean	std	min	max	mean	std	min	max
f_1	1.38E06	7.85E05	4.81E05	4.39E06	1.44E06	6.64E05	3.84E05	3.10E06	6.42E09	6.12E09	1.97E10	3.10E08	1.55E06	1.10E06	5.17E05	5.28E06
f_2	4.36E05	1.27E06	7.62E05	5.32E06	1.62E05	3.65E05	4.47E03	1.88E06	2.18E12	1.10E13	4.33E05	6.14E13	3.26E05	1.37E06	2.79E03	7.65E06
f_3	2.59E03	1.97E03	5.67E02	9.83E03	2.51E03	1.71E03	5.54E02	8.09E03	1.74E04	9.02E03	4.20E04	6.72E03	2.44E03	1.59E03	6.99E02	7.70E03
f_4	4.09E02	1.21E01	4.00E02	4.69E02	4.13E02	1.49E02	4.01E02	4.57E02	7.52E02	4.60E02	2.31E03	4.35E02	4.11E02	1.37E01	4.00E02	4.67E02
f_5	5.37E02	1.11E01	5.11E02	5.63E02	5.43E02	1.12E01	5.18E02	5.70E02	5.67E02	2.04E01	5.20E02	6.11E02	5.38E02	9.92E00	5.14E02	5.65E02
f_6	6.13E02	7.79E00	6.00E02	6.29E02	6.17E02	6.29E00	6.04E02	6.33E02	6.38E02	1.05E01	6.14E02	6.61E02	6.15E02	8.07E00	6.03E02	6.36E02
f_7	7.37E02	5.74E00	7.23E02	7.49E02	7.36E02	5.64E00	7.26E02	7.49E02	7.51E02	9.53E01	7.54E02	1.08E03	7.36E02	5.78E00	7.22E02	7.48E02
f_8	8.21E02	5.68E00	8.13E02	8.34E02	8.21E02	5.47E00	8.11E02	8.33E02	8.39E02	1.37E01	8.17E02	8.80E02	8.20E02	5.18E00	8.10E02	8.29E02
f_9	9.12E02	2.84E02	9.00E02	1.03E03	9.06E02	1.13E01	9.00E02	9.40E02	1.52E03	3.48E02	9.00E02	2.44E03	9.10E02	2.60E01	9.00E02	1.04E03
f_{10}	1.98E03	1.91E02	1.48E03	2.28E03	2.01E03	2.47E02	1.43E03	2.55E03	2.04E03	3.82E02	1.50E03	2.95E03	1.96E03	2.93E02	1.32E03	2.50E03
f_{11}	1.15E03	3.77E01	1.11E03	1.25E03	1.14E03	2.99E01	1.11E03	1.28E03	1.64E03	6.23E02	4.12E03	1.12E03	1.13E03	1.73E01	1.11E03	1.17E03
f_{12}	8.09E05	7.21E05	4.67E04	2.75E06	1.22E06	1.26E06	1.30E05	6.23E06	6.03E06	1.70E07	9.29E04	9.70E07	5.09E05	6.25E05	3.55E04	3.07E06
f_{13}	8.00E03	2.79E03	2.35E03	1.54E04	8.71E03	3.82E03	3.03E03	2.09E04	1.29E04	3.70E03	2.90E04	5.62E03	7.50E03	2.92E03	2.71E03	1.44E04
f_{14}	1.96E03	7.55E02	1.44E03	4.23E03	2.34E03	1.32E03	1.49E03	8.45E03	2.54E03	1.13E03	1.47E03	5.73E03	1.99E03	8.66E02	1.44E03	6.13E03
f_{15}	4.12E03	2.32E03	1.89E03	1.16E04	4.15E03	1.64E03	1.85E03	3.25E03	3.25E03	9.22E02	1.82E03	5.45E03	3.88E03	1.83E03	1.67E03	8.49E03
f_{16}	1.90E03	9.21E01	1.69E03	2.05E03	1.89E03	8.27E01	1.74E03	2.02E03	1.91E03	9.81E01	1.73E03	2.11E03	1.89E03	1.02E02	1.61E03	2.01E03
f_{17}	1.75E03	1.42E01	1.72E03	1.79E03	1.75E03	1.25E01	1.72E03	1.78E03	1.78E03	3.24E01	1.73E03	1.86E03	1.76E03	1.19E02	1.73E03	1.79E03
f_{18}	6.42E03	5.73E03	2.31E03	2.74E03	5.81E03	4.31E03	2.15E03	2.19E03	1.27E04	7.65E03	3.31E03	4.18E04	6.23E03	3.73E03	1.96E03	1.69E04
f_{19}	3.09E03	1.40E03	1.94E03	7.63E03	3.14E03	1.33E03	1.93E03	8.12E03	4.09E03	2.51E03	1.94E03	1.29E04	3.42E03	1.41E03	1.95E03	8.04E03
f_{20}	2.12E03	4.97E01	2.04E03	2.19E03	2.12E03	4.79E01	2.05E03	2.20E03	2.14E03	6.69E03	2.02E03	2.28E03	2.12E03	5.49E03	2.03E03	2.20E03
f_{21}	2.28E03	5.75E03	2.20E03	2.35E03	2.30E03	5.58E03	2.30E03	2.36E03	2.33E03	4.46E01	2.21E03	2.40E03	2.30E03	4.49E01	2.20E03	2.35E03
f_{22}	2.30E03	1.22E01	2.24E03	2.31E03	2.15E03	2.15E00	2.15E03	2.30E03	2.54E03	3.57E02	2.28E03	3.65E03	2.30E03	3.21E00	2.30E03	2.32E03
f_{23}	2.65E03	4.08E01	2.46E03	2.69E03	2.66E03	2.01E01	2.63E03	2.72E03	2.77E03	5.28E01	2.65E03	2.87E03	2.65E03	6.45E01	2.32E03	2.71E03
f_{24}	2.64E03	1.35E02	2.50E03	2.81E03	2.65E03	1.26E02	2.50E03	2.82E03	2.78E03	1.42E02	2.78E03	2.93E03	2.64E03	1.26E02	2.50E03	2.81E03
f_{25}	2.92E03	2.21E01	2.89E03	2.94E03	2.91E03	5.82E01	2.61E03	2.94E03	3.18E03	3.00E02	3.18E03	3.99E03	2.92E03	2.16E01	2.89E03	2.94E03
f_{26}	3.02E03	3.59E02	2.61E03	3.91E03	3.02E03	3.51E02	2.62E03	4.24E03	3.89E03	5.16E02	4.24E03	4.87E03	3.11E03	3.64E02	2.60E03	4.28E03
f_{27}	3.13E03	2.39E01	3.10E03	3.19E03	3.16E03	2.88E01	3.11E03	3.22E03	3.19E03	5.82E00	3.19E03	3.20E03	3.15E03	3.22E01	3.10E03	3.24E03
f_{28}	3.28E03	1.42E02	2.93E03	3.48E03	3.39E03	1.18E02	3.10E03	3.49E03	3.29E03	8.29E00	0.82E00	3.30E03	3.31E03	1.35E02	3.10E03	3.48E03
f_{29}	3.24E03	3.31E01	3.18E03	3.31E03	3.24E03	3.75E01	3.18E03	3.34E03	3.33E03	8.19E01	3.33E03	3.49E03	3.26E03	4.82E01	3.19E03	3.38E03
f_{30}	4.20E05	4.19E05	1.38E04	1.94E06	6.45E05	5.52E05	3.24E04	2.00E06	3.18E05	5.64E05	3.94E03	2.74E06	5.28E05	4.94E05	5.30E04	2.16E06

Table 2. Statistical results for dimension 30 (mean, std. dev., min., max.)

Function	Hard				Random				Hypersphere				Reflection			
	mean	std. dev.	min.	max.	mean	std. dev.	min.	max.	mean	std. dev.	min.	max.	mean	std. dev.	min.	max.
f_1	1.02E10	1.90E09	7.20E09	1.42E10	1.07E10	2.39E10	7.00E09	1.64E10	1.21E11	1.71E11	9.19E10	1.65E11	1.03E10	2.85E09	5.89E09	1.82E10
f_2	1.95E34	5.28E34	5.88E28	2.24E35	8.16E33	2.54E34	8.37E27	1.34E35	1.58E53	8.77E53	7.08E43	4.88E54	5.98E34	2.20E35	5.15E28	1.16E36
f_3	6.46E04	1.39E04	3.81E04	9.88E04	5.59E04	1.06E04	3.84E04	7.90E04	1.84E05	3.36E04	1.32E05	2.64E05	6.05E04	9.94E03	4.49E02	8.10E04
f_4	2.23E03	4.67E02	1.36E03	3.49E03	2.46E03	4.65E02	1.69E03	3.80E03	4.25E04	1.04E04	2.37E04	6.63E04	2.30E03	4.98E02	1.44E03	3.90E03
f_5	7.89E02	2.33E01	7.50E02	8.50E02	7.90E02	1.51E01	7.49E02	8.11E02	1.12E03	5.41E01	1.02E03	1.20E03	7.92E02	2.19E01	7.21E02	8.29E02
f_6	6.60E02	6.41E03	6.49E02	6.73E02	6.61E02	4.39E00	6.50E02	6.69E02	7.14E02	8.65E00	6.95E02	7.31E02	6.60E02	5.40E00	6.48E02	6.72E02
f_7	1.08E03	3.78E01	1.01E03	1.15E03	1.06E03	3.40E01	1.00E05	1.13E03	3.19E03	2.91E02	2.42E03	3.83E03	1.07E03	2.94E01	9.93E02	1.13E03
f_8	1.05E03	2.06E01	1.01E03	1.09E03	1.06E03	1.51E01	1.02E03	1.09E03	1.34E03	2.90E01	1.28E03	1.40E03	1.05E03	1.55E01	1.03E03	1.10E03
f_9	5.54E03	1.00E03	3.58E03	7.98E03	5.17E03	6.77E02	3.28E03	6.74E03	2.20E04	3.26E03	1.36E04	2.93E04	5.10E03	8.09E02	3.72E03	7.08E03
f_{10}	8.11E03	5.25E02	6.53E03	8.93E03	8.10E03	4.61E02	6.84E03	8.82E03	9.08E03	3.20E02	7.92E03	9.57E03	8.07E03	3.82E02	6.88E03	8.69E03
f_{11}	3.19E03	9.12E02	2.06E03	5.87E03	3.29E03	6.67E02	2.00E03	4.66E03	2.28E04	6.89E03	1.17E04	3.73E04	3.57E03	1.20E03	2.13E03	6.84E03
f_{12}	7.77E08	2.98E08	2.75E08	1.33E09	1.01E09	3.55E08	3.77E08	1.99E09	2.20E10	6.24E09	9.69E09	3.16E10	8.29E08	3.48E08	2.87E08	1.67E09
f_{13}	1.80E07	9.75E06	4.25E06	5.10E07	1.89E07	9.93E06	4.91E06	4.85E07	8.34E09	5.93E09	5.78E08	2.08E10	2.00E07	1.15E07	6.51E06	5.17E07
f_{14}	1.35E05	1.12E05	1.39E04	3.84E05	2.76E05	2.74E05	1.80E04	1.17E06	2.13E06	3.05E06	8.41E04	1.29E07	1.58E05	1.12E05	7.61E03	4.33E05
f_{15}	1.37E06	1.13E06	2.09E05	6.76E06	1.13E06	8.47E05	1.78E05	3.53E06	1.32E08	2.26E08	1.84E06	1.17E09	1.30E06	7.37E05	1.49E05	3.83E06
f_{16}	3.31E03	2.73E02	2.72E03	3.80E03	3.27E03	2.07E02	2.72E03	3.60E03	7.52E03	1.84E03	4.95E03	1.43E04	3.18E03	2.39E02	2.72E03	3.55E03
f_{17}	2.18E03	1.26E02	2.00E03	2.49E03	2.21E03	1.62E02	1.92E03	2.55E03	4.36E03	1.19E03	2.66E03	8.19E03	2.18E03	1.18E02	1.96E03	2.44E03
f_{18}	6.62E05	4.75E05	1.48E05	1.98E06	6.19E05	3.83E05	1.30E05	1.84E06	1.04E08	1.28E08	5.71E05	5.38E08	8.79E05	8.66E05	1.63E05	4.66E06
f_{19}	3.35E06	1.96E06	8.50E05	8.56E06	3.42E06	2.43E06	7.65E05	1.06E07	1.03E09	1.13E09	1.59E06	4.05E09	3.54E06	2.09E06	5.62E05	9.40E06
f_{20}	2.58E03	1.14E02	2.38E03	2.84E03	2.53E03	1.20E02	2.35E03	2.80E03	3.07E03	1.84E02	2.67E03	3.39E03	2.52E03	1.15E02	2.36E03	2.86E03
f_{21}	2.52E03	4.76E01	2.33E03	2.57E03	2.52E03	3.97E01	2.38E03	2.58E03	2.88E03	4.66E01	2.72E03	2.96E03	2.53E03	4.14E01	2.34E03	2.58E03
f_{22}	3.19E03	4.25E02	2.68E03	4.90E03	3.41E03	4.66E02	2.76E03	4.82E03	1.03E04	3.44E02	9.15E03	1.08E04	3.42E03	4.51E02	2.77E03	5.13E03
f_{23}	3.01E03	6.04E01	2.81E03	3.09E03	3.09E03	4.45E01	3.02E03	3.20E03	3.80E03	1.27E02	3.50E03	4.01E03	3.04E03	4.73E01	2.94E03	3.14E03
f_{24}	3.13E03	2.90E01	3.07E03	3.19E03	3.19E03	4.26E01	3.13E03	3.30E03	4.06E03	1.49E02	3.71E03	4.28E03	3.16E03	4.85E01	3.08E03	3.27E03
f_{25}	3.15E03	6.21E01	3.05E03	3.32E03	3.14E03	4.54E01	3.05E03	3.24E03	1.55E04	3.67E03	9.10E03	2.70E04	3.13E03	4.83E01	3.04E03	3.24E03
f_{26}	6.03E03	7.90E02	4.48E03	7.34E03	6.00E03	4.29E03	3.50E03	7.69E03	1.60E04	1.62E03	1.26E04	1.87E04	5.83E03	7.22E02	4.26E03	7.23E03
f_{27}	3.47E03	4.33E01	3.39E03	3.55E03	3.61E03	5.43E01	3.50E03	3.74E03	3.20E03	6.16E-5	3.20E03	3.20E03	3.20E03	1.49E-4	3.20E03	3.20E03
f_{28}	3.67E03	1.10E02	3.44E03	3.89E03	3.75E03	9.27E01	3.49E03	3.91E03	3.30E03	7.85E-5	3.30E03	3.30E03	3.30E03	1.28E-4	3.30E03	3.30E03
f_{29}	4.47E03	1.52E02	4.20E03	4.74E03	4.54E03	1.88E02	4.22E03	4.86E03	2.05E04	2.68E04	5.35E03	1.20E05	4.55E03	1.94E02	3.88E03	4.95E03
f_{30}	1.14E07	5.08E06	5.78E06	2.47E07	9.77E06	5.23E06	2.36E06	2.61E07	1.67E09	1.06E09	1.13E08	4.50E09	1.01E07	4.51E06	4.26E06	1.98E07

lowest mean rank). The critical distance (CD) value for this experiment has been calculated as 0.8586; according to the definition given in (13) and value $q_a = 2.5758$; using $k = 4$ boundary methods and a number of data sets $N = 30$ (30 repeated runs). From the results, it is noticeable, that the hard border and the reflective boundaries are the most favorable methods among the four compared.

$$CD = q_a \sqrt{k\,(k+1)\,/\,(6N)} \tag{13}$$

The illustrative comparisons depicted in Figs. 2, 3, 4 and 5 supported by the results of Friedmann rank tests lend weight to the argument that the hypersphere strategy often gives the much slower convergence speed. Although, there are two exceptions to this statement (Figs. 4 and 5). The other strategies frequently reach almost the same results. The differences between these strategies become noticeable with the increase of the dimension size.

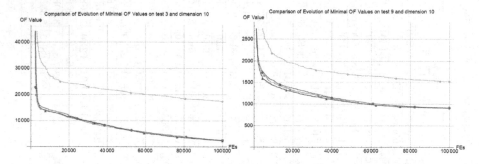

Fig. 2. Convergence plots of CEC2017 test functions *f3* (left) and *f9* (right) in 10*D*. The blue line stands for Hard borders strategy, the orange line is for Random position, the Hypersphere is in green color and the Reflection is in red. (Color figure online)

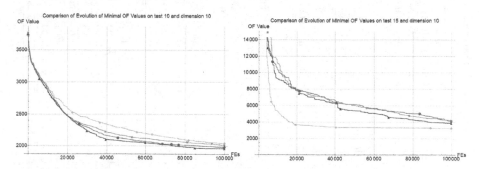

Fig. 3. Convergence plots of CEC2017 test functions *f10* (left) and *f15* (right) in 10*D*. The blue line stands for Hard borders strategy, the orange line is for Random position, the Hypersphere is in green color and the Reflection is in red. (Color figure online)

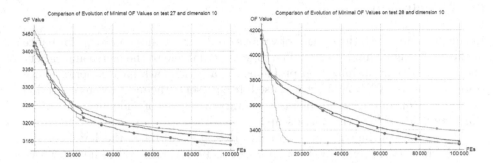

Fig. 4. Convergence plots of CEC2017 test functions *f27* (left) and *f28* (right) in 10*D*. The blue line stands for Hard borders strategy, the orange line is for Random position, the Hypersphere is in green color and the Reflection is in red. (Color figure online)

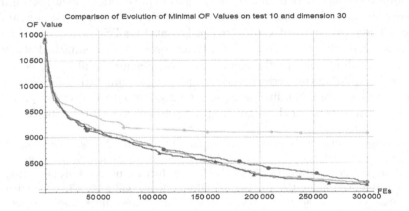

Fig. 5. Convergence graph for f_{10} dimension 30. The blue line stands for Hard borders strategy, the orange line is for Random position, the Hypersphere is in green color and the Reflection is in red. (Color figure online)

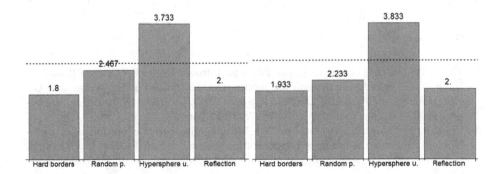

Fig. 6. Friedmann rank test comparison on CEC2017 test functions in 10*D* (left) and 30*D* (right) in 10*D*.

6   Conclusion

In this original study, the impact of various border strategies on the performance of the firefly algorithm is tested. The topic is actual due to the increasing variety and complexity of optimization problems. As a benchmark for the performance comparisons, the CEC 2017 set was used. It represents the most recent collection of artificial optimization problems that vary in terms of modality and other characteristics of the fitness landscape.

It may be concluded, that according to statistical data, the hard borders and the reflection boundary strategy seem to be favorable over the other two (random with slightly worse performance and hypersphere).

However, it seems that in the most cases, the border strategy does not have a significant impact on the performance of the method (especially in lower dimensions). The hypersphere boundary model stands out, mostly in the negative way. Despite the fact that remaining strategies behave almost identical on most problems, the most favorable strategies could be either the reflection or random position. These two strategies are often picked also for PSO [8].

Despite that, the results of this study are useful as an empirical study for researchers dealing with firefly algorithm. This research will continue in the future with exploring the performance of firefly algorithm with different boundary strategies on different fitness landscape models and real-world problems, especially with a focus on the algorithm setup to achieve the best performance.

Acknowledgements. This work was supported by the Ministry of Education, Youth and Sports of the Czech Republic within the National Sustainability Programme Project no. LO1303 (MSMT-7778/2014), further by the European Regional Development Fund under the Project CEBIA-Tech no. CZ.1.05/2.1.00/03.0089 and by Internal Grant Agency of Tomas Bata University under the Projects no. IGA/CebiaTech/2018/003. This work is also based upon support by COST (European Cooperation in Science & Technology) under Action CA15140, Improving Applicability of Nature-Inspired Optimisation by Joining Theory and Practice (ImAppNIO), and Action IC406, High-Performance Modelling and Simulation for Big Data Applications (cHiPSet).

References

1. Yang, X.S.: Algorithms N.I.M., pp. 242–246. Luniver Press, Beckington (2008)
2. Yang, X.-S.: Firefly algorithms for multimodal optimization. In: Watanabe, O., Zeugmann, T. (eds.) SAGA 2009. LNCS, vol. 5792, pp. 169–178. Springer, Heidelberg (2009). https://doi.org/10.1007/978-3-642-04944-6_14
3. Oosumi, R., Tamura, K., Yasuda, K.: Novel single-objective optimization problem and firefly algorithm-based optimization method. In: 2016 IEEE International Conference on Systems, Man, and Cybernetics (SMC), pp. 001011–001015. IEEE (2016)
4. Yang, X.S.: Multiobjective firefly algorithm for continuous optimization. Eng. Comput. **29**(2), 175–184 (2013)

5. Yang, X.S.: Firefly algorithm, lévy flights and global optimization. In: Bramer, M., Ellis, R., Petridis, M. (eds.) Research and Development in Intelligent Systems XXVI, pp. 209–218. Springer, London (2010). https://doi.org/10.1007/978-1-84882-983-1_15
6. dos Santos Coelho, L., Mariani, V.C.: Firefly algorithm approach based on chaotic tinkerbell map applied to multivariable PID controller tuning. Comput. Math. Appl. **64**(8), 2371–2382 (2012)
7. Helwig, S., Branke, J., Mostaghim, S.: Experimental analysis of bound handling techniques in particle swarm optimization. IEEE Trans. Evol. Comput. **17**(2), 259–271 (2013)
8. Kadavy, T., Pluhacek, M., Viktorin, A., Senkerik, R.: Comparing border strategies for roaming particles on single and multi-swarm PSO. In: Silhavy, R., Senkerik, R., Kominkova Oplatkova, Z., Prokopova, Z., Silhavy, P. (eds.) CSOC 2017. AISC, vol. 573, pp. 528–536. Springer, Cham (2017). https://doi.org/10.1007/978-3-319-57261-1_52
9. Awad, N., Ali, M., Liang, J., Qu, B., Suganthan, P.: Problem definitions and evaluation criteria for the CEC 2017 special session and competition on single objective bound constrained real-parameter numerical optimization. Technical Report. NTU, Singapore (2016)
10. Kadavy, T., Pluhacek, M., Viktorin, A., Senkerik, R.: Hypersphere universe boundary method comparison on HCLPSO and PSO. In: Martínez de Pisón, F.J., Urraca, R., Quintián, H., Corchado, E. (eds.) HAIS 2017. LNCS (LNAI), vol. 10334, pp. 173–182. Springer, Cham (2017). https://doi.org/10.1007/978-3-319-59650-1_15
11. Barthelemy, P., Bertolotti, J., Wiersma, D.S.: A lévy flight for light. Nature **453**(7194), 495 (2008)

A New Binary Encoding Scheme
in Genetic Algorithm for Solving
the Capacitated Vehicle Routing Problem

Stanley Jefferson de A. Lima$^{(\boxtimes)}$ and Sidnei Alves de Araújo

Informatics and Knowledge Management Graduate Program,
Universidade Nove de Julho – UNINOVE, São Paulo, SP, Brazil
stanleyjefferson@outlook.com, saraujo@uni9.pro.br
http://www.uninove.br

Abstract. In the last decades the Vehicle Routing Problem (VRP) and
its ramifications, including the Capacitated Vehicle Routing Problem
(CVRP), have attracted the attention of researchers mainly because their
presence in many practical situations. Due to the difficulties encountered
in their solutions, such problems are usually solved by means of heuristic
and metaheuristics algorithms, among which is the Genetic Algorithm
(GA). The solution of CVRP using GA requires a solution encoding step,
which demands a special care to avoid high computational cost and to
ensure population diversity that is essential for the convergence of GA
to global optimal or sub-optimal solutions. In this work, we investigated
a new binary encoding scheme employed by GA for solving the CVRP.
Conducted experiments demonstrated that the proposed binary encoding
is able to provide good solutions and is suitable for practical applications
that require low computational cost.

Keywords: Genetic Algorithm · Solution encoding
Chromosome representation · Capacitated Vehicle Routing Problem

1 Introduction

Optimization of the logistics system has become one of the most important
aspects of the supply chain during the last three decades [1]. In this context,
many researchers have invested their efforts in solving various problems in this
segment, among them is the Vehicle Routing Problem (VRP).

In general, the VRP consists in defining the routes that a set of vehicles must
follow to supply the demand of certain customers, respecting the operational
restrictions imposed by the context that they are inserted. The most common
objectives of the VRP are minimize the total distance traveled, improve the
transport time, minimize the number of vehicles needed and reduce the total
cost of the routes [2]. One of the main ramifications of the VRP is the Capacitated Vehicle Routing Problem (CVRP), which is considered in this work and
explained in detail in Sect. 2.1.

© Springer International Publishing AG, part of Springer Nature 2018
P. Korošec et al. (Eds.): BIOMA 2018, LNCS 10835, pp. 174–184, 2018.
https://doi.org/10.1007/978-3-319-91641-5_15

In the literature there are several proposals to solve the VRP (and its ramifications) using different heuristic and meta-heuristics techniques, among which
are: Tabu Search, Genetic Algorithms, Simulated Annealing, Ant Colony Optimization, Particle Swarm Optimization, Variable Neighborhood Search, and
Hybrid Meta-Heuristics [3]. The Genetic Algorithm (GA) stand out by its versa-
tility of construction and the good results that it has been demonstrated in solving complex problems, including VRP, as can be seen in Lau et al. [4]; Bermudez
et al. [5]; Wang and Lu [6]; Lee and Nazif [2]; Tasan and Gen [7]; Ursani et al.
[8]; Lu and Vincent [9]; Kuo et al. [10]; Vidal et al. [11]; Reiter and Gutjahr [12];
Osaba et al. [13] and Lima et al. [14].

A trivial way of encoding solutions for the VRP using GA is through a three-
dimensional binary matrix in which the rows are associated with the vehicles, the
columns with the costumers and the depth with the visitation order. However,
this encoding scheme demands high computational cost and may be inefficient
in terms of population diversity, which is essential to promote the convergence
to global optimum or sub-optimal solutions. Thus, many studies found in the
literature has shown concern about how to encode VRP solutions.

In this context, and differently from all above mentioned works which explore
improvements in the heuristic and meta-heuristic algorithms, this work is focused
in more efficient ways to encode solutions in GA. Specifically, we are proposing
a new binary encoding scheme in GA for Solving the CVRP, which constitutes
the main contribution of this work.

2   Theorectical Background

2.1   Capacitated Vehicle Routing Problem (CVRP)

The CVRP is one of the most basic version of VRP. In this problem all customers
have their demands previously defined which must be attend entirely by a fleet
of homogeneous vehicles, all of them running from only distribution center. In
the CVRP, just the vehicle capacity restriction is imposed [15], that is, the sum
of the demand of all customers belonging to a route does not exceed the capacity
of vehicle used to execute that route. Figure 1 illustrates an example of CVRP,
which involves two vehicles for meeting the demands of eighteen geographically
dispersed customers.

Let be $G = (V, E)$ a graph in which $V = 0 \ldots n$ is the set of vertices that
represent the customers and E the set of edges, representing the paths connecting
the customers to each other and to the distribution center. Each edge (v_i, vj) has
associated a cost C_{ij} of the path between the costumers represented by vertices
i and j. When $C_{ij} = C_{ji}$, the problem is known as symmetrical, otherwise the
problem is identified as asymmetrical. A set of K identical vehicles with capacity
c_v is allocated to the distribution center. For each customer v is associated a
demand d_v, and for the distribution center is defined $d_0 = 0$.

In summary, the CVRP consists of finding a set of routes, where each route
is traveled by a vehicle, with the objective to minimize the total cost of the
routes (TC), respecting the following restrictions: (1) each route must start and

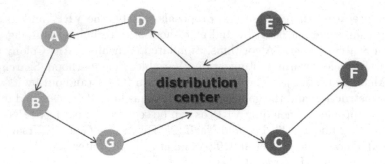

Fig. 1. Example of routing with the vehicles starting from a distribution center.

finish at the distribution center; (2) each customer must be visited just only time and (3) the sum of the customers' demands included in a route cannot exceed the vehicle's capacity. According to Vieira [3] the CVRP can be mathematically formulated as follows:

$$\text{Minimize } TC = \sum_{i=0}^{nc} \sum_{j=0, j\neq i}^{nc} \sum_{k=1}^{K} C_{ij} x_{ijk} \tag{1}$$

$$\text{Subject to } \sum_{k=1}^{K} \sum_{j=1}^{nc} x_{0jk} \leq K \tag{2}$$

$$\sum_{j=1}^{nc} x_{0jk} = \sum_{j=1}^{nc} x_{j0k} = 1, k = 1, \ldots, K \tag{3}$$

$$\sum_{k=1}^{K} \sum_{j=0}^{nc} x_{ijk} = 1, i = 1, \ldots, nc \tag{4}$$

$$\sum_{j=0}^{nc} x_{ijk} - \sum_{j=0}^{nc} x_{ijk} = 0, k = 1, \ldots, K i = 1, \ldots, nc \tag{5}$$

$$\sum_{k=1}^{K} \sum_{i \in S} \sum_{j \in S} x_{ijk} \leq |S| - v(S), \forall S \subseteq V/\{0\}, |S| \geq 2 \tag{6}$$

$$\sum_{i=1}^{nc} d_i \sum_{i=0, j\neq i} x_{ijk} \leq cv, k = 1, \ldots, K \tag{7}$$

$$x_{ijk} \in \{0,1\}, i = 1, \ldots, nc, j = 1, \ldots, nc, k = 1, \ldots, K \tag{8}$$

where: d_i is the demand of customer i; k: vehicle; K: set of vehicles; S: set of customers; nc: Number of customers; $v(S)$: Minimum number of vehicles to attend S; cv: Capacity of vehicles; c_{ij}: cost of the path from customer i to customer j; TC: total cost of the routes; x_{ijk}: path from customer i to customer j with vehicle k.

The Eq. 2 ensures that K vehicles will be used, while the Eq. 3 guarantees that each route has its beginning and ending at the distribution center. Equation 4 defines that customers must be attended exactly one time and the Eq. 5 keeps the flow ensuring that a vehicle arrives at a customer and out of it, preventing that the route ends prematurely. The Eq. 6 prevents the formulation of routes that do not include the distribution center. In this restriction, $v(S)$ represents the minimum number of vehicles required to attend a set of customers S. To ensure that the number of vehicles used to attend the customers of set S is not less than $v(S)$, the restriction 6 establishes, indirectly, that the capacity of the vehicle is not exceeded. However, to let this explicit, the Eq. 7 is used to formulate the capacity restriction.

Finally, the Eq. 9 is used to evaluate the solutions generated by GA. It reflects the value of the objective function (OF) or fitness and involves the number of vehicles used in the solution, violated restrictions (Eqs. 2 to 7) and the total cost of routes (Eq. 1).

$$OF = TC + KW_v + nrW_r \qquad (9)$$

where: W_v is the weight assigned to the number of vehicles used in the solution; nr is the number of violated restrictions and W_r is the weight given to the violated restrictions.

2.2   Genetic Algorithm (GA)

The GA is an evolutionary computational technique that simulates the mechanisms of natural selection, genetics and evolution. In the last decades it has been employed in several applications to solve complex optimization problems. Its bias is how much better an individual adapts to its environment, the greater their chances of surviving and generating offspring [16]. A GA individual represents a solution to the problem being solved. Each individual is defined as a chromosome, consisting of genes, which represent variables of the problem, and each position of a gene is defined as an allele.

In GA, the crossover operation consists in recombination of genes from selected individuals, responsible to reproduce descendants more adapted to the next generation. After a certain number of generations, it is common to occur the loss of population diversity, which results in the premature stopping of the GA leading to local optimum solutions. To avoid this problem, the mutation is applied at a given rate of individuals (usually by randomly changing the alleles), aiming to change the characteristic of the genes [17].

Other concepts associated with GAs are:

- **Genotype:** is related to the population in the computation space, in which the solutions are represented to be easily understood and manipulated by computers [18,19].

- **Phenotype:** is related to the population in the real world solution space, in which the solutions are represented to be interpreted in real world situations [18,19].
- **Encoding and Decoding:** in the most cases, the phenotype and genotype spaces are different. Encoding is an operation that transforms a solution from the phenotype to genotype space, while decoding is responsible by transforming a solution from the genotype to the phenotype space. The main encoding schemes are: Binary, Value (integer, float, string, etc.), Permutation and Tree [19,20]. Since these operations are carried out repeatedly during the fitness value calculation (evaluation) in a GA, as illustrated in Fig. 2, they need to be simple and fast.

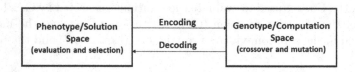

Fig. 2. Encoding/decoding operations.

Based on the above explanation, it is observed that the encoding solution scheme is an important step in the development of GA, since it is directly related to the quality of the solutions found, as well as the computational time spent to find them.

2.3   Some Recent Encoding Schemes Used in GA for Solving the VRP and Its Ramifications

As observed in the recent literature, the most commonly used schemes for VRP solution encoding are permutation and value (integer). Such representations can be found, for example, in the works of Lu and Vincent [9], Lau et al. [4], Lee and Nazif [2], Bermudez et al. [5] and Lima et al. [14].

Lu and Vincent [9] proposed a simple mixed encoding scheme (permutation and integer), illustrated in Fig. 3, which encapsulates a main chromosome (permutation of costumers) and a 'subchromosome' formed by integer values representing the number of customers on each route.

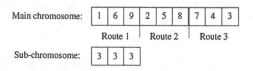

Fig. 3. Encoding scheme proposed by Lu and Vincent [9].

Lau et al. [4] adopted an encoding scheme similar to that presented in [9], for the Multidepot VRP, in which the subchromosome (first chromosome positions) represents the number of costumers that each vehicle must attend, as well as the depot each vehicle will depart to make deliveries (see Fig. 4).

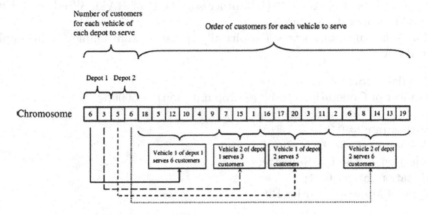

Fig. 4. Encoding scheme proposed by Lau et al. [4].

It is important to note that in these cases additional mechanisms must be used for route separation and also to bypass the problem of generating non-feasible solutions after applying the crossover and mutation operators. However, this latter mechanism is not clearly described in the above mentioned works.

Recently, Lima et al. [14] proposed a short binary encoding scheme for CVRP in which the chromosome represents the set of customers that must be attended by each vehicle, as can be seen in Fig. 5, while the sequence for visiting the customers is solved by the Nearest Neighbor algorithm.

Customers	A	B	C	D	E	F	G
Vehicle 1	1	1	0	1	0	0	1
Vehicle 2	0	0	1	0	1	1	0

Fig. 5. Binary encoding scheme proposed by Lima et al. [14].

In this encoding scheme the alleles with value of 1 indicate the customers that will be attended by a vehicle, that is represented by each line of the binary matrix.

3   Materials and Methods

In the development of proposed encoding scheme, the programming language C/C++ and GAlib library [21] were used. The GAlib is a free library widely used for solving combinatorial optimization problems. For evaluating the proposal, experiments were performed and the results obtained were compared with the best results found in the literature for a set of instances extracted from Christofides and TSPLIB libraries, with up to 30 customers.

In the experiments we employed a desktop computer with the following configurations: Intel Celeron 1.40 GHz processor; 4 GB of RAM; Windows 7 Ultimate 32-bits operating system.

The following parameters (empirically defined) were employed by implemented GA:

- Population Size = 1200;
- Number of Generations (used as stop criterion) = 5000;
- Population rate of replacement = 0.8;
- Elitism rate = 0.2;
- Crossover rate = 0.8;
- Selection Method = Roulette;
- Mutation rate = 0.01;
- Type of Mutation = Flip Bit.

4 Proposed Binary Encoding Scheme

The encoding scheme proposed in this work consists of a binary matrix of $M = nc * 2 - 1$ columns by K rows. The example shown in Fig. 6 illustrates the solution encoding of a CVPR instance that involves $nc = 7$ costumers and $K = 2$ vehicles (as depicted in Fig. 1). The first nc columns of each row indicate the costumers to be served by a vehicle, while the last $nc - 1$ columns consist of a vector that indicates the permutations to be made in a matrix of integers (Fig. 7), called permutation matrix, representing the order that the costumers will be visited by the K vehicles.

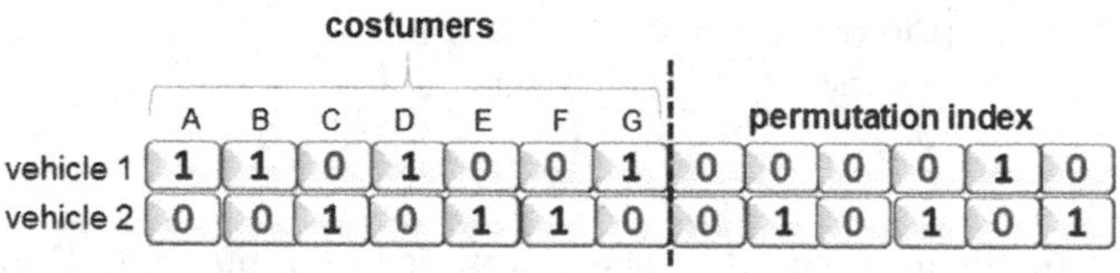

Fig. 6. Proposed binary encoding scheme for CVPR.

The permutation matrix (that can be understood as a seed) containing nc columns and K rows, shown in Fig. 7, is unique and must be generated before the execution of GA using random permutations or some heuristic algorithm. Thus, when it is combined with a GA chromosome (indicating the costumers to be visited and how the visitation order will be permuted), a solution for CVRP is generated, as shown in Fig. 8.

permutation matrix

vehicle 1 | 4 | 5 | 1 | 3 | 6 | 2 | 7
vehicle 2 | 6 | 2 | 7 | 5 | 3 | 1 | 4

Fig. 7. Permutation matrix (seed).

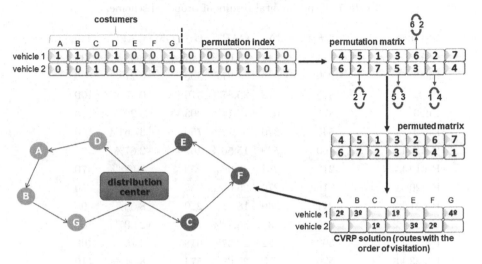

Fig. 8. Combining a permutation matrix with a chromosome to generate a solution for CVRP.

In summary, combining a unique seed with the GA chromosomes a set of different solutions for the CVRP is generated, each one providing the set of customers to be visited by each vehicle as well as the order they will be visited.

It is valid to mention that the encoding scheme described here was inspired by the work of Grassi [22], who proposed a similar way to represent solutions to the Job-shop Scheduling Problem (FJSP), and is very different from those employed in the VRP solution found in the literature, including the schemes described in Sect. 2.3.

5   Experimental Results

To evaluate the proposed encoding scheme we executed the GA ten times for each instance. Then, the results obtained were compared with the best solutions found in the literature. To this end, we considered the optimal solutions presented by Reinelt and Wenger [23] and by Ralphs et al. [24], respectively, for instances extracted from Christofides and TSPLIB.

The quality of obtained solutions was evaluated by a measure known as GAP, which is widely used in the literature to express how far the result obtained for a problem is from the best result reported in the literature for that problem. In our case, $GAP = (OF - OF_{Best})/OF_{Best}$, being OF the best value of objective function (Eq. 9) obtained in the 10 executions of GA and OF_{Best} the best solution found in the literature. In addition, we present in Table 1 results considering the population initiated in a random way (GA) and including in it a feasible solution generated by Gillet & Miller heuristic (GA+GM).

Table 1. Experimental results of proposed scheme.

Instance	OF_{Best}	GA	GAP%	GA+GM	GAP%	Time (s)
Eil7	114	114	0.00%	114	0.00%	30
Eil13	290	316	8.97%	308	6.21%	50
Eil22	375	472	25.87%	376	0.27%	100
Eil23	875	1025	17.14%	903	3.20%	110
Eil30	545	840	54.13%	750	37.61%	150
P-n16-k8	450	520	15.56%	462	2.67%	60
P-n19-k2	212	284	33.96%	255	20.28%	70
P-n20-k2	216	270	25.00%	255	18.06%	80
P-n21-k2	211	249	18.01%	229	8.53%	90
P-n22-k2	216	338	56.48%	268	24.07%	100
P-n22-k8	590	722	22.37%	618	4.75%	100
P-n23-k8	529	675	27.60%	574	8.51%	110
E-n13-k4	247	306	26.89%	302	22.27%	50
E-n22-k4	375	462	23.20%	390	4.00%	100
E-n23-k3	569	892	56.77%	690	21.27%	110
E-n30-k3	534	880	64.76%	687	28.65%	150
Average GAP%	–	–	**29.6%**	–	**13.14%**	–

As shown in Table 1, the proposed scheme provided good performance regarding the quality of the solutions. Considering the results of GA+GM, the GAP in most cases (except for instances "Eil30" and "E-n30-k3") did not exceed 25%, being that for 56% of tested instances the GAP was less than 10%. Still analyzing the GAP, the average value did not exceed 14%, highlighting the good performance of our proposed approach.

With respect to computational cost, as can be seen in Table 1, the processing time ranges from 30 s for the smallest instance ("Eil7") to 150 s for larger instances ("Eil30" and "E-n30-k3"). In addition, the results showed that the use of Gillett & Miller heuristic to generate a feasible solution in the initial population helps the GA to converge quickly to promising points in the search space, generating solutions with good quality. It should be noted that the average time spent in the execution of the Gillett & Miller algorithm was on average 1.7 s, which shows that it does not compromise the computational cost of GA.

Despite the good results obtained by our approach, many improvements can still be made in the proposed encoding scheme, such as: the use of more than one seed (matrix of permutation), the use of local search operators (k-opt, OR-opt, k-Point Move and Cross-Exchange) and also by incorporating some local search algorithm to refine the solutions generated by GA.

6 Conclusions

In this work we presented a new binary encoding scheme for GA to solve the CVRP. From the computational experiments carried out with instances of Christofides and TSPLIB, it was possible to conclude that the proposed scheme provided good results considering the computational cost and the quality of solutions. In addition, it was found that the chromosome representation is suitable to met the specific characteristics of the CVRP, besides it is simple to interpret and adapt. The experiments also pointed out that the use of Gillett & Miller heuristic helped the convergence of GA to promising points in the search space. In future works some improvements in the proposed scheme will be investigated, such as: (i) the use of Clarke and Wright heuristic to generate feasible solutions to be injected into the initial population of the GA; (ii) the use of local search operators (k-opt, OR-opt, k-Point Move and Cross-Exchange), aiming to generate different solutions from the same seed; (iii) incorporate some local search algorithm to refine the solutions generated by GA and (iv) apply the proposed scheme in a large number of instances found in the literature, in order to evaluate the applicability of our approach in real scenarios.

Acknowledgements. The authors would like to thank UNINOVE, FAPESP–São Paulo Research Foundation by financial support (#2017/05188-9) and CNPq–Brazilian National Research Council for the scholarship granted to S. A. Araújo (#311971/2015-6).

References

1. Dalfard, V.M., Kaveh, M., Nosratian, N.E.: Two meta-heuristic algorithms for two-echelon location-routing problem with vehicle fleet capacity and maximum route length constraints. Neural Comput. Appl. **23**(7–8), 2341–2349 (2013)
2. Nazif, H., Lee, L.S.: Optimised crossover genetic algorithm for capacitated vehicle routing problem. Appl. Math. Model. **36**(5), 2110–2117 (2012)
3. Vieira, H.P.: Metaheuristic to solve vehicles routing problems with time windows (2013)
4. Lau, H.C., Chan, T., Tsui, W., Pang, W.: Application of genetic algorithms to solve the multidepot vehicle routing problem. IEEE Trans. Autom. Sci. Eng. **7**(2), 383–392 (2010)
5. Bermudez, C., Graglia, P., Stark, N., Salto, C., Alfonso, H.: Comparison of recombination operators in panmictic and cellular GAs to solve a vehicle routing problem. Intel. Artif. Rev. Iberoam. de Intel. Artif. **14**(46), 34–44 (2010)
6. Wang, C.H., Lu, J.Z.: An effective evolutionary algorithm for the practical capacitated vehicle routing problems. J. Intell. Manuf. **21**(4), 363–375 (2010)
7. Tasan, A.S., Gen, M.: A genetic algorithm based approach to vehicle routing problem with simultaneous pick-up and deliveries. Comput. Ind. Eng. **62**(3), 755–761 (2012)

8. Ursani, Z., Essam, D., Cornforth, D., Stocker, R.: Localized genetic algorithm for vehicle routing problem with time windows. Appl. Soft Comput. **11**(8), 5375–5390 (2011)
9. Lu, C.C., Vincent, F.Y.: Data envelopment analysis for evaluating the efficiency of genetic algorithms on solving the vehicle routing problem with soft time windows. Comput. Ind. Eng. **63**(2), 520–529 (2012)
10. Kuo, R., Zulvia, F.E., Suryadi, K.: Hybrid particle swarm optimization with genetic algorithm for solving capacitated vehicle routing problem with fuzzy demand – a case study on garbage collection system. Appl. Math. Comput. **219**(5), 2574–2588 (2012)
11. Vidal, T., Crainic, T.G., Gendreau, M., Lahrichi, N., Rei, W.: A hybrid genetic algorithm for multidepot and periodic vehicle routing problems. Oper. Res. **60**(3), 611–624 (2012)
12. Reiter, P., Gutjahr, W.J.: Exact hybrid algorithms for solving a bi-objective vehicle routing problem. Cent. Eur. J. Oper. Res. **20**(1), 19–43 (2012)
13. Osaba, E., Diaz, F., Onieva, E.: Golden ball: a novel meta-heuristic to solve combinatorial optimization problems based on soccer concepts. Appl. Intell. **41**(1), 145–166 (2014)
14. Lima, S.J.A., Araújo, S.A., Schimit, P.H.: A hybrid approach based on genetic algorithm and nearest neighbor heuristic for solving the capacitated vehicle routing problem. Acta Scientiarum Technology (2018)
15. Laporte, G.: The vehicle routing problem: an overview of exact and approximate algorithms. Eur. J. Oper. Res. **59**(3), 345–358 (1992)
16. Goldberg, D.E.: Genetic Algorithms in Search, Optimization, and Machine Learning. Addison-Wesley, Reading (1989)
17. Banzhaf, W., Nordin, P., Keller, R.E., Francone, F.D.: Genetic Programming: An Introduction, vol. 1. Morgan Kaufmann, San Francisco (1998)
18. Brooker, R.: Concepts of Genetics. McGraw-Hill Higher Education, New York (2012)
19. Kumar, R.: Novel encoding scheme in genetic algorithms for better fitness. Int. J. Eng. Adv. Technol. **1**(6), 214–219 (2012)
20. Kumar, A.: Encoding schemes in genetic algorithm. Int. J. Adv. Res. IT Eng. **2**(3), 1–7 (2013)
21. Wall, M.: GAlib: a C++ library of genetic algorithm components (1996)
22. Grassi, F.: Optimization by genetic algorithms of the sequencing of production orders in job shop environments. Master's Dissertation, Industrial Engineering Post Graduation Program, Universidade Nove de Julho (UNINOVE) (2014)
23. Reinelt, G., Wenger, K.M.: Maximally violated mod-p cuts for the capacitated vehicle-routing problem. INFORMS J. Comput. **18**(4), 466–479 (2006)
24. Ralphs, T., Pulleyblank, W., Trotter Jr., L.: On capacitated vehicle routing. Problem, Mathematical Programming (1998)

Ensemble and Fuzzy Techniques Applied to Imbalanced Traffic Congestion Datasets: A Comparative Study

Pedro Lopez-Garcia[1,2]([✉]), Antonio D. Masegosa[1,2,3], Enrique Onieva[1,2],
and Eneko Osaba[1]

[1] DeustoTech-Fundacion Deusto, Deusto Foundation, 48007 Bilbao, Spain
{p.lopez,ad.masegosa,e.onieva,e.osaba}@deusto.es
[2] Faculty of Engineering, University of Deusto, 48007 Bilbao, Spain
[3] IKERBASQUE, Basque Foundation for Science, 48011 Bilbao, Spain

Abstract. Class imbalance is among the most persistent complications which may confront the traditional supervised learning task in real-world applications. Among the different kind of classification problems that have been studied in the literature, the imbalanced ones, particularly those that represents real-world problems, have attracted the interest of many researchers in recent years. In order to face this problems, different approaches have been used or proposed in the literature, between then, soft computing and ensemble techniques. In this work, ensembles and fuzzy techniques have been applied to real-world traffic datasets in order to study their performance in imbalanced real-world scenarios. KEEL platform is used to carried out this study. The results show that different ensemble techniques obtain the best results in the proposed datasets.

Keywords: Intelligent Transportation Systems · Imbalanced data
Ensemble techniques · Fuzzy techniques · Soft Computing techniques
Classification

1 Introduction

Class imbalance is among the most persistent complications which may confront the traditional supervised learning task in real-world applications [1]. The problem appears when the number of instances in one of the classes significantly outnumbers the number of instances in the other ones. This situation is a handicap when trying to identify the minority class, as the learning algorithms are not usually adapted to such characteristics. Without the loss of generality, it can be assumed that the class of interest is the minority class, while the other ones are the majority ones. Various applications demonstrate this characteristic of high class imbalance, such as bioinformatics, e-business, information security, and national security.

Among the different kind of classification problems that have been studied in the literature, the imbalanced ones, particularly those that represents real-world

© Springer International Publishing AG, part of Springer Nature 2018
P. Korošec et al. (Eds.): BIOMA 2018, LNCS 10835, pp. 185–196, 2018.
https://doi.org/10.1007/978-3-319-91641-5_16

problems, have attracted the interest of many researchers in recent years [2, 3]. In particular, in traffic environments, the apparition of a particularly complicated state of the road (i.e. traffic congestion) will represent a minority class for prediction algorithms, while its proper detection in advance is a topic of interest for administrations and users.

One of the most problematic issues in the development of actual cities is road traffic. This problem is actually one of the most important study focuses of the Intelligent Transportation Systems (ITS) field. In the last decades, intelligent techniques such as those mentioned before have been applied to solve this problem. In particular fuzzy systems are used in [4] to infer the future state of the road by combining several systems in a hierarchical way. In addition different metaheuristics have been used in order to optimize systems, such as Support Vector Machines [5] (SVM); Genetic Algorithms (GA) are used in [6], while Particle Swarm Optimization (PSO) is implemented in [7], among others.

Recently, ensemble learning is a popular and significant research in data mining and machine learning area. Ensemble classifiers have received considerable attention in applied statistics and machine learning for over a decade [8]. Several studies demonstrate that the practice of combining several models into a aggregated one leads to significant gains in performance over its constituent members [9].

The principal aim is to make a comparative study between the performance of ensembles and fuzzy recent approaches in traffic state prediction, which is a multi-classification problem with a high imbalance between classes. Data used in this work come from two sources. The first one comes from cameras in the city of Helmond (The Netherlands) collected by TASS International company[1] and took part of the developing of different models for traffic systems in Horizon 2020 TIMON project[2] (Enhanced real time services for optimized multimodal mobility relying on cooperative networks and open data). Another data source used for the development of this work is the data obtained in Lisbon (Portugal) A5 highway, and used in the European Project ICSI (Intelligent Cooperative Sensing for Improved Traffic Efficiency).

The rest of the paper is structured as follow. Section 2 contains the state of the art of the two kind of techniques applied in this work: ensembles and metaheuristics. Section 3 is dedicated to the descriptions of the different methods used for this comparative study. In Sect. 4 information about the datasets used and its comparative is shown. Finally, in Sect. 5 the conclusions obtained for this study are collected.

2   Background

In this section, a brief study of the state of the art is presented in order to show the contributions of the community to the imbalance data problem using ensembles (Sect. 2.1), in specially boosting and bagging algorithms, and metaheuristics (Sect. 2.2).

---

[1] https://www.tassinternational.com/.
[2] https://www.timon-project.eu/.

2.1 Ensembles

Ensemble learning is defined as the use of multiple learning algorithms to obtain better predictive performance that could be obtained from any of these algorithms alone [10]. Over the last decade, this kind of approach has been used in different themes such as optimization [11], medicine [12], or ITS [13]. Focusing in imbalance classification problems, these algorithms can be found in many articles. For example, in [14], Lim et al. propose a evolutionary cluster-based oversampling ensemble framework. This method is based on contemporary ideas of identifying oversampling regions using clusters. The evolutionary part of the ensemble is used to optimize the parameters of the data generation method and to reduce the overall computational cost. The proposal is applied to a set of 40 imbalance datasets.

Among the different ensemble techniques, two of them can be frequently found in the literature applied to several themes: bagging and boosting techniques [15]. While in bagging several models are created using different subsets of the training set [16], in boosting, a set of weak learning algorithms create a single strong learner and produce only one model [17]. Both kind of methods have been used in imbalance classification.

Authors in [9] analyze different corrective and total corrective boosting algorithms in order to present its own boosting algorithm adding a strong classifier to the linear constraints of LPBoost. Besides, in [18], an Adaboost algorithm to learn fuzzy-rule-based classifiers is proposed. Adaboost approach is applied to approximate and descriptive fuzzy-rule bases, and the performance of the proposed method is compared with other classification schemes applied on a set of benchmark classification tasks.

Other example can be found in [19]. This article presents a research about the Roughly Balanced Bagging and its basic properties that can influence its classification performance. Variables such as the number of component classifiers, their diversity, and ability to deal with difficult types of the minority examples are studied. The experiments are carried out using synthetic and real life data.

The number of articles related with this theme is wide extended in the literature, which means that it is an active issue. In this section, some interesting examples have been exposed, but, in order to give more information and related articles about the problem we are dealing with, interested reader are referred to [20–22] for different surveys about this issue.

2.2 Soft Computing Techniques Applied to Imbalance Datasets

Soft Computing techniques have been widely used since its presentation in 90's by Zadeh [23]. Machine Learning, Fuzzy Logic, and Evolutionary Computation methods are inside the vast group of Soft Computing techniques. Techniques such as GAs, SVM, Fuzzy Rule Based Systems, PSO and so on, have been developed and applied to different themes along the years, showing their good performance and the huge range of possibilities that they offer.

Regarding Fuzzy Logic techniques, fuzzy logic methods have been used in imbalance cases of study along the years. For example, in [24], a fuzzy technique is developed to predict heart diseases. The technique is divided in three phases: first, a fuzzy c-means clustering algorithm is used. Then, rules are generated from the rough set theory, and those rules are used for prediction with the fuzzy classifier.

Another case can be found in [25], where linguistic Fuzzy Rule Based Systems have been applied to imbalance datasets to deal with the overlapping problems between the concepts to be learned. This problem is more severe in imbalance datasets due to the most of the techniques try to correctly classify the majority class and, in cases of imbalance distribution of the data, it is the minority class where the most important data can be found. Datasets used are extracted from KEEL dataset repository.

Finally, authors of this study are aware of the huge amount of related papers that can be found in the literature. In this work, we have mentioned some of the most interesting research papers, in order to give an idea of the activity that is being carried out in the community. For further information, we recommend the reading of any of the review papers that can be found in the literature, such as [26], or [27]. In this work, fuzzy methods will be used to study their performance in a real imbalance scenario.

3   Techniques Used for the Comparative Study

As mentioned in previous sections, one of the aims of this work is to study the performance of ensembles and fuzzy meta-heuristic techniques when they are applied to imbalanced problems. A total of 10 techniques are chosen, divided in two principal groups: six ensemble techniques, and four fuzzy ones. Due to the limited space, only the name of the techniques as well as a brief description of them are listed below:

– Ensemble techniques
  1. AdaBoost (I) [28] is an adaptation of general Adaboost for imbalance datasets.
  2. MSSMOTE Bagging [29] oversamples minority class instances using MSMOTE preprocessing algorithm. In this method both classes contribute to each bag with N instances.
  3. MSSMOTE Boosting [30] introduces synthetic instances in each iteration of AdaBoost technique, using the MSMOTE data preprocessing algorithm.
  4. RUSBoost [31] removes instances from the majority class by random undersampling the data-set in each iteration.
  5. SMOTE Bagging [32] oversamples minority class instances using SMOTE preprocessing algorithm.
  6. SMOTE Boosting [33] introduces synthetic instances in each iteration of AdaBoost technique, using the SMOTE data preprocessing algorithm.

All ensemble techniques used in this work have C4.5 algorithm as base classifier.

– Fuzzy Classification techniques

1. AdaBoost (C) [34] is a boosting algorithm, which repeatedly invokes a learning algorithm to successively generate a committee of simple, low-quality classifiers.

2. LogitBoost [35] is a backfitting algorithm, which repeatedly invokes a learning algorithm to successively generate a committee of simple, low-quality classifiers.

3. FARCHD-C [36] mines fuzzy association rules limiting the order of the associations in order to obtain a reduced set of candidate rules with less attributes in the antecedent.

4. C4.5 [37] is a decision tree generating algorithm that it induces classification rules in the form of decision trees from a set of given examples. C4.5 is based on ID3 algorithm.

It is important to remark that the different between $AdaBoost(C)$ and $AdaBoost(I)$ is the base classifier. While the first one counts with fuzzy classifiers, the second one uses a C4.5 algorithm as base classifier.

4   Experimentation

This section compiles the experimentation carried out in this work. Datasets used in this work as well as the information related to them are exposed in Sect. 4.1 while the results, and statistic methods applied are summarized in Sect. 4.2.

4.1   Datasets and Preprocessing

Datasets used in this work contains real data from traffic cameras in the city of Helmond (The Netherlands). This data is provided by TASS international (see footnote 1) and used in the Horizon 2020 project TIMON project (see footnote 2) (Enhanced real time services for optimized multimodal mobility relying on cooperative networks and open data). Congestion in the road is used as class variable. In the raw data, this variable can take four different values: Normal, Increasing, Dense and Congestion. In order to simplify and make the problem equal to the techniques mentioned in the previous section, the classes have been reduced by two: Normal (majority class) and Congestion value (minority class), which includes Increasing, Dense and Congestion instances. Each dataset counts with a total of 22 variables, which includes not only information about the speed, the number of vehicles or the occupancy of the road, but the weather when data was taken. Data used in this work are collected during two months by four cameras, and divided in four different horizons of time (15, 30, 45 and 60 min respectively), which makes a total of 16 datasets.

Besides, data collected from Lisbon highway A5 used in EU project ICSI[3] have been also used. This highway is a 25 km long motorway in Portugal that

---

[3] http://www.ict-icsi.eu.

connects Lisbon to Cascais. Data used in this work was collected from seven sensors displayed in the road and transformed into datasets. As well as in Helmond datasets, congestion in the road is taken as class variable. In this case, this class contains a value of congestion that appear in the next hour at a certain point and can take as values *LOW*, if the number of vehicles are below the percentile 15; *MED* (Medium), if the it is between percentiles 15 and 30; and *HIGH* otherwise. Following the same logic applied to previous datasets, *LOW* and *MED* instances have been labeled as Normal (majority class) while *HIGH* instances have been changed to Congestion label (minority class). Data was collected during a month. The three first weeks are used as training data while the last week of the month is used to validate the solutions. These datasets are called BRISA datasets along the rest of the work.

Information about Imbalance Ratio (IR) and number of instances in each dataset are shown in Table 1.

Table 1. Information about the datasets used in this work

	Name of dataset	N. instances	IR
TASS datasets	C1	5333	8.1
	C2	5338	8.2
	C28	5348	8.16
	C47	5449	7
Brisa datasets	CL_{600}	721	2.04
	CL_{1980}	1441	2.26
	CL_{3600}	721	5.43
	CL_{4000}	1441	2.57
	CL_{6800}	721	2.13
	CL_{8050}	1441	2.25
	CL_{9400}	721	2.53

4.2   Results

KEEL software [38] has been used to carry out the experiments. In the case we are dealing with, the module for imbalanced techniques are used. The experimentations have been executed in a Intel Xeon E5 2.30 GHz with a RAM memory of 32 GB. Related with the configuration of the techniques used in the experimentation, the default configuration given by KEEL has been retained. The Area Under the Curve (AUC) has been used as error metric. To show TASS dataset results, datasets are divided by id of the camera and horizon of time. Those results are shown in Table 2. Bold values represent the two best results obtained in each dataset.

Table 2. AUC values obtained for each technique in each dataset and horizon of time for TASS datasets

Techniques	C1				C2				C28				C47			
	15	30	45	60	15	30	45	60	15	30	45	60	15	30	45	60
C4.5	**.968**	.958	.956	**.963**	**.970**	.954	**.955**	**.955**	**.963**	.949	.958	**.962**	**.958**	**.964**	.940	.953
FARCHD	.805	.727	.642	.623	.788	.729	.612	.575	.808	.723	.667	.500	.829	.732	.642	.622
AdaBoost(C)	.549	.563	.508	.500	.564	.614	.507	.501	.560	.540	.510	.500	.566	.541	.512	.501
LogitBoost	.672	.668	.585	.537	.703	.678	.594	.548	.659	.657	.567	.531	.685	.662	.604	.560
AdaBoost(I)	.939	.950	.957	.941	.951	.940	.950	.953	.952	.952	.938	.941	.950	.945	.930	.952
MSMOTEBagging	.872	.942	.943	.941	.886	.939	.932	.929	.903	.945	.947	.936	.912	.937	.926	.927
MSMOTEBoost	.916	.948	.935	.932	.936	.939	.925	.918	.939	.942	.940	.934	.935	.952	.934	.930
RUSBoost	**.976**	**.973**	**.971**	**.968**	**.973**	**.972**	**.967**	**.965**	**.972**	**.977**	**.968**	**.971**	**.971**	**.973**	**.968**	**.969**
SMOTEBagging	.916	.953	.936	.938	.923	.941	.934	.923	.937	.947	.943	.932	.893	.945	.926	.937
SMOTEBoost	.956	**.963**	**.960**	.954	.946	**.954**	.954	.946	.946	**.961**	**.959**	.955	.952	.960	**.958**	**.955**

As it can be seen, three techniques stand out from the rest: RUSBoost, SMOTEBoost, and C4.5. In case of RUSBoost, it obtains one of the two best results in every dataset used, being the first one in each one of them. For SMOTE-Boost, it gets one of the two best AUC values in 7 out of 16 datasets. Finally, for C4.5, it achieves a value between the best two in 10 out of 16 datasets, especially in C2 dataset. About the rest of the techniques, in general, ensemble techniques obtain better results than fuzzy ones. Focusing in the fuzzy techniques, though FARCHD and C4.5 achieves good performance in this problem without changing anything in its execution, AdaBoost(C) and LogitBoost do not obtain a considerable performance. In fact, AdaBoost(C) obtain the lowest AUC values in every dataset in comparison with the rest of techniques. If both AdaBoost techniques presented in this experimentation are compared, ensemble version of AdaBoost (AdaBoost(I)) outperforms the fuzzy one. On the other hand, taking into account ensemble techniques, RUSBoost outperforms the rest of them, followed by SMOTEBoost. However, all the techniques obtain a good performance in every dataset and horizon of time, which always achieve an AUC value higher than 0.9. About the horizon of time, the increasing of this value does not seem to affect to the performance of the techniques significantly. Only AdaBoost(C) and LogitBoost notice the change of this value. The rest of the techniques obtains almost the same performance when the horizon of time is 15 min than when it takes the value 60 min. Some of them (SMOTEBagging, C1 dataset) even improve its performance between these two horizons.

Table 3 contains the results obtained by each one of the techniques for each BRISA dataset. As in the previous results, the two best values are highlighted in bold.

The results show that MSMOTEBagging is the best technique so far in these datasets, obtaining 4 out of 7 best values, following by RUSBoost and SMOTE-Bagging, which both obtain 3 out of 7 best results. For the rest of the techniques, about fuzzy techniques used, only AdaBoost (C) and LogitBoost obtain bold values. Although their performance is not far from those obtained by the best techniques, they do not reach the high AUC value obtained by the rest of

Table 3. AUC values obtained for each technique in each Lisbon dataset

	CL_{600}	CL_{1980}	CL_{3600}	CL_{4000}	CL_{6800}	CL_{8050}	CL_{9400}
C4.5	.893	.919	.898	.945	.872	.940	.875
FARCHD	.830	.955	.906	.928	.893	.951	.954
AdaBoost(C)	.882	.938	.808	.938	.864	.948	**.979**
LogitBoost	.853	.951	.891	.945	.884	.945	**.975**
AdaBoost(I)	.886	.954	.859	.941	.852	.957	.892
MSMOTE-Bagging	**.924**	**.961**	.928	.941	**.909**	.962	.867
MSMOTE-Boost	.884	.957	.899	.954	.881	**.965**	.871
RUSBoost	.902	.955	**.919**	**.955**	**.909**	.951	.896
SMOTEBagging	.914	**.958**	**.935**	**.958**	.901	.954	.875
SMOTEBoost	**.928**	.934	.915	.941	.897	.940	.921

the techniques. Adaboost (C) and LogitBoost obtain one bold value, in dataset CL_{9400}, being the two best techniques in the mentioned dataset. Comparing the results obtained in the previous datasets, in this case, bagging techniques overpass boosting techniques, being RUSBoost the only one that can be compared with the results obtained by them (Table 3).

In order to assess if the differences in performance among the techniques studied here are significantly different we employed non-parametric tests following the guidelines given by García et al. in [39]. The procedure carried out is described next. We first apply Friedman's non-parametric test for multiple comparison at a significance level $\alpha \leq 0.05$ to assess if we can reject the null hypothesis of similar performance among all algorithms. If so, then we evaluate if the performance of the best algorithm according to Friedman's averaged ranking versus the other classifiers is significantly better. To this end, we apply Holm's [40] and Finner's [41] post-hoc tests at a significance level $\alpha \leq 0.05$ using the best method as control algorithm. Following this procedure, we analyse the performance of the algorithms globally over the two datasets.

We do the exercise of evaluating the performance of the methods over all datasets. According to Friedman's tests there exists significant differences among algorithms. The averaged ranking displayed in Table 4 confirm that RUSBoost is the most robust classifier followed by SMOTEBoost. On the contrary, the three fuzzy algorithms are clearly the ones that show a worse performance, whereas the result of the rest of algorithms is very similar. Using RUSBoost as control algorithm for the Holm's and Finner's post-hoc tests, we observe in Table 5 that, taking into account all datasets, it obtains significantly better AUC values that the other studied methods, excepting SMOTEBoost, although even in this case the significance level is quite near to the threshold, being equal to 0.07.

Table 4. Average rankings of the algorithms provided by Friedman's non-parametric test for multiple comparisons over all datasets

Algorithm	Ranking
AdaBoost(I)	4.9783
C4.5	4.2391
FARCHD	7.5652
AdaBoost(C)	9.1739
LogitBoost	8.1087
MSMOTEBagging	5.2609
MSMOTEBoost	5.3913
RUSBoost	1.8043
SMOTEBagging	5.0652
SMOTEBoost	3.413

Table 5. Adjusted p-value returned by Holm's and Finner's post-hoc tests for all datasets

Algorithm	Adjusted p-value Holm	Adjusted p-value Finner
AdaBoost(C)	0	0
LogitBoost	0	0
FARCHD	0	0
MSMOTEBoost	0.000353	0.000132
MSMOTEBagging	0.000541	0.000195
SMOTEBagging	0.001039	0.00039
AdaBoost(I)	0.001134	0.000486
C4.5	0.012778	0.007185
SMOTEBoost	0.07157	0.07157

5   Conclusions

In this work, ensemble and fuzzy rules techniques have been applied to imbalance real traffic datasets in order to classify correctly the state of the road in a real scenario. In this case, data collected from cameras in the city of Helmond (The Netherlands), and from A5 Highway in Lisbon are used. Data from cameras was collected by TASS international and used in II2020 TIMON project. In case of A5 highway, this data was used in ICSI project. The aim of this article is to compare the performance of ensemble and fuzzy techniques in imbalance real scenarios.

As results, in Helmond datasets, ensemble techniques outperform those fuzzy techniques used in the experimentation, with two techniques between the best ones. Three techniques stand out the rest: RUSBoost, SMOTEBoost, and C4.5. Among all, RUSBoost obtained at least one of the two best values in every dataset used. For SMOTEBoost and C4.5, they obtained 7 out of 16 and 10 out of 16 best values respectively. Regarding Lisbon datasets, ensemble techniques again, specially Bagging techniques and RUSBoost, obtain better performance than fuzzy techniques. All these results are checked using different statistical tests.

As future works, other techniques for both groups can be used. Besides, the experimentation could be applied to more datasets and other horizons of time. Regarding this, one future work to take into account is to adapt ensemble techniques to work with multiclass classification. This will increase the difficulty of the problem as well as the IR of each dataset, making the data a good real benchmark to use in comparatives like the presented in this paper.

Acknowledgements. This work has been supported by TIMON project (Enhanced real time services for optimized multimodal mobility relying on cooperative networks and open data) which received funding from the European Unions Horizon 2020 research and innovation programme under grant agreement No. 636220. E. Osaba performed his contribution when he was working on the University of Deusto.

References

1. López, V., Fernández, A., Moreno-Torres, J.G., Herrera, F.: Analysis of prepro- cessing vs. cost-sensitive learning for imbalanced classification. Open problems on intrinsic data characteristics. Expert Syst. Appl. **39**, 6585–6608 (2012)
2. Sardari, S., Eftekhari, M.: A fuzzy decision tree approach for imbalanced data classification, pp. 292–297 (2016)
3. Savetratanakaree, K., Sookhanaphibarn, K., Intakosum, S., Thawonmas, R.: Bor- derline over-sampling in feature space for learning algorithms in imbalanced data environments. IAENG Int. J. Comput. Sci. **43**, 363–373 (2016)
4. Lopez-Garcia, P., Onieva, E., Osaba, E., Masegosa, A.D., Perallos, A.: A hybrid method for short-term traffic congestion forecasting using genetic algorithms and cross entropy. IEEE Trans. Intell. Transp. Syst. **17**, 557–569 (2016)
5. Guo, L., Ge, P.S., Zhang, M.H., Li, L.H., Zhao, Y.B.: Pedestrian detection for intel- ligent transportation systems combining adaboost algorithm and support vector machine. Expert Syst. Appl. **39**, 4274–4286 (2012)
6. Cervantes, J., Li, X., Yu, W.: Imbalanced data classification via support vector machines and genetic algorithms. Connect. Sci. **26**, 335–348 (2014)
7. Xu, Z., Watada, J., Wu, M., Ibrahim, Z., Khalid, M.: Solving the imbalanced data classification problem with the particle swarm optimization based support vector machine. IEEJ Trans. Electron. Inf. Syst. **134**, 788–795 (2014)
8. Bauer, E., Kohavi, R.: An empirical comparison of voting classification algorithms: bagging, boosting, and variants. Mach. Learn. **36**, 105–139 (1999)
9. Fang, Y., Fu, Y., Sun, C., Zhou, J.: Improved boosting algorithm using combined weak classifiers. J. Comput. Inf. Syst. **7**, 1455–1462 (2011)
10. Rokach, L.: Ensemble-based classifiers. Artif. Intell. Rev. **33**, 1–39 (2010)
11. Nama, S., Saha, A.: An ensemble symbiosis organisms search algorithm and its application to real world problems. Decis. Sci. Lett. **7**, 103–118 (2018)
12. Zhao, Z., Liu, Y., Li, J., Wang, J., Wang, X.: A study of fuzzy clustering ensemble algorithm focusing on medical data analysis. In: Yen, N., Hung, J. (eds.) FC 2016. LNEE, vol. 422, pp. 383–396. Springer, Singapore (2018). https://doi.org/10.1007/ 978-981-10-3187-8_37
13. Pescaru, D., Curiac, D.I.: Ensemble based traffic light control for city zones using a reduced number of sensors. Transp. Res. Part C: Emerg. Technol. **46**, 261–273 (2014)
14. Lim, P., Goh, C., Tan, K.: Evolutionary cluster-based synthetic oversampling ensemble (ECO-Ensemble) for imbalance learning. IEEE Trans. Cybern. **47**, 2850– 2861 (2017)
15. Kotsiantis, S.B.: Bagging and boosting variants for handling classifications prob- lems: a survey. Knowl. Eng. Rev. **29**, 78–100 (2014)
16. Breiman, L.: Bagging predictors. Mach. Learn. **24**, 123–140 (1996)
17. Freund, Y., Schapire, R.E., et al.: Experiments with a new boosting algorithm, vol. 96, pp. 148–156 (1996)
18. Del Jesus, M., Hoffmann, F., Navascués, L., Sánchez, L.: Induction of fuzzy-rule- based classifiers with evolutionary boosting algorithms. IEEE Trans. Fuzzy Syst. **12**, 296–308 (2004)
19. Lango, M., Stefanowski, J.: Multi-class and feature selection extensions of roughly balanced bagging for imbalanced data. J. Intell. Inf. Syst. **50**(1), 97–127 (2018)
20. Jurek, A., Bi, Y., Wu, S., Nugent, C.: A survey of commonly used ensemble-based classification techniques. Knowl. Eng. Rev. **29**(5), 551–581 (2013)

21. Mokeddem, D., Belbachir, H.: A survey of distributed classification based ensemble data mining methods. J. Appl. Sci. **9**, 3739–3745 (2009)
22. Wang, S., Yao, X.: Multiclass imbalance problems: analysis and potential solutions. IEEE Trans. Syst. Man Cybern. Part B Cybern. **42**, 1119–1130 (2012)
23. Zadeh, L.A.: Fuzzy logic, neural networks, and soft computing. Commun. ACM **37**, 77–85 (1994)
24. Antonelli, M., Ducange, P., Marcelloni, F.: An experimental study on evolutionary fuzzy classifiers designed for managing imbalanced datasets. Neurocomputing **146**, 125–136 (2014)
25. Harandi, F., Derhami, V.: A reinforcement learning algorithm for adjusting antecedent parameters and weights of fuzzy rules in a fuzzy classifier. J. Intell. Fuzzy Syst. **30**, 2339–2347 (2016)
26. Kotsiantis, S., Kanellopoulos, D., Pintelas, P., et al.: Handling imbalanced datasets: a review. GESTS Int. Trans. Comput. Sci. Eng. **30**, 25–36 (2006)
27. Ramyachitra, D., Manikandan, P.: Imbalanced dataset classification and solutions: a review. Int. J. Comput. Bus. Res. (IJCBR) **5** (2014)
28. Freund, Y., Schapire, R.E.: A desicion-theoretic generalization of on-line learning and an application to boosting. In: Vitányi, P. (ed.) EuroCOLT 1995. LNCS, vol. 904, pp. 23–37. Springer, Heidelberg (1995). https://doi.org/10.1007/3-540-59119-2_166
29. Galar, M., Fernandez, A., Barrenechea, E., Bustince, H., Herrera, F.: A review on ensembles for the class imbalance problem: bagging-, boosting-, and hybrid-based approaches. IEEE Trans. Syst. Man Cybern. Part C (Appl. Rev.) **42**, 463–484 (2012)
30. Hu, S., Liang, Y., Ma, L., He, Y.: MSMOTE: improving classification performance when training data is imbalanced. In: Second International Workshop on Computer Science and Engineering, WCSE 2009, vol. 2, pp. 13–17. IEEE (2009)
31. Seiffert, C., Khoshgoftaar, T.M., Van Hulse, J., Napolitano, A.: RUSBoost: a hybrid approach to alleviating class imbalance. IEEE Trans. Syst. Man Cybern.-Part A: Syst. Hum. **40**, 185–197 (2010)
32. Wang, S., Yao, X.: Diversity analysis on imbalanced data sets by using ensemble models. In: IEEE Symposium on Computational Intelligence and Data Mining, CIDM 2009, pp. 324–331. IEEE (2009)
33. Chawla, N.V., Lazarevic, A., Hall, L.O., Bowyer, K.W.: SMOTEBoost: improving prediction of the minority class in boosting. In: Lavrač, N., Gamberger, D., Todorovski, L., Blockeel, H. (eds.) PKDD 2003. LNCS (LNAI), vol. 2838, pp. 107–119. Springer, Heidelberg (2003). https://doi.org/10.1007/978-3-540-39804-2_12
34. Del Jesus, M.J., Hoffmann, F., Navascués, L.J., Sánchez, L.: Induction of fuzzy-rule-based classifiers with evolutionary boosting algorithms. IEEE Trans. Fuzzy Syst. **12**, 296–308 (2004)
35. Otero, J., Sánchez, L.: Induction of descriptive fuzzy classifiers with the Logitboost algorithm. Soft Comput.- Fus. Found. Methodol. Appl. **10**, 825–835 (2006)
36. Alcala-Fdez, J., Alcala, R., Herrera, F.: A fuzzy association rule-based classification model for high-dimensional problems with genetic rule selection and lateral tuning. IEEE Trans. Fuzzy Syst. **19**, 857–872 (2011)
37. Quinlan, J.R.: C4.5: Programming for Machine Learning, vol. 38. Morgan Kaufmann, Burlington (1993)
38. Alcalá-Fdez, J., Fernández, A., Luengo, J., Derrac, J., García, S., Sánchez, L., Herrera, F.: KEEL data-mining software tool: data set repository, integration of algorithms and experimental analysis framework. J. Mult.-Valued Log. Soft Comput. **17**, 255–287 (2011)

39. García, S., Herrera, F., Shawe-taylor, J.: An extension on "statistical comparisons of classifiers over multiple data sets" for all pairwise comparisons. J. Mach. Learn. Res. **9**, 2677–2694 (2008)
40. Holm, S.: A simple sequentially rejective multiple test procedure. Scand. J. Stat. **6**(2), 65–70 (1979)
41. Finner, H.: On a monotonicity problem in step-down multiple test procedures. J. Am. Stat. Assoc. **88**, 920–923 (1993)

Multi-objective Design
of Time-Constrained Bike Routes
Using Bio-inspired Meta-heuristics

Eneko Osaba[1]([⊠]), Javier Del Ser[1,2,3], Miren Nekane Bilbao[2],
Pedro Lopez-Garcia[4], and Antonio J. Nebro[5]

[1] TECNALIA, Derio, Spain
eneko.osaba@tecnalia.com
[2] University of the Basque Country (UPV/EHU), Bilbao, Spain
[3] Basque Center for Applied Mathematics (BCAM), Bilbao, Spain
[4] Deusto Institute of Technology (DeustoTech), University of Deusto, Bilbao, Spain
[5] Dept. de Lenguajes y Ciencias de la Computación, Universidad de Málaga,
Málaga, Spain

Abstract. This paper focuses on the design and implementation of a
bike route optimization approach based on multi-objective bio-inspired
heuristic solvers. The objective of this approach is to produce a set of
Pareto-optimal bike routes that balance the trade-off between the length
of the route and its safety level, the latter blending together the slope of
the different street segments encompassing the route and their average
road velocity. Additionally, an upper and lower restriction is imposed on
the time taken to traverse the route, so that the overall system can be
utilized for planning bike rides during free leisure time gaps. Instead of
designing a discrete route encoding strategy suitable for heuristic operators, this work leverages a proxy software – Open Trip Planner, OTP –
capable of computing routes based on three user-level preference factors
(i.e. safety, inclination and duration), which eases the adoption of off-the-
shelf multi-objective solvers. The system has been assessed in a realistic
simulation environments over the city of Bilbao (Spain) using multi-
objective bio-inspired approaches. The obtained results are promising,
with route sets trading differently distance for safety of utmost utility
for bike users to exploit fully their leisure time.

Keywords: Bike route planning · Multi-objective optimization
Time-constrained routing · Open Trip Planner · jMetal

1 Introduction

Thanks to the rapid advance of technology, transportation networks have become
increasingly complex along the last decade. This fact has led the mobility to be
a crucial aspect for society, affecting its quality of life directly. In this way, the
necessity for efficient transport means has increased the demand for Intelligent

© Springer International Publishing AG, part of Springer Nature 2018
P. Korošec et al. (Eds.): BIOMA 2018, LNCS 10835, pp. 197–210, 2018.
https://doi.org/10.1007/978-3-319-91641-5_17

Transportation Systems (ITS), lying at the core of many initiatives focused on shedding smartness and intelligence in different paradigms related to transportation and mobility [1].

Among such paradigms, route planning has gained more and more importance in the last years [2]. It is an undoubted fact that daily transits (e.g. from home to work and return) have become a habit for many people worldwide. In this context, by virtue of well-connected, advanced transport networks, travelers and commuters change from one transportation mode to another every day. Taking the underground, then the bus, and finishing the travel on foot is an example of the typical traveling routine for many people nowadays. This *multimodal* transport aims at providing the traveler feasible routes between a certain origin and destination, involving diverse public and private transportation modes connected throughout different schedules [3].

In this context the so-called *mono-modal* route planning, which correspondingly consists of routes performed by a single transport type, are also demanded by people for very diverse purposes, not only by the need for reaching their jobs as postulated above. Mono-modal routes performed by car, bike or foot are often developed for leisure, last-mile packet delivery schedules, and public transport planning, among others [4,5]. As in any other routing construction process several route planners are available in the market or in the Web to help users design optimal routes according to their needs and requirements. The study presented in this work focuses in this latter case, specifically, in routes performed by bike.

In the last couple of decades a growing number of route planning systems have been developed, which are freely available for the community of users. These tools, mostly accessible from different platforms (with deployable versions for computers, smartphones or tablets), are flexible enough to let users comfortably query routes in any place and time. In all cases, one of the characteristics shared by all route planners is that the provided portfolio of routes are strictly based on parameters that the user enters as an input. However, it is intuitive to think that the user could tolerate a certain degree of flexibility in his/her inputs to the routing system, should this flexibility lead to better routes under a certain optimality criterion (e.g. distance, travel time or exposure to traffic). As surveyed next, the relative scarcity of contributions in the literature exploring the implications of this flexibility in bike routes is what motivates to conduct this study.

1.1 Related Work

Some studies can be found in the literature focused on bike route planning. To begin with, a web-based platform is presented in [6] to help cyclists determine safe and efficient routes. The system developed in that study calculates routes using a weighted combination of five different metrics, which are considered to optimize a trade-off among various safety and distance-related factors. A heuristic multi-modal route planning system is introduced in [7], in which cycling trips are considered. The system in that work enforces the user to select both origin and destination of the route, along with other preferences. One of the tested scenarios is bike route from work to home in an energy-efficient manner. In any case, authors use a single objective aggregating all route metrics.

Most existing planning systems for bike routing do not formulate the optimality of explored routes from a multi-criteria or multi-objective approach, but rather opt for aggregate metric models as the ones mentioned above. As a result, planning systems cannot provide the users with diverse sets of suggested routes, hence narrowing the amount and diversity of information provided to cyclists for their decision making. A few exceptions have been published recently, as in [8], where a multi-criteria bicycle routing problem is tackled. In this work, authors develop a set of heuristics for speeding up the multi-criteria route search. Concretely, the objectives to optimize in this problem are the comfort, duration and inclination of the route. Additionally, the heuristic presented in that paper is an extension of the standard multi-criteria label-setting algorithm [9]. Another interesting example of this kind is the one proposed by Caggiani *et al.* in [10]. In this work, a multi-objective biking route choice model is proposed for a bike-sharing mobile application. One of the research challenges addressed therein is to offer the user the appropriate starting and ending bike hiring station. To this end, the suggested origin station is set to the nearest one satisfying the requirements of the user, whereas a similar criterion is applied for selecting the destination station. The system developed in [10] informs the user with the starting and ending bike sharing stations, and the best path to follow according to time, distance, pollution and safety. Additionally, users can select an alternative route according to the parameter that they are willing to prioritize.

1.2   Research Contribution

This manuscript aims at contributing to the observed scarcity of references dealing with multi-objective bike route planning by undertaking the design and practical implementation of an bike path planning system for random bike routes generation, grounded on multi-objective bio-inspired optimization heuristics. Several novel ingredients are introduced in our problem formulation, the most relevant being (1) the consideration of lower and upper trip time constraints to model the case where the planning system is used for e.g. leisure/sport; (2) the derivation of a quantitative metric to evaluate the degree of safety associated to a given route with respect to its topological profile and the speed of motor vehicles along its segments; and (3) four different bio-inspired multi-objective solvers (namely, NSGA-II [11], MOEA/D [12], SMS-EMOA [13], and SMPSO [14]) to efficiently balance the Pareto trade-off between the safety level and the distance of the route, always subject to the imposed time constraints. The (pseudo) Pareto-optimal set of routes produced by any of these can be informed to the user if the system so that he/she has the freedom to choose the one that matches best his/her preferences with respect to the considered objectives.

The proposed system has been assessed in a realistic environment using Open Trip Planner (OTP [15]) as the simulation framework. Experimental results from three different use cases located in the city of Bilbao (Spain) are presented and discussed, all using real data sources, namely, the Open Street Map of the city and its Digital Elevation Model (DEM). The analysis of the obtained route portfolios evinces the practicality of the proposed approach, and paves the way towards extending the problem formulation so as to accommodate other manifold route metrics.

The rest of the paper is structured as follows. Section 2 formulates the bi-objective optimization problem considered in this study, whereas Sect. 3 elaborates on the considered multi-objective heuristics. Section 4 describes in detail the deployed simulation environment. Next, the experimentation performed is shown and discussed in Sect. 5. Finally, Sect. 6 ends the paper and outlines future research.

2   Problem Definition

As has been explained beforehand, the problem tackled in this work is the optimization of bike routes, bearing in mind two different objectives (distance and safety of the route) and the compliance with lower and upper time constraints. According to Fig. 1, the scenario model on which this problem is formulated gravitates on the position $(lat^{\circlearrowleft}, lon^{\circlearrowleft})$ where all bike routes depart from, emulating e.g. a bike ride that a user is willing to enjoy from home within his/her limited leisure time. For simplicity in subsequent algorithmic explanations, we assume that $(lat^{\circlearrowleft}, lon^{\circlearrowleft}) \in [lat_{min}, lat_{max}] \times [lon_{min}, lon_{max}]$, i.e. the scenario and the produced routes themselves are located within a maximum square area.

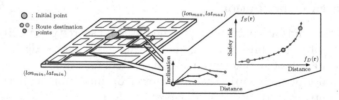

Fig. 1. Schematic diagram of the routing scenario tackled in this paper.

In this scenario a route $\mathbf{r}_i$ will be given by a variable-length sequence of *segments* $(\mathbf{s}_i^1, \ldots, \mathbf{s}_i^{N_i})$, where $\mathbf{s}_i^j$ denotes the j-th segment of route $\mathbf{r}_i$ and N_i the overall number of segments of the entire route. Each segment $\mathbf{s}_i^j$ is composed by a set of parameters,

$$\mathbf{s}_i^j \doteq \{(lat_i^{j,o}, lon_i^{j,o}), (lat_i^{j,d}, lon_i^{j,d}), d_i^j, t_i^j, \alpha_i^j, v_i^{j,max}\} \tag{1}$$

that characterize the segment in terms of its latitude/longitude extremes (^{o}: origin, ^{d}: destination), its length $d_i^j \in \mathbb{R}^+$, the time $t_i^j \in \mathbb{R}^+$ taken to traverse it by bike, its inclination profile $\alpha_i^j \in \mathbb{R}[0, 90]$, and maximum speed $v_i^{j,max} \in \mathbb{R}[0, V^{max}]$ of the road traffic along the segment, where V^{max} is the maximum admissible road vehicle speed as per the legislation of the scenario at hand.

Given that we seek continuous routes, they should all fulfill $(lat_i^{1,o}, lon_i^{1,o}) = (lat^{\circ}, lon^{\circ})$ and

$$(lat_i^{j,d}, lon_i^{j,d}) = (lat_i^{j+1,o}, lon_i^{j+1,o}), \quad \forall j = 1, \ldots, N_i - 1. \tag{2}$$

Based on the above notation, the overall distance and time of the route will be given by $f_D(\mathbf{r}_i) \doteq \sum_{j=1}^{N_i} d_i^j$ and $T(\mathbf{r}_i) \doteq \sum_{j=1}^{N_i} t_i^j$, i.e. the sum of segments' distance/time.

Intuitively, the level of safety when a bike traverses route $\mathbf{r}_i$ should be driven by two different aspects: first, the inclination of its segments should be as close to 0 as possible (namely, a flat segment) so that the rider does not loose control of the bike due to either a high speed and risk to encounter unavoidable moving obstacles along the segment (downhill), or a physically demanding uphill segment that could put in danger the health of the biker and his/her capability to react against vehicles in the opposite direction. All in all, it should be clear that the inclination of the segment as per α_i^j plays a crucial role when quantifying the degree of safety of a segment. Based on this rationale and the notation introduced above, we propose a measure of route safety as

$$f_S(\mathbf{r}_i) \doteq \sum_{j=1}^{N_i} \left(d_i^j / \cos \alpha_i^j\right)^{v_i^{j,max}/V^{max}} \tag{3}$$

from where it is straightforward to note that the higher the value of $f_S(\mathbf{r}_i)$ is, the less safe route $\mathbf{r}_i$ will be. In other words, $f_S(\mathbf{r}_i)$ must be conceptually conceived as a measure of the risk assumed by the biker when traversing route $\mathbf{r}_i$, which should be minimized in the problem formulation. The baseline user parameters required for stating the problem also include an upper bound T^{max} for the trip time $T(\mathbf{r}_i)$ needed to complete route $\mathbf{r}_i$. Routes $\mathbf{r}_{i'}$ for which $T(\mathbf{r}_i) > T^{max}$ should not be allowed to appear in the eventually output set of routes. Correspondingly, the minimum trip time is defined as a fraction $\rho \in \mathbb{R}[0,1]$ of T^{max}, such that a feasible route $\mathbf{r}_i$ should meet $T(\mathbf{r}_i) \geq \rho \cdot T^{max}$ in all cases. This parameter ρ is input by the user to reflect his/her tolerance respect to the admissible maximum time for the bike ride.

This notation being defined, the bike routing problem addressed in this paper can be formulated as the discovery of a set of routes that balances their safety and distance values in a Pareto optimal fashion satisfying, at the same time, lower and upper bounds in regards to their total duration. Mathematically:

$$\underset{\mathbf{R} \in \mathcal{R}}{\text{minimize}} \quad f_S(\mathbf{r}), \quad \underset{\mathbf{R} \in \mathcal{R}}{\text{maximize}} \quad f_D(\mathbf{r}), \tag{4a}$$

$$\text{subject to} \quad T(\mathbf{r}_i) \leq T^{max}, \tag{4b}$$

$$T(\mathbf{r}_i) \geq T^{min} = \rho \cdot T^{max}, \tag{4c}$$

$$(lat_i^{1,o}, lon_i^{1,o}) = (lat^{\circ}, lon^{\circ}) \, \forall \mathbf{r}_i \in \mathbf{R},, \tag{4d}$$

$$(lat_i^{j,d}, lon_i^{j,d}) = (lat_i^{j+1,o}, lon_i^{j+1,o}), \, \forall j = 1, \ldots, N_i - 1, \tag{4e}$$

where $\mathbf{R}$ denotes a variable-length set of trip routes rooted on $(lat^{\circ}, lon^{\circ})$, and $\mathcal{R}$ the number of all possible route sets satisfying this latter constraint.

3   Considered Solvers

We have chosen four population-based bio-inspired algorithms to solve the above bi-objective problem in a computationally efficient fashion. As a result, not only we obtain an insight of the solutions that can be obtained, but we can also determine which solver provides routes with best Pareto quality in terms of convergence and diversity.

However, before proceeding with the explanation of the utilized solvers, we delve into the strategy adopted to encode routes so that they can be handled by their heuristic operators. In this regard the numerical encoding does not represent a route by itself, but rather a set of factors that can be used to calculate a route by means of the OTP route generation engine. This way, each candidate route ($\mathbf{r}_p$) within the P-sized populations these algorithms is a vector comprising the following five values:

- *Latitude* $lat_p^{N_p}$ and *longitude* $lon_p^{N_p}$ of the destination location of route $\mathbf{r}_p$. Rather than using the true coordinates in the candidate, the relative difference between the origin location (lat°, lon°) and the coordinates ($lat_p^{N_p}, lon_p^{N_p}$) is instead used.
- *Safety preference* ($S_p \in \mathbb{R}[0,1]$), which stands for the priority that the OTP route planner should grant to the safety of the route. If this value is high, routes with a high safety will be better rated and output by the engine.
- *Inclination preference* ($I_p \in \mathbb{R}[0,1]$): the importance that the planner endows to the aggregate inclination of the route.
- *Duration preference* ($D_p \in \mathbb{R}[0,1]$): the importance that the route planner gives to the duration of the route.

These values are modified along the execution by means of the bio-inspired operators of every solver, repaired to ensure that $S_p + I_p + D_p = 1$ $\forall \mathbf{r}_p$ in the population, and delivered to the OTP engine as new routing requests to produce routes based on the new set of preferences. Once created, every newly produced route is evaluated in terms of safety and distance, and then ranked and sorted as defined by the heuristic algorithm at hand.

In this regard, three of the selected algorithms are NSGA-II [11], MOEA/D [12], and SMS-EMOA [13], which are archetypal of Pareto dominance based, decomposition based, and indicator based evolutionary algorithms, respectively. We also added a particle swarm optimization technique, SMPSO [14], which has shown a remarkable performance in solving continuous multi-objectives problems as the one we are dealing with. We briefly describe these metaheuristics next:

- NSGA-II (Non-dominated Sorting Genetic Algorithm II) is a generational genetic algorithm which has become the most well-known and widely used multi-objective algorithm since it was first proposed. It applies a Pareto ranking scheme to foster the convergence to the Pareto front and the crowding distance density estimator to promote the diversity of the front of solutions it is managing.

- MOEA/D (Multi-Objective Evolutionary Algorithm Based on Decomposition) is a steady-state evolutionary algorithm based on an aggregative approach with the aim of decomposing a multi-objective problem in a set of single-objective subproblems that are solved at the same time by taking into account information of a number of neighbors. We use in this paper the MOEA/DE version [16], which uses differential evolution instead of the mutation and crossover operators of the original proposal.
- SMS-EMOA (S-Metric Selection EMOA) is also an steady-state evolutionary algorithm which is based on NSGA-II but, instead of using the crowding distance density estimator, it applies the concept of hypervolume contribution. The idea is that, after applying the ranking procedure, the solution belonging to the last rank having the lowest contribution to the hypervolume of the set of solutions of that rank is removed.
- SMPSO (Speed-constrained Multi-objective PSO) is particle swarm optimization algorithm whose main features is the use of a velocity constraint mechanism, to avoid the particles to fly beyond the limits of the search space, and an external bounded-sized archive to store the non-dominated solutions found during the search. This archive is used also for leader selection and the crowding distance density estimator is used to remove solutions when it becomes full.

4   Description of the Simulation Environment

As has been mentioned in previous sections, the developed route planning system hinges on the route generation functionality provided by the OTP platform, an open source framework for mono and multi-modal journey planning. It follows a client-server model, and provides a map-based web and smartphone interface, as well as a REST API for its use with third-party applications. OTP operates with different open data standards, such as GeoTIFF, Protocol Buffers, General Transit Feed Specification (GTFS) and Open Street Map (OSM). Different reason have motivated the use of this platform:

- OTP is open source in its entirety, easing its adaptation to the specific simulation scenarios considered in this study.
- OTP efficiently works with OSM, providing the structure to automatically build the street network.
- OTP is well documented, updated, with an active, growing community of developers. These situation facilitates the understanding and maintenance of the platform.

The simulation platform developed in this study and architecturally illustrated in Fig. 2 relies on the Java project of OTP available in [15]. Specifically, this repository contains the complete code of the OTP system and the client for testing purposes. As can be read in the documentation of the project, *"it includes a REST API for journey planning as well as a map-based Javascript client. Open Trip Planner can also create travel time contour visualizations and*

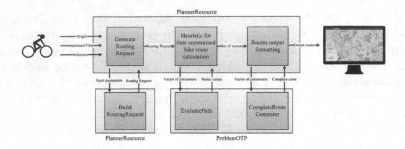

Fig. 2. Architecture of the deployed system.

compute accessibility indicators for planning and research applications". As OTP is open source, both parts have been adapted and modified to accommodate the requirements of this study and to enable constraining the routes in time, and the output of all segments comprising the generated route. Consequently, several classes have been created in order to deploy these functionalities.

In order to focus the scope of this manuscript strictly on the heuristic domain, implementation details on the modified OTP Java classes are not provided. Instead, we just mention and describe two newly developed methods, which are crucial for the understanding of the whole system: (1) `evaluatePath()`, recurrently called by the algorithm to return the length and safety of the route provided as an input; and (2) `completeRouteGenerator()`, which returns the entire path calculated by the OTP engine from its encoded representation for visualization and further analysis. Finally, it should be noted that the architecture also integrates the jMetal framework [17] jointly with OTP for implementing the considered multi-objective solvers.

5   Experimental Setup

In order to shed light on the empirical performance of the 4 multi-objective optimization algorithms considered to deal with the posed routing problem, several computer experiments have been carried out over different square areas located in the city of Bilbao (Spain), bounded by coordinates $(lat^{min}, lat^{max}) = (lat^{\circlearrowleft} - 0.1425, lat^{\circlearrowleft} + 0.1425)$ and $(lon^{min}, lon^{max}) = (lon^{\circlearrowleft} - 0.0665, lon^{\circlearrowleft} + 0.0665)$. Differences between scenarios yield from the selection of different initial points $(lon^{\circlearrowleft}, lat^{\circlearrowleft})$ for the routes, so that topological changes in the urban areas enclosed by such squares are expected to arise from the performed experiments. These selected scenarios are characterized by a flat, a highly slopped (hilly) and a hybrid terrain profile. This tailored choice permits to verify how the proposed system and the considered heuristic solvers behave in geographically diverse setups. Two different open data sources have been used for the deployment of these real-world scenarios:

– *OSM map files*: the maps and street networks of the simulated scenarios have been retrieved in the form of OSM map files from the Planet OSM public repository [18], using the open tool BBBike [19] to download them in Protocolbuffer Binary Format (PBF). The downloaded OSM tiles contain all nodes, ways and relations required to build the map. OSM files are directly consumed by OTP, which automatically constructs the full road network.

- *Digital Elevation Model*: the elevations of the streets of Bilbao is downloaded from SRTM Tile Grabber[1] and directly consumed by OTP in GeoTIFF format. This format is a public domain metadata standard, which allows georeferencing information to be embedded within a TIFF file [20]. OTP uses these files for assigning the corresponding elevation to the entire street network, and it is employed for calculating the route flatness and safety.

Table 1. Parameter setting of the heuristics considered in the experimental benchmark.

Algorithm	Parameter	Value
All	*Population/swarm size*	100 individuals/particles
	Evaluations	5000
	Independent runs	15
	Mutation	Polynomial mutation
	| *Probability*	0.2 (once per every 5 decision variables)
	| *Distribution index* η_m	20.0
NSGA-II SMS-EMOA	*Crossover*	Simulated binary crossover
	| *Probability*	1.0
	| *Distribution index* η_m	20
MOEA/D	Differential evolution scheme	rand/1/bin
	| *CR*	1.0
	| *F*	0.5
	Neighborhood size	20
	Neighborhood selection probability	0.9
	Max. number of replaced solutions	2
SMPSO	*Archive size*	100
	Density estimator	Crowding distance

As the bike routing is a continuous optimization problem, we have configured the algorithms with commonly accepted settings, without any attempt at finding their best parameter configuration. A summary of the parameters is included in Table 1. All the algorithms have a population size of 100 individuals (or particles in the case of SMPSO) and use a polynomial mutation operator which is applied

---

[1] http://dwtkns.com/srtm/.

with a probability of 0.2 (according to the typical value of 1.0 / L, where $L = 5$ is the number of decision variables of the problem) and a distributed index equal to 20.0; the maximum number of function evaluations has been fixed to 5000. Both NSGA-II and SMS-EMOA apply a simulated binary crossover, with a probability of 1.0 and a distributed index equal to 20.0. MOEA/D follows a rand/1/bin differential evolution scheme, with parameters $CR = 1.0$ and $F = 0.5$. The values of the neighborhood size, the neighborhood selection probability, and maximum number of replace solutions are 20, 0.9, and 2, respectively. SMSPO has an external archive of a maximum size of 100 particles and applies the crowding distance density estimator.

For proving the robustness of the methods and extracting fair and rigorous conclusions, 15 independent runs have been made per algorithm for all problem scenarios (see next section). To assess the performance of the algorithms, we have used the so-called hypervolume [21], a Pareto compliant quality indicator that takes into account both the convergence and diversity of the Pareto front approximations returned by the solvers included in the benchmark.

Since we deal with an optimization problem whose true Pareto front is unknown, we have generated a reference Pareto front for each instance by combining all the non-dominated solutions computed in all the executions of all the algorithms. This front will be used as a reference to compute the hypervolume. Furthermore, in order to assess whether the differences between the algorithm results have statistical significance, we have applied the Wilcoxon rank-sum text, a non-parametric statistical hypothesis test which allows for a pairwise comparison between two samples. A significance level of 5% has been considered, meaning that the differences are unlikely to have occurred by chance with a probability of 95%.

5.1   Results and Discussion

To illustrate the fronts that each of the four compared algorithms have produced, we include in Fig. 3 (next page) the approximations corresponding to the best hypervolume values for the flat (first row), hybrid (second row) and hilly scenario (third row). To ease the visualization of the solutions, the reference Pareto front is included as a continuous line. We can observe how SMPSO excels at generating a set of solutions that are on top of the reference Pareto front and that are uniformly spread, including the extreme solutions. By contrast, MOEA/D fails to generate a front with accurate convergence and widespread diversity.

The results of the hypervolume values obtained by the four metaheuristics are presented in Table 2, which includes the median and interquartile range of the 15 independent runs per algorithm and problem instance. Those cells with a dark and light gray backgrounds indicates, respectively, the best and second best indicator values. We can observe that the particle swarm optimization algorithm SMPSO has produced the best (highest) values in the three considered scenarios. NSGA-II and SMS-EMOA have yielded, respectively, two and one second best values.

Table 2. Median and Inter Quartile Range (IQR) of the hypervolume values obtained by the algorithms. Best and second best median results have dark and light gray backgrounds, respectively.

	SMPSO	NSGA-II	MOEA/D	SMS-EMOA
Flat scenario	$5.80e-01_{8.8e-03}$	$5.68e-01_{6.2e-03}$	$5.27e-01_{7.5e-03}$	$5.64e-01_{1.2e-02}$
Hybrid scenario	$5.95e-01_{3.8e-03}$	$5.79e-01_{1.0e-02}$	$5.30e-01_{1.8e-02}$	$5.74e-01_{1.2e-02}$
Hilly scenario	$7.00e-01_{8.4e-03}$	$6.13e-01_{5.0e-02}$	$5.71e-01_{2.2e-02}$	$6.20e-01_{8.2e-02}$

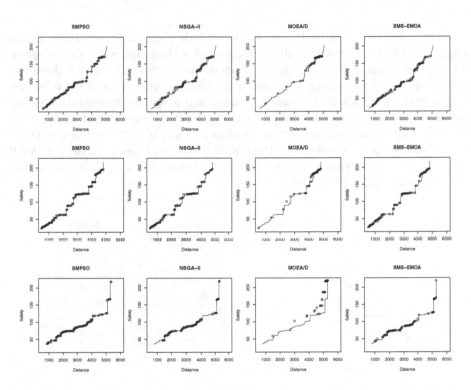

Fig. 3. Estimated Pareto fronts with the best hypervolume values obtained by the four compared algorithms for the flat (first row), hybrid (second row) and hilly (third row) scenarios. The line stands for the reference Pareto front approximation.

To determine whether the differences between pair of algorithms are statistically significant, we have applied the Wilcoxon rank-sum test; the obtained results are included in Table 3. In each cell, the three considered scenarios (plain, medium, and high) are represented with one of the following symbols: "–" indicates that there not statistical significance between the algorithms, "▲" means that the algorithm in the row has yielded better results than the algorithm in the column with confidence, and "∇" is used when the algorithm in the column is statistically better than the algorithm in the row. We can observe that all the differences are significant but the results of NSGA-II and SMS-EMOA, so we can claim that SMPSO is the algorithm providing the best overall performance in the context of the study carried out.

Table 3. Wilcoxon test results. Each cell contains a symbol per problem (flat, hybrid, hilly).

	NSGA-II	MOEA/D	SMS-EMOA
SMPSO	▲ ▲ ▲	▲ ▲ ▲	▲ ▲ ▲
NSGA-II		▲ ▲ ▲	– – –
MOEA/D			▽ ▽ ▽

The results provided by the hypervolume indicator are quantitative, in the sense that they indicate which algorithm generates the fronts with better degrees of convergence and diversity. However, they do not provide any insight about the quality of the solutions. For that reason, we next include in Fig. 4 the reference Pareto fronts for each of the three scenarios, and a visual representation of the routes corresponding to the points in the estimated Pareto front of the hilly scenario. Indeed differences are visually clear in regards to the distance of every route: interesting is to note that the one in green traverses a urban area with sharp slopes (namely, the urban core of the town of Portugalete within the metropolitan area of *Gran Bilbao*).

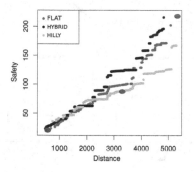 

Fig. 4. (Left) Reference Pareto fronts obtained for the three considered scenarios; (Right) routes corresponding to the colored points in the reference Pareto front of the hilly scenario. (Color figure online)

6   Conclusions and Further Work

In this work the design of time-constrained bike routes has been studied and approached from a multi-criteria perspective. The focus has been placed on generating a group of open-destination bike routes based on three input parameters: origin, maximum trip time and tolerance. The problem has been modeled as a bi-objective paradigm balancing two conflicting objectives: the distance of the route and its safety level, the latter blending together the inclination of segments composing the route, their length and the speed of vehicles along each segment.

For efficiently tackling this problem, four bio-inspired multi-objective optimization methods have been used (namely, NSGA-II, SMS-EMOA, MOEA/D, and SMPSO), and applied to three different real-world scenarios placed in Bilbao, Spain. Experiments have been conducted in a realistic simulation environment based on Open Trip Planner as the software simulation platform. The obtained results reveal that the SMPSO solver outperforms its counterparts in the benchmark in terms of Pareto optimality as gauged by their hypervolume indicator.

Several research lines will be tackled in the near future. In short term, additional bio-inspired approaches are planned to be included in the benchmark to assess whether they get to obtain better results in terms of Pareto spread and dominance. In the longer term we intend to extend the problem formulation to add new objectives such as the energy consumed by the user and air pollution in the route. Real open data will be utilized to model this improved setup.

Acknowledgments. E. Osaba and J. Del Ser would like to thank the Basque Government for its funding support through the EMAITEK program. This work is also partially funded by Grants TIN2017-86049-R and TIN2014-58304 (Ministerio de Ciencia e Innovación), and P11-TIC-7529 and P12-TIC-1519 (Plan Andaluz I+D+I).

References

1. Wang, F.Y.: Scanning the issue and beyond: transportation and mobility transformation for smart cities. IEEE Trans. Intell. Transp. Syst. **16**(2), 525–533 (2015)
2. Bast, H., Delling, D., Goldberg, A., Müller-Hannemann, M., Pajor, T., Sanders, P., Wagner, D., Werneck, R.F.: Route planning in transportation networks. In: Kliemann, L., Sanders, P. (eds.) Algorithm Engineering. LNCS, vol. 9220, pp. 19–80. Springer, Cham (2016). https://doi.org/10.1007/978-3-319-49487-6_2
3. Zografos, K.G., Androutsopoulos, K.N.: Algorithms for itinerary planning in multimodal transportation networks. IEEE Trans. Intell. Transp. Syst. **9**(1), 175–184 (2008)
4. Staunton, C.E., Hubsmith, D., Kallins, W.: Promoting safe walking and biking to school: the marin county success story. Am. J. Public Health **93**(9), 1431–1434 (2003)
5. Wang, S., Lin, W., Yang, Y., Xiao, X., Zhou, S.: Efficient route planning on public transportation networks: a labelling approach. In: Proceedings of the 2015 ACM SIGMOD International Conference on Management of Data, pp. 967–982. ACM (2015)
6. Turverey, R.J., Cheng, D.D., Blair, O.N., Roth, J.T., Lamp, G.M., Cogill, R.: Charlottesville bike route planner. In: Systems and Information Engineering Design Symposium, pp. 68–72. IEEE (2010)
7. Bucher, D., Jonietz, D., Raubal, M.: A heuristic for multi-modal route planning. In: Gartner, G., Huang, H. (eds.) Progress in Location-Based Services 2016. LNGC, pp. 211–229. Springer, Cham (2017). https://doi.org/10.1007/978-3-319-47289-8_11
8. Hrnčíř, J., Žilecký, P., Song, Q., Jakob, M.: Practical multicriteria urban bicycle routing. IEEE Trans. Intell. Transp. Syst. **18**(3), 493–504 (2017)
9. Martins, E.Q.V.: On a multicriteria shortest path problem. Eur. J. Oper. Res. **16**(2), 236–245 (1984)

10. Caggiani, L., Camporeale, R., Ottomanelli, M.: A real time multi-objective cyclists route choice model for a bike-sharing mobile application. In: IEEE International Conference on Models and Technologies for Intelligent Transportation Systems, pp. 645–650. IEEE (2017)
11. Deb, K., Pratap, A., Agarwal, S., Meyarivan, T.: A fast and elitist multiobjective genetic algorithm: NSGA-II. IEEE Trans. Evol. Comput. **6**(2), 182 197 (2002)
12. Zhang, Q., Li, H.: MOEA/D: a multiobjective evolutionary algorithm based on decomposition. IEEE Trans. Evol. Comput. **8**(11), 712–731 (2008)
13. Beume, N., Naujoks, B., Emmerich, M.: SMS-EMOA: multiobjective selection based on dominated hypervolume. Eur. J. Oper. Res. **181**(3), 1653–1669 (2007)
14. Nebro, A.J., Durillo, J.J., Garcia-Nieto, J., Coello, C.C., Luna, F., Alba, E.: SMPSO: a new PSO-based metaheuristic for multi-objective optimization. In: IEEE Symposium on Computational Intelligence in Multi-criteria Decision-Making (MCDM 2009), pp. 66–73. IEEE Press (2009)
15. Open Trip Planner. https://github.com/opentripplanner. Accessed 30 Nov 2017
16. Li, H., Zhang, Q.: Multiobjective optimization problems with complicated pareto sets, MOEA/D and NSGA-II. IEEE Trans. Evol. Comput. **12**(2), 284–302 (2009)
17. Durillo, J.J., Nebro, A.J.: jMetal: a java framework for multi-objective optimization. Adv. Eng. Softw. **42**(10), 760–771 (2011)
18. Planet OSM. https://planet.osm.org/. Accessed 30 Nov 2017
19. BBBike tool. https://extract.bbbike.org/. Accessed 30 Nov 2017
20. Hart, C., Koupal, J., Giannelli, R.: EPA's onboard analysis shootout: Overview and results. Technical report, United States Environmental Protection Agency (2002)
21. Zitzler, E., Thiele, L.: Multiobjective evolutionary algorithms: a comparative case study and the strength pareto approach. IEEE Trans. Evol. Comp. **3**(4), 257–271 (1999)

Ensemble of Kriging with Multiple Kernel Functions for Engineering Design Optimization

Pramudita Satria Palar$^{(\boxtimes)}$ and Koji Shimoyama

Institute of Fluid Science, Tohoku University,
Sendai, Miyagi Prefecture 980-8577, Japan
pramudita.satria.palar.a5@tohoku.ac.jp

Abstract. We introduce the ensemble of Kriging with multiple kernel functions guided by cross-validation error for creating a robust and accurate surrogate model to handle engineering design problems. By using the ensemble of Kriging models, the resulting ensemble model preserves the uncertainty structure of Kriging, thus, can be further exploited for Bayesian optimization. The objective of this paper is to develop a Kriging methodology that eliminates the needs for manual kernel selection which might not be optimal for a specific application. Kriging models with three kernel functions, that is, Gaussian, Matérn-3/2, and Matérn-5/2 are combined through a global and a local ensemble technique where their approximation quality are investigated on a set of aerodynamic problems. Results show that the ensemble approaches are more robust in terms of accuracy and able to perform similarly to the best performing individual kernel function or avoiding misspecification of kernel.

1 Introduction

The computationally expensive nature of many real-world engineering optimizations hinders the crude of use of evolutionary algorithms (EA) and other meta-heuristics for obtaining highly optimized designs. To this end, surrogate models are now commonly deployed to act as a replacement for black-box functions in order to accelerate the optimization process. There are basically two frameworks to apply surrogate models, that is, to utilize them either as a global or local surrogate model. Global surrogate models are particularly useful when the number of design variables is low to moderate under the constraint of a limited computational budget. On the other hand, local surrogate models are typically used under the condition of high-dimensionality and moderate computational budget, such as to assist the local search for memetic algorithm [1,2]. For a comprehensive review of this topic, readers are referred to Jin [3] and Viana et al. [4].

Kriging is one of the most widely used types of surrogate model for approximating engineering functions. One powerful aspect of Kriging models is that they provide a measure of estimation error that could be used to guide Bayesian

© Springer International Publishing AG, part of Springer Nature 2018
P. Korošec et al. (Eds.): BIOMA 2018, LNCS 10835, pp. 211–222, 2018.
https://doi.org/10.1007/978-3-319-91641-5_18

optimization or error-based refinement in order to improve the approximation quality [5]. The most widely used kernel function for constructing Kriging models in the context of engineering design is the Gaussian kernel function. On the other hand, Stein recommends that Matérn kernel function should be used instead of Gaussian since the smoothness of Gaussian function is unrealistic for many real-world processes [6]. It is worth noting that the best kernel function is highly problem dependent; therefore, it is of utmost importance to correctly deploy a proper kernel for optimum approximation accuracy.

One approach to combine or take the best from multiple surrogate models is to perform an ensemble of surrogate models [7–11]. Traditionally, various surrogate models such as radial basis function (RBF), Kriging, and support vector regression are combined together, which results in the inapplicability of Bayesian optimization (e.g., efficient global optimization [5]). Bayesian optimization can be performed with the ensemble model if each of the constituent models possesses an uncertainty structure. In this paper, we propose to combine multiple Kriging models with multiple kernel functions. The advantage of the ensemble of Kriging models with various kernel functions is that the uncertainty structure is still conserved. We tested the proposed framework on a set of aerodynamic problems using various ensemble methods. In this paper, we limit the research scope to only analyzing the approximation accuracy of the ensemble Kriging models and compared them to those with single kernel function.

Note that the mixture of Kriging with kernel function is not totally a new idea; in fact, this idea was first proposed by Ginsbourger et al. [12]. Ginsbourger et al. approach uses the combination of Gaussian and exponential kernel function and mix them globally with Akaike weights; while in this paper, we utilize the cross-validation (CV) error to mix the Kriging model with Gaussian and advanced Matérn kernel function using both the global and local ensemble. Moreover, Ginsbourger et al.'s method was only tested on Branin function while we directly used engineering functions in our study.

2   Ensemble of Kriging

2.1   Kriging Model

We are interested in approximating a black box function $y = f(\boldsymbol{x})$ with a Kriging surrogate model, where $\boldsymbol{x} = \{x_1, x_2, \ldots, x_m\}$ and m is the dimensionality of the decision variables. The Kriging approximation is modeled as a realization of a stationary Gaussian process $Y(\boldsymbol{x})$ reads as

$$Y(\boldsymbol{x}) = \sum_{i=0}^{P-1} \alpha_i \Psi_i(\boldsymbol{x}) + Z(\boldsymbol{x}), \tag{1}$$

where $\boldsymbol{\Psi}(\boldsymbol{x}) = \{\Psi_0(\boldsymbol{x}), \ldots, \Psi_{P-1}(\boldsymbol{x})\}$ is a collection of regression polynomial functions, $\boldsymbol{\alpha} = \{\alpha_0(\boldsymbol{x}), \ldots, \alpha_{P-1}(\boldsymbol{x})\}$ is the vector of regression coefficients, and Z is a stochastic process. In this paper, we use the ordinary Kriging which assumes that the trend is a constant Ψ_0.

One building block of Kriging is the covariance function which represents the similarity between two input points in the design space. There are several choices to model this similarity using different types of kernel function. In this paper, we opt for the Gaussian and Matérn class function due to their robustness and popularity in various applications. We do not opt for the exponential function since based on our experiment in aerodynamic functions, it did not yield a satisfactory accuracy. These kernel functions are explained in detail below.

Gaussian. The Gaussian kernel function is defined as

$$R(h, \theta) = \exp\left(-\sum_{k=1}^{m} \left(\frac{h}{\theta}\right)^2\right),$$ (2)

where $\boldsymbol{\theta} = \{\theta_1, \ldots, \theta_m\}$ are the vector of hyperparameters that needs to be estimated and $h = |\boldsymbol{x} - \boldsymbol{x}'|$.

Matérn Class. The general form of Matérn kernel function is expressed as

$$R(h, \theta, \nu) = \frac{1}{2^{\nu-1}\Gamma(\nu)}\left(2\sqrt{\nu}\frac{|h|}{\theta}\right)\mathcal{K}_\nu\left(2\sqrt{\nu}\frac{|h|}{\theta}\right),$$ (3)

where $\nu \geq 1/2$ is the shape parameter, Γ is the Gamma function, and $\mathcal{K}_\nu$ is the modified Bessel function of the second kind.

For $\nu = 3/2$, the formulation of Matérn kernel function is defined as

$$R(h, \theta, \nu = 3/2) = \left(1 + \frac{\sqrt{3}|h|}{\theta}\right)\exp\left(-\frac{\sqrt{3}|h|}{\theta}\right),$$ (4)

while for $\nu = 5/2$ is defined as

$$R(h, \theta, \nu = 5/2) = \left(1 + \frac{\sqrt{5}|h|}{\theta} + \frac{5h^2}{3\theta^2}\right)\exp\left(-\frac{\sqrt{5}|h|}{\theta}\right).$$ (5)

The Matérn$-3/2$ and Matérn$-5/2$ are two forms that are widely used to model real-world processes. We, therefore, used these two forms of Matérn kernel function in our study and compare it with the standard Gaussian.

A set of n observations points $\mathcal{X} = \{\boldsymbol{x}^{(1)}, \ldots, \boldsymbol{x}^{(n)}\}$ and the responses $\boldsymbol{y} = \{y^{(1)}, \ldots, y^{(n)}\} = \{f(\boldsymbol{x}^{(1)}), \ldots, f(\boldsymbol{x})^{(n)}\}$ are collected first in order to create a Kriging surface. As opposed to the majority of the types of surrogate model, Kriging allows the computation of both the prediction $\hat{y}(\boldsymbol{x})$ and the mean-squared error $\hat{s}^2(\boldsymbol{x})$.

The ordinary Kriging prediction for an arbitrary input variable reads as

$$\hat{y}(\boldsymbol{x}) = \mu_{KR} + \boldsymbol{r}(\boldsymbol{x})^T \boldsymbol{R}^{-1}(\boldsymbol{y} - \boldsymbol{1}),$$ (6)

with the mean-squared error of the Kriging prediction $\hat{s}(\boldsymbol{x})$ reads as:

$$\hat{s}^2(\boldsymbol{x}) = \sigma^2\left(1 - (\boldsymbol{r}(\boldsymbol{x})^T \boldsymbol{R}^{-1}\boldsymbol{r}(\boldsymbol{x})) + \left(1 - \boldsymbol{1}^T \boldsymbol{R}^{-1}\boldsymbol{r}(\boldsymbol{x})\right)^2 \left(\boldsymbol{1}^T \boldsymbol{R}^{-1}\boldsymbol{1}\right)^{-1}\right).$$ (7)

Here, R is the $n \times n$ matrix with the (i, j) entry is $\mathrm{corr}[Z(\boldsymbol{x}^{(i)}), Z(\boldsymbol{x}^{(j)})]$, $\boldsymbol{r}(\boldsymbol{x})$ is the correlation vector between $\boldsymbol{x}$ and $\mathcal{X}$ whose $(i, 1)$ entry is $\mathrm{corr}[Z(\boldsymbol{x}^{(i)}), Z(\boldsymbol{x})]$, and $\mathbf{1}$ is the vector of ones with length n. As we can see from this formulation, the choice of kernel function enters the formulation through R and $\boldsymbol{r}(\boldsymbol{x})$. In this paper, we opt for the standard technique of maximizing the likelihood function to determine the hyperparameters. We do not go too much into details of the Kriging method; readers are referred to other literatures such as [5,13].

Since the determination of a proper kernel function is not trivial, we advocate the use of the ensemble of Kriging models with various kernel functions instead of choosing just one specific kernel. We hypothesized that this would improve the robustness and accuracy of Kriging models while still preserving the uncertainty structure through the law of total expectation and total variance [12].

2.2   Ensemble of Kriging Models

Assuming that we possess K different surrogate models, the general form of the ensemble of surrogate models reads as

$$\hat{f}_{ens}(\boldsymbol{x}) = \sum_{i=1}^{K} w_i(\boldsymbol{x}) \hat{f}_i(\boldsymbol{x}) \tag{8}$$

where $\hat{f}_1(\boldsymbol{x}), \ldots, \hat{f}_K(\boldsymbol{x})$ are K surrogate models to be combined into one model and $\boldsymbol{w}(\boldsymbol{x}) = \{w_1(\boldsymbol{x}), \ldots, w_K(\boldsymbol{x})\}$ are the weights that define the contribution of each surrogate model to the ensemble function.

To perform the ensemble of surrogates, we need the information of the CV error, i.e., $\boldsymbol{e}$ for each Kriging model. We firstly define $\boldsymbol{e}_i = \{e_i^{(1)}, \ldots, e_i^{(n)}\}$, where $e^{(j)} = y(\boldsymbol{x}^{(j)}) - \hat{y}^{(-j)}(\boldsymbol{x}^{(j)})$ is the CV error for sample j with the sample j is removed from the experimental design, as the CV errors for surrogate i. For Kriging models, the CV error can be obtained analytically without the need to construct Kriging n times [14]. The simplest approach is to directly select the Kriging model with the lowest CV error, where in this paper we opt for the root-mean-squared error (RMSE) to compute the CV error for each surrogate. However, as argued by Viana et al. [8], the ensemble of surrogate models is the better approach since it uses all information from each constituent surrogate model instead of directly choosing the best one in terms of the CV error.

There are two techniques to ensemble the function, that is, the global and local ensemble approach which are explained below.

Global Ensemble. The global ensemble approach employs a constant weight for each surrogate model in the range of the design space. In this paper, we opt for Acar and Rohani's approach [9] to construct the global ensemble. Here, the constant weight $\boldsymbol{w}$ is found by solving the following minimization problem

$$\min_{\boldsymbol{w}} \mathrm{MSE}_{ens} = \mathbb{E}\big(e_{\mathrm{WAS}}^2(\boldsymbol{x})\mathrm{d}\boldsymbol{x}\big) = \mathbf{w}^T \mathbf{C} \mathbf{w}, \tag{9}$$

where MSE_{ens} is the mean squared error of the global ensemble, $\mathbf{C}$ is the matrix of CV error and e_{WAS}^2 is the mean-squared error of the weighted average surrogate. Following Viana et al.'s suggestion [8], we only used the diagonal matrix of $\mathbf{C}$ to compute $\mathbf{w} = \{w_1, w_2, \ldots, w_K\}$ using Lagrange multipliers.

Local Ensemble. One downside of the global ensemble approach, in spite of its simplicity, is its inability to cope with the locality of the response surface. There are situations where Kriging with one type of kernel function is accurate in a certain region while another kernel is more suitable in other regions of the design space. To this end, the local ensemble is probably more suitable since it allows a non-constant weight function to be used. In this paper, we opt for Liu et al.'s approach [11] which originally proposed the method for creating the local ensemble of radial basis function models; readers are also referred to this paper for a more detail explanation about the method. Using Liu et al.'s approach, the weight for surrogate j at a certain design point is calculated by

$$w_j(\boldsymbol{x}) = \begin{cases} \text{if } \boldsymbol{x} \neq \boldsymbol{x}_i & : \sum_{i=1}^{n} \frac{d_i^{-B_i \Theta}}{\sum d_i^{-B_i \Theta}}, \\ \text{if } \boldsymbol{x} = \boldsymbol{x}_i & : W_{ij} \end{cases} \tag{10}$$

where Θ is the attenuation coefficient that is automatically selected using CV error, d_i is the distance between $\boldsymbol{x}$ and $\boldsymbol{x}_i$, B_i is the normalized global accuracy of the constituent model that yields the the lowest error at $\boldsymbol{x}_i$, and $\boldsymbol{W}$ is the observed weight matrix.

According to the law of total expectation, the prediction and variance from the mixture of multiple Kriging models can be computed through the law of total expectation and total variance [12], respectively. In this paper, we use the UQLab open source software to construct the Kriging model [15].

3   Applications to Aerodynamic Problems

We consider two engineering test cases in order to demonstrate the efficacy of the ensemble methods. The two problems considered are the subsonic and transonic airfoil (i.e., the cross-section of an aircraft wing) design, with two subcases for the subsonic airfoil problem. Here, the output of interest for all cases is the drag coefficient (C_d), computed by a computational fluid dynamics method, which measures the efficiency of aerodynamic bodies. For each test case, we compared the Kriging model with Gaussian, Matérn-3/2, and Matérn-5/2 kernel functions, the scheme that yields the lowest CV error (i.e., model selection), local ensemble, and global ensemble. The Kriging quality is measured by the squared correlation coefficient, i.e., R^2. We also use the average performance score (APS) [16] to compare various Kriging methods. APS indicates the number of other methods that strictly dominate the method being investigated; thus, low APS value denotes a good performing method.

3.1 Subsonic Airfoil Problem

Design optimization of an airfoil in subsonic flow regime for low-speed is highly useful for such applications as unmanned aerial vehicles or low-speed training aircraft. For the subsonic airfoil problem, we used the PARSEC airfoil parameterization technique [17] (see Fig. 1 and Table 1) and we set the Reynolds and Mach number to 3×10^6 and 0.3, respectively. Here, the first and second subcase considers a fixed angle of attack of 2° and fix $C_l = 0.5$, respectively. The lower and upper bound (i.e., l_b and u_b, respectively) for the subsonic airfoil problem are shown in Table 1. Since this case is cheap, we could evaluate a large number of samples for the training and validation set. We used training sample points with $n = 40$ and $n = 80$ generated by Latin hypercube sampling with 1000 validation samples.

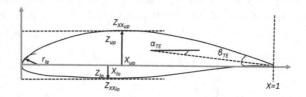

Fig. 1. Illustration of PARSEC airfoil parameterization.

Table 1. The upper and lower bounds for the subsonic airfoil problem.

Variable	Definition	l_b	u_b
r_{le}	Leading edge radius	0.0108	0.0162
X_{up}	Upper crest position in horizontal coordinates	0.3288	0.4932
Z_{up}	Upper crest position in vertical coordinates	0.0830	0.1245
$Z_{XX_{up}}$	Upper crest curvature	−0.8700	−0.5800
X_{lo}	Lower crest position in horizontal coordinates	0.3254	0.4881
Z_{lo}	Lower crest position in vertical coordinates	−0.0690	−0.0460
$Z_{XX_{lo}}$	Lower crest curvature	0.3086	0.4629
α_{te}	Trailing edge direction	−0.2286	−0.1524
β_{te}	Trailing edge wedge angle	0.1120	0.1680

Results for Subcase 1. The R^2 results for the first subsonic case are shown in Fig. 2. Comparison of Kriging models with single kernel function shows that Gaussian is the most suitable kernel function for this particular problem, followed by Matérn-5/2 and Matérn-3/2. The global ensemble and model selection are the most robust multiple kernel approaches that can match the approximation quality of the Kriging with the Gaussian kernel. On the other hand, the local ensemble is outperformed by two methods on a high number of sample points (i.e., $n = 80$).

The weight distribution obtained from all 30 independent runs for $n = 40$ and $n = 80$ are shown in Figs. 3 and 4, respectively. First, the model selection has a very strong tendency to select Gaussian kernel over the others for both n; this indicates that the approximation quality of Kriging with the Gaussian kernel is far superior over the Matérn kernels for this problem. For the global ensemble scheme, there is a fairer distribution of kernel, where the kernel with the highest portion is Gaussian followed by Matérn-5/2 and Matérn-3/2. We observe a difference between the proportion of kernels for the global and local ensemble, that is, the latter tends to favor Matérn-3/2 over Matérn-5/2. This means that the Kriging model with Matérn-3/2 kernel is able to produce a locally accurate approximation near the design points over the Matérn-3/2 kernel; this trend is stronger with higher sample size. However, such scheme is not as optimal as the global ensemble for this particular problem.

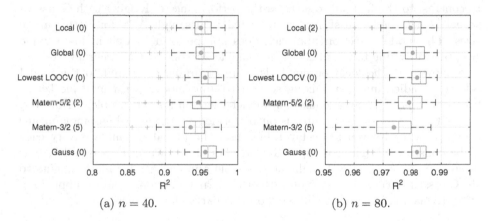

(a) $n = 40$.   (b) $n = 80$.

Fig. 2. R^2 results for the first subcase of subsonic airfoil problem. The number inside the bracket shows the corresponding APS value.

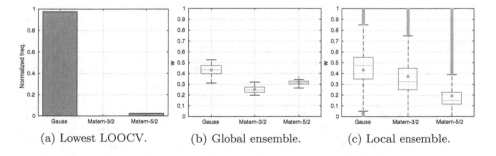

(a) Lowest LOOCV.   (b) Global ensemble.   (c) Local ensemble.

Fig. 3. Distribution of the weights for the first subsonic case with $n = 40$.

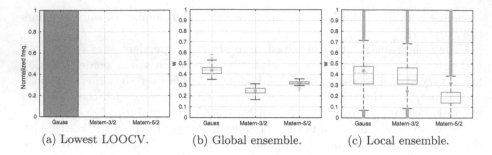

(a) Lowest LOOCV.   (b) Global ensemble.   (c) Local ensemble.

Fig. 4. Distribution of the weights for the first subsonic case with $n = 80$.

Result for Subcase 2. The results for subsonic case 2 (see Fig. 5) reveal that the global ensemble is able to compete with the two best-performing methods for this problem, that is, Kriging with Matérn-3/2 and Matérn-5/2 kernel function. In contrast to the first subsonic case, the performance of Kriging with Gaussian kernel is not really satisfying as indicated by its high APS for both sample sizes. The model selection approach does not perform so well in low sample size, primarily due to the effect of low sample size on the CV accuracy. Results also show that the local ensemble is more favorable compared to the model selection, indicating that mixing several Kriging models with multiple kernel function is more advantageous than model selection for this problem. However, the fact that the local ensemble is outperformed by the global ensemble means that the latter is even more favorable; also, the global ensemble is very easy to be constructed. The corresponding weights are shown in Figs. 6 and 7. It is interesting to see that although the ensemble approaches give more weights to the Gaussian kernel, combination with other kernel functions yields a suppressing effect to the inadequacy of Gaussian on this particular problem.

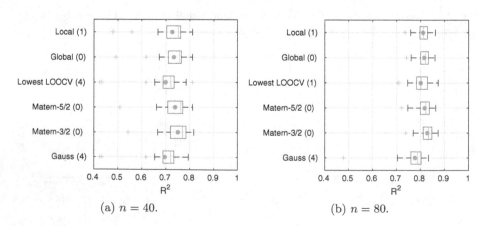

(a) $n = 40$.   (b) $n = 80$.

Fig. 5. R^2 results for the second subsonic airfoil case. The number inside the bracket shows the performance score.

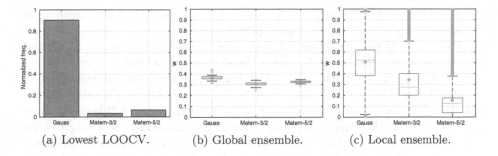

(a) Lowest LOOCV.   (b) Global ensemble.   (c) Local ensemble.

Fig. 6. Distribution of the weights for the second subsonic case with $n = 80$.

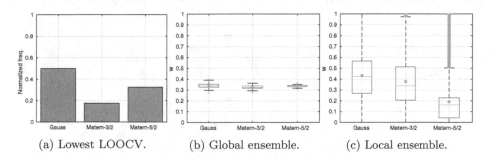

(a) Lowest LOOCV.   (b) Global ensemble.   (c) Local ensemble.

Fig. 7. Distribution of the weights for the second subsonic case with $n = 80$.

3.2 Inviscid Transonic Airfoil Problem

The second sub-case is the design of inviscid (i.e., no friction) transonic airfoil problem in Mach number of 0.73, which is the flying regime of a modern commercial aircraft, and angle of attack of 2°. The airfoil shape for the transonic problem is parameterized by the Class Shape Transformation (CST) [18] method with a total of 16 variables (i.e., 8 variables for each upper and lower surface). We used the RAE 2822 airfoil shape as the datum and then varied the CST shape parameters by ±20%. We set n to $n = 50$ and $n = 100$ by taking a subset of random samples from the available 400 samples and then use the other subset as validation samples.

The R^2 results are depicted in Fig. 8 while the distributions of the generated weight are shown in Figs. 9 and 10. We observe that the Gaussian kernel strictly outperforms Matérn kernels, especially Matérn-3/2. Due to this significant performance difference, the performance of the model selection scheme successfully mimics that of the Kriging model with the Gaussian kernel. On the other hand, the local and the global ensemble approach are outperformed by the model selection and Kriging with the Gaussian kernel; however, it is worth noting that the ensemble schemes successfully avoid the relatively poor performance of Kriging with Matérn-3/2 kernel and are also better than that of Matérn-5/2. In this regard, the ensemble schemes act as a safeguard that prevents a misspecification of kernel that yields a relatively poor performance.

The trend of the weighting for the kernels shows a similar trend to that of the subsonic airfoil case. In the inviscid transonic airfoil case, the weight of Matérn-5/2 in the global ensemble scheme is more dominant than that of Matérn-3/2, while it is the opposite case for the local ensemble. Especially on the first subsonic and transonic airfoil case, Kriging with Matérn-5/2 kernel is more globally accurate than that of Matérn-3/2; which explains why the local ensemble scheme is less accurate than the global one since the former tends to give more reward to the Matérn-3/2 kernel. However, when Bayesian optimization is to be performed, there is a chance that the local ensemble scheme would be better than the global ensemble due to that a local accuracy is more important for optimization; empirical experiments are needed to test this hypothesis.

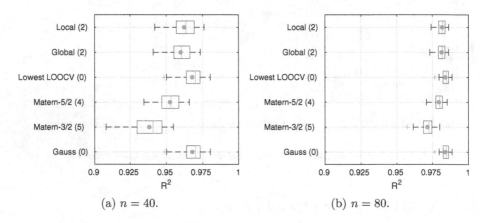

(a) $n = 40$.   (b) $n = 80$.

Fig. 8. R^2 results for the inviscid transonic airfoil case. The number inside the bracket shows the performance score.

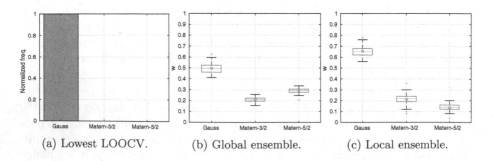

(a) Lowest LOOCV.   (b) Global ensemble.   (c) Local ensemble.

Fig. 9. Distribution of the weights for the inviscid transonic airfoil case with $n = 50$.

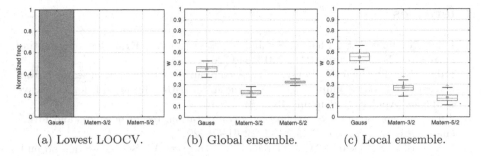

(a) Lowest LOOCV.   (b) Global ensemble.   (c) Local ensemble.

Fig. 10. Distribution of the weights for the inviscid transonic airfoil case with $n = 100$.

4   Conclusions and Future Works

In this paper, we studied the efficacy of the ensemble of Kriging with multiple kernel functions for approximating black-box engineering functions. Our research is motivated by the need to create a robustly accurate surrogate models without eliminating the advantage of uncertainty structure that can be used for Bayesian sequential optimization strategy. To this end, we extend the previous work in the ensemble of Kriging with multiple kernel functions by introducing advanced kernel functions (i.e., Matérn class) besides the widely used Gaussian. Further, we implement the global and the local ensemble technique to mix multiple Kriging models. Since our primary objective is for engineering design, we directly tested the approach on aerodynamic problems as representatives for general engineering problems. It is shown that for the airfoil problems, the local and ensemble approaches are robust in terms of the approximation quality, in the sense that they could mimic the performance of the best performing kernel or at least avoiding misspecification of the kernel. Comparing the two ensemble approaches, the global ensemble is better in mixing multiple Kriging models than the local ensemble; further, this also comes with a simpler method for computing the weights. The model selection approach (i.e., select the model with the lowest LOOCV error), although might outperform ensemble approaches when a single kernel function is strictly better than the others, is prone to the misguidance of the CV error in selecting the best model as shown in the results from the second subsonic airfoil case.

For future works, benchmarking of the ensemble of Kriging models and those with single-kernel function should be performed within the Bayesian optimization context. Furthermore, the capability of the aforementioned approach should also be investigated for applications besides optimization (e.g., uncertainty quantification and global sensitivity analysis).

References

1. Le, M.N., Ong, Y.S., Menzel, S., Jin, Y., Sendhoff, B.: Evolution by adapting surrogates. Evol. comput. **21**(2), 313–340 (2013)
2. Palar, P.S., Tsuchiya, T., Parks, G.T.: A comparative study of local search within a surrogate-assisted multi-objective memetic algorithm framework for expensive problems. Appl. Soft Comput. **43**, 1–19 (2016)
3. Jin, Y.: Surrogate-assisted evolutionary computation: recent advances and future challenges. Swarm Evol. Comput. **1**(2), 61–70 (2011)
4. Viana, F.A., Simpson, T.W., Balabanov, V., Toropov, V.: Special section on multidisciplinary design optimization: metamodeling in multidisciplinary design optimization: how far have we really come? AIAA J. **52**, 670–690 (2014)
5. Jones, D.R., Schonlau, M., Welch, W.J.: Efficient global optimization of expensive black-box functions. J. Glob. optim. **13**(4), 455–492 (1998)
6. Stein, M.L.: Interpolation of Spatial Data: Some Theory for Kriging. Springer Science & Business Media, Heidelberg (2012)
7. Goel, T., Haftka, R.T., Shyy, W., Queipo, N.V.: Ensemble of surrogates. Struct. Multidisc. Optim. **33**(3), 199–216 (2007)
8. Viana, F.A., Haftka, R.T., Steffen, V.: Multiple surrogates: how cross-validation errors can help us to obtain the best predictor. Struct. Multidisc. Optim. **39**(4), 439–457 (2009)
9. Acar, E., Rais-Rohani, M.: Ensemble of metamodels with optimized weight factors. Struct. Multidisc. Optim. **37**(3), 279–294 (2009)
10. Song, X., Sun, G., Li, G., Gao, W., Li, Q.: Crashworthiness optimization of foam-filled tapered thin-walled structure using multiple surrogate models. Struct. Multidisc. Optim. **47**(2), 221–231 (2013)
11. Liu, H., Xu, S., Wang, X., Meng, J., Yang, S.: Optimal weighted pointwise ensemble of radial basis functions with different basis functions. AIAA J. **54**(10), 3117–3133 (2016)
12. Ginsbourger, D., Helbert, C., Carraro, L.: Discrete mixtures of kernels for kriging-based optimization. Qual. Reliab. Eng. Int. **24**(6), 681–691 (2008)
13. Sacks, J., Welch, W.J., Mitchell, T.J., Wynn, H.P.: Design and analysis of computer experiments. Stat. Sci. **4**(4), 409–423 (1989)
14. Dubrule, O.: Cross validation of kriging in a unique neighborhood. Math. Geol. **15**(6), 687–699 (1983)
15. Marelli, S., Sudret, B.: UQLab: a framework for uncertainty quantification in Matlab. In: Vulnerability, Uncertainty, and Risk: Quantification, Mitigation, and Management, pp. 2554–2563 (2014)
16. Bader, J., Zitzler, E.: HypE: an algorithm for fast hypervolume-based many-objective optimization. Evol. comput. **19**(1), 45–76 (2011)
17. Sobieczky, H.: Parametric airfoils and wings. In: Fujii, K., Dulikravich, G.S. (eds.) Recent Development of Aerodynamic Design Methodologies. NNFM, vol. 65, pp. 71–87. Springer, Heidelberg (1999). https://doi.org/10.1007/978-3-322-89952-1_4
18. Kulfan, B.M.: Universal parametric geometry representation method. J. Aircr. **45**(1), 142–158 (2008)

Path Planning Optimization Method Based on Genetic Algorithm for Mapping Toxic Environment

Luis Piardi[1,2(✉)], José Lima[2,4,5], Ana I. Pereira[2,4,6], and Paulo Costa[3,5]

[1] Federal University of Technology - Paraná, Toledo, Brazil
luis.fp.piardi@alunos.ipb.pt
[2] Instituto Politécnico de Bragança, Bragança, Portugal
{jllima,apereira}@ipb.pt
[3] Faculty of Engineering of University of Porto, Porto, Portugal
paco@fe.up.pt
[4] Research Centre in Digitalization and Intelligent Robotics (CeDRI),
Instituto Politécnico de Bragança, Bragança, Portugal
[5] Centre for Robotics in Industry and Intelligent Systems, INESC-TEC,
Porto, Portugal
[6] Algoritmi R&D Centre, University of Minho, Braga, Portugal

Abstract. The ionizing radiation is used in the nuclear medicine field during the execution of diagnosis exams. The administration of nuclear radio pharmaceutical components to the patient contaminates the environment. The main contribution of this work is to propose a path planning method for scanning the nuclear contaminated environment with a mobile robot optimizing the traveled distance. The Genetic Algorithm methodology is proposed and compared with other approaches and the final solution is validated in simulated and real environment in order to achieve a closer approximation to reality.

Keywords: Genetic Algorithm · Mobile robot · Path planning
Optimization

1 Introduction

Medical imaging is an area of knowledge with continuous technological innovation, that develops new techniques for the medical diagnosis in order to provide an image of the anatomy of the human body and its functions [1]. According to NUMDAB (Nuclear Medicine Database), there are 1490 nuclear medicine institutions in the world, of which 1288 are active. Actually, 0.69 million PET (Positron Emission Tomography) and PET-CT (Computed Tomography) annual examinations are registered in the world [2].

The nuclear medicine provides diagnosis tests that detect with some precision when a certain part of the body has a change in the metabolism. The administration of nuclear radio pharmaceutical components to the patient must be carefully done by specialists. Unfortunately, the patient can contaminate the environment with physiologic needs. Moreover, environment and the patient should

© Springer International Publishing AG, part of Springer Nature 2018
P. Korošec et al. (Eds.): BIOMA 2018, LNCS 10835, pp. 223–233, 2018.
https://doi.org/10.1007/978-3-319-91641-5_19

be isolated by a period of time regarding the decay of nuclear properties. The inspection of the clearance of the environment is mainly made by human beings that are exposed to the ionizing radiation that may cause the damage in the organs and tissues. The scanning and measurement of the radiation can be done resorting to a mobile robot that performs the acquisition based on a Geiger counter. The path planning of the robot should guarantee that the complete scan is performed and ensure the environment is clean and technicians can enter the room. The presented paper addresses a path planning method that scans the desired environment while optimizing the mobile robot travelled distance. This optimization, based on Genetic Algorithm, is implemented in simulation and real robot scenario and compared with other approaches that validates the proposed methodology.

The paper is organized as follows: After a brief introduction, Sect. 2 presents the related work. Then, Sect. 3 addresses problem formulation of path planning to scan the environment. Section 4 presents the developed Genetic algorithm and its operations. Section 5 presents the obtained numerical results and compares it with a heuristic method for path planning. Finally, last section concludes the paper and presents some future work.

2   Related Work

Path planning is crucial for autonomous mobile robots in various environments with the presence of obstacles [3]. In the literature, path planning is defined as: "Given a map and a goal location, path planning involves identifying a trajectory that will cause the robot to reach the goal location when executed. Path planning is a strategic problem-solving competence, as the robot must decide what to do over the long term to achieve its goals" [4].

This subject is widely discussed by the academic community. The task of moving the robot from a starting point to a target point avoiding obstacles and running an optimized or near optimal path is a complex computational process. Complexity increases as the environment has more known, unknown or dynamic obstacles.

Several algorithms are used for the mobile robot path planning problem, e.g, visibility chart [5], Voronoi diagrams [6,7], cell decomposition [8], potential field [9], A* [10] and other methods found in the literature. According to [3] "Each method differs in its effectiveness depending on the type of application environment and each one of them has its own strength and weaknesses".

Another approach used in the search to optimize path planning is based on Genetic Algorithms [3,11–14]. In [3] this methodology was used with search algorithm to carry out the path planning of starting point and end point avoiding obstacles and collisions in the environment (static or dynamic where was used an optimization in the mutation operator to optimize the path or seek a path near the optimum). Already in [12], applying crossover and mutations to search for an optimized path, using a connectivity grid to represent the plant where the robot is inserted, the objective is to find the lowest path between the start and end points, avoiding repeating cells along the way, simplifying the fitness function by analyzing path length.

Many approaches in path planning, even using Genetic Algorithm, seek only to make the shortest, or most efficient, path between two distinct points (start and target). However, our problem has a different framework, similar to the classic travelling salesman problem (TSP). Considering a range of n cities where the purpose of this problem is to start the route in city defined, visiting the other cities only once, and them returning to the first city [15]. Considering the possibility of the existence of several cities, the TSP becomes complex with $(n-1)!$ possible routes to be calculated. The differences between our problem and the travelling salesman's problem is that the starting and ending points are different and the robot must avoid collision with obstacles.

In the present work, we will adapt a Genetic Algorithm to find the smallest path to perform a scan in the environment represented by a connectivity grid. An example with this applicability is found in [16,17] works. We will initially restrict the problem to static environments, and future work will address dynamic environments where there are unknown obstacles by the robot.

3 Problem Formulation

The challenge of path planning for robots is usually formulated as follows: given a mobile robot and a description of an environment, we need to find a route between two specified locations, the start and the end point. During the execution of the path the robot can not collide with obstacles and the optimization criterion must be satisfied (i.e., shortest path) [13].

To simplify the path planning problem, it is necessary to make some assumptions. They are as follows:

– A path will be selected, always starting from a start point to a target point, as show in Fig. 1.
– Known obstacles are mapped and represent a cell in the connectivity grid.
– The proposed algorithm acts on a connectivity grid arranged in a two dimensional space (2D) or IR^2 space.
– The robot does not perform movements in diagonal directions. It only moves between interconnected points in horizontal and vertical directions in the grid of connectivity, as show in Fig. 1.
– The robot should visit all cells, or points, that are free of obstacles in the grid of connectivity at least once.

3.1 Problem Space Representation

Many works developed in the area of path planning for mobile robots, use a graph grid of connectivity to represent the environment and obstacles. In the present work we use a similar approach as presented in the papers [3,14], where we modify the order of the values as shown in Fig. 1. The dark color represents

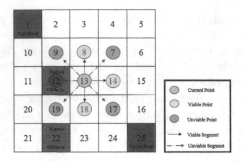

Fig. 1. Connectivity grid (5×5) and an example of possible points and segments. Without an obstacle the 12 point will be a reachable point. (Color figure online)

obstacles, while the lighter colors represent obstacle-free cells. It is important to remind that the size of the connectivity grid can vary, according to the resolution of the desired scan.

4   Genetic Algorithm

In this section we will present the Genetic Algorithm (GA) used to solve the path planning problem described in the section above. To facilitate understanding, when referring to a gene, we are indicating a cell in the grid of connectivity. When a chromosome is pronounced, it indicates a set of cells that connects the start point to the end point.

4.1   Encoding Representation

The encoding method is one of the key steps in the GA design. The representation of the possible paths to be realized by the robot, is known as chromosome [3,11, 14]. The path is encoded in a sequence of adjacent cells. This sequence is started with the start cell (upper left corner) and ended with the destination (bottom right corner) cell. The path consists of a variable number of segments formed between two cells or waypoints. Each segment is a straight line which can be vertical or horizontal. Diagonal segments are invalid. Figure 2 shows a possible chromosome generated from the connectivity grid of Fig. 1.

Fig. 2. Possible chromosome of the GA initial population.

4.2   Initial Population

The initial population is generated in order to respect the criteria of horizontal and vertical movement allowed. The initial population is composed by a set of chromosomes that are subjected to a random process, where each chromosome starts at the start point and ends at the target point (see Figs. 1 and 2), and each chromosome describes a path that should visit all the points of the grid of connectivity at least once.

With the intention to reducing the search time of the evolutionary algorithm, all the chromosomes generated by the initial population represent an executable path, as in the papers [3,14,18].

To generate a chromosome of the initial population, the algorithm applies a mask with an unitary cross as shape, where the center represents the current point and the extremity of the cross represents the directions allowed for the path. Each direction has a probability of choice according to the amount of visits already undertaken. In other words, a point that was less visited is more likely to be visited compared to its neighbors that were most visited. In this way, all points have a probability of being chosen, guaranteeing a great diversity for the initial population. The mask can be seen in Fig. 3a, where the possible configurations are also shown depending on the availability of neighboring points or in case the mask is centered at the end of the grid.

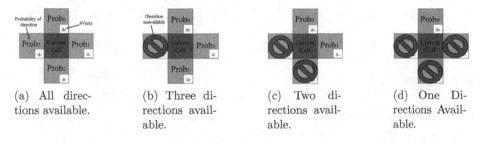

(a) All direc-
tions available.

(b) Three di-
rections avail-
able.

(c) Two di-
rections avail-
able.

(d) One Di-
rections Avail-
able.

Fig. 3. Geometry of the mask for the generation of the initial population.

The probability of each direction $Prob_i$, for $i = 0, \ldots, 3$, is a function of the visit cell number (a_i) and n, that represents the number of available directions. $Prob_i$, for $i = 0, \ldots, 3$, can be defined as:

$$Prob_i = \begin{cases} \dfrac{\sum_{k=0}^{n-1} a_k - a_i}{(n-1) \cdot \sum_{k=0}^{n-1} a_k}, & for \quad n > 1 \\ \quad\quad 1, & for \quad n = 1 \end{cases} \tag{1}$$

The procedure ends when all cells are visited and the path terminates at the end point of the connectivity grid.

4.3   Crossover Operation

Crossover can be defined as a process of taking two parent solutions to produce a child. After reproduction process, the population is enriched with better individuals. The goal of the operator is to find new structures that have a high probability of causing significant improvements [19].

In the developed algorithm, the crossover consider two parents, selected randomly, to produce two children. The first step of this process is to generate the characteristic path of these two selected parents. The characteristic path is a sequence of cells that are visited for the first time in the path. In this way, individual and distinct information is stored for each parent. Each characteristic path must begins at the starting point and ends at the endpoint (even if the endpoint was previously visited).

Between two consecutive cells of the characteristic path there may be several cells in the parent chromosome, which were already visited. Figure 4a illustrates a situation where two characteristic paths are generated for two parents, where a 3 × 3 grid was used to facilitate the understanding of this operation.

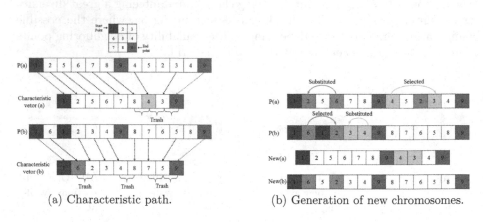

(a) Characteristic path.   (b) Generation of new chromosomes.

Fig. 4. Crossover operation details. (Color figure online)

Only the garbage ranges can be used to generate the new chromosomes (offsprings). Therefore a random point of the characteristic path is selected (in yellow in (a) and green in (b)), where between it and its subsequent point there is garbage to be replaced by the smaller interval in the opposite parents that generated the characteristic path. Figure 4b shows in detail the process of generating the new chromosomes.

4.4   Mutation Operation

Mutation operation prevents the algorithm from being trapped in a local minimum. Mutation is an operator to maintain genetic diversity in the population. It introduces new genetic structures in the population by randomly modifying some of its building blocks. It helps to escape from a local solution and maintains diversity in the population to find structures that improve the path planning [19]. All chromosomes are candidates to be submitted in the mutation process with a probability of $Prob_m$ [18].

In order to prevent a mutation parent producing a infeasible path, the developed algorithm for the mutation operator was established to avoid all such cases, i.e, all the paths generated after the mutation are feasible. As in the crossover operator, the first procedure performed is to generate a characteristic path. Then, a cell of the characteristic path is randomly chosen and its subsequent one where a random path between them will be inserted. The generated random path allows only horizontal and vertical movements. Figure 5 illustrates the operation for a 3×3 size connectivity grid.

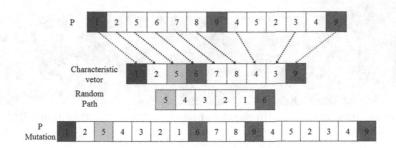

Fig. 5. Detail of mutation operator.

4.5 Selection Process

In our work the goal is to obtain an optimal path, i. e., a path with the shortest distance between the starting point and the end point by visiting all points of the connectivity grid. In order to evaluate the chromosomes, the amount of cells are analysed. The best path is the one with less cells in its chromosome. When one of the chromosomes has $(i \times j)$ cells, i.e. when all points are visited only once to accomplish all the visits, the path is fully optimized.

To get the best path it is necessary that the smallest paths are maintained and transferred to the next generations. A selection process is proposed to obtain the best parents and yet guarantee the diversity of the new populations. This process consists of ordering all the chromosomes obtained in the current iteration of the algorithm, considering the results of crossover and mutation operations, and classifying them in ascending order. After ordering the chromosomes the new population is selected, where 10% of the individuals are the ones with the smallest paths and the remaining 90% are selected randomly from the ordered chromosomes.

5 Numerical Results

In this section we will present the results obtained with the Genetic Algorithm for the path planning to the problem described above. In order to evaluate the obtained results, we will compare with the heuristic method proposed in [16]. This heuristic planning method is based on eight different priorities of directions for the robot, where the best priority is selected and executed by the robot.

To validate and test the results of the path planning algorithm, we used the SimTwo Simulator [20]. In the simulation environment (Fig. 6a), the robot follows the dimensions of real robot used in [17], as show Fig. 6b and c.

The test environment used has a dimension of 3 m long by 3 m wide. As explained above, the size of the connectivity grid can be changed and consequently the resolution of the scan as well. For the present work, an 8 × 8 grid was used.

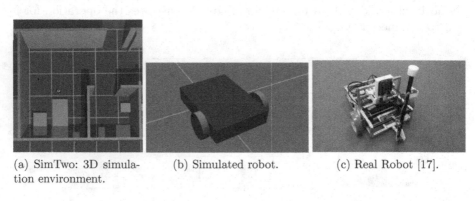

(a) SimTwo: 3D simula-   (b) Simulated robot.   (c) Real Robot [17].
tion environment.

Fig. 6. Tools used to test the developed algorithm.

In this work we test three different situations. Situation A where there are no obstacles and the optimal path is trivial. Situations B and C where there are some known obstacles and it is not obvious the optimal path. The Genetic Algorithm was executed ten times for each case, and the best result for each problem is presented.

Figure 7 presents the Situation A where connectivity grid has no obstacles. The performance of the Genetic Algorithm (GA) is presented in Fig. 7b where is analysed the evolution of the chromosomes generations during a GA run. The line referring to the heuristic method presents the number of waypoints visited when it is applied in path planning and the ideal line represents the number of obstacle-free waypoints present in the connectivity grid, i.e., the ideal size of the chromosome. Then it is possible to observe that the heuristic planning obtains better results when compared with the GA results in environments with simple layout (without obstacles). The obtained solution of the two tested procedures are illustrated in Fig. 7c and d.

Figure 8 presents the Situation B where connectivity grid has two known obstacles. The performance of the Genetic Algorithm (GA) is presented in Fig. 8b where is possible to observe that, after some iterations, the Genetic Algorithm is capable to identify a better path when compared with the heuristic planning procedure. The obtained solutions of the heuristic planning and Genetic Algorithm are illustrated in Fig. 8c and d, respectively.

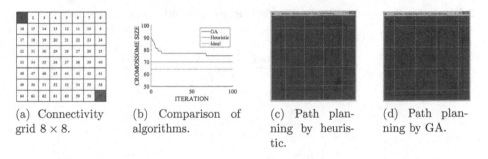

(a) Connectivity grid 8 × 8.

(b) Comparison of algorithms.

(c) Path planning by heuristic.

(d) Path planning by GA.

Fig. 7. Plan with a connectivity grid 8 × 8 without obstacles.

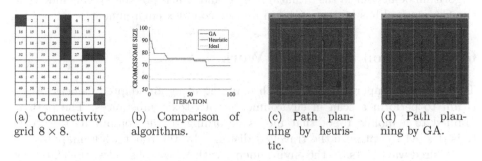

(a) Connectivity grid 8 × 8.

(b) Comparison of algorithms.

(c) Path planning by heuristic.

(d) Path planning by GA.

Fig. 8. Plan with a connectivity grid 8 × 8 with two known obstacles.

Figure 9 presents the Situation C where the connectivity grid has three known obstacles. The performance of the Genetic Algorithm (GA) is presented in Fig. 9b where it is possible to observe that GA obtains better solutions than the heuristic planning procedure starting from the initial iterations.

The obtained solutions of the heuristic planning and Genetic Algorithm are illustrated in Fig. 9c and d, respectively.

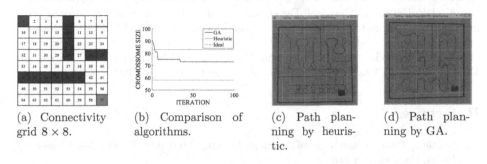

(a) Connectivity grid 8 × 8.

(b) Comparison of algorithms.

(c) Path planning by heuristic.

(d) Path planning by GA.

Fig. 9. Plan with a connectivity grid 8 × 8 with three known obstacles.

Table 1. Number of visited cells: Heuristic Procedure and Genetic Algorithm method comparison

Situation	HP	GA
A	70	75
B	75	71
C	83	72

The Table 1 presents the number of visited cells. So, analyzing the Genetic Algorithm behaviour in the Situations A, B and C it is possible to conclude that the GA method has better results in a more complex environment.

6   Conclusion and Future Work

The presented paper proposes a path planning using an adapted Genetic Algorithm to perform a scan in environments with toxic substances. The path is applied to a mobile robot that moves according to the computed trajectory. It is desired to optimize the travelled distance by the robot while mapping all the desired waypoints. In the environments with known obstacles, the efficiency of the proposed Genetic Algorithm is relevant, identifying the optimal path in complex situations. Thus, a more efficient trajectory is planned.

As future work we intend to apply the algorithm in dynamic environments with also unknown obstacles and replace the SimTwo by the real robot for a more realistic approach. Moreover, a real time constraint should be addressed to solve the path during the scan.

Acknowledgment. This work is financed by Project "TEC4Growth - Pervasive Intelligence, Enhancers and Proofs of Concept with Industrial Impact/NORTE-01-0145-FEDER-000020" financed by the North Portugal Regional Operational behaviour (NORTE 2020), under the PORTUGAL 2020 Partnership Agreement, and through the ERDF European Regional Development Fund through the Operational Programme for Competitiveness and Internationalisation - COMPETE 2020 Programme and by National Funds through the FCT Fundação para a Ciência e a Tecnologia (Portuguese Foundation for Science and Technology) within projects POCI-01-0145-FEDER-006961, POCI-01-0145-FEDER-007043 and UID/CEC/00319/2013.

References

1. Suetens, P.: Fundamentals of Medical Imaging, 2nd edn. Cambridge University Press, Cambridge (2009)
2. International Atomic Energy Agency (IAEA). http://nucmedicine.iaea.org/default.asp. Accessed 13 Dec 2017
3. Tuncer, A., Yildirim, M.: Dynamic path planning of mobile robots with improved genetic algorithm. Comput. Electr. Eng. **38**(6), 1564–1572 (2012)

4. Siegwart, R., Nourbakhsh, I.R.: Introduction to Autonomous Mobile Robots, 1st edn. The MIT Press, Cambridge (2004)
5. Ma, Y., Zheng, G., Perruquetti, W.: Cooperative path planning for mobile robots based on visibility graph. In: Proceedings of the 32nd Chinese Control Conference, pp. 4915–4920, July 2013
6. Dong, H., Li, W., Zhu, J., Duan, S.: The path planning for mobile robot based on Voronoi diagram. In: 2010 Third International Conference on Intelligent Networks and Intelligent Systems, pp. 446–449, November 2010
7. Yang, X., Zeng, Z., Xiao, J., Zheng, Z.: Trajectory planning for RoboCup MSL mobile robots based on Bézier curve and Voronoi diagram. In: 2015 IEEE International Conference on Information and Automation, pp. 2552–2557, August 2015
8. Kloetzer, M., Mahulea, C., Gonzalez, R.: Optimizing cell decomposition path planning for mobile robots using different metrics. In: 2015 19th International Conference on System Theory, Control and Computing (ICSTCC), pp. 565–570, October 2015
9. Yu, Z., Yan, J., Zhao, J., Chen, Z.F., Zhu, Y.: Mobile robot path planning based on improved artificial potential field method. Harbin Gongye Daxue Xuebao (J. Harbin Inst. Technol.) **43**(1), 50–55 (2011)
10. Moreira, A.P., Costa, P.J., Costa, P.: Real-time path planning using a modified A* algorithm. In: Proceedings of ROBOTICA 2009-9th Conference on Mobile Robots and Competitions (2009)
11. Hu, Y., Yang, S.X.: A knowledge based genetic algorithm for path planning of a mobile robot. In: Proceedings of the 2004 IEEE International Conference on Robotics and Automation 2004, ICRA 2004, vol. 5, pp. 4350–4355. IEEE (2004)
12. Ismail, A., Sheta, A., Al-Weshah, M.: A mobile robot path planning using genetic algorithm in static environment. J. Comput. Sci. **4**(4), 341–344 (2008)
13. Sedighi, K.H., Ashenayi, K., Manikas, T.W., Wainwright, R.L., Tai, H.M.: Autonomous local path planning for a mobile robot using a genetic algorithm. In: Proceedings of the 2004 Congress on Evolutionary Computation (IEEE Cat. No. 04TH8753), vol. 2, pp. 1338–1345, June 2004
14. Alnasser, S., Bennaceur, H.: An efficient genetic algorithm for the global robot path planning problem. In: 2016 Sixth International Conference on Digital Information and Communication Technology and its Applications (DICTAP), pp. 97–102, July 2016
15. Miller, C.E., Tucker, A.W., Zemlin, R.A.: Integer programming formulation of traveling salesman problems. J. ACM (JACM) **7**(4), 326–329 (1960)
16. Piardi, L., Lima, J., Costa, P., Brito, T.: Development of a dynamic path for a toxic substances mapping mobile robot in industry environment. In: Ollero, A., Sanfeliu, A., Montano, L., Lau, N., Cardeira, C. (eds.) ROBOT 2017. AISC, vol. 694, pp. 655–667. Springer, Cham (2018). https://doi.org/10.1007/978-3-319-70836-2_54
17. Lima, J., Costa, P.: Ultra-wideband time of flight based localization system and odometry fusion for a scanning 3 DoF magnetic field autonomous robot. In: Ollero, A., Sanfeliu, A., Montano, L., Lau, N., Cardeira, C. (eds.) ROBOT 2017. AISC, vol. 693, pp. 879–890. Springer, Cham (2018). https://doi.org/10.1007/978-3-319-70833-1_71
18. Moharam, R., Morsy, E.: Genetic algorithms to balanced tree structures in graphs. Swarm Evol. Comput. **32**, 132–139 (2017)
19. Sivanandam, S.N., Deepa, S.N.: Introduction to Genetic Algorithms. Springer
20. Costa, P., Gonçalves, J., Lima, J., Malheiros, P.: Simtwo realistic simulator: a tool for the development and validation of robot software. Theory Appl. Math. Comput. Sci. **1**(1), 17 (2011)

Tuning Multi-Objective Optimization Algorithms for the Integration and Testing Order Problem

Miha Ravber[✉], Matej Črepinšek, Marjan Mernik, and Tomaž Kosar

Faculty of Electrical Engineering and Computer Science,
University of Maribor, Maribor, Slovenia
miha.ravber@um.si

Abstract. Multi-Objective Evolutionary Algorithms (MOEAs) are one of the most used search techniques in Search-Based Software Engineering (SBSE). However, MOEAs have many control parameters which must be configured for the problem at hand. This can be a very challenging task by itself. To make matters worse, in Multi-Objective Optimization (MOO) different aspects of quality of the obtained Pareto front need to be taken in to account. A novel method called MOCRS-Tuning is proposed to address this problem. MOCRS-Tuning is a meta-evolutionary algorithm which uses a chess rating system with quality indicator ensemble. The chess rating system enables us to determine the performance of an MOEA on different problems easily. The ensemble of quality indicators ensures that different aspects of quality are considered. The tuning was carried out on five different MOEAs on the Integration and Test Order Problem (ITO). The experimental results show significant improvement after tuning of all five MOEAs used in the experiment.

Keywords: Multi-Objective Optimization · Evolutionary algorithms
Parameter tuning · Search-Based Software Engineering
Class Integration and Testing Order · Chess rating system

1 Introduction

Search-Based Software Engineering (SBSE) is an approach where search-based optimization algorithms are used to solve problems in software engineering [1]. One of the many areas that SBSE tackles is software testing [2]. Software testing plays an important role in the software development life cycle, since it has a direct impact on the quality of the software. However, generating tests is a very difficult and costly task [3]. Since software testing is so complex, and exact solutions cannot be found in reasonable time using deterministic methods, it is no surprise that SBSE algorithms were applied in industrial cases [4,5]. One of the most popular methods used in SBSE are Multi-Objective Evolutionary Algorithms (MOEAs), which return a Pareto fronts. This enables the users to choose a solution with the best trade-off between different objectives. However,

P. Korošec et al. (Eds.): BIOMA 2018, LNCS 10835, pp. 234–245, 2018.
https://doi.org/10.1007/978-3-319-91641-5_20

evolutionary algorithms have different control parameters. The choice of control parameters has a great impact on the performance of an evolutionary algorithm [6]. Setting control parameters can be very challenging, and is known as a parameter tuning problem [7]. Tuning of algorithms is very important. It can find good control parameters which improve the algorithms performance. Also, with tuned algorithms we can perform a fair comparison [8]. Algorithms with default parameters perform well on benchmark problems, but this is usually not the case for real-world problems, since they are not studied in literature and we have little knowledge about them.

To tackle this problem, we propose Tuning with a Chess Rating System (CRSTuning) [8], adapted for Multi-Objective Optimization called MOCRS-Tuning. The tuning process is guided by a self-adaptive Differential Evolution (jDE) [9], which searches for optimal control parameter. By using a self-adaptive algorithm, we removed the additional parameters needed for the tuning process. The solutions in the population are evaluated with a Chess Rating System with a Quality Indicator Ensemble (CRS4MOEA/QIE) [10]. The Quality Indicator Ensemble ensures that the outcome of each candidate solution is evaluated with different Quality Indicators (QIs), making sure that different aspects of quality are taken into account [11]. We know by the No Free Lunch (NFL) theorem [12] that it is not possible to find optimal parameter settings, but this holds only if all possible search problems are considered. In our experiments, we limited ourselves to the Integration and Testing Order (ITO) problem [13], which has been shown that MOEAs can solve efficiently [14]. The ITO problem is concerned with the order in which software components are to be integrated and tested, such that the stubbing cost is minimised [15].

In our experiments, we applied the novel MOCRS-Tuning method to five different MOEAs. The tuning was conducted on 8 real-world object-oriented and aspect-oriented systems [4,13,14]. The comparison was conducted using the Evolutionary Algorithms Rating System (EARS) framework [16]. The EARS framework uses a chess rating system to rank and compare evolutionary algorithms. The results show significant improvement of all five MOEAs with tuned control parameters compared with the non-tuned (default) versions.

The remainder of the paper is organised as follows. A brief description of the ITO problem is given in Sect. 2. The chess rating system for evolutionary algorithms is described in Sect. 3. Section 4 describes the proposed tuning method. The execution of the experiment and results are presented in Sect. 5. Finally, the paper concludes in Sect. 6.

2   Integration and Testing Order

When performing a unit test in order to detect interaction problems between units, they need to be integrated and tested in order. If a unit is required by other units but is not yet available, it has to be emulated. An emulated unit is called a stub, and it imitates some or all functions of the actual unit [15]. A stub must be created for each unit that is not available during the integration process.

Stubs are not desired for three reasons. First, stubs can be more complex than the code they simulate. Second, since they require understanding of the semantics of the simulated functions their generation cannot be fully automated. Third, some stubs may be more error prone than their real counterparts [17]. Therefore, to reduce the stubbing cost, such a sequence must be determined that it minimises the stubbing cost [14]. This, however, is not a trivial task, and is known as the Integration and Testing Order problem [13]. Since different factors (objectives) influence the stubbing process, the problem should be treated as multi-objective [14]. This makes it very suitable to be solved by MOEAs [13]. In our experiments we used two objectives: Number of attributes and number of methods, which have to be emulated in the stub if the dependencies between two modules are to be broken. We used eight real systems in our experiments: MyBatis, AJHSQLDB (HyperSQL DataBase), BCEL (Byte Code Engineering Library), JHotDraw, HealthWatcher, JBoss, AJHotDraw, TollSystems. Information about the systems such as number of dependencies, classes, aspects, and Lines of Code (LOC) is given in Table 1.

Table 1. Details of the systems used for the ITO problem in the experiments.

Name	Dependencies	Classes	Aspects	LOC
AJHotDraw	1592	290	31	18586
AJHSQLDB	1338	276	15	68550
MyBatis	1271	331	-	23535
JHotDraw	809	197	-	20273
JBoss	367	150	-	8434
HealthWatcher	289	95	22	5479
BCEL	289	45	-	2999
TollSystems	188	53	24	2496

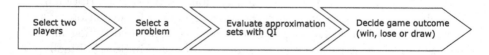

Fig. 1. A single game in CRS4MOEA/QIE.

3   Chess Rating System for Evolutionary Algorithms

For comparing and evaluating MOEAs we used a novel method called Chess Rating System with a Quality Indicator Ensemble (CRS4MOEA/QIE) [10]. CRS4MOEA/QIE uses the Glicko-2 system [18] to rate and rank players. A chess rating system is used to estimate a chess player's skill level. Although it was initially intended to rank chess players, it can be applied to any competitor-versus-competitor game. In our case, players are MOEAs. Figure 1 shows a single game between two players (MOEAs). Each MOEA returns an approximation set for the given problem. The two approximation sets are evaluated with a QI from the ensemble, and the outcome of the game is decided. In a tournament players play multiple games against all participating players for each given problem. A tournament can have multiple independent runs. The outcomes of the games are used to update each player's rating R and rating deviation RD [18]. Each unrated player has his rating set to 1500 and RD to 350 before the tournament starts. The rating represents a player's skill; the higher the rating, the higher the skill. If the player performs better than expected his rating increases, and decreases if they perform worse than expected. The rating deviation indicates how reliable a player's rating is. A small RD means a player plays often and has a reliable rating. In contrast, if the RD is high, his rating is unreliable. The chess rating system was used for comparison of MOEAs and for their evaluation in the tuning process.

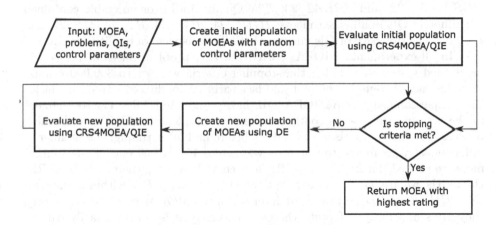

Fig. 2. MOCRS-tuning flowchart.

4   MOCRS-Tunning Method

Proposed method (MOCRS-Tunning) uses a meta-evolutionary approach in order to tune the control parameters of MOEAs. Figure 2 shows a simple flowchart of the tuning process. As input, we give it an MOEA, the problems for which it will be tuned, QIs for evaluation of results, and control parameters with their ranges to be tuned. First an initial population is created where the control parameters are generated randomly. The initial population is then evaluated using CRS4MOEA/QIE. In the tournament, multiple versions of the given MOEA with different control parameters are competing with each other on the given problems. At the end of the tournament, each version of MOEA receives its rating R, which reflects its performance (fitness). In the main loop, the tuning process takes place and is guided by jDE and CRS4MOEA/QIE. jDE is used to produce new solutions (MOEAs with different control parameters) and CRS4MOEA/QIE to evaluate the newly produced solutions. In order to evaluate the new solution it plays in a tournament with the old population. If the new solution has a higher rating compared to its current version, it will be added to the new population, otherwise the current solution is added. The new population needs to be evaluated, since the rating of a player depends on its current opponents. When the stopping criteria is meet the MOEA with the highest rating in the population is returned.

5   Experiment

The experiment consists of three parts: Comparing MOEAs with their 'default' control parameters, tuning of MOEAs, and comparing MOEAs with tuned control parameters against MOEAs with default parameters. The experiment was performed on five MOEAs: $IBEA$ [19], $MOEAD$ [20], $NSGA - II$ [21], $PESA - II$ [22] and $SPEA2$ [23]. The Quality Indicator ensemble contained five different QIs in all experiments: IGD^+ [24], HV [25], $R2$ [26], MS [27] and $I_{\epsilon+}$ [28]. The diversity of QIs ensures that all the aspects of quality are covered [10]. In all experiments, MOEAs solved the ITO problem on eight previously mentioned systems for which the stopping criteria was set to 300,000 evaluations for each system. In the first and last parts we conducted a tournament for the comparison using CRS4MOEA/QIE incorporated in EARS. The tournament in the first and third parts contained the same problems and QIs as the tuning process. For the comparison of MOEAs before and after tuning, the number of independent runs in the tournament was set to 15. At the end of the tournament we plotted Rating Intervals (RI) of each MOEA using their rating and RD. Using RIs, we are 95% confident that the player's rating R is within an interval $[R - 2RD, R + 2RD]$. If the rating intervals of two MOEAs do not overlap, then they are significantly different, whereas, conversely, it is not necessarily true.

5.1   Comparing MOEAs with Default Control Parameters

Finding default parameters can be challenging, since they depend on the type of problem. The default values are commonly provided by the author. However they are usually available only for continuous types of problems, and rarely for combinatorial types such as the ITO problem. Therefore, we set the default values of control parameters for all MOEAs based on the source code of combinatorial operators found in the jMetal framework [29]. We limited the tuning process to three control parameters: Population size μ, crossover probability η_c and mutation probability η_m. Based on the jMetal framework, the default values of the parameters are 100 for μ, 1.0 for η_c and 0.2 for η_m. The results of the tournament are displayed in the form of Rating Intervals. The RD value of all participating MOEAs reached its minimum value (50) [30]. The Rating Intervals of all MOEAs with default control parameters are shown in Fig. 3. The algorithms are ranked based on the rating, where the algorithm with the highest rating is first. From the results, we can observe that $NSGAII$ performed the best, and is significantly better (Rating Intervals do not overlap) than $MOEAD$. $PESAII$, $IBEA$ and $SPEA2$ have a very similar rating and, consequently, their intervals overlap almost entirely. There is a high probability that the order of these three MOEAs would change if the tournament were repeated.

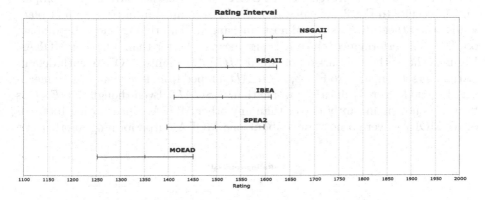

Fig. 3. 95% rating intervals of all MOEAs with default parameters.

Table 2. Control parameters of all five MOEAs after tuning.

	μ	η_c	η_m
$IBEA$	173	0.63	0.9
$MOEAD$	192	0.50	0.98
$NSGAII$	108	1.00	0.86
$PESAII$	110	0.37	1.0
$SPEA2$	190	0.74	0.87

5.2   Tuning MOEAs

In the tuning process we limited the search space of control parameters. For population size the lower bound is set to 10 and the upper bound to 200. Mutation and crossover probability have the same lower bound 0.1 and upper bound 1.0. The population size (number of MOEAs) for jDE was set to 20, and the stopping criteria was set to 20 generations. Table 2 shows the parameters of each MOEA after the tuning process. We can observe that different MOEAs have very different control parameters, except for mutation η_m. All MOEAs seem to prefer a higher mutation probability, meaning that higher exploitation is required for the given problems.

5.3 Comparing MOEAs with Tuned Control Parameters

After all MOEAs underwent tuning, we repeated the tournament from the first part of the experiment for each MOEA. In each tournament, an MOEA with tuned control parameters played against MOEAs which had their default parameters. This enabled us to detect performance improvement of each MOEA easily. The resulting Rating Intervals are displayed in Figs. 4 to 8. The first Figure (Fig. 4), shows the improvement of $IBEA$ with tuned parameters. By comparing the results to Fig. 3, we can see that $IBEA$ jumped from third to first place whilst the other MOEAs are almost unchanged. The tuning had a big impact on $IBEA$'s performance, since it is significantly better than all other MOEAs. Figure 5 shows the comparison of tuned $MOEAD$ against MOEAs with default parameters. Compared to Fig. 3, $MOEAD$ jumped from last to first place meaning, it is no longer significantly worse than $NSGAII$. Even though $MOEAD$ is first, it is not significantly better than any other MOEA. Since Rating Intervals of all MOEAs overlap no claims about one MOEA outperforming another can

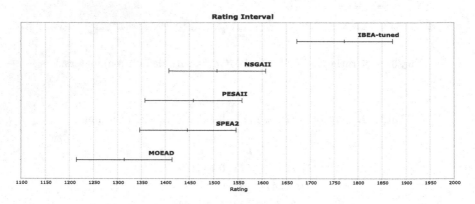

Fig. 4. Comparing $IBEA$ with tuned parameters to MOEAs with default parameters.

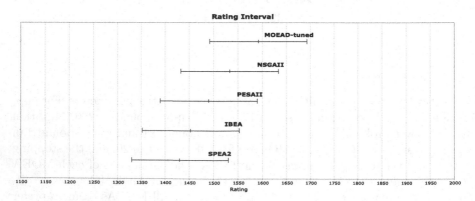

Fig. 5. Comparing $MOEAD$ with tuned parameters to MOEAs with default parameters.

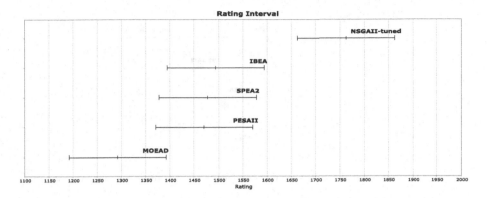

Fig. 6. Comparing *NSGAII* with tuned parameters to MOEAs with default parameters.

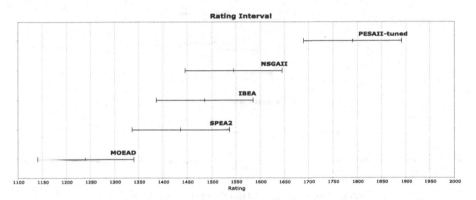

Fig. 7. Comparing *PESAII* with tuned parameters to MOEAs with default parameters.

be made. Figure 6 shows the performance of the tuned *NSGAII*. With default parameters it was already first, and significantly better than *MOEAD*. As we can see from the results, this does not mean it cannot be improved. With tuned parameters it performs significantly better than the rest. As we can see from Fig. 7, tuning also had a positive effect on *PESAII*. It took the first place from *NSGAII*, and is significantly better than the other MOEAs. The tuning of *PESAII* also had an effect on the rating of *MOEAD*. It is no surprise that *MOEAD* is outperformed by *PESAII*, since it is tuned and it was already outperformed by *NSGAII*. However, now it is also outperformed by *IBEA*, and the Rating Intervals are barely overlapping with *SPEA2*. This means that a bigger portion of *MOEAD*s rating can be attributed to victories against *PESAII*. Figure 8 show the performance improvement of tuned *SPEA2*. As with all other MOEAs, it also jumped to the first place. With tuned parameters it outperforms every MOEA except *NSGAII*. The improvement of *SPEA2* also had a bigger impact on the rating of *MOEAD*. Its Rating Interval shifted to the left, but not

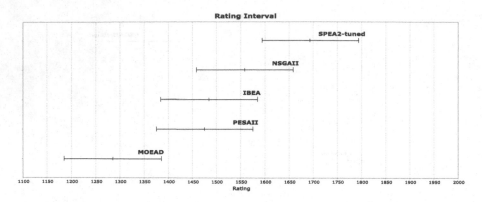

Fig. 8. Comparing $SPEA2$ with tuned parameters to MOEAs with default parameters.

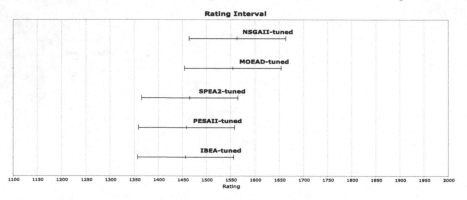

Fig. 9. Comparing all tuned versions of MOEAs.

as much when compared with the tuned version of $SPEA2$. For a better comparison we performed a tournament where all tuned versions of MOEAs played against each other. The resulting Rating intervals are displayed in Fig. 9. We can see that tuning had the biggest impact on $MOEAD$. It is on par $NSGAII$, whereas with default parameters it performed significantly worse (Fig. 3). The remaining MOEAs improved almost identically. The order of $SPEA2$, $PESAII$ and $IBEA$ has switched, but their intervals overlap like they do with default parameters. However, the end user is most interested in the obtained approximation set. Therefore, we plotted the approximation set for system AJHSQLDB obtained by $MOEAD$ with default and tuned parameters on Fig. 10. The results show that the approximation set obtained with tuned $MOEAD$ has both better convergence as spread. Overall, we can observe that MOCRS-Tuning was very successful at improving the performance of MOEAs, which was reflected in their rating and obtained approximation sets. The drastic changes in the performance after tuning implies that control parameters play a very important role in their execution, giving us a good reason as to why tuning is important, not only in real-world applications, but also when conducting comparisons amongst MOEAs.

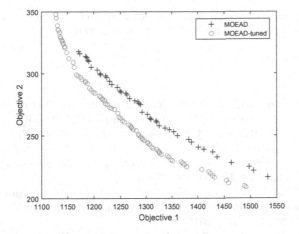

Fig. 10. Comparing approximation fronts of *MOEAD* with *MOEAD – tuned* for system AJHSQLDB.

6   Conclusion

In this paper we presented a novel tuning method for multi-objective algorithms called MOCRS-Tuning. The method uses a jDE for the search of optimal parameters and a chess rating system with a Quality Indicator Ensemble for evaluation of MOEAs. The tuning was performed on five different MOEAs. All MOEAs were tuned for the real-world ITO problem on eight systems. All experiments were conducted in the EARS framework. For the comparison between MOEAs before and after tuning, and for the evaluation of solutions in the tuning process, we used CRS4MOEA/QIE. The results have shown that tuned versions of MOEAs have improved significantly compared to their versions with default parameters. This has proven that every MOEA has a benefit when tuning is performed, and that more emphasis needs to be given to control parameters when using MOEAs. Since the tuning process incorporated a Quality Indicator Ensemble, we have assured that different aspects of quality were considered in the tuning process. Because we used eight systems in the tuning process, it was extremely time-consuming. Therefore, each algorithm was tuned only once. The tuning process for one MOEA takes approximately 23 h on a computer with an Intel(R) Core(TM) i7-4790 3.60 GHz CPU and 16 GB of RAM.

For future work, we would like to speed up the tuning process, which would enable additional tuning runs. In order to know with greater certainty whether the parameters are suitable for a wider set of problems, tuned MOEAs need to be run on additional systems which were not included in the tuning process. We also intend to compare the results of tuned MOEAs with a state-of-the-art method called Hyper-heuristic for the Integration and Test Order Problem (HITO) [4]. This would show us if a well tuned MOEA can compete with a state-of-the-art algorithm. Additionally, we would like to tune MOEAs on problems with higher numbers of objectives, to see how the number of objectives affects the tuning process of control parameters.

Acknowledgement. The authors acknowledge the financial support from the Slovenian Research Agency (research core funding No. P2-0041).

References

1. Harman, M., Mansouri, S.A., Zhang, Y.: Search-based software engineering: trends, techniques and applications. ACM Comput. Surv. (CSUR) **45**(1), 11 (2012)
2. Afzal, W., Torkar, R., Feldt, R.: A systematic review of search-based testing for non-functional system properties. Inf. Softw. Technol. **51**(6), 957–976 (2009)
3. McMinn, P.: Search-based software test data generation: a survey. Softw. Test. Verification Reliab. **14**(2), 105–156 (2004)
4. Guizzo, G., Vergilio, S.R., Pozo, A.T., Fritsche, G.M.: A multi-objective and evolutionary hyper-heuristic applied to the integration and test order problem. Appl. Soft Comput. **56**, 331–344 (2017)
5. Vos, T.E., Baars, A.I., Lindlar, F.F., Kruse, P.M., Windisch, A., Wegener, J.: Industrial scaled automated structural testing with the evolutionary testing tool. In: 2010 Third International Conference on Software Testing, Verification and Validation (ICST), pp. 175–184. IEEE (2010)
6. Eiben, A.E., Smit, S.K.: Parameter tuning for configuring and analyzing evolutionary algorithms. Swarm Evol. Comput. **1**(1), 19–31 (2011)
7. Karafotias, G., Hoogendoorn, M., Eiben, Á.E.: Parameter control in evolutionary algorithms: trends and challenges. IEEE Trans. Evol. Comput. **19**(2), 167–187 (2015)
8. Veček, N., Mernik, M., Filipič, B., Črepinšek, M.: Parameter tuning with chess rating system (CRS-tuning) for meta-heuristic algorithms. Inf. Sci. **372**, 446–469 (2016)
9. Brest, J., Zumer, V., Maucec, M.: Self-adaptive differential evolution algorithm in constrained real-parameter optimization. In: IEEE Congress on Evolutionary Computation, CEC 2006, pp. 215–222. IEEE (2006)
10. Ravber, M., Mernik, M., Črepinšek, M.: Ranking multi-objective evolutionary algorithms using a chess rating system with quality indicator ensemble. In: 2017 IEEE Congress on Evolutionary Computation (CEC), pp. 1503–1510. IEEE (2017)
11. Ravber, M., Mernik, M., Črepinšek, M.: The impact of quality indicators on the rating of multi-objective evolutionary algorithms. In: 7th International Conference on Bioinspired Optimization Methods and their Applications (BIOMA 2016), pp. 119–130 (2016)
12. Wolpert, D.H., Macready, W.G.: No free lunch theorems for optimization. IEEE Trans. Evol. Comput. **1**(1), 67–82 (1997)
13. Assunção, W.K.G., Colanzi, T.E., Vergilio, S.R., Pozo, A.: A multi-objective optimization approach for the integration and test order problem. Inf. Sci. **267**, 119–139 (2014)
14. Assunção, W.K.G., Colanzi, T.E., Pozo, A.T.R., Vergilio, S.R.: Establishing integration test orders of classes with several coupling measures. In: Proceedings of the 13th annual conference on Genetic and evolutionary computation, pp. 1867–1874. ACM (2011)
15. Beizer, B.: Software Testing Techniques. Dreamtech Press, New Delhi (2003)
16. EARS: Evolutionary algorithms rating system (GitHub) (2016). https://github.com/UM-LPM/EARS

17. Hashim, N.L., Schmidt, H.W., Ramakrishnan, S.: Test order for class-based integration testing of Java applications. In: Fifth International Conference on Quality Software (QSIC 2005), pp. 11–18. IEEE (2005)
18. Glickman, M.E.: Example of the Glicko-2 System. Boston University, Boston (2012)
19. Zitzler, E., Künzli, S.: Indicator-based selection in multiobjective search. In: Yao, X., Burke, E.K., Lozano, J.A., Smith, J., Merelo-Guervós, J.J., Bullinaria, J.A., Rowe, J.E., Tiňo, P., Kabán, A., Schwefel, H.-P. (eds.) PPSN 2004. LNCS, vol. 3242, pp. 832–842. Springer, Heidelberg (2004). https://doi.org/10.1007/978-3-540-30217-9_84
20. Zhang, Q., Li, H.: MOEA/D: a multiobjective evolutionary algorithm based on decomposition. IEEE Trans. Evol. Comput. 11(6), 712–731 (2007)
21. Deb, K., Pratap, A., Agarwal, S., Meyarivan, T.: A fast and elitist multiobjective genetic algorithm: NSGA-II. IEEE Trans. Evol. Comput. 6(2), 182–197 (2002)
22. Corne, D.W., Jerram, N.R., Knowles, J.D., Oates, M.J., et al.: PESA-II: region-based selection in evolutionary multiobjective optimization. In: Proceedings of the Genetic and Evolutionary Computation Conference (GECCO 2001), pp. 124–130 (2001)
23. Zitzler, E., Laumanns, M., Thiele, L., Zitzler, E., Zitzler, E., Thiele, L., Thiele, L.: SPEA2: improving the strength Pareto evolutionary algorithm (2001)
24. Ishibuchi, H., Masuda, H., Tanigaki, Y., Nojima, Y.: Difficulties in specifying reference points to calculate the inverted generational distance for many-objective optimization problems. In: IEEE Symposium on Computational Intelligence in Multi-criteria (MCDMDecision-Making), pp. 170–177. IEEE (2014)
25. Zitzler, E., Thiele, L.: Multiobjective evolutionary algorithms: a comparative case study and the strength Pareto approach. IEEE Trans. Evol. Comput. 3(4), 257–271 (1999)
26. Hansen, M.P., Jaszkiewicz, A.: Evaluating The Quality of Approximations to the Non-dominated set. IMM, Technical University of Denmark, Department of Mathematical Modelling (1998)
27. Yen, G.G., He, Z.: Performance metric ensemble for multiobjective evolutionary algorithms. IEEE Trans. Evol. Comput. 18(1), 131–144 (2014)
28. Zitzler, E., Thiele, L., Laumanns, M., Fonseca, C.M., Da Fonseca, V.G.: Performance assessment of multiobjective optimizers: an analysis and review. IEEE Trans. Evol. Comput. 7(2), 117–132 (2003)
29. Durillo, J.J., Nebro, A.J.: jMetal: a Java framework for multi-objective optimization. Adv. Eng. Soft. 42(10), 760–771 (2011)
30. Veček, N., Mernik, M., Črepinšek, M.: A chess rating system for evolutionary algorithms: a new method for the comparison and ranking of evolutionary algorithms. Inf. Sci. 277, 656–679 (2014)

Surrogate-Assisted Particle Swarm with Local Search for Expensive Constrained Optimization

Rommel G. Regis$^{(\boxtimes)}$ (iD)

Saint Joseph's University, Philadelphia, PA 19131, USA
rregis@sju.edu

Abstract. This paper develops a surrogate-assisted particle swarm optimization framework for expensive constrained optimization called *CONOPUS (CONstrained Optimization by Particle swarm Using Surrogates)*. In each iteration, CONOPUS considers multiple trial positions for each particle in the swarm and uses surrogate models for the objective and constraint functions to identify the most promising trial position where the expensive functions are evaluated. Moreover, the current overall best position is refined by finding the minimum of the surrogate of the objective function within a neighborhood of that position and subject to surrogate inequality constraints with a small margin and with a distance requirement from all previously evaluated positions. CONOPUS is implemented using radial basis function (RBF) surrogates and the resulting algorithm compares favorably to alternative methods on 12 benchmark problems and on a large-scale application from the auto industry with 124 decision variables and 68 inequality constraints.

Keywords: Particle swarm optimization · Constrained optimization
Surrogate model · Radial basis function · Expensive function

1 Introduction

In many engineering optimization problems, the objective and constraint functions are *black-box* in that their mathematical expressions are not explicitly available. Moreover, accurate gradient information is often not available and so classical optimization methods are not applicable. Particle swarm optimization (PSO) (Kennedy and Eberhart [1]) is among the most popular metaheuristics for solving these problems. In the PSO paradigm, the population of solutions simulates the behavior of a swarm of agents or particles, such as a flock of birds or a school of fish, as they collectively attempt to find some optimal state.

Numerous variants of PSO have been proposed and shown to be effective on a wide variety of problems (e.g., [2–5]). Moreover, many PSO methods have been developed to handle constraints (e.g., [6–9]). Now there are many optimization problems for which the objective and constraint function values are obtained

© Springer International Publishing AG, part of Springer Nature 2018
P. Korošec et al. (Eds.): BIOMA 2018, LNCS 10835, pp. 246–257, 2018.
https://doi.org/10.1007/978-3-319-91641-5_21

from time-consuming computer simulations. In these situations, only a relatively small number of simulations can be carried out for the optimization process. Hence, surrogates have been used to assist PSO by reducing the number of function evaluations needed to obtain good solutions (e.g., Parno et al. [10], Jiang et al. [11], Tang et al. [12], Sun et al. [13]). These surrogate-assisted PSO methods are designed for bound-constrained problems where only the objective function is expensive. There are very few, if any, surrogate-assisted PSO approaches where surrogates are used to approximate both the objective and constraint functions. Moreover, there are relatively few surrogate-assisted PSO methods that can be used for high-dimensional problems with over 100 decision variables (e.g., Sun et al. [13]). However, there are surrogate-assisted evolutionary algorithms for constrained problems (e.g., Regis [14]) and non-evolutionary methods that use surrogates to model the objective and constraints (e.g., Basudhar et al. [15], Regis [16], Bagheri et al. [17]).

This paper solves constrained optimization problems of the form:

$$\min \{f(x) : G(x) = (g_1(x), \ldots, g_m(x)) \leq 0, \ell \leq x \leq u\} \tag{1}$$

where $f, g_1, \ldots, g_m$ are functions whose values at an input $x \in \mathbb{R}^d$ are obtained from a deterministic and expensive computer simulation. The region $[\ell, u] \subset \mathbb{R}^d$ defined by the bounds is referred to as the *search space* for problem (1). Here, one *simulation* for a given input $x \in [\ell, u]$ yields the values of $f(x)$ and $G(x)$. This paper assumes that accurate gradient information for the objective and constraint functions are not available. Problem (1) is denoted by CBOP$(f, G, [\ell, u])$.

Since standard PSO is not expected to be effective when the objective and constraint functions are expensive, this paper develops a surrogate-based approach called *CONOPUS (CONstrained Optimization by Particle swarm Using Surrogates)* to reduce the number of simulations in PSO for constrained problems. This method can be used for problems involving hundreds of decision variables and many black-box inequality constraints. In each iteration, CONOPUS considers multiple trial positions for each particle in the swarm and then uses surrogate models for the objective and constraint functions to identify the most promising trial position. The simulations yielding the objective and constraint function values are then performed only at these promising trial positions. Moreover, the current overall best position is refined by finding the minimum of the surrogate of the objective function within some search radius of that position and subject to surrogate inequality constraints with a small margin and with a distance requirement from previously visited positions. In the numerical experiments, CONOPUS is implemented using RBF surrogates and the resulting *CONOPUS-RBF* algorithm is compared to alternative methods, including APSO (Accelerated Particle Swarm Optimization) (Yang [18]) and another PSO for constrained problems, an RBF-assisted PSO without local refinement, and an RBF-assisted evolutionary algorithm called CEP-RBF (Regis [14]), on 12 benchmark problems and on the large-scale MOPTA08 problem from the auto industry (Jones [19]) with 124 decision variables and 68 black-box inequality constraints. The results show that CONOPUS-RBF outperforms the other PSO-based approaches and is competitive with CEP-RBF on the problems used.

2   Constrained Particle Swarm Using Surrogates

2.1   Overview of the Proposed Method

As mentioned above, the use of surrogates in PSO have mostly been limited to bound constrained problems where only the objective function is expensive. This paper develops a new surrogate-assisted PSO framework for constrained black-box optimization called *CONOPUS (CONstrained Optimization by Particle swarm Using Surrogates)* that extends the OPUS framework for bound-constrained black-box optimization (Regis [20]). As in OPUS, multiple trial positions for each particle are considered in each iteration. However, in CONOPUS, there are now surrogate models for each inequality constraint function in addition to the surrogate for the objective function. These surrogates are updated in every iteration and, for each particle, they are used to identify the most promising among a large number of trial positions for this particle. Then, each particle is moved to the most promising trial position and then the expensive simulation is carried out only at these promising positions. In addition, CONOPUS refines the current overall best position by finding a minimizer of the updated surrogate model of the objective function within a relatively small radius around that position (and within the bounds), subject to surrogate inequality constraints with a small margin, and subject to a distance requirement from previously evaluated points. The idea of a margin for the constraints was introduced in Regis [16] and it is meant to facilitate the generation of feasible sample points, while the distance requirement is meant to prevent the algorithm from generating sample points that are close to previous sample points. The solution to this optimization subproblem is referred to as a *local refinement point*. The expensive simulation is then also carried out at this point. Hence, CONOPUS is essentially an accelerated PSO for constrained problems with the surrogates guiding where each particle should go and helping to refine the current overall best position.

2.2   Algorithmic Framework

A constrained optimization algorithm needs to be able to compare two infeasible solutions in the search space $[\ell, u]$ and determine which one is more desirable. This can be accomplished by means of a *constraint violation (CV) function*, denoted by $V_G(x)$, which measures the degree of constraint violation of a point $x \in [\ell, u]$ with respect to the constraint function $G(x)$. Commonly used examples are $V_G(x) = \sum_{j=1}^{m} [\max\{g_j(x), 0\}]$ and $V_G(x) = \sum_{j=1}^{m} [\max\{g_j(x), 0\}]^2$, and here, the former is used. Now given the objective function f and a CV function V_G, the definition below clarifies what is meant by an improving solution.

Definition 1. *Let $[\ell, u] \subseteq \mathbb{R}^d$ be the search space and let $G(x)$ be the constraint function for problem (1). Moreover, let $\mathcal{D} = \{x \in \mathbb{R}^d : \ell \leq x \leq u, G(x) \leq 0\}$ be the feasible region of the problem. A point $x_1 \in [\ell, u]$ is an improvement over $x_2 \in [\ell, u]$ if one of the following conditions hold: (a) $x_1, x_2 \in \mathcal{D}$ and $f(x_1) < f(x_2)$; (b) $x_1 \in \mathcal{D}$ but $x_2 \notin \mathcal{D}$; or (c) $x_1, x_2 \notin \mathcal{D}$ and $V_G(x_1) < V_G(x_2)$.*

Below (Algorithm 1) is the CONOPUS framework for constrained PSO using surrogates that extends the OPUS framework in Regis [20] to constrained optimization. In every iteration of a PSO algorithm, each particle is represented as a point in the search space with an associated velocity vector. This velocity vector is updated by using a linear combination of the velocity in the previous iteration, the direction of the best position so far of the particle, and the direction of the best position so far of any of the particles. The weights for the last two components of this linear combination vary randomly from iteration to iteration to allow for the exploration of the search space. Assume for now that a feasible starting point is given but the method can be extended to deal with infeasible starting points by considering a two-phase approach as in Regis [16] where the first phase consists of finding a feasible point while the second phase proceeds in the same manner described below.

In the notation below, s denotes the number of particles and t denotes the time period. Here, only discrete time periods $t = 0, 1, 2, \ldots$ are considered. Moreover, $x^{(i)}(t)$ represents the position of particle i, where $i = 1, \ldots, s$, during time t and $x_j^{(i)}(t)$ represents the jth coordinate or component of $x^{(i)}(t)$, where $j = 1, \ldots, d$. That is, $x^{(i)}(t) = (x_1^{(i)}(t), x_2^{(i)}(t), \ldots, x_d^{(i)}(t))$. Moreover, $y^{(i)}(t)$ is the best position visited by particle i while $\widehat{y}(t)$ is the best position visited by any of the particles up to time t. In addition, $v^{(i,\ell)}(t)$ and $x^{(i,\ell)}(t)$ are the ℓth trial velocity and ℓth trial position, respectively, for particle i during time t.

The CONOPUS framework begins by evaluating the points of the given space-filling design over the search space $[\ell, u]$ (Step 1). Then the initial swarm positions are selected to be the s best points of the space-filling design with respect to the objective function f and constraint violation function V_G (Step 2). In Step 3, the initial particle velocities are determined using the half-diff method [21]. Next, in Step 4, the best position for each particle is initialized to the starting position of the particle. Moreover, the overall best position is initialized to the best position among the starting positions in terms of f and V_G. In addition, the collection of local refinement points $\mathcal{E}_0$ is initialized to the empty set.

Next, Step 5 fits $m + 1$ surrogate models $s_t^{(0)}(x), s_t^{(1)}, \ldots, s_t^{(m)}$, one for the objective function and one for each of the constraint functions, using all available data points. These data points come from all positions visited by any particle (given by $\bigcup_{j=0}^{t} \bigcup_{i=1}^{s} \{x^{(i)}(j)\}$) and from all local refinement points (given by $\mathcal{E}_t$). Then, Step 6 determines the new position of each particle by first considering multiple trial velocities within the velocity limits for that particle (Step 6.1(a)), generating the corresponding trial positions (Step 6.1(b)), projecting the trial positions into the bounds in case they leave the search space (Step 6.1(c)), and then using the surrogate to select the most promising among the trial positions and then choosing this to be the new position of the given particle (Step 6.2). Once the new positions for the particles have been determined, the simulator is then run at these positions to obtain the objective and constraint function values (Step 7). Again, the best position for each particle and the overall best position by any particle are updated (Step 8).

Algorithm 1. CONstrained Optimization by Particle swarm Using Surrogates.

Inputs: (1) CBOP($f, G, [\ell, u]$); (2) CV function $V_G(x)$; (3) population size: s; (4) space-filling design: $\{z^{(1)}, \ldots, z^{(k)}\} \subseteq [\ell, u]$ with $k \geq s$; (5) inertial weighting factor for each iteration: $i(t)$, where t is the iteration number; (6) cognition parameter: μ; (7) social parameter: ν; (8) minimum and maximum velocities: v_{min} and v_{max}; (9) number of trial positions for each particle: r; (10) type of surrogate model; (11) optimization solver for local refinement; (12) search radius for local refinement: $\Delta > 0$; (13) distance requirement from previous sample points: $\xi > 0$; (14) initial margin for the surrogate inequality constraints: $\epsilon > 0$; (15) distance threshold to determine if points are too close: $\delta > 0$; (16) maximum iterations: T_{max}

Output: The best point found by the algorithm.

1. **Evaluate Design.** For $i = 1, \ldots, k$, run simulator to obtain $f(z^{(i)})$ and $G(z^{(i)})$.
2. **Determine Initial Swarm Positions.** Choose initial swarm positions $x^{(1)}(0), \ldots, x^{(s)}(0)$ to be the s best points from $\{z^{(1)}, \ldots, z^{(k)}\}$ according to f and V_G.
3. **Determine Initial Particle Velocities.** For $i = 1, \ldots, s$, generate $u^{(i)}$ uniformly at random on $[\ell, u]$ and set $v^{(i)}(0) = \frac{1}{2}(u^{(i)} - x^{(i)}(0))$.
4. **Initialize Best Position for Each Particle and Overall Best.** Set $y^{(i)}(0) = x^{(i)}(0)$, $i = 1, \ldots, s$, and let $\hat{y}(0)$ be the best point in $\{y^{(1)}(0), \ldots, y^{(s)}(0)\}$ with respect to f and V_G. Set the iteration counter $t = 0$ and $\mathcal{E}_t = \emptyset$.

5. **Fit Surrogates.** Use all previous sample points $\left(\bigcup_{j=0}^{t} \bigcup_{i=1}^{s} \{x^{(i)}(j)\} \right) \bigcup \mathcal{E}_t$ to build surrogates $s_t^{(0)}(x), s_t^{(1)}, \ldots, s_t^{(m)}$ for the objective and constraint functions.
6. **Determine New Particle Positions.** For $i = 1, \ldots, s$
    6.1 Generate Trial Positions. For $\ell = 1, \ldots, r$
    (a) **(Generate Trial Velocities)** For $j = 1, \ldots, d$
    $$v_j^{(i,\ell)}(t+1) = i(t)v_j^{(i)}(t) + \mu\omega_{1,j}^{(i)}(t)(y_j^{(i)}(t) - x_j^{(i)}(t))$$
    $$+ \nu\omega_{2,j}^{(i)}(t)(\hat{y}_j(t) - x_j^{(i)}(t)), \text{ where } \omega_{1,j}^{(i)}(t), \ \omega_{2,j}^{(i)}(t) \sim U[0,1]$$
    $$v_j^{(i,\ell)}(t+1) = \min(\max(v_{min}, v_j^{(i,\ell)}(t+1)), v_{max})$$
    End for.
    (b) **(Generate Trial Positions)** $x^{(i,\ell)}(t+1) = x^{(i)}(t) + v^{(i,\ell)}(t+1)$
    (c) **(Project Trial Positions)** $x^{(i,\ell)}(t+1) = \text{proj}_{[\ell,u]}(x^{(i,\ell)}(t+1))$
    End for.
    6.2 Select Promising Position Using Surrogate. Use the surrogate model $s_t(x)$ to select the most promising trial position for particle i among the points $\{x^{(i,1)}(t+1), x^{(i,2)}(t+1), \ldots, x^{(i,r)}(t+1)\}$. Let $x^{(i)}(t+1)$ be the most promising trial position and let $v^{(i)}(t+1)$ be the associated trial velocity.
7. **Evaluate Swarm Positions.** For each $i = 1, \ldots, s$, run the simulator to obtain $f(x^{(i)}(t+1))$ and $G(x^{(i)}(t+1))$.
8. **Update Best Position for Each Particle and Overall Best.** Set $\hat{y}(t+1) = \hat{y}(t)$. For $i = 1, \ldots, s$
    (a) If $x^{(i)}(t+1)$ is an improvement over $y^{(i)}(t+1)$, then
       Set $y^{(i)}(t+1) = x^{(i)}(t+1)$.
       If $y^{(i)}(t+1)$ is an improvement over $\hat{y}(t+1)$, then $\hat{y}(t+1) = y^{(i)}(t+1)$.
    (b) Else
       Set $y^{(i)}(t+1) = y^{(i)}(t)$.
    End if.

9. **Refit Surrogates.** Use all previous sample points $\left(\bigcup_{j=0}^{t+1} \bigcup_{i=1}^{s} \{x^{(i)}(j)\} \right) \bigcup \mathcal{E}_t$ to refit surrogates $s_t^{(0)}(x), s_t^{(1)}, \ldots, s_t^{(m)}$ for the objective and constraint functions.

Algorithm 1. CONOPUS algorithm (continued)

---

10. Perform Local Refinement of Overall Best Position. Relabel all previous sample points by $v_1, \ldots, v_n$ and let v_n^* be the best feasible point so far. Solve the subproblem:

$$
\begin{aligned}
\min \ & s_t^{(0)}(x) \\
\text{s.t.} \ & x \in \mathbb{R}^d, \ \ell \le x \le u \\
& \|x - v_n^*\| \le \Delta, \quad \|x - v_j\| \ge \xi, \ j = 1, \ldots, n \\
& s_t^{(i)}(x) + \epsilon \le 0, \ i = 1, 2, \ldots, m
\end{aligned}
\tag{2}
$$

11. Check if Feasible Solution to Subproblem was Found. If a feasible solution is found for Problem (2), then let x_{t+1}^* be the solution obtained. Otherwise, let x_{t+1}^* be the best solution with respect to f and V_G (infeasible for (2)) among a set of randomly generated points within the search region $\{x \in [\ell, u] : \|x - v_n^*\| \le \Delta\}$.

12. Determine if Minimizer of Surrogate is Far From Previous Points. If x_{t+1}^* is at least of distance δ from all previously evaluated points, then do

12.1 Evaluate Minimizer of Surrogate. Run the simulator to obtain $f(x_{t+1}^*)$ and $G(x_{t+1}^*)$.

12.2 Update Overall Best Position and Local Refinement Points. If x_{t+1}^* is an improvement over $\widehat{y}(t+1)$, then $\widehat{y}(t+1) = x_{t+1}^*$ and set $\mathcal{E}_{t+1} = \mathcal{E}_t \cup \{x_{t+1}^*\}$. Else, set $\mathcal{E}_{t+1} = \mathcal{E}_t$.

13. Check Termination Condition. If $t < T_{max}$, then reset $t \leftarrow t + 1$ and go back to Step 5. Else, STOP.

The algorithm then refits the surrogate models $s_t^{(0)}(x), s_t^{(1)}, \ldots, s_t^{(m)}$ to incorporate the newly evaluated points (Step 9) in preparation for local refinement of the overall best point (Step 10). In this step, an optimization solver finds a global minimizer x_{t+1}^* of the surrogate for the objective $s_t^{(0)}(x)$ within a ball of radius Δ centered at the current overall best point $\widehat{y}(t+1)$, within the search space, subject to surrogate inequality constraints with a margin ϵ, and with a distance requirement of ξ from all previous sample points. In the numerical implementation, it is enough to find an approximate solution to this optimization subproblem. If the subproblem solution (local refinement point) is not too close to any previous sample point (at least distance δ), then the simulator is run at this point (Step 12.1), and then the overall best position and the set of local refinement points are also updated (Step 12.2). Finally, the algorithm goes back to Step 5 if the termination condition has not been satisfied. Otherwise, the algorithm stops and returns the overall best position found (Step 13).

2.3   A Radial Basis Function Model

CONOPUS can be implemented using any type of surrogate model that is continuously differentiable and whose gradients are easy to calculate. This study uses the radial basis function (RBF) interpolation model in [22] and the resulting algorithm is referred to as CONOPUS-RBF. This RBF model has been used in various surrogate-based optimization methods (e.g., [14,16]). Fitting this model involves solving a linear system with good theoretical properties and it differs from the typical training methods for RBF networks in machine learning.

Suppose we are given n distinct points $u^{(1)}, \ldots, u^{(n)} \in \mathbb{R}^d$ with function values $h(u^{(1)}), \ldots, h(u^{(n)})$, where h is the objective or one of the constraint functions. CONOPUS-RBF uses an interpolant of the form

$$s(x) = \sum_{i=1}^{n} \lambda_i \phi(\|x - u^{(i)}\|) + p(x), \qquad x \in \mathbb{R}^d, \tag{2}$$

where $\| \cdot \|$ is the Euclidean norm, $\lambda_i \in \mathbb{R}$ for $i = 1, \ldots, n$, $p(x)$ is a linear polynomial in d variables, and ϕ has the *cubic* form: $\phi(r) = r^3$. Other possible choices for ϕ include the thin plate spline, multiquadric and Gaussian forms. We use a cubic RBF because of previous success with this model (e.g., [14,20]).

3   Numerical Experiments

CONOPUS-RBF is compared with alternative methods on the MOPTA08 benchmark problem [19] from the auto industry. The MOPTA08 problem involves finding the values of the decision variables (e.g., shape variables) that minimize the mass of the vehicle subject to performance constraints (e.g., crashworthiness, durability). It has one black-box objective function to be minimized, 124 decision variables that take values on a continuous scale from 0 to 1, and 68 black-box inequality constraints that are well normalized [19]. A Fortran code for this problem is available at http://www.miguelanjos.com/jones-benchmark.

CONOPUS-RBF is also compared with the alternative methods on 12 test problems used in Regis [14]. These include G7, G8, G9, G10, four 30-D problems from the CEC 2010 benchmark [23] (C07, C08, C14 and C15) and four design problems, namely, Welded Beam, GTCD (Gas Transmission Compressor Design), Pressure Vessel, and Speed Reducer. The number of decision variables, number of inequality constraints, the region defined by the bounds, and the best known feasible objective values for these problems are given in Regis [14].

To evaluate the effectiveness of the RBF surrogate strategy, CONOPUS-RBF is compared with CONPSO, which is a standard PSO for constrained problems obtained by removing the trial solutions and RBF surrogates in CONOPUS-RBF and also the local refinement phase. To assess the effectiveness of the local refinement strategy, CONOPUS-RBF is also compared with an RBF-assisted extension of CONPSO without local refinement called CONPSO-RBF. Moreover, it is compared with an RBF-assisted evolutionary algorithm called CEP-RBF [14] and with Accelerated Particle Swarm Optimization (APSO) [18].

All computational runs are carried out in Matlab 8.2 on an Intel(R) Core(TM) i7-4770 CPU 3.40 GHz 3.00 GHz desktop machine. Each method is run for 30 trials on all problems. The RBF-assisted methods are all initialized using an affinely independent Latin Hypercube Design (LHD) with $d+1$ points. The initial population of particles is chosen as a subset of the LHD with the best objective function values. If there are not enough LHD points to form the initial population, it is augmented by uniform random points over the search space. The LHD is not needed by CONPSO and other non-surrogate methods. However, experiments on the test problems suggest that the performance of PSO when initialized by uniform random points over the search space is similar to its performance when initialized by an LHD. To ensure fair comparison, all methods use the same LHD in a given trial, but different LHDs are used in different trials.

In the numerical experiments, the population size for CONOPUS-RBF, CONPSO-RBF and CONPSO is set to $s = 5, 10, 20$ (e.g., [7]). In some PSO implementations, the inertial weighting factor $i(t)$ varies with the iterations from a high value (close to 1) to a low value. Here, it is fixed at $i(t) = 0.72984$ and the cognition and social parameters are set to $\mu = \nu = 1.496172$ as recommended in [24]. The minimum and maximum values for the components of the velocity vectors are set to $\mp \min_{1 \leq i \leq d} (u_i - \ell_i)/4$, respectively. For CONOPUS-RBF, the number of trial positions for each particle is $r = 10d$, the search radius for local refinement is $\Delta = 0.05 \min_{1 \leq i \leq d} (u_i - \ell_i)$, the distance requirement from previous sample points is $\xi = 0.0005 \min_{1 \leq i \leq d} (u_i - \ell_i)$, and $\delta = \xi$. For CEP-RBF, the parameters are $\mu = 5$ parent solutions in each generation, and the number of trial offspring for each parent in each generation is $\nu = \min(1000d, 10000)$.

Parameter tuning can be used to obtain better algorithm performance when the computational budget is limited [25]. However, for truly expensive functions, this may not always be feasible and one can use parameter settings that are reasonable based on previous algorithm performance. Besides, finding the best parameter settings for CONOPUS-RBF is beyond the scope of this paper, and our goal is *not* to show that it always outperforms other methods. Rather, we wish to demonstrate that surrogates dramatically improve the performance of PSO on constrained problems and that the resulting CONOPUS-RBF is a promising approach when the number of simulations is limited.

4   Results and Discussion

CONOPUS-RBF is compared with alternatives on the 12 test problems using data profiles [26]. To make it easier to present the results, two sets of comparisons are performed: (1) CONOPUS-RBF vs CONPSO-RBF with different population sizes ($s = 5, 10, 20$); and (2) CONOPUS-RBF vs other methods including APSO, CONPSO, CONPSO-RBF and CEP-RBF.

Now the *data profile of a solver s* [26] is the function

$$d_s(\alpha) = |\{p \in \mathcal{P} : t_{p,s} \leq \alpha(n_p + 1)\}| / |\mathcal{P}|, \qquad \alpha > 0, \tag{3}$$

where $t_{p,s}$ is the number of simulations required by solver s to satisfy the convergence test defined below on problem p and n_p is the number of variables in problem p. For a given solver s and any $\alpha > 0$, $d_s(\alpha)$ is the fraction of problems "solved" by s within $\alpha(n_p + 1)$ simulations (equivalent to α simplex gradient

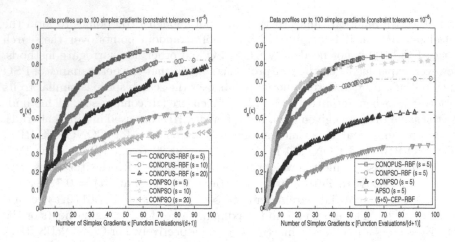

Fig. 1. Data profiles for optimization methods on the test problems.

estimates [26]). Here, "solved" means the solver generated a point satisfying the convergence test in Moré and Wild [26]. This test uses a tolerance $\tau > 0$ and the minimum feasible objective function value f_L obtained by *any* of the solvers on a particular problem within a given number of simulations μ_f and it checks if a feasible point x obtained by a solver satisfies $f(x^{(0)}) - f(x) \geq (1-\tau)(f(x^{(0)}) - f_L)$, where $x^{(0)}$ is the feasible starting point corresponding to the given problem. Here, x is required to achieve a reduction that is $1 - \tau$ times the best possible reduction $f(x^{(0)}) - f_L$. In this study, $\tau = 0.05$.

Figure 1 shows the data profiles of the various solvers on the test problems. These profiles clearly show that CONOPUS-RBF is a dramatic improvement over CONPSO for each of the population sizes $s = 5, 10, 20$. Moreover, for the test problems considered and when the computational budget is limited, the best results for CONOPUS-RBF and CONPSO are obtained when $s = 5$, followed by $s = 10$ and then $s = 20$. A possible explanation for this is that with a smaller population size, these algorithms are able to perform more iterations.

Next, Fig. 1 shows that CONOPUS-RBF with $s = 5$ is slightly better than (5+5)-CEP-RBF after about 40 simplex gradient estimates and it is much better than both CONPSO and CONPSO-RBF with $s = 5$. In particular, after 100 simplex gradient estimates, CONOPUS-RBF with $s = 5$ satisfied the convergence test for about 85% of the problems compared to about 82% for (5+5)-CEP-RBF, about 72% for CONPSO-RBF with $s = 5$, about 53% for CONPSO and 35% for APSO. Additional comparisons between CONOPUS-RBF and CONPSO-RBF for $s = 5, 10, 20$ (not shown here) indicate that local refinement improves performance when the population size is small.

Friedman's nonparametric statistical test followed by a multiple comparison procedure was also performed to determine if the mean rank of CONOPUS-RBF is significantly better than that of other algorithms when $s = 5$ at a fixed computational budget of $15(d+1)$ for the CEC 2010 problems and $30(d+1)$ for the

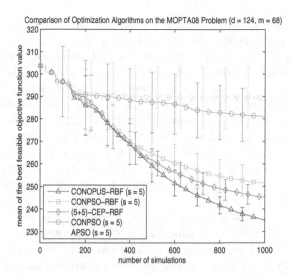

Fig. 2. Mean of the best feasible objective function value (over 10 trials) vs number of simulations for various optimization methods on the MOPTA08 optimization problem. Error bars represent 95% t-confidence intervals for the mean.

other test problems. The results show that CONOPUS-RBF is significantly better than CONPSO and APSO on most of the test problems and it is significantly better than CEP-RBF on three of the four CEC 2010 problems used.

Figure 2 shows the plot of the mean of the best objective function value (over 10 trials) obtained by each algorithm on the MOPTA08 problem as the number of simulations increases. The error bars are 95% t confidence intervals for the mean. This plot shows that on the MOPTA08 problem, CONOPUS-RBF with $s = 5$ is better than $(5 + 5)$-CEP-RBF followed by CONPSO-RBF with $s = 5$ and these RBF-assisted methods are dramatically much better than CONPSO and APSO with $s = 5$.

The advantage of CONOPUS-RBF over CEP-RBF may be partly due to the local refinement procedure. Incorporating local refinement in CEP-RBF might also improve its performance and the resulting algorithm might even outperform CONOPUS-RBF. However, the results suggest that CONOPUS-RBF will still be competitive with CEP-RBF with local refinement.

5   Summary and Future Work

This paper introduced the CONOPUS framework for a surrogate-assisted PSO for computationally expensive constrained optimization. This method generates a large number of trial positions for each particle in the swarm and uses surrogates for the objective and constraint functions to identify the most promising trial position for each particle. The function evaluations are then carried out only on the promising trial positions. Moreover, at the end of each iteration, CONOPUS refines the current best position of all particles by finding an approximate minimizer of the surrogate of the objective function within some neighborhood of that best position and subject to surrogate inequality constraints with a small margin and with a distance requirement from all previously visited positions. CONOPUS was implemented using RBF surrogates and was shown to outperform the APSO algorithm and another constrained PSO with and without RBF surrogates (CONPSO and CONPSO-RBF) for small population sizes of $s = 5, 10$ and 20 on the test problems. Moreover, CONOPUS-RBF with $s = 5$ is competitive with a surrogate-assisted evolutionary algorithm CEP-RBF with the same population size. In addition, CONOPUS-RBF with $s = 5$ outperforms all these other alternatives on the large-scale MOPTA08 problem with 124 decision variables and 68 black-box inequality constraints. Overall, CONOPUS-RBF is a promising algorithm for constrained expensive black-box optimization.

Future work will explore other ways to incorporate surrogates within the PSO framework for constrained optimization and compare with other approaches such as CEP-RBF with local refinement. Moreover, one can consider extensions of the CONOPUS framework to multiobjective optimization and to problems where there is noise in the objective and constraint functions. Finally, one can also apply CONOPUS to other real-world optimization problems.

References

1. Kennedy, J., Eberhart, R.: Particle swarm optimization. In: Proceedings of the 1995 IEEE International Conference on Neural Networks, pp. 1942–1948. IEEE Service Center, Piscataway (1995)
2. Ismail, A., Engelbrecht, A.P.: Self-adaptive particle swarm optimization. In: Bui, L.T., Ong, Y.S., Hoai, N.X., Ishibuchi, H., Suganthan, P.N. (eds.) SEAL 2012. LNCS, vol. 7673, pp. 228–237. Springer, Heidelberg (2012). https://doi.org/10.1007/978-3-642-34859-4_23
3. Qu, B.Y., Liang, J.J., Suganthan, P.N.: Niching particle swarm optimization with local search for multi-modal optimization. Inf. Sci. **197**, 131–143 (2012)
4. Poli, R., Kennedy, J., Blackwell, T.: Particle swarm optimization: an overview. Swarm Intell. **1**(1), 33–57 (2007)
5. Banks, A., Vincent, J., Anyakoha, C.: A review of particle swarm optimization, part I: background and development. Nat. Comput. **6**(4), 467–484 (2007)
6. He, Q., Wang, L.: A hybrid particle swarm optimization with a feasibility-based rule for constrained optimization. Appl. Math. Comput. **186**(2), 1407–1422 (2007)
7. Hu, X., Eberhart, R.C.: Solving constrained nonlinear optimization problems with particle swarm optimization. In: Callaos, N. (ed.) Proceedings of the Sixth World Multiconference on Systemics, Cybernetics and Informatics, pp. 203–206 (2002)
8. Munoz-Zavala, A.E., Aguirre, A.H., Diharce, E.R.V.: Constrained optimization via particle evolutionary swarm optimization algorithm (PESO). In: Beyer, H.G. (ed.) Proceedings of the Genetic and Evolutionary Computation Conference (GECCO 2005), vol. 1, pp. 209–216. ACM Press, New York (2005)
9. Toscano-Pulido, G., Coello, C.A.C.: A constraint-handling mechanism for particle swarm optimization. In: Proceedings of the Congress on Evolutionary Computation 2004 (CEC 2004), vol. 2, pp. 1396–1403. IEEE Service Center, Piscataway (2004)

10. Parno, M.D., Hemker, T., Fowler, K.R.: Applicability of surrogates to improve efficiency of particle swarm optimization for simulation-based problems. Eng. Optim. **44**(5), 521–535 (2012)
11. Jiang, P., Cao, L., Zhou, Q., Gao, Z., Rong, Y., Shao, X.: Optimization of welding process parameters by combining Kriging surrogate with particle swarm optimization algorithm. Int. J. Adv. Manuf. Technol. **86**(9), 2473–2483 (2016)
12. Tang, Y., Chen, J., Wei, J.: A surrogate-based particle swarm optimization algorithm for solving optimization problems with expensive black box functions. Eng. Optim. **45**(5), 557–576 (2013)
13. Sun, C., Jin, Y., Cheng, R., Ding, J., Zeng, J.: Surrogate-assisted cooperative swarm optimization of high-dimensional expensive problems. IEEE Trans. Evol. Comput. **21**, 644–660 (2017)
14. Regis, R.G.: Evolutionary programming for high-dimensional constrained expensive black-box optimization using radial basis functions. IEEE Trans. Evol. Comput. **18**(3), 326–347 (2014)
15. Basudhar, A., Dribusch, C., Lacaze, S., Missoum, S.: Constrained efficient global optimization with support vector machines. Struct. Multidiscip. Optim. **46**(2), 201–221 (2012)
16. Regis, R.G.: Constrained optimization by radial basis function interpolation for high-dimensional expensive black-box problems with infeasible initial points. Eng. Optim. **46**(2), 218–243 (2014)
17. Bagheri, S., Konen, W., Emmerich, M., Bäck, T.: Self-adjusting parameter control for surrogate-assisted constrained optimization under limited budgets. Appl. Soft Comput. **61**, 377–393 (2017)
18. Yang, X.S.: Nature-Inspired Metaheuristic Algorithms, 2nd edn. Luniver Press, Bristol (2010)
19. Jones, D.R.: Large-scale multi-disciplinary mass optimization in the auto industry. In: Modeling and Optimization: Theory and Applications Conference, Ontario, Canada, MOPTA 2008, August 2008
20. Regis, R.G.: Particle swarm with radial basis function surrogates for expensive black-box optimization. J. Comput. Sci. **5**(1), 12–23 (2014)
21. Helwig, S., Wanka, R.: Theoretical analysis of initial particle swarm behavior. In: Rudolph, G., Jansen, T., Beume, N., Lucas, S., Poloni, C. (eds.) PPSN 2008. LNCS, vol. 5199, pp. 889–898. Springer, Heidelberg (2008). https://doi.org/10.1007/978-3-540-87700-4_88
22. Powell, M.J.D.: The theory of radial basis function approximation in 1990. In: Light, W. (ed.) Advances in Numerical Analysis, Volume 2: Wavelets, Subdivision Algorithms and Radial Basis Functions, pp. 105–210. Oxford University Press, Oxford (1992)
23. Mallipeddi, R., Suganthan, P.N.: Problem definitions and evaluation criteria for the CEC 2010 competition on constrained real-parameter optimization. Technical report, Nanyang Technological University, Singapore (2010)
24. Bratton, D., Kennedy, J.: Defining a standard for particle swarm optimization. In: 2007 IEEE Swarm Intelligence Symposium, pp. 120–127, April 2007
25. Cáceres, L.P., López-Ibáñez, M., Stützle, T.: Ant colony optimization on a limited budget of evaluations. Swarm Intell. **9**, 103–124 (2015)
26. Moré, J.J., Wild, S.M.: Benchmarking derivative-free optimization algorithms. SIAM J. Optim. **20**(1), 172–191 (2009)

Indicator-Based Versus Aspect-Based Selection in Multi- and Many-Objective Biochemical Optimization

Susanne Rosenthal[1](✉) and Markus Borschbach[1,2](✉)

[1] Steinbeis Innovation Center "Intelligent and Self-Optimizing Software Assistance Systems", Paracelsusstr. 9, Bergisch Gladbach, Germany
{Susanne.Rosenthal,Markus.Borschbach}@stw.de
[2] University of Applied Sciences (FHDW), Hauptstr. 2, Bergisch Gladbach, Germany
{Susanne.Rosenthal,Markus.Borschbach}@fhdw.de

Abstract. The identification of qualified peptides as ligands for diagnostic and therapeutic interventions requires the solution of multi- and many-objective biochemical optimization problems. A MOEA has been designed for molecular optimization with a combined indicator- and Pareto-based selection strategy that encounters common classification problems of the solutions' quality with the rise of the problem dimension. Therefore, a sophisticated selection strategy is presented in this work that selects the individuals for the succeeding generation related to two general aspects in biochemical optimization: the first aspect reflects the peptide quality and the second one the genetic dissimilarity among the peptides in a population. The search behavior of this aspect-based selection is compared to the traditional selection on generic 3- to 6-dimensional physiochemical optimization problems and the impact of the reference point in the aspect-based selection is investigated.

Keywords: Aspect-based selection
Multi- and many-objective biochemical optimization

1 Introduction

Peptides have several attractive features as they are highly selective, of low toxicity and are very effective in binding to targets. Due to these facts, peptides are highly suitable as applicants for diagnostic and therapeutic agents. Peptides as drug components have to fulfill several additional properties simultaneously like a good cell permeability, high molecule stability and insoluble in aqueous solutions [1].

The synthesis and laboratory analysis of peptides is a time and cost consuming process. In [2], a single-objective evolutionary algorithm for molecular optimization has been reported revealing exponential fitness improvement of candidate molecules within 10 iterations. A sophisticated version of this approach for multi-objective molecular optimization, referred to as COSEA-MO, has been

© Springer International Publishing AG, part of Springer Nature 2018
P. Korošec et al. (Eds.): BIOMA 2018, LNCS 10835, pp. 258–269, 2018.
https://doi.org/10.1007/978-3-319-91641-5_22

reported and benchmarked in [3] identifying a selected number of highly qualified molecules within a very low number of generations in the case of 3- and 4-dimensional physiochemical optimization problems. COSEA-MO is evolved as *in silico* drug design process to identify a selected number of improved molecules providing a wide range of genetic diversity. Molecule properties are determined in the laboratory as numerical approximation models are challenging, therefore only a very low iteration number of the process is performed (<10). COSEA-MO uses dynamic deterministic variation operators and a mating pool of the actual population and the offspring is generated after variation. A combined indicator-based and fitness-proportionate selection determines the individuals of the succeeding generation. The Pareto dominance principle as a part of the selection strategy potentially induces problems in the case of Many-objective Optimization Problems (MaOPs), referring to problems with more than three objectives. A potential idea to overcome this is a sophisticated selection strategy recently introduced in [4] to enhance COSEA-MO for many-objective molecular optimizations. This selection strategy applies the Pareto dominance principle not directly to the optimization problem, but to a two-dimensional problem covering two generic aspects of molecular optimization: the first aspect measures the peptides' quality, the second one measures the genetic dissimilarity of a peptide relative to the current population. Since the aspect-based selection strategy is not comprehensively analyzed so far, this work analyses the search behavior of COSEA-MO with the aspect-based selection compared to the traditional selection on generic 3- to 6-dimensional physiochemical optimization problems as well as the impact of the reference point in the aspect-based selection strategy.

The outline of this work is as follows: Sect. 2 references related work of enhanced MOEA for MaOPs. Section 3 introduces the molecular optimization problems and COSEA-MO with the traditional as well as aspect-based selection. Section 4 presents the simulation onsets and the experimental results, which are discussed in Sect. 5.

2   Related Work

MOEAs nowadays are categorized as Pareto-based, decomposition-based and indicator-based methods and have a high potential to achieve excellent performance in optimization problems with two or three objectives. Otherwise, MOEA have substantial difficulties to solve MaOPs [5]. These difficulties are to be found in the selection operators, the computational cost and visualization of the solutions. Pareto-based MOEA like NSGA-II [6] experience a low efficiency in terms of convergence as the selection criteria of NSGA-II is primary Pareto-based. The consequence is a significant increase of the non-dominated solutions as the Pareto principle has difficulties in distinguishing the individuals of a population. As the term convergence is neglected, diversity is predominant, see e.g. [5]. For decomposition-based methods like MOEA/D [7], assigning of weight vector values or a reference point in high dimensions is challenging. Indicator-based problems like HypeE [8] produce highly increasing computational complexity caused by the hypervolume indicator. Improvement of these algorithms for many-objective optimizations have been published addressing the challenge of convergence and diversity by methods of objective reduction, incorporation and preferences, modified dominance definitions and the introduction of additional selection criteria:

Dimensionality reduction methods have been published dealing with redundant objectives: In [9], a technique of selecting a subset of conflicting objectives using a correlation-based ordering of objectives is presented. In [10], objective reduction is formulated as a multi-objective search problem. Three formulations are introduced of this problem: two formulations base on preservation of dominance structure and one formulation utilizes the correlation between the objectives. NSGA-II is applied to generate Pareto front subsets that offer decision support to the user.

Preference-based many-objective evolutionary algorithms are developed providing a decision-maker search for user's preferred solutions. In [11], a brushing method is proposed to focus on a subset of Pareto optimal solutions on user's preference. In [12], a preference-inspired coevolutionary algorithm is proposed applying the concept of a set of decision-makers preferences together with a population of candidate solutions.

Alternative Pareto dominance principles have been proposed modifying the definition of Pareto dominance. Alternative rules such as ϵ-dominance [13], L-dominance [14], fuzzy- [15] and grid-dominance [16] have been published.

An established and improved MOEA for many-objective optimization is NSGA-III [17]. The primary Pareto-based selection of NSGA-II is improved by using the non-dominated sorting for the first aspect and a more complex niching operator based on a set of predefined reference directions, termed weight vectors, to address diversity. It is a challenge to design the weight vectors in real-world applications. Furthermore, MOEA/DD and Two-Arch2 achieved excellent performance in MaOPs [18]. MOEA/DD uses the Pareto dominance principle and decomposition; Two-Arch2 is also based on Pareto dominance and an indicator.

3   Designed MOEA for Molecular Optimization

3.1   Physiochemical Optimization Problems

Four optimization problems with 3 up to 6 objective functions are applied predicting physiochemical peptide properties. The optimization problems comprise molecular properties like charge, solubility in aqueous solutions, molecule size, molecule stability and structure. The six physiochemical functions are generic in the sense that the physiochemical properties are determined by descriptor values of the amino acids in the molecule sequence and are provided by the open source BioJava library [19]. A description of the determination methods is also available here [19]: Needleman Wunsch Algorithm (NMW), Molecular Weight (MW), Average Hydrophilicity (Hydro), Instability Index (InstInd), Isoelectric Point (pI) and Aliphatic Index (aI).

NMW is a well known and used method for the global sequence alignment of a solution to a pre-defined reference individual. This algorithm refers to the common hypothesis that a high similarity between molecules refers to similar molecular properties [20].

MW is an important peptide property as a minimized MW ensures a good cell permeability. MW of a peptide sequence of the length l is determined by the sum of the mass of each amino acid (a_i) plus a water molecule:
$\sum_{i=1}^{l} mass(a_i) + 17.0073(OH) + 1.0079(H)$, where O (oxygen) and H (hydrogen) are the elements of the periodic system.

A common challenge of drug peptides is the solubility in aqueous solutions, especially peptides with stretches of hydrophobic amino acids. Therefore, Hydro is calculated by the hydrophilicity scale of Hopp and Woods [21] with a window size equal to the peptide length l. An average hydrophilicity value is assigned to each candidate peptide using the scales for each amino acid a_i: $\frac{1}{l} \cdot (\sum_{i=1}^{l} hydro(a_i))$.

The use of molecules as therapeutic agents is potentially restricted by their instability and their potential degradation by enzymes in systemic application. The stability is addressed by the InstInd as stability is a very important feature of drug components. InstInd is determined by the Dipeptide Instability Weight Values (DIWV) of each two consecutive amino acids in the peptide sequence. DIWV are provided by the GRP-Matrix [22]. These values are summarized and the final sum is normalized by the peptide length l: $InstInd = \frac{10}{l} \sum_{i=1}^{l} DIWV(x_i, x_{i+1})$.

pI of a peptide is defined as the pH at which a peptide has a net charge of zero. A peptide has its lowest solubility at its pI. Therefore, the charge of a peptide influence the solubility in aqueous solutions. The pI value is calculated as follows: Firstly, the net charge for $pH = 7.0$ is determined. If this charge is positive, the pH at $7 + 3.5$ is calculated; otherwise the pH at $7 - 3.5$ is determined. This process is repeated until the modules of the charge is less or equal 0.0001.

aI of a peptide is defined as the relative volume occupied by aliphatic side chains consisting of the amino acids alanine (Ala), valine (Val), isoleucine (Ile) and leucine (Leu). aI is regarded as a positive factor for the increase of thermostability of globular molecules. aI is calculated according to the formula: $aI = X(Ala) + a \cdot X(Val) + b \cdot (X(Ile) + X(Leu))$,
where $X(Ala)$, $X(Val)$, $X(Ile)$ and $X(Leu)$ are mole percent of the amino acids. The coefficients a and b are the relative volume at the valine side chain ($a = 2.9$) and Lei, Ile side chains ($b = 3.9$) to the side chain Ala.

Table 1. Physiochemical functions of the different optimization problems

Dimension	Abbr.	Objective functions
3D	3D-MOP	NMW, MW, Hydro
4D	4D-MaOP	NMW, MW, Hydro, InstInd
5D	5D-MaOP	NMW, MW, Hydro, InstInd, pI
6D	6D-MaOP	NMW, MW, Hydro, InstInd, pI, aI

Table 1 presents the composed physiochemical optimization problems with the used abbreviations. These six objective functions comparatively act to reflect the similarity of a particular peptide and a pre-defined reference peptide: $f(\text{CandidatePeptide}) := |f(\text{CandidatePeptide}) - f(\text{ReferencePeptide})|$. Therefore, the four objective functions have to be minimized and the optimization problems are minimization problems.

3.2 Algorithm COSEA-MO

The presented COmponent-Specific Evolutionary Algorithm for Molecule Optimization (COSEA-MO) [3] is designed to complement an *in vitro* drug design process with a computer-assisting system aimed at the specific requirements of such combined *in vitro* and *in silico* process: Firstly, several molecular properties are not predictable by numerical approximation models or descriptor value sets and have to be determined in an *in vitro* process. As a consequence, the evolutionary process has to provide a selected number of high-qualified peptides within a very low number of generations and objective evaluations. Secondly, the proposed optimized peptides have to be highly diverse in its primary genetic structure and therefore, the algorithm has to propose the whole range from very similar to very diverse peptide sequences in each iteration. Thirdly, the algorithm has to be independent of problem-specific parameters as these are either usually unknown or expert rule of thumbs in real-world application problems.

The algorithms briefly described in the following make use of a combination of deterministic dynamic variation operators and a selection strategy for the determination of the individuals for the succeeding generation. The traditional selection concept is tournament-based and a combination of fitness-proportionate and indicator-based selection. The procedure of the proposed algorithm is similar to NSGA-II. The initial population of COSEA-MO is generated by N random individuals. Individuals are selected randomly from the actual population for variation. Parent and offspring sets are combined to a set of size $2N$. The succeeding generation of size N is generated by optionally applying either the proposed indicator-based selection strategy, or the aspect-based selection procedure.

The individuals in COSEA-MO represent peptides of length 20 consisting of the 20 canonical amino acids. The individuals are encoded as character strings. This encoding presents all feasible and only feasible solutions, which have an equal probability to be presented. Tools for the determination of physiochemical peptide properties often make use of this character encoding. Therefore, this encoding does not require a conversion of the data format based on a character set representing an amino acid chain.

The mutation and recombination operator are motivated by a suitable balance of global and local search. Deterministic dynamic variation operators are suitable operators to achieve this purpose. The characteristic of deterministic dynamic operators is the adaptation of mutation and recombination rates by a predefined functional reduction with the iteration progress.

The recombination operator varies the number of recombination points over the generations via a linearly decreasing function: $x_R(t) = \frac{l}{2} - \frac{l/2}{T} \cdot t$, which depends on the length of the individual l, the total number of the generations T and the index of the current generation t. Three parents are used for recombination.

An adapted version of the deterministic dynamic operator of Bäck and Schütz [4] determines the mutation probabilities via the following function with $a = 5$ $p_{BS} = (a + \frac{l-2}{T-1}t)^{-1}$. The mutation rates of the traditional operator have been adapted to a lower starting mutation rate by the parameter $a = 5$.

3.3   Indicator-Based Selection Strategy

The traditional selection concept of COSEA-MO starts with the tournament selection of ts individuals from the population. These individuals are ranked according to the Pareto dominance principle and the volume of each individual to the zero point as ideal reference point is calculated. From this ranked tournament set, the individuals with the lowest volume values are selected for the succeeding generation with a probability p_0, with the aim of guiding the search process in direction of high quality solutions. With a probability $1 - p_0$, the individuals are chosen from different fronts via Stochastic Universal Sampling (SUS). The number of pointers in front-based SUS is equal to the number of fronts detected in the ranking process. The segments are equal in size to the number of individuals in each front. These steps repeat until the succeeding filial generation is complete. Consequently, this selection strategy has two parameters, the tournament size and the probability p_0 for choosing the individuals from the first front. Default values are $ts = 10$ and $p_0 = 50\%$ according to previous simulation runs.

3.4   General Aspect-Based Selection

This section describes the alternative aspect-based selection strategy. A MaOP is given by $f : P \longrightarrow \mathbb{R}^m$, $p \longrightarrow (f_1(p), f_2(p), \ldots, f_m(p))$, whereby $m > 3$ is the number of objectives f_i as molecular functions which have to be minimized, and P is the quantity of feasible molecules. The procedure of the novel selection strategy is described in Algorithm 1. The strategy is ranked and binary tournament based. The Pareto principle used for ranking is not directly applied on the objective values but on a two-dimensional aspect-based minimization problem (line 4). The first aspect reflects the solutions' quality by the calculation of the L_p-norm of the objective values to a reference point (RP) (line 2), which is either determined by the minimum of each objective provided by the population members (line 1). Therefore, this reference point varies with the population. Alternatively, in the experiments the zero point is selected as ideal reference point RP. The second aspect refers to the general idea of maintaining a high genetic dissimilarity within the populations. Needleman Wunsch Algorithm [23] is chosen as global sequence alignment (line 3). COSEA-MO with aspect-based selection is further termed nCOSEA-MO. The N-best individuals are selected in the succeeding generation based on the rank (line 5) and the volume dominance principle via binary tournament selection (line 6). L_2-norm or Euclidean-norm is used here in the experiments.

Algorithm 1. Pseudo code of the aspect-based selection strategy

---

Input: Current population P_t with $|P_t| = 2N$, $P_{t+1} = \{\}$
Calculation of the two indicator values for each solution:
1: $RP := (min_{i_1} f_1(p_{i_1}), min_{i_2} f_2(p_{i_2}), \ldots, min_{i_m} f_m(p_{i_m}))$;
2: $\forall p \in P_t: f_{L_{p-norm}}(p) = L_p(f(p), RP)$;
3: $\forall p \in P_t: diss(p) = \frac{1}{|P_t|} \sum_{p \in P_t} SequenceAlignment(p, P_t - p)$;

Selection process:
4: Ranking of P_t according to $(f_{L_p-norm}, diss)$ into fronts F_i;
5: **while** $|P_{t+1}| + |F_i| < N$ **do**
    $\quad | \quad P_{t+1} = P_{t+1} \cup F_i$;   i++;
end
6: binary tournament selection: **while** $|P_{t+1}| < N$ **do**
    $\quad$ select $p_1, p_2 \in P_t \setminus \{P_{t+1}\}$:
    $\quad$ **if** $(f_{L_p}(p_1) * diss(p_1) < f_{L_p}(p_2) * diss(p_2))$ add p_1 to P_{t+1} ;
    $\quad$ **else** add p_2 to P_{t+1};
end

---

4   Experimental Studies

The experiments are generally performed with the default population size of 100 motivated by previous experimental studies; the start population is randomly initialized. The individuals are 20-mer peptides composed of the 20 canonical amino acids. Short peptides of length 20 are of specific interest because of their favorable properties as drugs. For statistical reasons, each configuration is repeated 30 times with 10 iterations. Firstly, the approximate Pareto optimal sets (PFs) of COSEA-MO and nCOSEA-MO in each generation are compared in terms of the established C-metric [24]

$$C(PF_1, PF_2) := \frac{|\{b \in PF_2 \mid \exists a \in PF_1 : a \preceq b\}|}{|PF_2|}. \tag{1}$$

$C(PF_1, PF_2) = 0$ means that no solution of PF_2 is weakly dominated by at least one solution of PF_1, whereas $C(PF_1, PF_2) = 1$ implicate that all points of PF_2 are weakly dominated by PF_1. This metric is usually not symmetric, consequently $C(PF_1, PF_2)$ and $C(PF_2, PF_1)$ have to be determined. Therefore, the C-metric value reflects the percentage of solutions that are weakly dominated by one individual of the other approximate Pareto set.

PF of COSEA-MO is determined according to the molecular optimization problem, whereas PF of COSEA-MO is determined according to the aspect-based problem. The C-metric values are determined according to the objective values as usual. Tables 2, 3, 4, 5, 6 and 7 depict the C-metric values $C_1 = C(\text{nCOSEA-MO, COSEA-MO})$ and $C_2 = C(\text{COSEA-MO, nCOSEA-MO})$ for the 3D-MOP to 6D-MaOP with different selection parameter settings p_0 and reference point (RP) based on empirical and experimental findings.

4.1   Experimental Results

The experimental results are analyzed according to the following questions: firstly, does a higher problem dimension have a different impact on the

Table 2. 3D-MOP: (a) $p_0 = 50\%$, $RP = min$ || (b) $p_0 = 50\%$, $RP = 0$

	G1	G2	G3	G4	G5	G6	G7	G8	G9	G10	G1	G2	G3	G4	G5	G6	G7	G8	G9	G10
C_1	0.88	0.87	0.9	0.9	0.81	0.73	0.73	0.5	0.68	0.7	0.78	0.83	0.83	0.79	0.64	0.67	0.69	0.58	0.6	0.6
C_2	0.69	0.75	0.73	0.65	0.68	0.61	0.69	0.7	0.56	0.55	0.72	0.69	0.66	0.64	0.65	0.55	0.55	0.68	0.48	0.5

Table 3. 4D-MaOP: (a) $p_0 = 50\%$, $RP = min$ || (b) $p_0 = 50\%$, $RP = 0$

	G1	G2	G3	G4	G5	G6	G7	G8	G9	G10	G1	G2	G3	G4	G5	G6	G7	G8	G9	G10
C_1	0.55	0.55	0.6	0.63	0.64	0.53	0.67	0.58	0.7	0.6	0.71	0.65	0.7	0.72	0.64	0.65	0.46	0.62	0.52	0.32
C_2	0.55	0.45	0.44	0.51	0.46	0.53	0.51	0.48	0.5	0.56	0.51	0.55	0.56	0.46	0.5	0.49	0.54	0.54	0.46	0.52

Table 4. 5D-MaOP: (a) $p_0 = 50\%$, $RP = min$ || (b) $p_0 = 50\%$, $RP = 0$

	G1	G2	G3	G4	G5	G6	G7	G8	G9	G10	G1	G2	G3	G4	G5	G6	G7	G8	G9	G10
C_1	0.48	0.36	0.38	0.38	0.33	0.29	0.24	0.22	0.18	0.22	0.5	0.45	0.35	0.32	0.3	0.22	0.3	0.23	0.21	0.17
C_2	0.6	0.6	0.65	0.64	0.63	0.6	0.59	0.66	0.62	0.64	0.59	0.66	0.63	0.63	0.68	0.67	0.68	0.62	0.54	0.55

Table 5. 5D-MaOP: (a) $p_0 = 70\%$, $RP = min$ || (b) $p_0 = 70\%$, $RP = 0$

	G1	G2	G3	G4	G5	G6	G7	G8	G9	G10	G1	G2	G3	G4	G5	G6	G7	G8	G9	G10
C_1	0.4	0.33	0.34	0.35	0.3	0.2	0.18	0.15	0.12	0.18	0.55	0.45	0.32	0.31	0.26	0.16	0.3	0.2	0.16	0.08
C_2	0.59	0.52	0.62	0.61	0.61	0.56	0.56	0.64	0.58	0.62	0.57	0.57	0.62	0.56	0.58	0.55	0.55	0.46	0.47	0.5

Table 6. 6D-MaOP: (a) $p_0 = 50\%$ and $RP = min$ || (b) $p_0 = 50\%$ and $RP = 0$

	G1	G2	G3	G4	G5	G6	G7	G8	G9	G10	G1	G2	G3	G4	G5	G6	G7	G8	G9	G10
C_1	0.32	0.26	0.43	0.29	0.26	0.24	0.25	0.25	0.22	0.25	0.4	0.4	0.41	0.38	0.37	0.36	0.28	0.19	0.28	0.37
C_2	0.51	0.55	0.76	0.51	0.52	0.51	0.45	0.54	0.61	0.54	0.57	0.61	0.72	0.6	0.46	0.55	0.52	0.6	0.56	0.48

Table 7. 6D-MaOP: (a) $p_0 = 70\%$ and $RP = min$ || (b) $p_0 = 70\%$ and $RP = 0$

	G1	G2	G3	G4	G5	G6	G7	G8	G9	G10	G1	G2	G3	G4	G5	G6	G7	G8	G9	G10
C_1	0.34	0.3	0.36	0.3	0.22	0.23	0.21	0.15	0.16	0.14	0.4	0.38	0.36	0.37	0.35	0.31	0.23	0.14	0.2	0.25
C_2	0.46	0.5	0.42	0.48	0.56	0.58	0.56	0.55	0.6	0.54	0.53	0.54	0.48	0.53	0.52	0.59	0.57	0.61	0.52	0.5

performance of either or both selection strategies, indicator- or aspect-based? Secondly, is there an impact of the selection parameters p_0 or RP observable? Thirdly, is there a fundamental difference in the search behavior of the different selection configurations?

Tables 2, 3, 4, 5, 6 and 7 depict the C-metric values of nCOSEA-MO and COSEA-MO with different parameter settings on the four optimization problems. A significant difference is observable comparing Tables 3(b), 4 and 5(a) with Tables 5(b), 6 and 7(b): in the case of 3D-MOP and 4D-MaOP, C_1 values are generally higher than those of C_2, revealing that more candidate solutions identified by nCOSEA-MO weakly dominate the solutions of COSEA-MO than vice versa within each of the 10 generations. Otherwise, in the case of 5D-MaOP and 6D-MaOP, C_2 values are generally higher than those of C_1, revealing that more solutions of COSEA-MO weakly dominate solutions of nCOSEA-MO

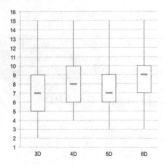

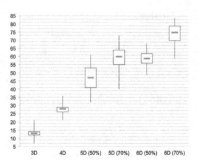

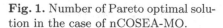

Fig. 1. Number of Pareto optimal solution in the case of nCOSEA-MO.

Fig. 2. Number of Pareto optimal solution in the case of COSEA-MO.

independent of the parameter settings. Figures 1 and 2 give an insight into the number of approximate Pareto optimal solutions identified by COSEA-MO and nCOSEA-MO in the test runs. nCOSEA-MO provides a significantly lower and stable number of candidate solutions, whereas the solutions number of COSEA-MO is generally higher and increases with the problem dimension as a consequence of the Pareto dominance principle being directly applied to the objective values. The number of Pareto optimal solutions of COEA-MO is increasing linearly from 3D-MOP to 4D-MaOP and this increasing rate slows down by a further dimension increase. The average number of identified Pareto optimal solutions by COSEA-MO is generally higher in the case of $p_0 = 70\%$ than those of $p_0 = 50\%$. As the approximate Pareto optimal sets of COSEA-MO are significantly larger than those of nCOSEA-MO, the probability of identified promising peptides in the sets of COSEA-MO is clearly higher than in the case of nCOSEA-MO.

Referring to the second question, there is no significant impact of the choice of RP. Consequently, RP has no impact on the selection pressure independent of the problem dimension. In the case of 5D-MOP and 6D-MaOP, the probability of p_0 and therefore the selection probability of the individuals for the succeeding generation by the indicator is increased with the aim of raising the selection pressure. A slight influence of the raise is observable as the C-metric values are mainly slightly lower in the case of $p_0 = 70\%$, revealing that more peptides of the approximate Pareto optimal sets are indifferent to each other.

To address the third question, a specific mapping method is applied to visualize the peptide quality of each generation equally for all optimization problems with the aim of analyzing the search behavior. The peptide quality of each generation is mapped into a point $(x; y)$, where x is the volume of the gravity point of the scatter plot to zero point as an ideal reference point. The coordinate y is the standard deviation of the scatter plot points to the calculated reference point symbolizing the average distance of the solutions points in each generation to the calculated gravity point of these solutions. Scatter plots of these points are depicted in Figs. 3, 4, 5 and 6 for each optimization problem. Generally, it is observable that nCOSEA-MO has higher volumes of the gravity point in the generations independent of the problem dimension but lower standard

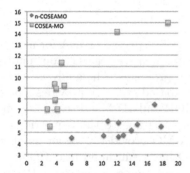

Fig. 3. 3D-MOP: peptide quality

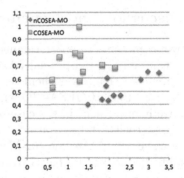

Fig. 4. 4D-MaOP: peptide quality

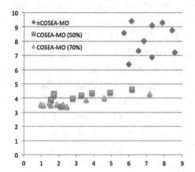

Fig. 5. 5D-MaOP: peptide quality

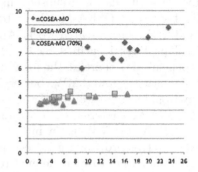

Fig. 6. 6D-MaOP: peptide quality

deviations of the peptides in each generation to the gravity point in the cases of 3D-MOP and 3D-MaOP. Figures 5 and 6 reveal that the results of nCOSEA are generally higher in the volume of the gravity points and die standard deviation. The results of COSEA-MO with the probabilities $p_0 = 50\%$ and $p_0 = 70\%$ are generally comparable in volume and standard deviation but remarkably low in both terms compared to nCOSEA-MO. The volume values of the configuration with $p_0 = 70\%$ are slightly lower, a consequence of the higher probabilities of the individuals to be selected into the succeeding generation by the ACV-indicator. The peptides identified by COSEA-MO are more clustered in the search space, which is a known property of the ACV-indicator. As a consequence, the indicator-based selection tends to identify higher quality solutions in the case of the 5D- and 6D-MaOP. nCOSEA-MO provides improved performance in the case of the 3D-MOP and 4D-MaOP. The analysis of the identified peptides of nCOSEA-MO and COSEA-MO according to their physiochemical function values reveals an interesting fact: the peptides identified by nCOSEA-MO are generally of significantly lower MW, but have a higher average hydrophilicity and higher pI values for 5D- and 6D-MaOP. As a consequence of the second aspect, the identified peptides of nCOSEA-MO tend to have lower NMW values and therefore provide a higher similarity to the reference peptide.

5   Discussion and Conclusion

This works presents the performance comparison of a specific MOEA for molecular optimization with optionally two different selection strategies in four multi- and many-objective physiochemical optimization problems. The analysis of the results reveal that nCOESA-MO with the aspect-based selection provides a performance improvement in the case of the 3D-MOP and 4D-MaOP compared to COSEA-MO with the indicator-based selection according to the C-metric values. In the cases of 5D- and 6D-MaOP, COSEA-MO provides a higher number of qualified peptides compared to nCOSEA-MO having in mind that COSEA-MO has significantly higher approximate optimal solution sets due to the Pareto dominance principle. A further selection method is required to eliminate worse candidate solutions for a subsequent laboratory analysis. Consequently, these optimal sets of COSEA-MO have to be determined by a more sophisticated method in further research work. An interesting point is the difference of the optimal peptides identified by COSEA-MO and nCOSEA-MO regarding the physiochemical properties: the identified peptides of nCOSEA-MO are generally of a significantly lower MW, better NMW values on average but higher average hydrophilicity as well as pI values in higher dimensions. This makes the use of nCOSEA-MO interesting in a practical sense even in the cases of 5D- and 6D-MaOP. A low MW is an important peptide property and therefore referenced objective providing good cell permeability. Better NMW values indicate a higher similarity to a predefined reference peptide and therefore potentially higher similarity in molecule properties.

A further improvement of nCOSEA-MO is therefore part of the future work as well as the evolution of a combination of these selection strategies for a robust and good performance of COSEA-MO in multi- and many-objective molecular optimization.

References

1. Otvos, L.: Peptide-Based Drug Design: Methods and Protocols. Humana Press Inc., New York (2000)
2. Röckendorf, N., Borschbach, M.: Molecular evolution of peptide ligands with custom-tailored characteristics. PLoS Comput. Biol. **8**(12), e1002800 (2012). https://doi.org/10.1371/journal.pcbi.1002800
3. Rosenthal, S., Borschbach, M.: Design perspectives of an evolutionary process for multi-objective molecular optimization. In: Trautmann, H., Rudolph, G., Klamroth, K., Schütze, O., Wiecek, M., Jin, Y., Grimme, C. (eds.) EMO 2017. LNCS, vol. 10173, pp. 529–544. Springer, Cham (2017). https://doi.org/10.1007/978-3-319-54157-0_36
4. Rosenthal, S., Borschbach, M.: General aspect-based selection concept for multi- and many-objective molecular optimization. In: International Conference on Genetic and Evolutionary Computation (GECCO 2017), pp. 45–46 (2017)
5. Ishibuchi, H., Akedo, N., Nojima, Y.: Behavior of multiobjective evolutionary algorithms on many-objective knapsack problems. IEEE Trans. Evol. Comput. **19**(2), 264–283 (2015)

6. Deb, K., Pratap, A., Agarwal, S., Meyarivan, T.: A fast and elitist multiobjective genetic algorithm: NSGA-II. IEEE Trans. Evol. Comput. **6**(2), 182–197 (2002)
7. Zhang, Q., Li, H.: MOEA/D: a multiobjective evolutionary algorithm based on decomposition. IEEE Trans. Evol. Comput. **11**(6), 712–731 (2007)
8. Bader, J., Zitzler, E.: HypE: analgorithm for fast hypervolume-based many-objective optimization. Evol. Comput. **19**(1), 45–76 (2011)
9. Bandyopadhyay, S., Mukherjee, A.: An algorithm for many-objective optimization with reduced objective computations: a study in differential evolution. IEEE Trans. Evol. Comput. **19**(3), 400–413 (2015)
10. Yuan, Y., Ong, Y.-S., Gupta, A., Xu, H.: Objective reduction in many-objective optimization: evolutionary multiobjective approaches and comprehensive analysis. IEEE Trans. Evol. Comput. **22**(2), 189–210 (2017). https://doi.org/10.1109/TEVC.2017.2672668
11. Wang, R., Purshouse, R., Giagkiozis, I., Fleming, P.: The iPICEA-g: a new hybrid evolutionary multi-criteria decision making approach using the brushing technique. Eur. J. Oper. Res. **243**(2), 442–453 (2015)
12. Wang, R., Purshouse, R., Fleming, P.: Preference-inspired coevolutionary algorithms for many-objective optimization. IEEE Trans. Evol. Comput. **17**(4), 474–494 (2013)
13. Laumanns, M., Thiele, L., Deb, K., Zitzler, E.: Combining convergence and diversity in evolutionary multiobjective optimization. Evol. Comput. **10**(3), 263–282 (2002)
14. Zou, X., Chen, Y., Liu, M., Kang, L.: A new evolutionary algorithm for solving many-objective optimization problems. IEEE Trans. Syst. Man Cybern. Part B (Cybern.) **38**(5), 1402–1412 (2008)
15. Wang, C., Jiang, H.: Fuzzy-dominance and its application in evolutionary many objective optimization. In: International Conference on Computational Intelligence and Security Workshops (CISW 2007), pp. 195–198. IEEE (2007)
16. Yang, S., Li, M., Liu, X., Zheng, J.: A grid-based evolutionary algorithm for many-objective optimization. IEEE Trans. Evol. Comput. **17**(5), 721–736 (2013)
17. Deb, K., Jain, H.: An evolutionary many-objective optimization algorithm using reference-point-based nondominated sorting approach, part I: solving problems with box constraints. IEEE Trans. Evol. Comput. **18**(4), 557–601 (2014)
18. Li, B., Li, J., Tang, K., Yao, X.: Many-objective evolutionary algorithms: a survey. ACM Comput. Surv. (CSUR) **48**(1), 13 (2015)
19. BioJava: CookBook, r. http://www.biojava.org/wiki/BioJava
20. Emmerich, M., Lee, B., Render, A.: Analyzing molecular landscapes using random walks and information theory. Chem. Cent. J. **3**(1), 20 (2009)
21. Hopp, T., Woods, K.: A computer program for predicting protein antigenic determinants. Mol. Immunol. **20**(4), 483–489 (1983)
22. Guruprasad, K., Reddy, B., Pandit, M.: Correlation between stability of a protein and its dipeptide composition: a novel approach for predicting in vivo stability of a protein from its primary structure. Protein Eng. **4**(2), 155–161 (1990)
23. Needleman, S., Wunsch, C.: A general method application to the research for similarities in the amino acid sequence of two proteins. J. Mol. Biol. **48**(3), 443–453 (1970)
24. Zitzler, E., Thiele, L.: Multiobjective optimization using evolutionary algorithms—a comparative case study. In: Eiben, A.E., Bäck, T., Schoenauer, M., Schwefel, H.-P. (eds.) PPSN 1998. LNCS, vol. 1498, pp. 292–301. Springer, Heidelberg (1998). https://doi.org/10.1007/BFb0056872

An Approach for Recovering Distributed Systems from Disasters

Ichiro Satoh[(✉)]

National Institute of Informatics, 2-1-2 Hitotsubashi, Chiyoda-ku, Tokyo, Japan
ichiro@nii.ac.jp

Abstract. This paper presents an approach to recovering distributed applications, which consist of software agents running on different computers from drastic damages by disasters. The approach is inspired from regeneration mechanisms in living things, e.g., tails of lizards. When an agent delegates a function to another agent coordinating with it, if the former has the function, this function becomes less-developed and the latter's function becomes well-developed like differentiation processes in cells. It can also initialize and restart differentiated software agents, when some agents cannot be delegated like regeneration processes. It is constructed as a general-purpose and practical middleware system for software agents on real distributed systems consisting of embedded computers or sensor nodes.

1 Introduction

Hundreds of natural disasters occur in many parts of the world every year, causing billions of dollars in damages. This fact may contrast with the availability of distributed systems. Distributed systems are often treated to be dependable against damages, because in distributed systems data can be stored and executed at multiple locations and processing must not be performed by only one computer. However, all existing distributed systems are not resilient to damages in the sense that if only one of the many computers fails, or if a single network link is down, the system as a whole may become unavailable. Furthermore, in distributed systems partially damaged by disasters surviving computers and networks have no ability to fill functions lost with damaged computers or networks.

On the other hand, several living things, including vertebrates, can *regenerate* their lost parts, where *regeneration* is one of developmental mechanisms observed in a number of animal species, e.g., lizard, earthworm, and hydra, because regeneration enables biological systems to recover themselves against their grave damages. For example, reptiles and amphibians can partially regenerate their tails, typically over a period of weeks after cutting the tails. *Regeneration* processes are provided by (de)differentiation mechanism by which cells in a multicellular organism become specialized to perform specific functions in a variety of tissues and organs. The key idea behind the approach proposed in this paper was inspired from *(de)differentiation* as a basic mechanism for regeneration like living things. The approach introduces a (de)differentiation mechanism

P. Korošec et al. (Eds.): BIOMA 2018, LNCS 10835, pp. 270–282, 2018.
https://doi.org/10.1007/978-3-319-91641-5_23

into middleware systems for distributed systems, instead of any simulation-based approaches.[1]

Our middleware system aims at building and operating distributed applications consisting of self-adapting/tuning software components, called agents, to regenerate/differentiate their functions according to their roles in whole applications and resource availability, as just like cells. It involves treating the undertaking/delegation of functions in agents from/to other agents as their differentiation factors. When an agent delegates a function to another agent, if the former has the function, its function becomes less-developed in the sense that it has less computational resources, e.g., active threads, and the latter's function becomes well-developed in the sense that it has more computational resources.

2 Example Scenario

Let us suppose a sensor network to observe a volcano. Its sensor nodes are located around the volcano. Each of the nodes have sensors to measure accelerations result from volcano tectonic earthquakes around it in addition to processors and wired or wireless network interfaces. The locations of sensor nodes tend to be irregular around the volcano.

A disaster may result in drastic damages in sensor networks. For example, there are several active or dormant volcanoes in Japan. Sensor networks to detect volcano ash and tremor are installed at several spots in volcanoes. Volcanic eruptions, including phreatic eruptions, seriously affect such sensor networks. More han half sensor nodes may be damaged by eruptions. Nevertheless, the sensor networks should continue to monitor volcano tectonic earthquakes with only their surviving nodes as much as possible.

Sensor nodes in a volcano are located irregularly, because it is difficult for people to place such nodes at certain positions in volcanoes, because there are many no-go zones and topographical constraints. Instead, they are distributed from manned airplanes or unmanned ones. Therefore, they tend to be overpopulated in several areas in the sense that the coverage areas of their sensors are overlap or contained. To avoid congestion in networks as well as to save energy consumption, redundant nodes should be inactivated.

3 Requirements

To support example scenarios discussed in the previous section, our approach needs to satisfy the following requirements: *Self-adaptation* is needed when environments and users' requirements change. To save computational resources and energy, distributed systems should adapt their own functions to changes in their systems and environments. *Saving resources* is important in distributed systems used in field, e.g., sensor networks, rather than data centers, including cloud

---

[1] There is often a gap between the real systems and simulations. We believe that adaptive distributed systems need more experiences in the real systems.

computing. Our approach should conserve limited computational resources, e.g., processing, storage resources, networks, and energy, at nodes as much as possible. *Non-centralized management* can support reliability and availability. Centralized management may be simple but can become a single point of failures. Therefore, our adaptation should be managed in a peer-to-peer manner. Distributed systems essentially lack no global view due to communication latency between computers. Software components, which may be running on different computers, need to coordinate them to support their applications with partial knowledge about other computers. Our approach should be practical so that it is implemented as a general-purpose middleware system. This is because applications running on distributed systems are various. Each of software components should be defined independently of our adaptation mechanism as much as possible. As a result, developers should be able to concentrate their application-specific processing.

4   Approach: Regeneration and Differentiation

The goal of the proposed approach is to introduce a *regeneration* mechanism into distributed systems like living things. Regenerations in living things need redundant information in the sense that each of their cells have genes as plans for other cells. When living things lose some parts of their bodies, they can regenerate such lost parts by encoding genes for building the parts with differentiation mechanisms. Differentiation mechanisms can be treated as selections of parts of genes to be encoded. Since a distributed application consists of software components, which may be running on different computers like cells, we assume that software components have program codes for functions, which they do not initially provide and our differentiation mechanisms can select which functions should be (in)activated or well/less-developed.

Each software component, called agent, has one or more functions with weights, where each weight indicates the superiority and development of its function in the sense that the function is assigned with more computational resources. Each agent initially intends to progress all its functions and periodically multicasts messages about its differentiation to other agents of which its distributed application consist. Such messages lead other agents to degenerate their functions specified in the messages and to decrease the superiority of the functions. As a result, agents complement other agents in the sense that each agent can provide some functions to other agents and delegate other functions to other agents that can provide the functions.

5   Design

Our approach is maintained through two parts: runtime systems and agents. The former is a middleware system for running on computers and the latter is a self-contained and autonomous software entity. It has three protocols for regeneration/differentiation.

5.1   Agent

Each agent consists of one or more functions, called the *behavior* parts, and its state, called the *body* part, with information for (de)differentiation, called the *attribute* part. The body part maintains program variables shared by its behaviors parts like instance variables in object orientation. When it receives a request message from an external system or other agents, it dispatches the message to the behavior part that can handle the message. The behavior part defines more than one application-specific behavior. It corresponds to a method in object orientation. As in behavior invocation, when a message is received from the body part, the behavior is executed and returns the result is returned via the body part. The attribute part maintains descriptive information with regard to the agent, including its own identifier. The attributes contains a database for maintaining the weights of its own behaviors and for recording information on the behaviors that other agents can provide.

5.2   Regeneration

We outline our differentiation processes for regeneration (Fig. 1). The Appendix describes the processes in more detail.

– *Invocation of behaviors:* Each agent periodically multicasts messages about the weights of its behaviors to other agents. When an agent wants to execute a behavior, even if it has the behavior, it compares the weights of the same or compatible behaviors provided in others and it. It select one of the behaviors, whose weights are the most among the weights of these behaviors. That is, the approach selects more developed behaviors than less developed behaviors.
– *Well/Less developing behaviors:* When a behavior is executed by other agents, the weight of the behavior increase and the weights of the same or behaviors provided from others decrease. That is, behaviors in an agent, which are delegated from other agents more times, are well developed, whereas other behaviors, which are delegated from other agents fewer times, in a cell are less developed.
– *Removing redundant behaviors:* The agent only provides the former behaviors and delegates the latter behaviors to other agents. Finally, when the weights of behaviors are zero, the behaviors become dormant to save computational resources.
– *Increasing resources for busy behaviors:* Each agent can create a copy of itself when the total weights of functions provided in itself is the same or more than a specified value. The sum of the total weights of the mother agent and those of the daughter agent is equal to the total weights of the mother agent before the agent is duplicated.
– *Reactivating dormant behaviors:* When an agent does not receive messages about the weights of behaviors provided in agents, treats such behaviors to be lost. When it has the same or compatible behaviors, which are dormant, it resets the wights of the behaviors, to their initial values. Therefore, they are regenerated and differentiated according to the above process again.

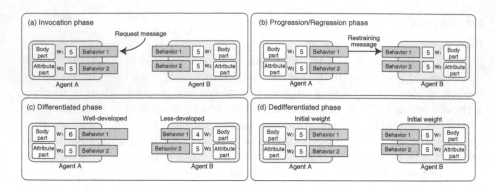

Fig. 1. Regeneration in agents

6 Implementation

To evaluate our proposed approach, we constructed it as a middleware system with Java (Fig. 2), which can directly runs on Java VM running on VMs in IaaS, e.g., Amazon EC2. It is responsible for executing duplicating, and deploying agents based on several technologies for mobile agent platforms. It is also responsible for executing agents and for exchanging messages in runtime systems on other IaaS VMs or PaaS runtime systems through TCP and UDP protocols. Messages for exchanging information about the weights of differentiation are transmitted as multicast UDP packets. Application-specific messages for invoking methods corresponding to behaviors in agents are implemented through TCP sessions.

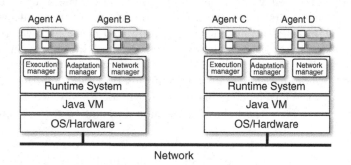

Fig. 2. Runtime system

Each agent is an autonomous programmable entity. The body part maintains a key-value store database, which is implemented as a hashtable, shared by its behaviors. We can define each agent as a single JavaBean, where each method in JavaBean needs to access the database maintained in the body parts. Each method in such a JavaBean-based agent is transformed into a Java class, which is called by another method via the body part, by using a bytecode-level modification technique before the agent is executed. Each body part is invoked from agents running on different computers via our original remote method invocation (RMI) mechanism, which can be automatically handled in network disconnection unlike Java's RMI library. The mechanism is managed by runtime systems and provided to agents to support additional interactions, e.g., one-way message transmission, publish-subscription events, and stream communications. Since each agent records the time the behaviors are invoked and the results are received, it selects behaviors provided in other agents according to the average or worst response time in the previous processing. When a result is received from another agent, the approach permits the former to modify the value of the behavior of the latter under its own control. For example, agents that want to execute a behavior quickly may increase the weight of the behavior by an extra amount, when the behavior returns the result too soon.

7 Evaluation

This section describes the performance evaluation of our implementation.

7.1 Basic Performance

Although the current implementation was not constructed for performance, we evaluated several basic operations in distributed systems consisting of eights embedded computers, where each computer is a Raspberry Pi computer, which has been one of the most popular embedded computers (its processor was Broadloom BCM2835 (ARM v6-architecture core with floating point) running at 700 MHz and it has 1 GB memory and SD card storage (16 GB SDHC), with a Linux operating system optimized to Raspberry Pi, and OpenJDK. The cost of transmitting a message through UDP multicasting was 17 ms. The cost of transmitting a request message between two computers was 28 ms through TCP. These costs were estimated from the measurements of round-trip times between computers. We assumed in the following experiments that each agent issued messages to other agents every 110 ms through UDP multicasting.

We evaluated the speed of convergence in our differentiation. Each computer had one agent having three functions, called behavior A, B and C, where behavior A invoked B and C behaviors every 200 ms and the B and C behaviors were null behaviors. We assigned at most one agent to each of the computers. B or C, selected a behavior whose weight had the highest value if its database recognized one or more agents that provided the same or compatible behavior, including itself. When it invokes behavior B or C and the weights of its and others behaviors were the same, it randomly selected one of the behaviors. We assumed in this experiment that the weights of the B and C behaviors of each agent would initially be five and the maximum of the weight of each behavior and the total maximum of weights would be ten.

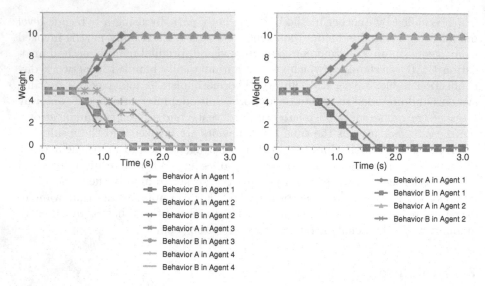

Fig. 3. Convergence in four agents with two behaviors (Left) and Convergence in eight agents with two behaviors (Right)

Differentiation started after 200 ms, because each agent knows the presence of other agents by receiving heartbeat messages from them. The right of Fig. 3 details the results obtained from our differentiation between four agents on four computers and The left of Fig. 3 between eight agents on eight computers. Finally, two agents provide behavior B and C respectively and the others delegate the two behaviors to the two agents in both the cases. Although the time of differentiation depended on the period of invoking behaviors, it was independent of the number of agents. This is important to prove that this approach is scalable.

7.2   Sensor Networks Recovering from Damaged by Disasters

Let us suppose a sensor-network system consisting of 15 × 15 nodes connected through a grid network, as shown in Fig. 4. The system was constructed on a commercial IaaS cloud infrastructure (225 instances of Amazon EC2 with Linux and JDK 1.7). This experiment permitted each node to communicate with its eights neighboring nodes and the diameter of a circle in each node represents the weight of a behavior. Nodes were connected according to the topology of the target grid network and could multicast to four neighboring runtime systems through the grid network. We assume that each agent monitors sensors in its current node and every node has one agent.

We put agents at all nodes and evaluated removing of redundant agents. Each agent has conflict with agents at its eights neighboring nodes, because it can delegate its function to them, vice versa. Figure 5(i) shows the initial weights of agents. (ii) and (iii) show the weights of behaviors in agents eight and

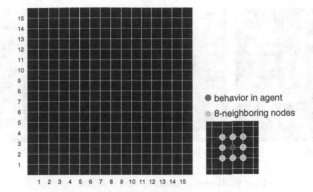

Fig. 4. 15 × 15-Grid network on cloud computing

sixteen seconds later. Even though differentiated behaviors were uneven, they could be placed within certain intervals, i.s., two edges on the grid network. This proved that our approach was useful in developing particular functions of software components at nodes.

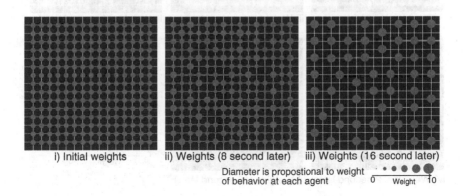

Fig. 5. Removing redundant agents

Figure 6(i) was the initial weights of agents on the network. We explicitly made a flawed part in the network (Fig. 6(ii)). Some agents dedifferentiate themselves in nodes when a flawed part made in the network. In the experiment agents around the hole started to activate themselves through dedifferentiation. The weights of their behaviors converged according to the weights of their behaviors to the behaviors of other newly activated agents in addition to existing agents. Finally, some agents around the hole could support the behaviors on behalf of · the dismissed agents with the flawed part. This result prove that our approach could remedy such a damage appropriately in a self-organized manner. This is useful for sensing catastrophes, e.g., earthquakes and deluges.

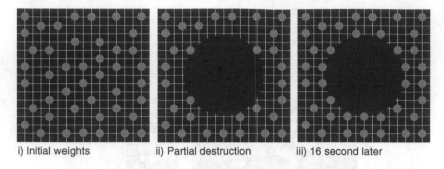

Fig. 6. Regeneration to recover damage

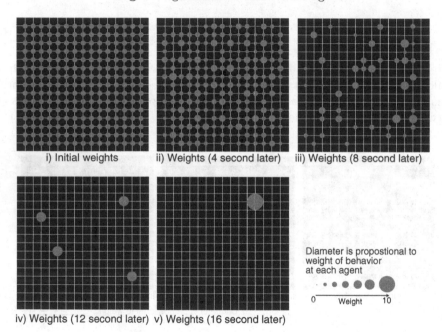

Fig. 7. Agents are differentiated in broadcasting to all agents

Next, we assume each node could multicast to all agents through the grid network. Figure 7 shows only one agent is activated and the others are inactivated after their differentiations, because the latter can delegate the function to the former. We partitioned the grid network as shown Fig. 8(ii). The above half has a well-developed behavior and the below half lacks such behavior. Therefore, all agents in the below half reset their weights as shown Fig. 8(iii) and they are differentiated. Finally, only one agent is activated on the below half part (Fig. 8(iv)).

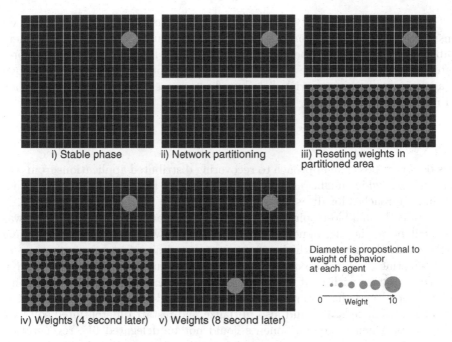

i) Stable phase   ii) Network partitioning   iii) Reseting weights in partitioned area

Diameter is propostional to weight of behavior at each agent

0   Weight   10

iv) Weights (4 second later)   v) Weights (8 second later)

Fig. 8. Agents are differentiated in network partitioning

8   Related Work

We compare between our approach and other existing bio-inspired approaches for distributed systems. The Anthill project [1] by the University of Bologna developed a bio-inspired middleware for peer-to-peer systems, which is composed of a collection of interconnected nests. Autonomous agents, called ants can travel across the network trying to satisfy user requests. The project provided bio-inspired frameworks, called Messor [2] and Bison [3]. Messor is a load-balancing application of Anthill and Bison is a conceptual bio-inspired framework based on Anthill. One of the most typical self-organization approaches to distributed systems is swarm intelligence [4,5]. Although there is no centralized control structure dictating how individual agents should behave, interactions between simple agents with static rules often lead to the emergence of intelligent global behavior. Suda et al. proposed bio-inspired middleware, called Bio-Networking, for disseminating network services in dynamic and large-scale networks where there were a large number of decentralized data and services [6,7]. Although they introduced the notion of energy into distributed systems and enabled agents to be replicated, moved, and deleted according to the number of service requests, they had no mechanism to adapt agents' behavior unlike ours. As most of their parameters, e.g., energy, tended to depend on a particular distributed system. so that they may not have been available in other systems. Our approach should be independent of the capabilities of distributed systems as much as possible.

Finally, we compare between our approach and our previous ones, because we constructed several frameworks for adaptive distributed systems. One of them enabled distributed components to be dynamically federated [8]. We also presented an early version of the proposed approach [9], but the version was designed for adaptive services over enrich distributed systems, e.g., cloud computing. They did not support any disaster management.

9   Conclusion

This paper proposed an approach to recovering distributed applications from violent damages, which might result from disasters. The approach is unique to other existing approaches for disaster-tolerant approaches for distributed systems. It was inspired from a bio-inspired mechanism, regeneration in living things. It was also available at the edge of networks, e.g., sensor networks and Internet-of-Thing (IoT). It enabled agents, which were implemented as software components, to be differentiated. When a component delegated a function to another component coordinating with it, if the former had the function, this function became less-developed and the latter's function became well-developed like differentiation processes in cells. It could also initialize and restart differentiated software components, when some components could not be delegated like regeneration processes in lizards. It was constructed as a general-purpose and practical middleware system for software components on real distributed systems consisting of embedded computers or sensor nodes.

Appendix

This appendix we describe our model for regenerating software components, called agents, by using a differentiation mechanism in detail. We specify from 1-th to n-th behaviors of k-th agent, as $b_1^k, \ldots, b_n^k$ and the weight of behavior b_i^k as w_i^k. Each agent (k-th) assigns its own maximum to the total of the weights of all its behaviors. The W_i^k is the maximum of the weight of behavior b_i^k. The maximum total of the weights of its behaviors in the k-th agent must be less than W^k. ($W^k \geq \sum_{i=1}^n w_i^k$), where $w_j^k - 1$ is 0 if w_j^k is 0. The W^k may depend on agents. In fact, W^k corresponds to the upper limit of the ability of each agent and may depend on the performance of the underlying system, including the processor.

Invocation of Behaviors

1. When an agent (k-th agent) receives a request message from another agent, it selects the behavior (b_i^k) that can handle the message from its behavior part and dispatches the message to the selected behavior (Fig. 1(a)).
2. It executes the behavior (b_i^k) and returns the result.
3. It increases the weight of the behavior, w_i^k.
4. It multicasts a restraining message with the signature of the behavior, its identifier (k), and the behavior's weight (w_i^k) to other agents (Fig. 1(b)).[2]

---

[2] Restraining messages correspond to cAMP in differentiation.

The key idea behind this approach is to distinguish between internal and external requests. When behaviors are invoked by their agents, their weights are not increased. If the total weights of the agent's behaviors, $\sum w_i^k$, is equal to their maximal total weight W^k, it decreases one of the minimal (and positive) weights (w_j^k is replaced by $w_j^k - 1$ where $w_j^k = \min(w_1^k, \ldots, w_n^k)$ and $w_j^k \geq 0$). The above phase corresponds to the degeneration of agents.

Well/Less Developing Behaviors

1. When an agent (k-th agent) wants to execute a behavior, b_i, it looks up the weight (w_i^k) of the same or compatible behavior and the weights ($w_i^j, \ldots, w_i^m$) of such behaviors ($b_i^j, \ldots, b_i^m$).
2. If multiple agents, including itself, can provide the wanted behavior, it selects one of the agents according to selection function ϕ^k, which maps from w_i^k and $w_i^j, \ldots, w_i^m$ to b_i^l, where l is k or $j, \ldots, m$.
3. It delegates the selected agent to execute the behavior and waits for the result from the agent.

The approach permits agents to use their own evaluation functions, ϕ, because the selection of behaviors often depends on their applications. Although there is no universal selection function for mapping from behaviors' weights to at most one appropriate behavior like a variety of creatures, we can provide several functions.

Removing Redundant Behaviors

1. When an agent (k-th agent) receives a restraining message with regard to b_i^j from another agent (j-th), it looks for the behaviors ($b_m^k, \ldots b_l^k$) that can satisfy the signature specified in the receiving message.
2. If it has such behaviors, it decreases their weights ($w_m^k, \ldots w_l^k$) and updates the weight (w_i^j) (Fig. 1(c)).
3. If the weights ($w_m^k, \ldots, w_l^k$) are under a specified value, e.g., 0, the behaviors ($b_m^k, \ldots b_l^k$) are inactivated.

References

1. Babaoglu, O., Meling, H., Montresor, A.: Anthill: a framework for the development of agent-based peer-to-peer systems. In: Proceedings of 22nd International Conference on Distributed Computing Systems (ICDCS 2002), Washington, D.C., USA, pp. 15–22. IEEE Computer Society (2002)
2. Montresor, A., Meling, H., Babaoğlu, Ö.: Messor: load-balancing through a swarm of autonomous agents. In: Moro, G., Koubarakis, M. (eds.) AP2PC 2002. LNCS (LNAI), vol. 2530, pp. 125–137. Springer, Heidelberg (2003). https://doi.org/10.1007/3-540-45074-2_12

3. Montresor, A., Babaoglu, O.: Biology-inspired approaches to peer-to-peer computing in BISON. In: Abraham, A., Franke, K., Köppen, M. (eds.) Intelligent Systems Design and Applications. ASC, vol. 23, pp. 515–522. Springer, Heidelberg (2003). https://doi.org/10.1007/978-3-540-44999-7_49
4. Bonabeau, E., Dorigo, M., Theraulaz, G.: Swarm Intelligence: From Natural to Artificial Systems. Oxford University Press, Oxford (1999)
5. Dorigo, M., Stützle, T.: Ant Colony Optimization. Bradford Company, Scituate (2004)
6. Nakano, T., Suda, T.: Self-organizing network services with evolutionary adaptation. IEEE Trans. Neural Netw. **16**(5), 1269–1278 (2005)
7. Suzuki, J., Suda, T.: A middleware platform for a biologically inspired network architecture supporting autonomous and adaptive applications. IEEE J. Sel. Areas Commun. **23**(2), 249–260 (2005)
8. Satoh, I.: Self-organizing software components in distributed systems. In: Lukowicz, P., Thiele, L., Tröster, G. (eds.) ARCS 2007. LNCS, vol. 4415, pp. 185–198. Springer, Heidelberg (2007). https://doi.org/10.1007/978-3-540-71270-1_14
9. Satoh, I.: Resilient architecture for complex computing systems. In: 18th International Conference on Engineering of Complex Computer Systems, pp. 256–259, July 2013

Population Diversity Analysis for the Chaotic Based Selection of Individuals in Differential Evolution

Roman Senkerik$^{(\boxtimes)}$ ⓘ, Adam Viktorin ⓘ, Michal Pluhacek ⓘ, and Tomas Kadavy ⓘ

Faculty of Applied Informatics, Tomas Bata University in Zlin,
T. G. Masaryka 5555, 760 01 Zlin, Czech Republic
{senkerik,aviktorin,pluhacek,kadavy}@utb.cz

Abstract. This research deals with the modern and popular hybridization of chaotic dynamics and evolutionary computation. It is aimed at the influence of chaotic sequences on the population diversity as well as the algorithm performance of the simple parameter adaptive Differential Evolution (DE) strategy: jDE. Experiments are focused on the extensive investigation of the different randomization schemes for the selection of individuals in DE algorithm driven by the nine different two-dimensional discrete chaotic systems, as the chaotic pseudo-random number generators. The population diversity and jDE convergence are recorded on the 15 test functions from the CEC 2015 benchmark.

Keywords: Differential Evolution · Complex dynamics
Deterministic chaos · Population diversity · Chaotic map

1 Introduction

This research deals with the mutual intersection of the two computational intelligence fields, which are the complex sequencing and dynamics given by the selected chaotic systems, and evolutionary computation techniques (ECT's).

Together with this persistent development in above-mentioned mainstream research topics, the popularity of hybridizing of chaos and metaheuristic algorithms is growing every year. Recent research in chaotic approach for metaheuristics uses various chaotic maps in the place of pseudo-random number generators (PRNG).

The initial concept of embedding chaotic dynamics into the evolutionary/swarm algorithms as chaotic pseudo-random number generator (CPRNG) is given in [1]. Firstly, the Particle Swarm Optimization (PSO) algorithm with elements of chaos was introduced as CPSO [2], followed by the introduction of chaos embedded Differential evolution (DE) [3], PSO with inertia weigh strategy [4], and PSO with an ensemble of chaotic systems [5]. Recently the chaos driven heuristic concept has been utilized in several swarm-based algorithms like ABC

ⓒ Springer International Publishing AG, part of Springer Nature 2018
P. Korošec et al. (Eds.): BIOMA 2018, LNCS 10835, pp. 283–294, 2018.
https://doi.org/10.1007/978-3-319-91641-5_24

algorithm [6], Firefly [7] and other metaheuristic algorithms [8–11], as well as many applications with DE [12].

The unconventional chaos-based approach is tightly connected with the importance of randomization within heuristics as compensation of a limited amount of search moves as stated in the survey paper [13]. This idea has been carried out in subsequent studies describing different techniques to modify the randomization process [14,15] and especially in [16], where the sampling of the points is tested from modified distribution. The importance and influence of randomization operations were also profoundly experimentally tested in simple control parameter adjustment DE strategy [17].

The focus of this research is the deeper insight into the population dynamics of the selected DE strategy (jDE) [18] when the directly embedded CPRNG is driving the indices selection. Currently, DE [13,19,20] is a well-known evolutionary computation technique for continuous optimization purposes solving many difficult and complex optimization problems. Many DE variants have been recently developed with the emphasis on control parameters self-adaptivity. DE has been modified and extended several times using new proposals of versions, and the performances of different DE variants have been widely studied and compared with other ECTs. Over recent decades, DE has won most of the evolutionary algorithm competitions in the leading scientific conferences [21–25], as well as being applied to several applications.

The organization of this paper is following: Firstly, the motivation for this research is proposed. The next sections are focused on the description of the concept of chaos driven jDE, and the experiment background. Results and conclusion follow afterward.

2   Motivation and Related Research

Recently, chaos with its properties like ergodicity, stochasticity, self-similarity, and density of periodic orbits became very popular and modern tool for improving the performance of various ECTs. Nevertheless, the questions remain, as to why it works, why it may be beneficial to use the chaotic sequences for pseudorandom numbers driving the selection, mutation, crossover or other processes in particular heuristics.

This research is an extension and continuation of the previous successful experiment with the single/multi-chaos driven PSO [5] and jDE [26], where the positive influence of hidden complex dynamics for the heuristic performance has been experimentally shown. This research is also a follow up to previous initial experiments with different sampling rates applied to the chaotic sequences resulting in keeping, partially/fully removing of traces of chaos [27].

The motivation and the novelty of the research are given by the investigating the influence of chaotic sequences to the population diversity, connected with the algorithm performance of the basic control parameter adjustment DE strategy: jDE. This strategy was selected as a compromise between original simple DE and the most recent Success-History based Adaptive Differential Evolution (SHADE) variants [25], where the influence of chaotic dynamics may be suppressed by the complex adaptive process and operations with the archive.

3   Differential Evolution

This section describes the basics of original DE and jDE strategies. The original DE [19] has four static control parameters – a number of generations G, population size NP, scaling factor F and crossover rate CR. In the evolutionary process of DE, these four parameters remain unchanged and depend on the initial user setting. jDE algorithm, on the other hand, adapts the F and CR parameters during the evolution. The mutation strategy for jDE is adapted from the original DE. The concept of essential operations in jDE algorithm is shown in following sections, for a detailed description on either original DE refer to [19] or for jDE see [18].

3.1   jDE

In this research, we have used jDE with original DE "rand/1/bin" (1) mutation strategy and binomial crossover (2).

Mutation Strategies and Parent Selection. The parent indices (vectors) are selected either by standard PRNG with uniform distribution or by CPRNG in case of chaotic versions. Mutation strategy "rand/1/bin" uses three random parent vectors with indexes $r1$, $r2$ and $r3$, where $r1 = U[1, NP]$, $r2 = U[1, NP]$, $r3 = U[1, NP]$ and $r1 \neq r2 \neq r3$. Mutated vector $v_{i,G}$ is obtained from three different vectors x_{r1}, x_{r2}, x_{r3} from current generation G with the help of scaling factor F_i as follows:

$$v_{i,G} = x_{r1,G} + F_i \left(x_{r2,G} - x_{r3,G} \right) \tag{1}$$

Crossover and Selection. The trial vector $u_{i,G}$ which is compared with original vector $x_{i,G}$ is completed by crossover operation (2). CR_i value in jDE algorithm is not static.

$$u_{j,i,G} = \begin{cases} v_{j,i,G} & \text{if } U[0,1] \leq CR_i \text{ or } j = j_{rand} \\ x_{j,i,G} & \text{otherwise} \end{cases} \tag{2}$$

Where j_{rand} is a randomly selected index of a feature, which has to be updated ($j_{rand} = U[1, D]$), D is the dimensionality of the problem.

The vector which will be placed into the next generation $G+1$ is selected by elitism. When the objective function value of the trial vector $u_{i,G}$ is better than that of the original vector $x_{i,G}$, the trial vector will be selected for the next population. Otherwise, the original will survive (3).

$$x_{i,G+1} = \begin{cases} u_{i,G} & \text{if } f\left(u_{i,G}\right) < f\left(x_{i,G}\right) \\ x_{i,G} & \text{otherwise} \end{cases} \tag{3}$$

3.2   Parameter Adjustment in jDE

The generated ensemble of two control parameters F_i and CR_i is assigned to each i-th individual of the population and survives with the solution if an individual is transferred to the new generation. The initialization of values of F and CR is designed to be either fully random with uniform distribution for each individual in the population or can be set according to the recommended values in the literature. If the newly generated solution is not successful, i.e., the trial vector has worse fitness than the compared original active individual; the new (possibly) reinitialized control parameters values disappear together with not successful solution. The both aforementioned DE control parameters may be randomly mutated with predefined probabilities τ_1 and τ_2. If the mutation condition happens, a new random value of $CR \in [0, 1]$ is generated, possibly also a new value of F which is mutated in $[F_l, F_u]$. These new control parameters are after that stored in the new population. Input parameters are typically set to $F_l = 0.1, F_u = 0.9, \tau_1 = 0.1$, and $\tau_2 = 0.1$ as originally given in [13, 18].

4   Chaotic Systems for CPRNGs

Following nine well known and frequently utilized discrete dissipative chaotic maps were used as the CPRNGs for jDE. With the settings as in Table 1, systems exhibit typical chaotic behavior [28].

Table 1. Definition of chaotic systems used as CPRNGs

Chaotic system	Notation	Parameters values
Arnold cat map	$X_{n+1} = X_n + Y_n (mod 1)$ $Y_{n+1} = X_n + kY_n (mod 1)$	$k = 2.0$
Burgers map	$X_{n+1} = aX_n - Y_n^2$ $Y_{n+1} = bY_n + X_n Y_n$	$a = 0.75$ and $b = 1.75$
Delayed logistic	$X_{n+1} = AX_n (1 - Y_n)$ $Y_{n+1} = X_n$	$A = 2.27$
Dissipative standard map	$X_{n+1} = X_n + Y_{n+1} (mod 2\pi)$ $Y_{n+1} = bY_n + k \sin X_n (mod 2\pi)$	$b = 0.1$ and $k = 8.8$
Hénon map	$X_{n+1} = a - x_n^2 + by_n$ $Y_{n+1} = x_n$	$a = 1.4$ and $b = 0.3$
Ikeda map	$X_{n+1} = \gamma + \mu(X_n \cos \phi + Y_n \sin \phi)$ $Y_{n+1} = \mu(X_n \sin \phi + Y_n \cos \phi)$ $\phi = \beta - \alpha / (1 + X_n^2 + Y_n^2)$	$\alpha = 6, \beta = 0.4, \gamma = 1$ and $\mu = 0.9$
Lozi map	$X_{n+1} = 1 - a|X_n| + bY_n$ $Y_{n+1} = X_n$	$a = 1.7$ and $b = 0.5$
Sinai map	$X_{n+1} = X_n + Y_n + \delta \cos 2\pi Y_n (mod 1)$ $Y_{n+1} = X_n + 2Y_n (mod 1)$	$\delta = 0.1$
Tinkerbell map	$X_{n+1} = X_n^2 - Y_n^2 + aX_n + bY_n$ $Y_{n+1} = 2X_n Y_n + cX_n + dY_n$	$a = 0.9, b = -0.6, c = 2$ and $d = 0.5$

5   The Concept of ChaosDE with Discrete Chaotic System as Driving CPRNG

The general idea of CPRNG is to replace the default PRNG with the chaotic system. As the chaotic system is a set of equations with a static start position, we created a random start position of the system, to have different start position for different experiments. Thus we are utilizing the typical feature of chaotic systems, which is extreme sensitivity to the initial conditions, popularly known as "butterfly effect." This random position is initialized with the default PRNG, as a one-off randomizer. Once the start position of the chaotic system has been obtained, the system generates the next sequence using its current position. Used approach is based on the following definition (4):

$$rndreal = \text{mod} \left(\text{abs} \left(rndChaos \right), 1.0 \right) \qquad (4)$$

5.1   Experiment Design

For the population diversity analysis and performance comparisons in this research, the CEC 15 benchmark was selected. The dimension D was set to 10. Every instance was repeated 51 times with the maximum number of objective function evaluations set to 100 000 ($10,000 \times D$). The convergence and population diversity were recorded for all tested algorithm – original jDE and nine versions of C_jDE with different CPRNGs. All algorithms used the same set of control parameters: population size $NP = 50$ and initial settings $F = 0.5$, $CR = 0.8$. Experiments were performed in the environment of *Java*; jDE, therefore, has used the built-in *Java linear congruential pseudorandom number generator* representing traditional pseudorandom number generator in comparisons. The Population Diversity (PD) measure used in this paper was described in [29] and is based on the sum of deviations (6) of individual's components from their corresponding means (5).

$$\overline{x_j} = \frac{1}{NP} \sum_{i=1}^{NP} x_{ij} \qquad (5)$$

$$PD = \sqrt{\frac{1}{NP} \sum_{i=1}^{NP} \sum_{j=1}^{D} (x_{ij} - \overline{x_j})^2} \qquad (6)$$

Where i is the population member iterator and j is the vector component iterator.

6   Results

Statistical results for the comparisons are shown in comprehensive Tables 2 and 3. Table 2 shows the mean results, with the highlighting based on the *Wilcoxon sum-rank test* with the significance level of 0.05; performed for each pair of original jDE and C_jDE. Ranking of the algorithms given in Fig. 1 was evaluated based on the Friedman test with Nemenyi post hoc test. Figures 2, 3, 4 and 5

Table 2. Results comparisons for the mean results of jDE and C_jDE; CEC 2015 Benchmark set, 10D, 51 runs

System\f	1	2	3	4	5	6	7	8	9	10	11	12	13	14	15
jDE	9.79E-08	**0.**	19.7916	4.1515	**126.70**	6.1719	0.1724	**0.2298**	100.207	**218.29**	**101.59**	101.839	27.96	3613.67	**100.**
Arnold C_jDE	2.74E-07	**0.**	18.8335	4.2794	145.24	9.4381	0.1567	0.5323	100.209	219.42	107.41	101.839	27.62	3544.63	**100.**
Burgers C_jDE	*4.4106*†	**0.**	19.2706	4.0942	*173.63*†	*54.0442*†	0.2997	*10.2154*†	*100.226*†	*243.52*†	*148.95*†	101.995	28.56	*4406.91*†	**100.**
DeLo C_jDE	*0.5832*†	**0.**	**18.3945**	**3.8806**	*166.44*†	*33.1935*†	0.1855	1.9563	**100.204**	*233.58*†	*154.45*†	101.884	28.68	3777.18	**100.**
Dissipative C_jDE	*3.62E-05*†	**0.**	19.6439	4.0253	139.11	9.7203	0.1662	0.5663	100.205	219.95	136.56	101.815	27.91	3756.54	**100.**
Henon C_jDE	*3.22E-06*†	**0.**	18.4531	4.1839	126.96	**2.4113**	0.1728	*0.9548*†	*100.218*†	219.42	124.95	101.851	**27.53**	3488.54	**100.**
Ikeda C_jDE	*3.55E-05*†	**0.**	19.7317	3.9634	137.59	6.1798	0.1592	1.5255	100.210	219.03	*154.26*†	101.820	27.71	3557.67	**100.**
Lozi C_jDE	*1.32E-04*†	**0.**	18.9552	4.1586	134.54	6.9613	**0.1561**	1.3641	100.215	219.59	142.43	101.859	28.09	3688.73	**100.**
Sinai C_jDE	**9.54E-08**	**0.**	*18.4859*‡	3.9828	127.20	10.3090	0.1569	1.3596	100.208	219.34	130.81	101.880	27.73	**3466.09**	**100.**
Tinkerbell C_jDE	*24.6343*†	**0.**	19.1244	3.9863	148.39	*39.4389*†	0.2460	*8.5815*†	100.215	*231.44*†	*125.99*†	**101.798**	28.06	*4417.27*†	**100.**

The bold values in Table 2 depict the best-obtained results (based on the mean values); italic values are considered to be significantly different (according to the Wilcoxon sum-rank test with the significance level of 0.05; performed for each pair of original jDE and C_jDE; †- performance of C_JDE was significantly worse, ‡- significantly better).

Table 3. The best (minimum found) results for jDE and C-jDE; CEC 2015 Benchmark set, 10D, 51 runs

System\f	1	2	3	4	5	6	7	8	9	10	11	12	13	14	15	Total
jDE	9.79E-08	0.	19.7916	4.1515	126.703	6.1719	0.1724	0.2298	100.207	218.286	101.59	101.839	27.961	3613.67	**100.**	2
Arnold C-jDE	0.	0.	**2.50E-09**	1.2559	37.1301	0.	0.0369	7.11E-07	100.152	**216.537**	0.4638	101.245	24.006	2935.54	**100.**	6
Burgers C-jDE	7.01E-04	0.	0.1154	0.	**10.3074**	2.14E-03	0.0197	6.37E-06	100.154	216.556	1.6532	101.308	**21.749**	2935.54	**100.**	5
DeLo C-jDE	4.92E-07	0.	5.5139	0.	25.7866	0.2081	0.0310	3.69E-06	**100.121**	**216.537**	1.0906	100.994	23.384	2935.54	**100.**	5
Dissipative C-jDE	0.	0.	6.5179	1.1008	37.3398	0.	0.0464	1.69E-05	100.108	**216.537**	0.7982	100.948	23.818	2935.54	**100.**	5
Henon C-jDE	0.	0.	2.39E-04	1.2774	14.2125	0.	0.0549	9.69E-05	100.134	**216.537**	0.9954	100.928	23.614	**100.**	**100.**	6
Ikeda C-jDE	0.	0.	11.9019	1.8199	40.4215	0.	0.0331	3.29E-06	**100.121**	**216.537**	0.8272	100.801	24.465	**100.**	**100.**	7
Lozi C-jDE	0.	0.	6.4830	1.5781	33.1746	0.	0.0497	3.38E-04	100.129	**216.537**	**0.4429**	101.238	25.882	2935.54	**100.**	6
Sinai C-jDE	0.	0.	3.24E-04	1.1066	23.3597	0.	0.0333	**3.38E-07**	100.126	**216.537**	0.5749	101.067	23.732	2935.54	**100.**	6
Tinkerbell C-jDE	3.15E-04	0.	7.3022	1.0075	33.8032	0.	**0.0093**	1.30E-04	100.148	216.539	1.1523	**100.409**	23.073	**100.**	**100.**	6

The bold values in Table 3 depict the best-obtained results (based on the min. values).

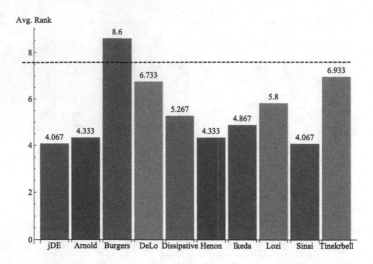

Fig. 1. Ranking of the all algorithms based on the 51 runs and 15 functions of CEC2015 benchmark in 10D. Dashed line represents the Nemenyi Critical Distance.

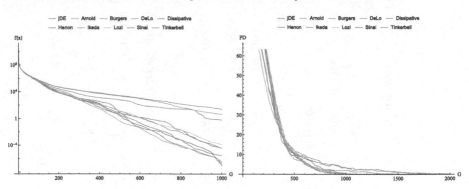

Fig. 2. Convergence plot (left) and population diversity plot (right) of CEC2015 $f1$ in 10D.

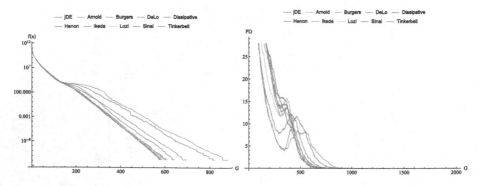

Fig. 3. Convergence plot (left) and population diversity plot (right) of CEC2015 $f2$ in 10D.

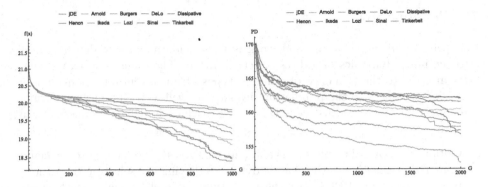

Fig. 4. Convergence plot (left) and population diversity plot (right) of CEC2015 *f3* in 10*D*.

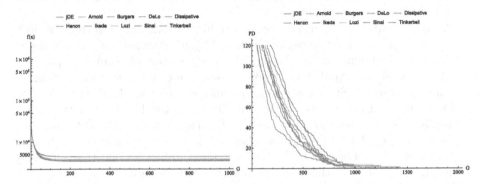

Fig. 5. Convergence plot (left) and population diversity plot (right) of CEC2015 *f14* in 10*D*.

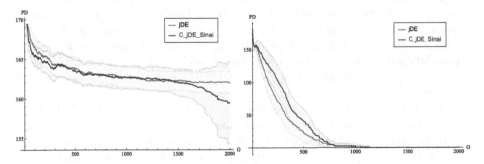

Fig. 6. Detailed population diversity plots for the selected pair of jDE and C_jDE driven by Sinai chaotic system (left *f3*) and (right *f14*), CEC2015 in 10*D*.

depict the graphical comparisons of the convergence plots and corresponding population diversity plots provided for the selected five benchmark functions. The Fig. 6 shows the detailed comparisons of population diversity plots (with confidence intervals) for the selected pair of jDE and C_jDE where the performance is different. The results discussion is in the next section.

7   Conclusions

The primary aim of this original work is to provide a more in-depth insight into the inner dynamics of indices selection in DE. The focus is to experimentally investigate the influence of different types of unconventional non-random (chaotic) sequences to the population diversity as well as to the performance of the simple parameter adjustment DE strategy, which is jDE. The findings can be summarized as:

- Obtained graphical comparisons and data in Tables 2 and 3 support the claim that jDE is sensitive to the chaotic dynamics driving the selection (mutation) process through CPRNG. At the same time, it is clear that (selection of) the best CPRNGs are problem-dependent. By using the CPRNG inside the heuristic, its performance is (significantly) different: either better or worse against other compared versions.
- The performance comparisons presented in Tables 2 and 3 reveal the fact that only in one case the performance of C_jDE is statistically significantly better (*f3* and Sinai map). Mostly the performance of compared pairs of jDE and C_jDE is similar, or in some cases, the chaotic versions performed significantly worse. Such a worse performance was repeatedly observed for two chaotic maps: Burgers and Tinkerbell. On the other hand, these two maps usually secured robust progress towards function extreme (local) followed by premature population stagnation phase, thus repeatedly secured finding of minimum values. Overall, C_jDE versions seem to be very effective regarding finding min. values of the objective function (See Table 3).
- The population diversity plots in Figs. 2, 3, 4 and 5 supports the above-mentioned facts. It is possible to identify 3 groups of population diversity behavior in comparison with original j_DE: less decreasing (Sinai, Henon, Ikeda maps), more decreasing (Lozi, Arnold, Dissipative maps) and significantly more decreasing (Delayed Logistic, Tinkerbell, Burgers maps).
- The selected paired diversity plots in Fig. 6 show that the diversity of the population is maintained higher for a longer period. Therefore the exploration phase supported by Sinai map based CPRNG is longer. This in return is beneficial for the result of the optimization.
- The population diversity analysis supports the theory, that unique features of the chaos transformed into the sequencing of CPRNG values may create the subpopulations (or inner neighborhood selection schemes, i.e., lower population diversity). Thus the metaheuristic can benefit from the searching within those sub-populations and quasi-periodic exchanges of information between individuals (see Fig. 3 for the sudden increase of diversity – the new search region was explored and attracted some (group) of individuals). However, lot of analyses and different scenarios (dimensional settings, etc.) are required in the future.

The research of randomization issues and insights into the inner dynamic of metaheuristic algorithms was many times addressed as essential and beneficial. The results presented here support the approach for multi-chaotic generators [30] or ensemble systems, where we can profit from the combined/selective population diversity (i.e. exploration/exploitation) tendencies, sequencing-based either stronger or moderate progress towards the function extreme, all given by the smart combination of multi-randomization schemes.

Acknowledgements. This work was supported by the Ministry of Education, Youth and Sports of the Czech Republic within the National Sustainability Programme Project no. LO1303 (MSMT-7778/2014), further by the European Regional Development Fund under the Project CEBIA-Tech no. CZ.1.05/2.1.00/03.0089 and by Internal Grant Agency of Tomas Bata University under the Projects no. IGA/CebiaTech/2018/003. This work is also based upon support by COST (European Cooperation in Science & Technology) under Action CA15140, Improving Applicability of Nature-Inspired Optimisation by Joining Theory and Practice (ImAppNIO), and Action IC406, High-Performance Modelling and Simulation for Big Data Applications (cHiPSet).

References

1. Caponetto, R., Fortuna, L., Fazzino, S., Xibilia, M.G.: Chaotic sequences to improve the performance of evolutionary algorithms. IEEE Trans. Evol. Comput. **7**(3), 289–304 (2003)
2. dos Santos Coelho, L., Mariani, V.C.: A novel chaotic particle swarm optimization approach using Hénon map and implicit filtering local search for economic load dispatch. Chaos Solitons Fractals **39**(2), 510–518 (2009)
3. Davendra, D., Zelinka, I., Senkerik, R.: Chaos driven evolutionary algorithms for the task of PID control. Comput. Math. Appl. **60**(4), 1088–1104 (2010)
4. Pluhacek, M., Senkerik, R., Davendra, D., Oplatkova, Z.K., Zelinka, I.: On the behavior and performance of chaos driven PSO algorithm with inertia weight. Comput. Math. Appl. **66**(2), 122–134 (2013)
5. Pluhacek, M., Senkerik, R., Davendra, D.: Chaos particle swarm optimization with Eensemble of chaotic systems. Swarm Evol. Comput. **25**, 29–35 (2015)
6. Metlicka, M., Davendra, D.: Chaos driven discrete artificial bee algorithm for location and assignment optimisation problems. Swarm Evol. Comput. **25**, 15–28 (2015)
7. Gandomi, A.H., Yang, X.S., Talatahari, S., Alavi, A.H.: Firefly algorithm with chaos. Commun. Nonlinear Sci. Numer. Simul. **18**(1), 89–98 (2013)
8. Wang, G.G., Guo, L., Gandomi, A.H., Hao, G.S., Wang, H.: Chaotic Krill Herd algorithm. Inf. Sci. **274**, 17–34 (2014)
9. Zhang, C., Cui, G., Peng, F.: A novel hybrid chaotic ant swarm algorithm for heat exchanger networks synthesis. Appl. Therm. Eng. **104**, 707–719 (2016)
10. Jordehi, A.R.: Chaotic bat swarm optimisation (CBSO). Appl. Soft Comput. **26**, 523–530 (2015)
11. Wang, G.G., Deb, S., Gandomi, A.H., Zhang, Z., Alavi, A.H.: Chaotic cuckoo search. Soft. Comput. **20**(9), 3349–3362 (2016)
12. dos Santos Coelho, L., Ayala, H.V.H., Mariani, V.C.: A self-adaptive chaotic differential evolution algorithm using gamma distribution for unconstrained global optimization. Appl. Math. Comput. **234**, 452–459 (2014)
13. Neri, F., Tirronen, V.: Recent advances in differential evolution: a survey and experimental analysis. Artif. Intell. Rev. **33**(1–2), 61–106 (2010)

14. Weber, M., Neri, F., Tirronen, V.: A study on scale factor in distributed differential evolution. Inf. Sci. **181**(12), 2488–2511 (2011)
15. Neri, F., Iacca, G., Mininno, E.: Disturbed exploitation compact differential evolution for limited memory optimization problems. Inf. Sci. **181**(12), 2469–2487 (2011)
16. Iacca, G., Caraffini, F., Neri, F.: Compact differential evolution light: high performance despite limited memory requirement and modest computational overhead. J. Comput. Sci. Technol. **27**(5), 1056–1076 (2012)
17. Zamuda, A., Brest, J.: Self-adaptive control parameters' randomization frequency and propagations in differential evolution. Swarm Evol. Comput. **25**, 72–99 (2015)
18. Brest, J., Greiner, S., Boskovic, B., Mernik, M., Zumer, V.: Self-adapting control parameters in differential evolution: a comparative study on numerical benchmark problems. IEEE Trans. Evol. Comput. **10**(6), 646–657 (2006)
19. Price, K., Storn, R.M., Lampinen, J.A.: Differential Evolution: A Practical Approach to Global Optimization. Springer Science & Business Media, Heidelberg (2006). https://doi.org/10.1007/3-540-31306-0
20. Das, S., Mullick, S.S., Suganthan, P.N.: Recent advances in differential evolution-an updated survey. Swarm Evol. Comput. **27**, 1–30 (2016)
21. Das, S., Abraham, A., Chakraborty, U.K., Konar, A.: Differential evolution using a neighborhood-based mutation operator. IEEE Trans. Evol. Comput. **13**(3), 526–553 (2009)
22. Mininno, E., Neri, F., Cupertino, F., Naso, D.: Compact differential evolution. IEEE Trans. Evol. Comput. **15**(1), 32–54 (2011)
23. Mallipeddi, R., Suganthan, P.N., Pan, Q.K., Tasgetiren, M.F.: Differential evolution algorithm with ensemble of parameters and mutation strategies. Appl. Soft Comput. **11**(2), 1679–1696 (2011)
24. Brest, J., Korošec, P., Šilc, J., Zamuda, A., Bošković, B., Maučec, M.S.: Differential evolution and differential ant-stigmergy on dynamic optimisation problems. Int. J. Syst. Sci. **44**(4), 663–679 (2013)
25. Tanabe, R., Fukunaga, A.S.: Improving the search performance of shade using linear population size reduction. In: 2014 IEEE Congress on Evolutionary Computation (CEC), pp. 1658–1665. IEEE (2014)
26. Senkerik, R., Pluhacek, M., Zelinka, I., Viktorin, A., Kominkova Oplatkova, Z.: Hybridization of multi-chaotic dynamics and adaptive control parameter adjusting jDE strategy. In: Matoušek, R. (ed.) ICSC-MENDEL 2016. AISC, vol. 576, pp. 77–87. Springer, Cham (2017). https://doi.org/10.1007/978-3-319-58088-3_8
27. Senkerik, R., Pluhacek, M., Zelinka, I., Davendra, D., Janostik, J.: Preliminary study on the randomization and sequencing for the chaos embedded heuristic. In: Abraham, A., Wegrzyn-Wolska, K., Hassanien, A.E., Snasel, V., Alimi, A.M. (eds.) Proceedings of the Second International Afro-European Conference for Industrial Advancement AECIA 2015. AISC, vol. 427, pp. 591–601. Springer, Cham (2016). https://doi.org/10.1007/978-3-319-29504-6_55
28. Sprott, J.C., Sprott, J.C.: Chaos and Time-Series Analysis, vol. 69. Citeseer (2003)
29. Poláková, R., Tvrdík, J., Bujok, P., Matoušek, R.: Population-size adaptation through diversity-control mechanism for differential evolution. In: MENDEL, 22th International Conference on Soft Computing, pp. 49–56 (2016)
30. Viktorin, A., Pluhacek, M., Senkerik, R.: Success-history based adaptive differential evolution algorithm with multi-chaotic framework for parent selection performance on CEC2014 benchmark set. In: 2016 IEEE Congress on Evolutionary Computation (CEC), pp. 4797–4803. IEEE (2016)

Robust Design with Surrogate-Assisted Evolutionary Algorithm: Does It Work?

Rodrigo C. P. Silva[1]($\boxtimes$), Min Li[1], Vahid Ghorbanian[1],
Frederico G. Guimarães[2], and David A. Lowther[1]

[1] McGill University, Montreal, Quebec, Canada
rodrigo.silva@mail.mcgill.ca
[2] Universidade Federal de Minas Gerais, Belo Horizonte, Minas Gerais, Brazil

Abstract. Recently, the use of surrogate models for robustness assessment has become popular in various research fields. In this paper, we investigate whether it is advantageous to use the sample data to build a model instead of computing the robustness measures directly. The results suggest that if the quality of the surrogate model cannot be guaranteed, their use can be harmful to the optimization process.

Keywords: Robust optimization · Surrogate models · SPM motor

1 Introduction

The goal of robust engineering design is to optimize performance criteria while minimizing the effect of manufacturing and operational uncertainties, i.e. finding a solution that is robust to uncertain conditions [1]. Often in computer-aided automated design based on finite element analysis (FEA), one solution evaluation may take from a few seconds to several hours of computation, and conventional robustness analysis (e.g. Monte-Carlo simulation) can require a large number of evaluations. For this reason, most robust design schemes are considered unrealistic for practical applications.

In this context, surrogate models have been used in lieu of expensive simulation code to estimate statistical measures of robustness [2–5]. The estimation of statistical quantities, e.g. mean and variance, is not trivial. For instance, [5] suggests that, in some circumstances, global surrogate models are not able to provide accurate estimates of the required quantities. Thus, in [2,5], instead of using a global surrogate model, local surrogates, fitted with samples in the neighborhood of the point of interest, are used to estimate robustness.

The use of surrogate models implies the existence of sample data. Besides, the use of local surrogate models implies the existence of data in the neighborhood of the point of interest. If that is the case, one has samples to estimate the robustness directly which in turn brings us to the following question: Do we need surrogate models at all?

In order to investigate this question, we test the framework introduced in [2,5] with 4 different types of surrogates plus a surrogate-less (direct calculation)

© Springer International Publishing AG, part of Springer Nature 2018
P. Korošec et al. (Eds.): BIOMA 2018, LNCS 10835, pp. 295–306, 2018.
https://doi.org/10.1007/978-3-319-91641-5_25

version in a set of benchmark analytical problems. In the tests, in addition to the type of surrogate, we also vary the number of variables and the number of samples selected for surrogate construction. We compare the surrogate models in terms of the accuracy of the provided estimates, the insensitivity to the number of samples and their distribution, and also in terms of the optimization algorithm effectiveness. Finally, we use the surrogate-assisted robust design method in a bi-objective robust optimization problem related to the design of a Surface-mounted Permanent Magnet (SPM) motor.

2   Robust Optimization

In mathematical terms a general optimization problem can be stated as:

$$\min\ f(\mathbf{x}) \qquad \text{s. t. } \mathbf{x} \in \mathcal{F} \tag{1}$$

where, $f(\mathbf{x})$ is the objective function, $\mathbf{x}$ is the vector of design variables and $\mathcal{F}$ represents the feasible region. The formulation shown in Eq. (1) does not take into account the effect of the uncertainties that often arise in real-world optimization problems. Thus, a more general definition for the objective function $f(\mathbf{x})$ would be: $f = f(\mathbf{x} + \delta, \alpha)$ where δ represents perturbations to the design variables which arise from production tolerances and α are the uncontrollable factors that arise from environmental and material uncertainties.

Robust optimization is a family of optimization approaches that tries to account for uncertainties as the ones defined above. The main goal is to find the, so called, robust solutions which present good performance and small variability with respect to the sources of uncertainty.

This loose definition of robustness can be translated to different formulations of the robust optimization problem such as, for instance, the minimization of the worst-case scenario. In some design problems, however, the worst-case approach can be regarded as too conservative, especially when the worst-cases are very unlikely to happen. Therefore, in this paper, we are going to focus on statistical measures of robustness.

The most commonly used statistical measure of the robustness of a given design is the expected value (mean) given by:

$$\mu_f(\mathbf{x}) = E[f|\mathbf{x}] = \int_{\mathcal{U}(\mathbf{x})} f(\mathbf{x} + \delta, \alpha) p(\delta, \alpha) d\delta d\alpha \tag{2}$$

where, $p(\delta, \alpha)$ is the joint probability distribution of the uncertainties and $\mathcal{U}(\mathbf{x})$ is an uncertainty set and defines the domain of δ and α for each $\mathbf{x}$.

Although the mean gives a more realistic measure of the expected performance, sometimes, it is also important to know the performance variability [4]. Therefore, in order to obtain robust solutions (designs) some measure of dispersion, such as the standard deviation σ, may also be incorporated in the problem formulation. σ is defined by:

$$\sigma_f(\mathbf{x}) = \sqrt{\int_{\mathcal{U}(\mathbf{x})} \left(f(\mathbf{x} + \delta, \alpha) - E[f|\mathbf{x}]\right)^2 p(\delta, \alpha) d\delta d\alpha} \tag{3}$$

3 Surrogate-Assisted Robust Optimization

An important concern in robust optimization is the computational cost related to the robustness estimation, which normally involves the use of Monte-Carlo sampling (MCS). When the sampling involves complex computational models, such as, finite element analysis (FEA), the estimation of robustness may become impractical. To reduce the computational cost, the framework described in Fig. 1 which uses an evolutionary algorithm (EA) as a search mechanism and surrogate models for robustness estimation was proposed in [2].

This algorithm keeps an archive with all the solutions ever evaluated. In step (6), a Latin-hypercube sampling plan (LHS) is generated in the uncertainty set, $\mathcal{U}$, of each offspring for robust assessment. The algorithm searches the archive for the closest neighbor of each point in the LHS. If two points have the same closest neighbor, the farther point from the point of interest in the archive is evaluated with expensive simulation code. Thus, the algorithm takes advantage of previously evaluated solutions and guarantees a reasonably well distributed set of samples. In the next sections a set of possible surrogate models is presented.

```
 1. initialize parent population
 2. initialize archive
 3. while not terminate do
 4.     generate offspring
 5.     for each offspring do
 6.         select archive points for surrogate construction
 7.         if no representative set of samples available then
 8.             get extra sample points
 9.             evaluate the extra sample points
10.             add extra points to the archive
11.         end if
12.         construct local surrogate
13.         evaluate robustness using surrogate
14.     end for
15.     select best offspring as new parent population
16. end while
```

Fig. 1. Surrogate-assisted algorithm for robust optimization

3.1 Polynomial Models

Given a $n \times 1$ vector of responses, $\mathbf{y}$, and a $n \times d$ matrix of observed variables, $\mathbf{X}$, where n is the number of samples, the relationship between $\mathbf{y}$ and $\mathbf{X}$ can be described as:

$$\mathbf{y} = \mathbf{X}\beta + \epsilon \tag{4}$$

where, β is the vector of regression coefficients, and ϵ the error vector.

The model "training" consists of finding the least squares estimators, $\mathbf{b}$, that minimize the loss function defined in Eq. (5).

$$L = \sum_{i=1}^{n} \epsilon_i^2 = \epsilon'\epsilon = (\mathbf{y} - \mathbf{X}\mathbf{b})^T (\mathbf{y} - \mathbf{X}\mathbf{b}) \tag{5}$$

By taking the derivatives of Eq. (5) with respect to the regression coefficients it is possible to find (see [6] for the detailed derivation) that the least squares estimators of β are given by:

$$\mathbf{b} = (\mathbf{X}^T\mathbf{X})^{-1}\mathbf{X}^T\mathbf{y} \tag{6}$$

Thus, a prediction at an unseen point $\mathbf{x}$ is $\hat{y}(\mathbf{x}) = \mathbf{x}\mathbf{b}$.

3.2 Kriging

Kriging [7] is an interpolation method that expresses the sought, unknown, function $y(\mathbf{x})$ as a combination of a global model β with local deviations $Z(\mathbf{x})$:

$$y(\mathbf{x}) = \beta + Z(\mathbf{x}) \tag{7}$$

where, β approximates the global trend of the original function while $Z(\mathbf{x})$ creates local deviations in order to approximate a possible multimodal behavior.

Mathematically, $Z(\mathbf{x})$ is the realization of a stochastic process with zero mean, variance σ^2 and covariance given by:

$$Cov[Z(\mathbf{x}_i), Z(\mathbf{x}_j)] = \sigma^2\mathbf{R} \tag{8}$$

$\mathbf{R}$ is the correlation matrix of all the observed data defined as:

$$\mathbf{R} = \begin{bmatrix} R(\mathbf{x}_1, \mathbf{x}_2) & \cdots & R(\mathbf{x}_1, \mathbf{x}_n) \\ \vdots & \ddots & \vdots \\ R(\mathbf{x}_1, \mathbf{x}_n) & \cdots & R(\mathbf{x}_n, \mathbf{x}_n) \end{bmatrix} \tag{9}$$

where, $R(\mathbf{x}_i, \mathbf{x}_j)$ is the correlation function defined as:

$$R(\mathbf{x}_i, \mathbf{x}_j) = \exp\left(-\sum_{l=1}^{k} \theta_l |x_{i_l} - x_{j_l}|^2 \right) \tag{10}$$

Predicted values at new points are given by:

$$\hat{y}(\mathbf{x}) = \hat{\beta} + \mathbf{r}(\mathbf{x})^T\mathbf{R}^{-1}(\mathbf{y} - \mathbf{1}\hat{\beta}) \tag{11}$$

where $\mathbf{1}$ is the unit vector, $\hat{\beta}$ is the estimated value of β given by Eq. (14), $\mathbf{y}$ contains the response values of the sample points and $\mathbf{r}^T$ is the correlation vector between an untried point $\mathbf{x}$ and the sampled data points $\mathbf{x}_i$, $i = 1, ..., n$.

$$\mathbf{r}(\mathbf{x})^T = [R(\mathbf{x}, \mathbf{x}_1), R(\mathbf{x}, \mathbf{x}_2), ..., R(\mathbf{x}, \mathbf{x}_n)] \tag{12}$$

Training the kriging model consists of maximizing the likelihood function, given by Eq. (13), in order to find the unknown parameters θ_l.

$$\ln(L(\theta)) = -\frac{n}{2}\ln(2\pi) - \frac{n}{2}\ln(\sigma^2) - \frac{n}{2}\ln(|\mathbf{R}(\theta)|)$$
$$- \frac{(\mathbf{y} - \mathbf{1}\hat{\beta})^T\mathbf{R}(\theta)^{-1}(\mathbf{y} - \mathbf{1}\hat{\beta})}{2\sigma^2} \tag{13}$$

$$\hat{\beta} = (\mathbf{1}^T\mathbf{R}(\theta)^{-1}\mathbf{y})/(\mathbf{1}^T\mathbf{R}(\theta)^{-1}\mathbf{1}) \tag{14}$$

$$\hat{\sigma}^2 = ((\mathbf{y} - \mathbf{1}\hat{\beta})^T\mathbf{R}(\theta)^{-1}(\mathbf{y} - \mathbf{1}\hat{\beta}))/n \tag{15}$$

3.3   Radial Basis Functions Neural Networks

Radial basis functions neural networks (RBFNN) can be implemented in numerous ways. Here, the RBFNN with Gaussian basis functions [3] will be used. This RBFNN has one hidden layer with n neurons, where n is also the sample size, and one output layer. Each neuron in the hidden layer has the following form:

$$\phi_k(\mathbf{x}, \mathbf{c}_k) = \exp\left(-\frac{\|\mathbf{x}-\mathbf{c}_k\|_2^2}{\sigma_k^2}\right) \quad 1 \le k \le N \tag{16}$$

where $\mathbf{x}$ is some input vector, $\mathbf{c}_k$ is the kth training point which is also the center of the basis function $\phi_k(\cdot)$, and σ_k^2 controls the basis function width.

The output layer is the weighted sum of the hidden layer outputs. Given a set of width parameters σ_k and training points T, consisting of input vectors $\mathbf{c}_i$ and targets $\mathbf{y}_i$, the RBFNN can be concisely expressed in matrix form as:

$$\Phi\mathbf{w} = \mathbf{Y} = [y_1, y_2, \cdots, y_N]^T \tag{17}$$

where,

$$\Phi = \begin{bmatrix} \phi(\mathbf{c}_1, \mathbf{c}_2) & \cdots & \phi(\mathbf{c}_1, \mathbf{c}_n) \\ \vdots & \ddots & \vdots \\ \phi(\mathbf{c}_1, \mathbf{c}_n) & \cdots & \phi(\mathbf{c}_n, \mathbf{c}_n) \end{bmatrix} \tag{18}$$

If all the centers are pairwise different, the matrix Φ is positive-definite and invertible [3]. Thus, the weight vector $\mathbf{w}$ can be computed through Eq. (17). Once the weights are computed, predictions at untried points $\mathbf{x}$ are given by:

$$\begin{aligned} \hat{y}(\mathbf{x}) &= \mathbf{r}(\mathbf{x}) \cdot \mathbf{w} \\ \mathbf{r}(\mathbf{x}) &= [\phi(\mathbf{x}, \mathbf{c}_1), \phi(\mathbf{x}, \mathbf{c}_2), \cdots, \phi(\mathbf{x}, \mathbf{c}_N)]^T \\ \mathbf{w} &= [w_1, w_2, \cdots, w_N]^T \end{aligned} \tag{19}$$

3.4   Generalized Regression Neural Network

The Generalized Regression Neural Network (GRNN) is a simple yet powerful regression model proposed in [8]. Different from other artificial neural networks (ANNs), GRNNs do not use backpropagation for training. Instead, the predictions are directly derived from the sampled data using the following formula:

$$\hat{y}(\mathbf{x}) = \frac{\sum_{i=1}^{n} y_i \exp\left(-\frac{(\mathbf{x}-\mathbf{x}_i)^T(\mathbf{x}-\mathbf{x}_i)}{2\sigma^2}\right)}{\sum_{i=1}^{n} \exp\left(-\frac{(\mathbf{x}-\mathbf{x}_i)^T(\mathbf{x}-\mathbf{x}_i)}{2\sigma^2}\right)} \tag{20}$$

where, $\mathbf{x}_i$s and y_is are the sampled input vector and the respective response values. σ is known as the smoothing parameter and controls the width of the Gaussian functions.

4   Computational Experiments

In order to test the described surrogates and the optimization framework described in Sect. 3, three benchmark functions proposed in [9] for robust optimization have been used. They are defined as follows:

$$f7a(\mathbf{x}) = H(x_2) \times \left(\sum_{i=3}^{D} 50x_i^2 - S(\mathbf{x}) \right) + 1.5$$
$$H(x) = \frac{1}{\sqrt{2\pi}}\pi e^{-0.5(\frac{x-1.5}{0.5})^2} + \frac{2}{\sqrt{2\pi}}\pi e^{-0.5(\frac{x-1.5}{0.1})^2}$$
$$S(\mathbf{x}) = \begin{cases} -x_1^{1.5}, & \text{if } x_2 < 0.8 \\ -x_1, & \text{if } x_2 \geq 0.8 \end{cases}$$
$$x_i \in [0.2, 1.8]$$

(21)

$$f10a(\mathbf{x}) = H(x_2) \times \left(\sum_{i=3}^{D} 50x_i^2 - x_1^{0.5} \right) + 1$$
$$H(x) = \frac{e^{-x^2}\cos(6\pi x) - x}{4} + 0.5$$
$$x_i \in [0.2, 0.8]$$

(22)

$$f16a(\mathbf{x}) = G(x)$$
$$\times \left(\left(1 - \sqrt{\frac{x_1}{G(x)}} - \frac{x_1}{G(x)}\sin(4\pi x_1) \right) + H(x_1) \right)$$
$$\times \left(\left(1 - \sqrt{\frac{x_2}{G(x)}} - \frac{x_2}{G(x)}\sin(4\pi x_2) \right) + H(x_2) \right) + 0.5$$
$$H(x) = \frac{e^{-2x^2}\sin(12\pi(x+\frac{\pi}{24})) - x}{3} + 0.5$$
$$G(\mathbf{x}) = 1 + 10\frac{\sum_{i=2}^{D} x_i}{D}$$
$$x_i \in [0.2, 0.8]$$

(23)

The uncertainty set is defined as $U(\mathbf{x}) = [\mathbf{x} - 0.2, \mathbf{x} + 0.2]$ for the three problems.

4.1   Surrogate Models for Robustness Assessment

The problem of estimating robustness using sampling is that the computed estimates will depend on the sample data. Hence, different results may be obtained for repeated evaluations at the same design parameter values. Such a noisy objective function may cause the following undesirable behavior [10]: (i) A superior candidate solution may be believed to be inferior and get eliminated; (ii) an inferior candidate may be believed to be superior and get selected for survival and reproduction; and (iii) the objective values may not monotonically improve over the generations.

Thus, a good methodology for robustness assessment should not only provide accurate estimates of the sought measures but also present small variability with respect to the number and the distribution of the samples.

With this in mind, in this section, the described surrogate models are evaluated in the estimation of statistical measures of robustness, more specifically the mean, μ_f, and the standard deviation, σ_f. In order to assess the quality of the surrogates, the average relative error, Eq. (24), is used to estimate the accuracy, and the average coefficient of variation, Eq. (25), is used to estimate the noise caused by the limited number of samples. These metrics are defined below.

$$e = \frac{\sum_{i=0}^{N} |\hat{s}_i - s_{ref}|/s_{ref}}{N} \tag{24}$$

where, $\hat{s}_i$ is the estimated value, s_{ref} is the reference value computed with a MCS of 10^6 samples and N is the number of experiments.

$$cv = \frac{\sum_{i=0}^{N} \sigma(\hat{\mathbf{s}}_i)/\mu(\hat{\mathbf{s}}_i)}{N} \tag{25}$$

where, $\hat{\mathbf{s}}_i$ is the collection of all estimates computed for $\mathbf{x}_i$. The experiment was designed as follows:

1. For each test function, 20 points were randomly selected in the design space;
2. For each selected point $\mathbf{x}_i$ a random sample of k points in $\mathcal{U}(\mathbf{x}_i)$ was generated and evaluated;
3. If surrogate models are used, the k samples are used to fit the surrogate (the values of σ used by GRNNs and RBFNNs were set to 1.201 as suggested in [11]). μ_f and σ_f are computed with a MCS of 10^6 samples evaluated with the surrogate;
4. If surrogate models are not used, μ_f and σ_f are computed directly from the k samples (DIRECT estimates);
5. This experiment was repeated 30 times for each $\mathbf{x}_i$.

Figure 2 illustrates this experiment for $f(x) = x \times sin(x) + 12$, where $\mathcal{U}(x) = [x - 2, x + 2]$. As mentioned before, the average relative error measures how accurate the estimates are. The average coefficient of variation measures, in some sense, the width of the shaded area ($max - min$ estimates of each point) which represents the noise.

Tables 1 and 2 show the average error and the coefficient of variation (in parenthesis) obtained in the estimation of μ_f and σ_f, respectively. Dunn's Test of Multiple Comparisons [12] was used for the statistical analysis. Surrogate-based estimates with average error significantly different ($\alpha - 95\%$) and better than *Direct* are shown in blue. Significantly different ($\alpha = 95\%$) and worse than *Direct* are shown in red. The column *Problem* consists of: *problem name/number of variables/number of samples (k)*.

Table 1 shows that, in some of the tested problems, the use of Kriging improved the accuracy of the estimates of μ_f. It has also reduced the noise throughout independent executions when compared to the other models. GRNN presented results close to the ones obtained when μ_f is directly estimated with the samples ("Direct"). When Polynomials and RBFNN were used, the accuracy decreased and the noise increased when compared with the other approaches.

As can be seen in Table 2, the estimation of σ_f with surrogates is more complicated than it is for μ_f. In the majority of the tested scenarios, there was no advantage in using surrogate models. Their use led, in most of the cases, to higher levels of noise and less accurate estimates. The exception was the problem *f7a* for which Kriging presented some improvement when compared with Direct.

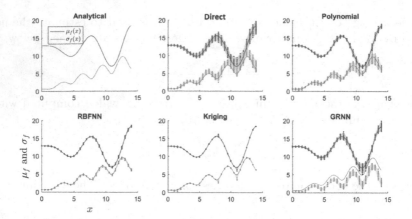

Fig. 2. Surrogate models for robustness estimation.

Table 1. Using surrogates for the estimation of μ_f.

Problem	Surrogate model				
	Direct	Kriging	RBFNN	GRNN	2nd-order polynomial
f7a/5/10	$0.095_{(0.118)}$	$0.044_{(0.060)}$	$0.092_{(0.121)}$	$0.102_{(0.125)}$	$0.083_{(0.106)}$
f7a/5/20	$0.069_{(0.084)}$	$0.008_{(0.011)}$	$0.068_{(0.096)}$	$0.068_{(0.084)}$	$0.124_{(0.244)}$
f7a/5/40	$0.050_{(0.061)}$	$0.003_{(0.003)}$	$0.049_{(0.068)}$	$0.047_{(0.059)}$	$0.016_{(0.019)}$
f7a/10/10	$0.096_{(0.117)}$	$0.090_{(0.114)}$	$0.129_{(0.189)}$	$0.092_{(0.113)}$	$0.179_{(0.257)}$
f7a/10/20	$0.066_{(0.081)}$	$0.039_{(0.058)}$	$0.064_{(0.088)}$	$0.064_{(0.078)}$	$0.066_{(0.081)}$
f7a/10/40	$0.050_{(0.061)}$	$0.008_{(0.015)}$	$0.042_{(0.054)}$	$0.043_{(0.053)}$	$0.053_{(0.070)}$
f10a/5/10	$0.150_{(0.189)}$	$0.130_{(0.161)}$	$0.458_{(0.676)}$	$0.144_{(0.180)}$	$1.243_{(5.228)}$
f10a/5/20	$0.109_{(0.133)}$	$0.052_{(0.072)}$	$0.571_{(0.993)}$	$0.104_{(0.131)}$	$0.328_{(0.446)}$
f10a/5/40	$0.076_{(0.095)}$	$0.015_{(0.019)}$	$0.541_{(0.783)}$	$0.073_{(0.090)}$	$0.102_{(0.130)}$
f10a/10/10	$0.141_{(0.175)}$	$0.140_{(0.173)}$	$0.405_{(0.627)}$	$0.150_{(0.189)}$	$0.427_{(0.583)}$
f10a/10/20	$0.101_{(0.122)}$	$0.087_{(0.114)}$	$0.242_{(0.315)}$	$0.097_{(0.121)}$	$0.249_{(0.330)}$
f10a/10/40	$0.072_{(0.090)}$	$0.032_{(0.048)}$	$0.207_{(0.277)}$	$0.073_{(0.091)}$	$0.209_{(0.268)}$
f16a/5/10	$0.057_{(0.072)}$	$0.063_{(0.078)}$	$0.196_{(0.320)}$	$0.058_{(0.073)}$	$0.140_{(0.197)}$
f16a/5/20	$0.042_{(0.052)}$	$0.041_{(0.050)}$	$0.223_{(0.334)}$	$0.044_{(0.055)}$	$0.362_{(0.849)}$
f16a/5/40	$0.030_{(0.037)}$	$0.025_{(0.031)}$	$0.325_{(0.515)}$	$0.029_{(0.037)}$	$0.043_{(0.055)}$
f16a/10/10	$0.057_{(0.071)}$	$0.059_{(0.073)}$	$0.155_{(0.247)}$	$0.056_{(0.071)}$	$0.161_{(0.230)}$
f16a/10/20	$0.039_{(0.049)}$	$0.042_{(0.052)}$	$0.092_{(0.121)}$	$0.042_{(0.050)}$	$0.089_{(0.115)}$
f16a/10/40	$0.029_{(0.036)}$	$0.027_{(0.033)}$	$0.079_{(0.110)}$	$0.030_{(0.037)}$	$0.086_{(0.110)}$

Table 2. Using surrogates for the estimation of σ_f.

Problem	Surrogate model				
	Direct	Kriging	RBFNN	GRNN	2nd-order polynomial
f7a/5/10	$0.173_{(0.215)}$	$0.206_{(0.314)}$	$0.184_{(0.223)}$	$0.982_{(0.356)}$	$0.252_{(0.212)}$
f7a/5/20	$0.119_{(0.149)}$	$0.039_{(0.041)}$	$0.186_{(0.163)}$	$0.982_{(0.253)}$	$0.700_{(0.414)}$
f7a/5/40	$0.079_{(0.098)}$	$0.013_{(0.012)}$	$0.120_{(0.103)}$	$0.983_{(0.188)}$	$0.035_{(0.038)}$
f7a/10/10	$0.160_{(0.207)}$	$0.915_{(3.112)}$	$0.238_{(0.299)}$	$0.978_{(0.304)}$	$0.723_{(0.469)}$
f7a/10/20	$0.120_{(0.148)}$	$0.570_{(1.078)}$	$0.163_{(0.189)}$	$0.981_{(0.249)}$	$0.290_{(0.182)}$
f7a/10/40	$0.080_{(0.101)}$	$0.122_{(0.282)}$	$0.088_{(0.102)}$	$0.982_{(0.180)}$	$0.416_{(0.170)}$
f10a/5/10	$0.177_{(0.228)}$	$0.461_{(0.621)}$	$1.128_{(0.682)}$	$0.986_{(0.405)}$	$7.103_{(1.262)}$
f10a/5/20	$0.117_{(0.149)}$	$0.179_{(0.254)}$	$2.130_{(0.682)}$	$0.989_{(0.367)}$	$1.153_{(0.484)}$
f10a/5/40	$0.085_{(0.106)}$	$0.043_{(0.050)}$	$2.234_{(0.575)}$	$0.990_{(0.302)}$	$0.229_{(0.229)}$
f10a/10/10	$0.157_{(0.202)}$	$0.947_{(3.786)}$	$0.787_{(0.608)}$	$0.983_{(0.306)}$	$1.695_{(0.572)}$
f10a/10/20	$0.101_{(0.125)}$	$0.743_{(1.569)}$	$0.557_{(0.406)}$	$0.986_{(0.261)}$	$1.114_{(0.324)}$
f10a/10/40	$0.070_{(0.086)}$	$0.294_{(0.555)}$	$0.586_{(0.338)}$	$0.989_{(0.241)}$	$2.109_{(0.321)}$
f16a/5/10	$0.190_{(0.235)}$	$0.573_{(0.703)}$	$1.270_{(0.814)}$	$0.986_{(0.416)}$	$1.120_{(0.526)}$
f16a/5/20	$0.137_{(0.168)}$	$0.401_{(0.375)}$	$2.153_{(0.619)}$	$0.988_{(0.339)}$	$6.191_{(0.995)}$
f16a/5/40	$0.093_{(0.115)}$	$0.291_{(0.222)}$	$3.186_{(0.795)}$	$0.989_{(0.267)}$	$0.215_{(0.238)}$
f16a/10/10	$0.189_{(0.238)}$	$0.952_{(3.196)}$	$0.698_{(0.607)}$	$0.982_{(0.347)}$	$1.607_{(0.630)}$
f16a/10/20	$0.133_{(0.166)}$	$0.795_{(1.527)}$	$0.581_{(0.505)}$	$0.985_{(0.286)}$	$0.999_{(0.334)}$
f16a/10/40	$0.090_{(0.113)}$	$0.521_{(0.673)}$	$0.559_{(0.359)}$	$0.988_{(0.250)}$	$1.869_{(0.310)}$

4.2   Surrogate-Assisted Robust Optimization

In this section, we compare the aforementioned robustness estimation schemes within the optimization framework presented in Sect. 3. Matlab's genetic algorithm (GA) [11] was used as search engine. Each version of the algorithm is used to minimize μ_f or σ_f for the 5-variable versions of $f7a$, $f10a$ and $f16a$. k is set to 20, the algorithm stops when the number of generations reaches 200 and 20 independent runs are performed for each version.

Figure 3 presents the convergence curves of the minimization problems regarding μ_f and σ_f for $f10a$ and $f16a$. To generate these curves, the best individual at each generation is evaluated using a Monte-Carlo simulation with 10000 samples. Given the 20 independent runs, the dots represent the average and the bars represent the range of the best individuals' fitness at that generation.

For the μ_f minimization problems, the framework versions with Kriging, GRNNs and direct estimates (without surrogate models) presented the best results which, in turn, can be explained by the error and coefficient of variation values in Table 1. For the σ_f minimization problems, as expected from the results in Table 2, the version with direct estimates outperformed the others.

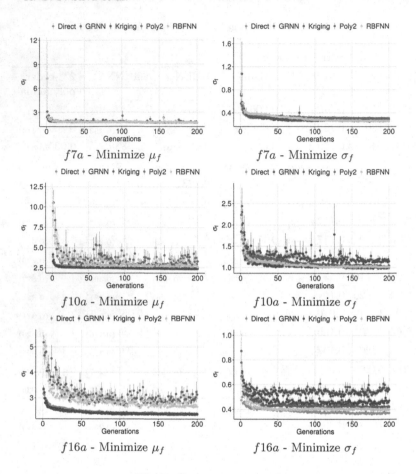

Fig. 3. Convergence curves

Interestingly, RBFNNs also presented good performance, despite the high prediction errors. This indicates that, for the tested problems, the prediction errors may have had minimal influence on the ranks of the candidate solutions in the GA. Overall, as can be seen in Fig. 3, the results presented by the framework with direct estimates were more consistent throughout the tested problems.

Figure 4(a) shows an example of a 3-phase 4-pole surface mounted permanent magnet (SPM) motor. SPM motors have been widely used in applications such as hybrid vehicles and robotics, and their performance highly depends on the produced average torque (T_{avg}) and cogging torque levels (T_{cog}).

It has been shown in [13] that an electrical machine's performance can be significantly affected by small tolerances in the manufacturing process. In this context, instead of optimizing for the nominal values, we optimize the expected (or mean) performance. In this formulation, the tolerances are set to 2% of the lower bound values, that is, $U(\mathbf{x}) = [\mathbf{x} - \mathbf{d}, \mathbf{x} + \mathbf{d}]$ where $d_i = 0.02 \times l_i$. The four design variables are indicated in Fig. 4(a).

To solve this problem, Kriging was combined with the Matlab multi-objective genetic algorithm (MOGA) [11]. Given the results presented in the previous section, Kriging seems to be the obvious choice for this kind of problem. For the sake of simplicity, from here on, this method is going to be called as robust multi-objective genetic algorithm (RMOGA).

Figure 4(b) shows the non-dominated solutions obtained using MOGA to solve the optimization problem without uncertainties (non-robust front) and RMOGA. The non-robust region is highlighted in the figure. It was observed that those solutions are clustered in a small region of the design space which means that a small change in the design variables is causing a large variation of the performance. In the robust front, on the other hand, the solutions are well distributed over the design space, representing the trade-offs between the two objectives. It is worth noting that the front of the optimal designs moves toward lower average torque and higher cogging torque levels if the robust approach is used. This demonstrates the trade-off between performance and robustness in this problem.

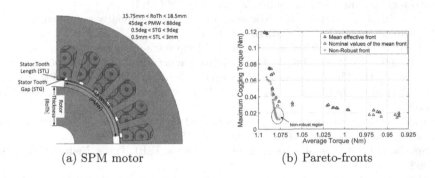

(a) SPM motor   (b) Pareto-fronts

Fig. 4. SPM motor layout and solutions

5 Conclusion

In this paper, the use of surrogate models for robustness assessment has been investigated. Although it has been shown that surrogate models may improve the accuracy and reduce the noise caused by the small sample sizes, that does not seem to happen very often. Even when the robustness estimation process was improved, the optimization results did not seem to be affected. In fact, in all the tested optimization problems, the surrogate-less method was either the best or among the best performing methods.

Although Kriging presented good performance for the mean related problems, for the general case, where no guarantees about the surrogate model's accuracy can be provided, it is safer to rely directly on the data acquired from the original problem set-up. If the surrogate model cannot be carefully constructed, it may end up introducing error and noise to the objective function instead of removing them. Although experiments in a larger set of problems with other types of surrogate models may be required to provide a definitive answer to the question proposed in the title, the results displayed here present a fair amount of evidence showing that, in general, the use of surrogate models is not advantageous.

Acknowledgements. Frederico G. Guimarães would like to thank the Minas Gerais State Agency for Research and Development (FAPEMIG).

References

1. Yoon, S.B., Jung, I.S., Hyun, D.S., Hong, J.P., Kim, Y.J.: Robust shape optimization of electromechanical devices. IEEE Trans. Magn. **35**(3), 1710–1713 (1999)
2. Kruisselbrink, J., Emmerich, M., Deutz, A., Back, T.: A robust optimization approach using Kriging metamodels for robustness approximation in the CMA-ES. In: 2010 IEEE Congress on Evolutionary Computation (CEC), pp. 1–8, July 2010
3. Yao, W., Chen, X., Huang, Y., van Tooren, M.: A surrogate-based optimization method with rbf neural network enhanced by linear interpolation and hybrid infill strategy. Optim. Methods Softw. **29**(2), 406–429 (2014)
4. Xiao, S., Li, Y., Rotaru, M., Sykulski, J.K.: Six sigma quality approach to robust optimization. IEEE Trans. Magn. **51**(3), 1–4 (2015)
5. Li, M., Silva, R., Lowther, D.: Global and local meta-models for the robust design of electrical machines. Int. J. Appl. Electromagnet Mech **51**(s1), 89–95 (2016)
6. Myers, R.H., Montgomery, D.C.: Response Surface Methodology: Process and Product in Optimization Using Designed Experiments, 2nd edn. Wiley, New York (2002)
7. Jones, D.R.: A taxonomy of global optimization methods based on response surfaces. J. Glob. Optim. **21**(4), 345–383 (2001)
8. Specht, D.F.: A general regression neural network. IEEE Trans. Neural Netw. **2**(6), 568–576 (1991)
9. Mirjalili, S., Lewis, A.: Novel frameworks for creating robust multi-objective benchmark problems. Inf. Sci. **300**, 158–192 (2015)
10. Rana, S., Whitley, L.D., Cogswell, R.: Searching in the presence of noise. In: Voigt, H.-M., Ebeling, W., Rechenberg, I., Schwefel, H.-P. (eds.) PPSN 1996. LNCS, vol. 1141, pp. 198–207. Springer, Heidelberg (1996). https://doi.org/10.1007/3-540-61723-X_984
11. MATLAB: version (R2015a). The MathWorks Inc., Natick, Massachusetts (2015)
12. Dinno, A.: Dunn's test of multiple comparisons using rank sums. Technical report (2017)
13. Lei, G., Wang, T., Zhu, J., Guo, Y., Wang, S.: System-level design optimization method for electrical drive systems - robust approach. IEEE Trans. Ind. Electron. **62**(8), 4702–4713 (2015)

How Distance Based Parameter Adaptation Affects Population Diversity

Adam Viktorin$^{(\boxtimes)}$ ⓘ, Roman Senkerik ⓘ, Michal Pluhacek ⓘ,
and Tomas Kadavy ⓘ

Faculty of Applied Informatics, Tomas Bata University in Zlin,
T. G. Masaryka 5555, 760 01 Zlin, Czech Republic
{aviktorin,senkerik,pluhacek,kadavy}@utb.cz

Abstract. This paper discusses the effect of distance based parameter adaptation on the population diversity of the Success-History based Adaptive Differential Evolution (SHADE). The distance-based parameter adaptation was designed to promote exploration over exploitation and provide better search capabilities of the SHADE algorithm in higher dimensional objective spaces. The population diversity is recorded on the 15 test functions from the CEC 2015 benchmark set in two-dimensional settings, $10D$ and $30D$, to provide the empiric evidence of a beneficial influence of the distance based parameter adaptation in comparison with the objective function value based approach.

Keywords: Distance-based parameter adaptation · SHADE
Population diversity

1 Introduction

The original Differential Evolution (DE) algorithm that was proposed for global optimization by Storn and Price in [1] has three main control parameters: population size NP, scaling factor F and crossover rate CR. As it was shown in [2,3], the setting of these control parameters is crucial for the performance of the algorithm, and there seems to be no universal setting, which is in accordance with the famous no free lunch theorem [4]. Due to this fact, researchers in the DE field are trying to overcome this problem with self-adaptive variants of DE, which do not require fine-tuning of the control parameters to the given optimization task. And since the DE research community is fairly active, there have been numerous updated and improved DE versions over the last few years. Various directions of the research were recently nicely surveyed in the Das, Mullick and Suganthan's paper [5].

One of the most successful novel variants of adaptive DE algorithm is Success-History based Adaptive Differential Evolution (SHADE) [6]. Its superiority was proved on the last five CEC competitions in continuous optimization, where SHADE or its updated variants placed on the top ranks (CEC2013 – SHADE

P. Korošec et al. (Eds.): BIOMA 2018, LNCS 10835, pp. 307–319, 2018.
https://doi.org/10.1007/978-3-319-91641-5_26

placed 3rd, CEC2014 – L-SHADE [7] placed 1st, CEC2015 – SPS-L-SHADE-EIG [8] placed 1st, CEC2016 – LSHADE_EpSin [9] placed on joint 1st place, CEC2017 – jSO [10] placed 1st). Therefore, the SHADE algorithm was selected as a basis for this study.

The adaptive mechanism in Tanabe and Fukunaga's SHADE is based on the improvement in objective function value from the original individual to the trial individual. Scaling factor and crossover rate values that were used for the generation of successful trial individuals are then subject to the comparison based on the objective function value improvement and the ones with the highest improvement have the highest weights in the forthcoming calculation of the values that will be stored in the algorithm's memory of successful control parameter settings. Thus, this approach benefits exploitation of the objective space rather than the exploration. Due to this fact, the algorithm is subject to premature convergence when solving optimization problems of higher dimensionalities. In this paper, a novel approach, which considers the distance between the original and trial individuals rather than the objective function improvement is analyzed from the perspective of performance and its effect on population diversity. Maintaining of the population diversity is an interesting task which was lately studied in numerous papers. In [11], auto-enhanced population diversity is proposed, which regenerates individuals components based on the detection of stagnation in respective dimension, in [12], a diversity-based population strategy serves for population size management, in [13], population diversity is maintained by scattering individuals from the centre of the population whenever the variance in objective function values of the population drops below certain level, and finally in [14], population diversity is maintained at a predefined value by increasing or decreasing the population size after each generation. The aforementioned approaches to population diversity maintaining are based on artificial changes to the population, whereas approach proposed in this paper is based on a different view at the information exchange between individuals, where the position change is more valuable for the optimization than the objective function improvement. Therefore, such approach does not lose any of the population shared knowledge, which might be lost in artificial changes of the population. Proposed distance based adaptation is also applicable to any SHADE-based algorithm.

The rest of the paper is structured as follows: The next Section describes original DE algorithm, the Section that follows provides the description of SHADE and Sect. 4 is devoted to the distance based parameter adaptation mechanism. Sections 5, 6 and 7 deal with experimental setting, results, their discussion and conclusion correspondingly.

2   Differential Evolution

The DE algorithm is initialized with a random population of individuals $\boldsymbol{P}$, that represent solutions of the optimization problem. The population size NP is set by the user along with other control parameters – scaling factor F and crossover rate CR.

In continuous optimization, each individual is composed of a vector x of length D, which is a dimensionality (number of optimized attributes) of the problem, and each vector component represents a value of the corresponding attribute, and of objective function value $f(x)$.

For each individual in a population, three mutually different individuals are selected for mutation of vectors and the resulting mutated vector v is combined with the original vector x in the crossover step. The objective function value $f(u)$ of the resulting trial vector u is evaluated and compared to that of the original individual. When the quality (objective function value) of the trial individual is better, it is placed into the next generation, otherwise, the original individual is placed there. This step is called selection. The process is repeated until the stopping criterion is met (e.g., the maximum number of objective function evaluations, the maximum number of generations, the low bound for diversity between objective function values in population).

The following sections describe four steps of DE: Initialization, mutation, crossover, and selection.

2.1   Initialization

As aforementioned, the initial population P with NP individuals is randomly generated. For this purpose, the individual vector xi components are generated by Random Number Generator (RNG) with uniform distribution from the range which is specified for the problem by lower and upper bound (1).

$$x_{j,i} = U\left[lower_j,\ upper_j\right] \text{ for } j = 1,\ \ldots,\ D \tag{1}$$

Where i is the index of a current individual, j is the index of current attribute and D is the dimensionality of the problem.

In the initialization phase, a scaling factor value F and crossover value CR has to be assigned as well. The typical range for F value is $[0,\ 2]$ and for CR, it is $[0,\ 1]$.

2.2   Mutation

In the mutation step, three mutually different individuals x_{r1}, x_{r2}, x_{r3} from a population are randomly selected and combined by the mutation strategy. The original mutation strategy of canonical DE is "rand/1" and is depicted in (2).

$$v_i = x_{r1} + F\left(x_{r2} - x_{r3}\right) \tag{2}$$

Where $r1 \neq r2 \neq r3 \neq i$, F is the scaling factor, and v_i is the resulting mutated vector.

2.3   Crossover

In the crossover step, the mutated vector v_i is combined with the original vector x_i to produce the trial vector u_i. The binomial crossover (3) is used in canonical DE.

$$u_{j,i} = \begin{cases} v_{j,i} & \text{if } U\left[0,1\right] \leq CR \text{ or } j = j_{rand} \\ x_{j,i} & \text{otherwise} \end{cases} \qquad (3)$$

Where CR is the used crossover rate value, and j_{rand} is an index of an attribute that has to be from the mutated vector v_i (this ensures generation of a vector with at least one new component).

2.4   Selection

The selection step ensures that the optimization will progress towards better solutions because it allows only individuals of better or at least equal objective function value to proceed into the next generation $G + 1$ (4).

$$x_{i,G+1} = \begin{cases} u_{i,G} & \text{if } f\left(u_{i,G}\right) \leq f\left(x_{i,G}\right) \\ x_{i,G} & \text{otherwise} \end{cases} \qquad (4)$$

Where G is the index of the current generation. The basic concept of the DE algorithm is depicted in pseudo-code below.

Algorithm pseudo-code 1: DE

Algorithm 1. DE

1: Set *NP, CR, F* and stopping criterion;
2: $G = 0$, $x_{best} = \{\}$;
3: Randomly initialize (1) population $P = (x_{1,G}, \dots, x_{NP,G})$;
4: $P_{new} = \{\}$, $x_{best} = $ best from population P;
5: **while** stopping criterion not met **do**
6:     **for** $i = 1$ to *NP* **do**
7:         $x_{i,G} = P[i]$;
8:         $v_{i,G}$ by mutation (2);
9:         $u_{i,G}$ by crossover (3);
10:        **if** $f(u_{i,G}) < f(x_{i,G})$ **then**
11:            $x_{i,G+1} = u_{i,G}$;
12:        **else**
13:            $x_{i,G+1} = x_{i,G}$;
14:        **end if**
15:        $x_{i,G+1} \rightarrow P_{new}$;
16:     **end for**
17:     $P = P_{new}$, $P_{new} = \{\}$, $x_{best} = $ best from population P;
18: **end while**
19: **return** x_{best} as the best found solution

---

3   SHADE

In SHADE, the only control parameter that can be set by the user is population size *NP*, the other two (*F, CR*) are adapted to the given optimization task, a new parameter H is introduced, which determines the size of F and CR value memories. The initialization step of the SHADE is, therefore, similar to DE. Mutation, however, is completely different because of the used strategy "current-to-$p$best/1" and the fact that it uses different scaling factor value F_i for each individual. Crossover is still binary, but similarly to the mutation and scaling factor values, crossover rate value CR_i is also different for each individual. The selection step is the same, and therefore following sections describe only the different aspects of initialization, mutation and crossover.

3.1 Initialization

As aforementioned, the initial population P is randomly generated as in DE, but additional memories for F and CR values are initialized as well. Both memories have the same size H and are equally initialized, the memory for CR values is titled M_{CR}, and the memory for F is titled M_F. Their initialization is depicted in (5).

$$M_{CR,i} = M_{F,i} = 0.5 \text{ for } i = 1, \dots, H \tag{5}$$

Also, the external archive of inferior solutions A is initialized. Since there are no solutions so far, it is initialized empty $A = \emptyset$, and its maximum size is set to NP.

3.2 Mutation

Mutation strategy "current-to-$p$best/1" was introduced in [15] and unlike "rand/1", it combines four mutually different vectors $pbest \neq r1 \neq r2 \neq i$ (6).

$$v_i = x_i + F_i (x_{pbest} - x_i) + F_i (x_{r1} - x_{r2}) \tag{6}$$

Where x_{pbest} is randomly selected from the best $NP \times p$ individuals in the current population. The p value is randomly generated for each mutation by RNG with uniform distribution from the range $[p_{min}, 0.2]$. Where $p_{min} = 2/NP$. Vector x_{r1} is randomly selected from the current population, and vector x_{r2} is randomly selected from the union of current population P and archive A. The scaling factor value F_i is given by (7).

$$F_i = C[M_{F,r}, 0.1] \tag{7}$$

Where $M_{F,r}$ is a randomly selected value (by index r) from M_F memory and C stands for Cauchy distribution, therefore the F_i value is generated from the Cauchy distribution with location parameter value $M_{F,r}$ and scale parameter value 0.1. If the generated value $F_i > 1$, it is truncated to 1, and if it is $F_i \leq 0$, it is generated again by (7).

3.3 Crossover

Crossover is the same as in (3), but the CR value is changed to CR_i, which is generated separately for each individual (8). The value is generated from the

Gaussian distribution with a mean parameter value of $M_{CR.r}$, which is randomly selected (by the same index r as in mutation) from $\boldsymbol{M}_{CR}$ memory and standard deviation value of 0.1.

$$CR_i = N\left[M_{CR,r}, 0.1\right] \tag{8}$$

3.4   Historical Memory Updates

Historical memories $\boldsymbol{M}_F$ and $\boldsymbol{M}_{CR}$ are initialized according to (5), but its components change during the evolution. These memories serve to hold successful values of F and CR used in mutation and crossover steps (successful regarding producing trial individual better than the original individual). During one generation, these successful values are stored in corresponding arrays $\boldsymbol{S}_F$ and $\boldsymbol{S}_{CR}$. After each generation, one cell of $\boldsymbol{M}_F$ and $\boldsymbol{M}_{CR}$ memories is updated. This cell is given by the index k, which starts at 1 and increases by 1 after each generation. When it overflows the memory size H, it is reset to 1. The new value of k-th cell for $\boldsymbol{M}_F$ is calculated by (9) and for $\boldsymbol{M}_{CR}$ by (10).

$$M_{F,k} = \begin{cases} \text{mean}_{WL}\left(\boldsymbol{S}_F\right) \text{ if } \boldsymbol{S}_F \neq \emptyset \\ M_{F,k} \qquad \text{otherwise} \end{cases} \tag{9}$$

$$M_{CR,k} = \begin{cases} \text{mean}_{WL}\left(\boldsymbol{S}_{CR}\right) \text{ if } \boldsymbol{S}_{CR} \neq \emptyset \\ M_{CR,k} \qquad \text{otherwise} \end{cases} \tag{10}$$

Where $\text{mean}_{WL}()$ stands for weighted Lehmer (11) mean.

$$\text{mean}_{WL}\left(\boldsymbol{S}\right) = \frac{\sum_{k=1}^{|S|} w_k \bullet S_k^2}{\sum_{k=1}^{|S|} w_k \bullet S_k} \tag{11}$$

Where the weight vector $\boldsymbol{w}$ is given by (12) and is based on the improvement in objective function value between trial and original individuals.

$$w_k = \frac{\text{abs}\left(f\left(\boldsymbol{u}_{k,G}\right) - f\left(\boldsymbol{x}_{k,G}\right)\right)}{\sum_{m=1}^{|S_{CR}|} \text{abs}\left(f\left(\boldsymbol{u}_{m,G}\right) - f\left(\boldsymbol{x}_{m,G}\right)\right)} \tag{12}$$

Moreover, since both arrays $\boldsymbol{S}_F$ and $\boldsymbol{S}_{CR}$ have the same size, it is arbitrary which size will be used for the upper boundary for m in (12).

The pseudo-code of the SHADE algorithm is depicted below.

4   Distance Based Parameter Adaptation

The original adaptation mechanism for scaling factor and crossover rate values uses weighted forms of means (11), where weights are based on the improvement in objective function value (12). This approach promotes exploitation over exploration, and therefore might lead to premature convergence, which could be a problem especially in higher dimensions.

Algorithm 2. SHADE

1: Set NP, H and stopping criterion;
2: $G = 0$, $\boldsymbol{x}_{best} = \{\}$, $k = 1$, $p_{min} = 2/NP$, $\boldsymbol{A} = \varnothing$;
3: Randomly initialize (1) population $\boldsymbol{P} = (\boldsymbol{x}_{1,G}, \ldots, \boldsymbol{x}_{NP,G})$;
4: Set $\boldsymbol{M}_F$ *and* $\boldsymbol{M}_{CR}$ according to (5);
5: $\boldsymbol{P}_{new} = \{\}$, $\boldsymbol{x}_{best}$ = best from population $\boldsymbol{P}$;
6: **while** stopping criterion not met **do**
7:     $\boldsymbol{S}_F = \varnothing$, $\boldsymbol{S}_{CR} = \varnothing$;
8:     **for** $i = 1$ to NP **do**
9:         $\boldsymbol{x}_{i,G} = \boldsymbol{P}[i]$;
10:        $r = U[1, H]$, $p_i = U[p_{min}, 0.2]$;
11:        Set F_i by (7) and CR_i by (8);
12:        $\boldsymbol{v}_{i,G}$ by mutation (6);
13:        $\boldsymbol{u}_{i,G}$ by crossover (3);
14:        **if** $f(\boldsymbol{u}_{i,G}) < f(\boldsymbol{x}_{i,G})$ **then**
15:            $\boldsymbol{x}_{i,G+1} = \boldsymbol{u}_{i,G}$;
16:            $\boldsymbol{x}_{i,G} \rightarrow \boldsymbol{A}$;
17:            $F_i \rightarrow \boldsymbol{S}_F$, $CR_i \rightarrow \boldsymbol{S}_{CR}$;
18:        **else**
19:            $\boldsymbol{x}_{i,G+1} = \boldsymbol{x}_{i,G}$;
20:        **end if**
21:        **if** $|\boldsymbol{A}| > NP$ **then**
22:            Randomly delete an ind. from $\boldsymbol{A}$;
23:        **end if**
24:        $\boldsymbol{x}_{i,G+1} \rightarrow \boldsymbol{P}_{new}$;
25:     **end for**
26:     **if** $\boldsymbol{S}_F \neq \varnothing$ and $\boldsymbol{S}_{CR} \neq \varnothing$ **then**
27:        Update $\boldsymbol{M}_{F,k}$ (9) and $\boldsymbol{M}_{CR,k}$ (10), k++;
28:        **if** $k > H$ **then**
29:            $k = 1$;
30:        **end if**
31:     **end if**
32:     $\boldsymbol{P} = \boldsymbol{P}_{new}$, $\boldsymbol{P}_{new} = \{\}$, $\boldsymbol{x}_{best}$ = best from population $\boldsymbol{P}$;
33: **end while**
34: **return** $\boldsymbol{x}_{best}$ as the best found solution

---

The distance approach is based on the Euclidean distance between the trial and the original individual, which slightly increases the complexity of the algorithm by replacing simple difference by Euclidean distance computation for the price of stronger exploration. In this case, scaling factor and crossover rate values connected with the individual that moved the furthest will have the highest weight (13).

$$w_k = \frac{\sqrt{\sum_{j=1}^{D} \left(u_{k,j,G} - x_{k,j,G}\right)^2}}{\sum_{m=1}^{|S_{CR}|} \sqrt{\sum_{j=1}^{D} \left(u_{m,j,G} - x_{m,j,G}\right)^2}} \tag{13}$$

Therefore, the exploration ability is rewarded, and this should lead to avoidance of the premature convergence in higher dimensional objective spaces. Such approach might also be useful for constrained problems, where constrained areas could be overcame by increased changes of individual's components.

5   Experimental Setting

The CEC 2015 benchmark set states that each function should be run 51 times and the stopping criterion should be set to $10{,}000 \times D$ objective function evaluations. These requirements were adhered to, and two-dimensional settings were selected $10D$ and $30D$ to provide a robust comparison. The convergence and population diversity were recorded for both versions of the tested algorithm – original SHADE and SHADE with distance based parameter adaptation abbreviated to Db_SHADE. The used population diversity measure is described in the next section.

Both algorithm variants had the same set of variable parameters – population size NP was set to 100, the maximum size of the optional archive $|A|$ was set to NP, and the historical memory size H was set to 10.

5.1   Population Diversity Measure

The Population Diversity (PD) measure used in this paper was described in [14] and is based on the sum of deviations (15) of individual's components from their corresponding means (14).

$$\overline{x_j} = \frac{1}{NP} \sum_{i=1}^{NP} x_{ij} \tag{14}$$

$$PD = \sqrt{\frac{1}{NP} \sum_{i=1}^{NP} \sum_{j=1}^{D} (x_{ij} - \overline{x_j})^2} \tag{15}$$

Where i is the population member iterator and j is the vector component iterator.

6   Results and Discussion

The comparative results for both dimensional settings are in Tables 1 and 2, where the last column depicts the result of the Wilcoxon rank-sum test with significance level of 0.05. No significant difference in performance between SHADE and Db_SHADE algorithm is represented by "=" sign when the SHADE algorithm performs significantly better; there would be "−" sign and when the distance based version performs significantly better, the "+" sign is used. As it can be seen from results in Table 1, the performance of both versions is comparable with only one win for the Db_SHADE algorithm. This was suspected as the dimensionality of the problem is quite low, and the SHADE algorithm does not

Table 1. SHADE vs. Db_SHADE on CEC2015 in 10D.

f	SHADE		Db_SHADE		Result
	Median	Mean	Median	Mean	
1	0.00E+00	0.00E+00	0.00E+00	0.00E+00	=
2	0.00E+00	0.00E+00	0.00E+00	0.00E+00	=
3	2.00E+01	1.89E+01	2.00E+01	1.92E+01	=
4	3.07E+00	2.97E+00	3.06E+00	2.98E+00	=
5	2.21E+01	3.42E+01	2.98E+01	4.52E+01	=
6	2.20E−01	2.97E+00	4.16E−01	8.08E−01	=
7	1.67E−01	1.88E−01	1.73E−01	1.91E−01	=
8	8.15E−02	2.69E−01	4.28E−02	2.06E−01	=
9	1.00E+02	1.00E+02	1.00E+02	1.00E+02	=
10	2.17E+02	2.17E+02	2.17E+02	2.17E+02	=
11	3.00E+02	1.66E+02	3.00E+02	2.01E+02	=
12	1.01E+02	1.01E+02	1.01E+02	1.01E+02	+
13	2.78E+01	2.78E+01	2.79E+01	2.76E+01	=
14	2.94E+03	4.28E+03	2.98E+03	4.66E+03	=
15	1.00E+02	1.00E+02	1.00E+02	1.00E+02	=

Table 2. SHADE vs. Db_SHADE on CEC2015 in 30D.

f	SHADE		Db_SHADE		Result
	Median	Mean	Median	Mean	
1	3.73E+01	2.62E+02	2.12E+01	2.42E+02	=
2	0.00E+00	0.00E+00	0.00E+00	0.00E+00	=
3	2.01E+01	2.01E+01	2.01E+01	2.01E+01	=
4	1.41E+01	1.41E+01	1.32E+01	1.31E+01	=
5	1.55E+03	1.50E+03	1.54E+03	1.52E+03	=
6	5.36E+02	5.73E+02	3.37E+02	3.48E+02	+
7	7.17E+00	7.26E+00	6.81E+00	6.74E+00	+
8	1.26E+02	1.21E+02	5.27E+01	7.38E+01	+
9	1.03E+02	1.03E+02	1.03E+02	1.03E+02	+
10	6.27E+02	6.22E+02	5.29E+02	5.32E+02	+
11	4.53E+02	4.50E+02	4.10E+02	4.16E+02	+
12	1.05E+02	1.05E+02	1.05E+02	1.05E+02	=
13	9.52E+01	9.50E+01	9.47E+01	9.50E+01	=
14	3.21E+04	3.24E+04	3.22E+04	3.24E+04	=
15	1.00E+02	1.00E+02	1.00E+02	1.00E+02	=

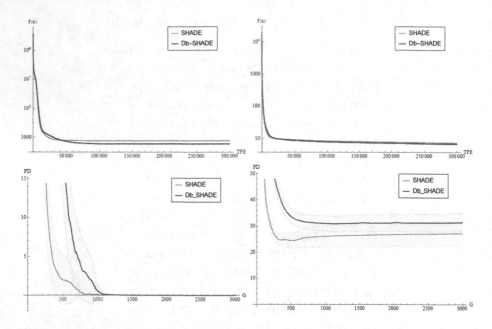

Fig. 1. Convergence plots (top) and population diversity plots (bottom) of CEC2015 test functions *f6* (left) and *f7* (right) in 30*D*.

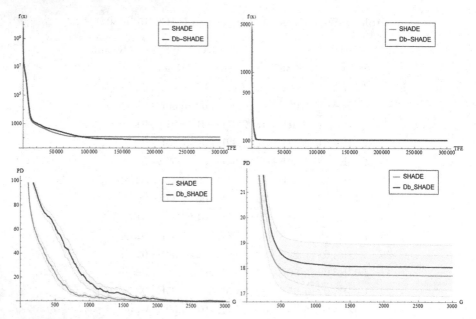

Fig. 2. Convergence plots (top) and population diversity plots (bottom) of CEC2015 test functions *f8* (left) and *f9* (right) in 30*D*.

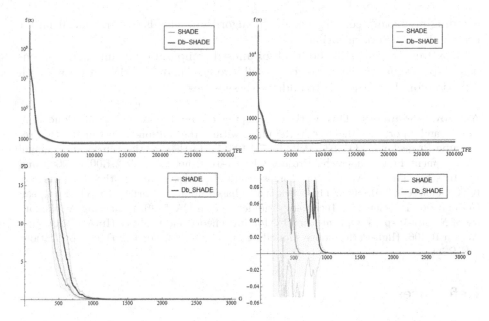

Fig. 3. Convergence plots (top) and population diversity plots (bottom) of CEC2015 test functions *f10* (left) and *f11* (right) in 30*D*.

tend to converge prematurely. The situation is more interesting in the second table, where there are 6 significantly different results in performance, and all of them are in favor of the Db_SHADE algorithm.

The convergence comparison plots and population diversity plots with confidence intervals are provided for the six functions in 30*D*, where the performance is significantly different in Figs. 1, 2 and 3. In these figures, it can be seen that the population diversity is maintained longer, which leads to a more explorative manner during the exploration phase of the algorithm, while the exploitation phase is still present in the later generations. As for the other functions from the benchmark with no significant difference in results, the population diversity is also higher in the case of Db_SHADE algorithm, but it does not help to improve the optimization result significantly. Therefore, the further study of the on-line effects of the distance based adaptation is needed.

7   Conclusion

This paper provided an analysis of the effect of distance based parameter adaptation in SHADE algorithm to population diversity. The analysis was done on two test cases – 15 test functions from the CEC2015 benchmark set in 10*D* and 30*D*. The presumption that the effect will be more visible in higher dimensional setting was confirmed. It can be seen, that the diversity of the population is maintained for a longer period, therefore prolonging the exploration phase and avoiding premature convergence of the algorithm. This is in turn beneficial for the result of the optimization.

However, there is still too much of unused computational time and the tendency for premature convergence is still strong. Therefore, the future research direction for the authors is to address these issues.

Acknowledgements. This work was supported by the Ministry of Education, Youth and Sports of the Czech Republic within the National Sustainability Programme Project no. LO1303 (MSMT-7778/2014), further by the European Regional Development Fund under the Project CEBIA-Tech no. CZ.1.05/2.1.00/03.0089 and by Internal Grant Agency of Tomas Bata University under the Projects no. IGA/CebiaTech/2018/003. This work is also based upon support by COST (European Cooperation in Science & Technology) under Action CA15140, Improving Applicability of Nature-Inspired Optimisation by Joining Theory and Practice (ImAppNIO), and Action IC406, High-Performance Modelling and Simulation for Big Data Applications (cHiPSet).

References

1. Price, K., Storn, R.: Differential evolution-a simple and efficient adaptive scheme for global optimization over continuous space. Technical report, International Computer Science Institute (1995)
2. Gämperle, R., Müller, S.D., Koumoutsakos, P.: A parameter study for differential evolution. Adv. Intell. Syst. Fuzzy Syst. Evol. Comput. **10**(10), 293–298 (2002)
3. Liu, J.: On setting the control parameter of the differential evolution method. In: Proceedings of the 8th International Conference on Soft Computing (MENDEL 2002), pp. 11–18 (2002)
4. Wolpert, D.H., Macready, W.G.: No free lunch theorems for optimization. IEEE Trans. Evol. Comput. **1**(1), 67–82 (1997)
5. Das, S., Mullick, S.S., Suganthan, P.N.: Recent advances in differential evolution-an updated survey. Swarm Evol. Comput. **27**, 1–30 (2016)
6. Tanabe, R., Fukunaga, A.: Success-history based parameter adaptation for differential evolution. In: 2013 IEEE Congress on Evolutionary Computation (CEC), pp. 71–78. IEEE (2013)
7. Tanabe, R., Fukunaga, A.S.: Improving the search performance of shade using linear population size reduction. In: 2014 IEEE Congress on Evolutionary Computation (CEC), pp. 1658–1665. IEEE (2014)
8. Guo, S.M., Tsai, J.S.H., Yang, C.C., Hsu, P.H.: A self-optimization approach for l-shade incorporated with eigenvector-based crossover and successful-parent-selecting framework on CEC 2015 benchmark set. In: 2015 IEEE Congress on Evolutionary Computation (CEC), pp. 1003–1010. IEEE (2015)
9. Awad, N.H., Ali, M.Z., Suganthan, P.N., Reynolds, R.G.: An ensemble sinusoidal parameter adaptation incorporated with l-shade for solving CEC 2014 benchmark problems. In: 2016 IEEE Congress on Evolutionary Computation (CEC), pp. 2958–2965. IEEE (2016)
10. Brest, J., Maučec, M.S., Bošković, B.: Single objective real-parameter optimization: algorithm jSO. In: 2017 IEEE Congress on Evolutionary Computation (CEC), pp. 1311–1318. IEEE (2017)

11. Yang, M., Li, C., Cai, Z., Guan, J.: Differential evolution with auto-enhanced population diversity. IEEE Trans. Cybern. **45**(2), 302–315 (2015)
12. Zhang, C., Zhao, Z., Yang, T., Fan, B.: Adaptive differential evolution with coordinated crossover and diversity-based population. In: 2016 12th IEEE International Conference on Control and Automation (ICCA), pp. 947–950. IEEE (2016)
13. Zhao, L., Sun, C., Huang, X., Zhou, B.: Differential evolution with strategy of improved population diversity. In: 2016 35th Chinese Control Conference (CCC), pp. 2784–2787. IEEE (2016)
14. Poláková, R., Tvrdík, J., Bujok, P.: Population-size adaptation through diversity-control mechanism for differential evolution. In: Proceedings of the 22nd International Conference on Soft Computing (MENDEL 2016), pp. 49–56 (2016)
15. Zhang, J., Sanderson, A.C.: JADE: adaptive differential evolution with optional external archive. IEEE Trans. Evol. Comput. **13**(5), 945–958 (2009)

Collaborative Variable Neighborhood Search

Nicolas Zufferey[1(✉)] and Olivier Gallay[2]

[1] Geneva School of Economics and Management, GSEM, University of Geneva,
Blvd du Pont-d'Arve 40, 1211 Geneva 4, Switzerland
n.zufferey@unige.ch
[2] Faculty of Business and Economics (HEC Lausanne), University of Lausanne,
Quartier UNIL-Dorigny, 1015 Lausanne, Switzerland
olivier.gallay@unil.ch

Abstract. Variable neighborhood search (VNS) is a well-known metaheuristic. Two main ingredients are needed for its design: a collection $M = (N_1, \ldots, N_r)$ of neighborhood structures and a local search LS (often using its own single neighborhood L). M has a diversification purpose (search for unexplored zones of the solution space S), whereas LS plays an intensification role (focus on the most promising parts of S). Usually, the used set M of neighborhood structures relies on the same type of modification (e.g., change the value of i components of the decision variable vector, where i is a parameter) and they are built in a nested way (i.e., N_i is included in N_{i+1}). The more difficult it is to escape from the currently explored zone of S, the larger is i, and the more capability has the search process to visit regions of S which are distant (in terms of solution structure) from the incumbent solution. M is usually designed independently from L. In this paper, we depart from this classical VNS framework and discuss an extension, Collaborative Variable Neighborhood Search (CVNS), where the design of M and L is performed in a collaborative fashion (in contrast with nested and independent), and can rely on various and complementary types of modifications (in contrast with a common type with different amplitudes).

Keywords: Metaheuristics · Variable neighborhood search

1 Introduction

As depicted in [1], modern methods for solving complex optimization problems are often divided into exact methods (e.g., dynamic programming, branch and bound) and metaheuristics [2]. An optimal solution can always be found with an exact method in a finite amount of time. Unfortunately, most real-life optimization problems are NP-hard, and therefore, exact methods would require too much computing time to find an optimal solution. For such difficult problems, it is thus better to quickly find a satisfying solution. A streamline heuristic can be

© Springer International Publishing AG, part of Springer Nature 2018
P. Korošec et al. (Eds.): BIOMA 2018, LNCS 10835, pp. 320–332, 2018.
https://doi.org/10.1007/978-3-319-91641-5_27

used if solution quality is not a crucial issue. Otherwise, a more advanced meta-heuristic is recommended. There are mainly two classes of metaheuristics: local search and population based methods. The former algorithms work iteratively on a single solution (e.g., descent local search, tabu search, variable neighborhood search), whereas the latter manage a set of solutions (e.g., genetic algorithms, ant colonies, adaptive memory algorithms).

A local search starts from an initial solution. Next, in each iteration, a *neighbor* solution s' is generated from the *current* solution s by performing a *move* on s (i.e., the structure of s is slightly modified to get s', according to predefined rules). In tabu search, to try to avoid cycling (i.e., coming back to an already visited solution), a *tabu list* forbids to perform the reverse of recently performed moves. The best non-tabu move is generally performed in each iteration. In most local search algorithms, only one neighborhood structure is used (i.e., a solution can only be modified according to a dedicated technique with a fixed ampli-tude, like changing one component of the solution). In contrast, Variable Neigh-borhood Search (VNS) [3] uses sequentially different neighborhood structures. A generic version of VNS is given in Algorithm 1, where $N_1, N_2, \ldots, N_r$ denote a finite set of neighborhoods, $N_i(s)$ is the set of solutions in the ith neighborhood of solution s, and L is the neighborhood structure used in the local search LS. In a classical VNS, the neighborhood structures $N_1, \ldots, N_r$ actually rely on the same type of move, but used with different amplitudes. For example, if a solu-tion s is a vector, N_i consists in changing the value of i components of s. The resulting collection M of neighborhood structures are thus dependent (i.e., they rely on the same type of modification) and nested (i.e., N_i is included in N_{i+1}).

Algorithm 1. Variable Neighborhood Search (VNS)

Generate an initial solution s and set $i = 1$

While no stopping criterion is met, **do**

1. *Shaking* (diversification): generate a neighbor solution s' in $N_i(s)$.
2. *Local search* (intensification): apply some local search method (with neighborhood L) with s' as initial solution, and let s'' be the returned solution.
3. *Relocate the search*: if s'' improves s, move there (set $s = s''$), and continue the search with N_1 (set $i = 1$); otherwise set $i = i + 1$, but if $i > r$, set $i = r$.

In this paper, starting from such a VNS framework, we discuss how the design of the neighborhood structures $N_1, \ldots, N_r$ and L can be enhanced in order to be performed in a collaborative and integrated fashion (note that integrated col-laboration also appears in some ant algorithms [4], but within a different frame-work). The resulting VNS is called CVNS (for Collaborative VNS). In contrast with the standard literature on VNS, depending on the involved problem struc-ture, the following features can appear in CVNS: (A) a strategic use of *destroying* neighborhood structures in M (i.e., moves which eliminate some pieces of the solution); (B) the use of a *central memory Mem* containing all the local minima encountered during the search, which is employed to design the stopping condition of *LS*. On the one hand, feature (A) allows for the joint action of moves of different types, resulting in a collaborative solution improvement process. On the other hand, feature (B) offers a way to collaboratively improve the performance of *LS* thanks to the sharing of information at a global level. In this contribution, we discuss the use of such features, and the performance of CVNS is highlighted with the use of three problems belonging to different fields: (1) job scheduling with time-window penalties (Sect. 2 relying on [5]); (2) nonlinear global optimization (Sect. 3 relying on [6]); (3) network design (Sect. 4 relying on [7]). Only a baseline study is given for each problem, and the reader is referred to the above three references to have more detailed information on the complexity issues, the literature review, the parameter setting, and a finer-grained presentation of the experiments, including the experimental conditions like the computer type, the programming language, etc. The main numerical results are highlighted in this work, which allows to observe the good performance of CVNS. A conclusion is provided in Sect. 5. For recent VNS variants, the reader is referred to [8–10].

2   Job Scheduling with Time-Window Penalties

2.1   Presentation of the Problem (P)

Make-to-order production systems are relevant to face the customized products requested at the clients level [11]. The associated just-in-time paradigm appears as a relevant approach to reduce the inventory costs. In such a context and because of the limited production capacity, scheduling jobs at the plant level can result in rejecting some orders [12]. Surprisingly, the literature on order acceptance problems involving earliness or tardiness penalties is limited [13,14]. Let (P) denote the considered NP-hard single-machine scheduling problem. It has the following features: sequence-dependent setup times and costs, earliness and tardiness penalties, and rejection penalties associated with the rejected jobs.

(P) can be presented as follows [15]. n jobs can be performed on a single machine, but two jobs cannot be processed concurrently. With each job j, the following information is associated: a due date d_j, a deadline $\bar{d}_j$, a rejection penalty u_j, an available date $\bar{r}_j$, a release date r_j, and a processing time p_j. Let S_j (resp. C_j) denote the starting time (resp. completion time) of job j. The following constraints are imposed for each job j: $S_j \geq \bar{r}_j$ and $C_j \leq \bar{d}_j$. If an accepted job j is not fully performed in time-window $[r_j, d_j]$, a penalty is encountered: if $S_j < r_j$ (resp. $C_j > d_j$), an earliness (resp. tardiness) penalty $E_j(S_j)$ (resp. $T_j(C_j)$) is paid, where $E_j(\cdot)$ (resp. $T_j(\cdot)$) is a non-increasing (resp. non-decreasing) function. In addition, a setup time (resp. cost) $s_{jj'}$ (resp. $c_{jj'}$) is encountered if two jobs j and j' of different families are consecutively performed. Idle times are allowed (indeed, they can have a positive impact on the earliness penalties), but preemptions are forbidden. Let $\sigma(s)$ (resp. $\Omega(s)$) be the sequence (resp. set) of accepted (resp. rejected) jobs associated with solution s. In order to measure the earliness/tardiness penalties of any solution s, it is necessary to first determine a starting time for each job of $\sigma(s)$. This is performed with a *timing procedure* [15] (this task is complex as idle times are allowed). The objective function to minimize is $f(s) = \sum_{j \in \sigma(s)} \left[E_j(S_j) + T_j(C_j) + c_{p_s(j)j} \right] + \sum_{j \in \Omega(s)} u_j$, where $p_s(j)$ is the predecessor of job j in $\sigma(s)$ (the predecessor of the first job is a dummy job representing the initial state of the machine).

2.2   CVNS for (P)

VNS has been applied to single-machine scheduling problems with different production environments [16]. When it is forbidden rejecting jobs, the neighborhood structures often consist in slightly changing the production sequence with move REINSERT or with move SWAP (as defined below). The strategic use of the move DROP (consisting in rejecting some jobs) is proposed in CVNS for (P).

Two methods are proposed for (P) in [15]: GR (a greedy heuristic) and TS (a tabu search using GR to generate an initial solution). GR consists in two phases: (1) sort the jobs by increasing slack times $(\bar{d}_j - \bar{r}_j - p_j)$; (2) sequentially insert the jobs in the solution s under consideration, at the position minimizing the augmentation of the costs (but a job is rejected if it is cheaper than to do it). Four types of moves are used in TS in order to modify the current solution s: ADD moves a job from $\Omega(s)$ to $\sigma(s)$; DROP moves a job from $\sigma(s)$ to $\Omega(s)$; REINSERT reschedules one job in $\sigma(s)$; SWAP exchanges the positions of two jobs in $\sigma(s)$. If a move leads to an unfeasible solution s' (as available dates or deadlines are not respected), s' is immediately repaired as follows: while s' remains unfeasible, the job whose rejection leads to the smallest cost is removed (and the starting/ending times are also updated with the timing procedure). Four tabu structures were employed after applying a move on solution s. The first forbids adding a dropped job for τ_1 (parameter) iterations. The second forbids dropping an added job for τ_2 iterations. The third forbids (during τ_3 iterations) moving again a job that has been swapped, reinserted or added. If j has been reinserted or swapped, the fourth tabu status forbids moving a job j between its two previous neighboring jobs (in $\sigma(s)$) for τ_4 iterations.

In CVNS for (P), the initial solution is also generated by GR. The way to switch from one neighborhood to another differs from the standard Algorithm 1. $N_i(s)$ consists in randomly dropping $i\%$ of the jobs from $\sigma(s)$ to $\Omega(s)$. Such a move DROP is used here to diversify the search. Parameter i is managed in order to focus the search away from the current solution when no improvement has been made for a long period. More precisely, the proportion of removed jobs grows exponentially with the number of iterations without improvement. In step (1) of Algorithm 1, the selected solution is the best among k (parameter) solutions generated randomly in $N_i(s)$. In step (2) of Algorithm 1, the above presented TS is applied for I (parameter) iterations, but without move DROP (as it appears in the shaking process).

2.3   Results

The uniform distribution was used to generate all the data. Two values are important for generating instances for (P): the number n of jobs, and a parameter α impacting the time interval within which release dates and due dates are generated. Formally, a value $Start$ is selected large enough, and End is computed as $Start + \alpha \sum_j p_j$. Next, each r_j (resp. d_j) is randomly chosen in $[Start, End]$ (resp. $[r_j + p_j, End]$). Linear and quadratic penalties are investigated. More precisely, the earliness (resp. tardiness) penalties are computed as $w_j(r_j - S_j)^{q_j}$ (resp. $w'_j(C_j - d_j)^{q'_j}$). The weights w_j and w'_j are randomly picked in $\{1, 2, 3, 4, 5\}$, whereas q_j and q'_j are selected in $\{1, 2\}$. p_j is an integer randomly generated in $[50, 100]$, and $u_j = \beta_j \cdot p_j$, where β_j is an integer randomly picked in interval $[50, 200]$. $\bar{d}_j$ and $\bar{r}_j$ are generated such that $T_j(\bar{d}_j) = E_j(\bar{r}_j) = u_j$. The number of job families is chosen randomly in $[10, 20]$. Finally, setup costs and setup times are related (as in practice): the setup time $s_{FF'}$ between jobs of families F and F' is selected randomly in $[50, 200]$, and the corresponding setup cost $c_{FF'}$ is computed as $\lfloor \gamma \cdot s_{FF'} \rfloor$, where γ is randomly chosen in interval $[0.5, 2]$.

The quick timing procedure proposed in [17] was adapted to evaluate a solution in TS and CVNS. GR, TS and CVNS were tested with a time limit $T(n)$ depending on n. As GR is quick, it is restarted as long as T is not reached, and it finally returns the best generated solution among the restarts. Table 1 summarizes the results. Column "Best-known" indicates the best-known objective function value for each instance (in \$). Next, for each method, the percentage gap between the average result (over 10 runs) and "Best-known" is given. Both local search approaches are better than GR, and CVNS outperforms TS. Indeed, CVNS obtains the best results for 11 instances out of 15, versus 5 for TS. In other words, a strategic use of move DROP appears to be a powerful exploration tool: the ingredients added to TS to derive CVNS are thus efficient.

Table 1. Results for a job scheduling problem

n	α	Best-known [\$]	GR [% gap]	TS [% gap]	CVNS [% gap]
25	0.5	46,860	0.4	0.13	0.05
	1	35,866	6.5	0	0
	2	8,172	21.25	0.75	1.33
50	0.5	137,567	6.47	4.26	2.32
	1	69,671	44.34	10.15	11.26
	2	6,123	166.39	30.91	19.52
75	0.5	198,633	19.68	6.52	6.06
	1	126,052	33.93	5.15	0.6
	2	11,199	246.3	41.58	32.86
100	0.5	332,731	21.32	8.36	6.63
	1	175,237	50.36	25.65	4.6
	2	20,459	124.39	39.34	17.98
150	0.5	561,422	23.49	3.92	4.8
	1	320,225	53.85	11.76	15.6
	2	66,585	16.34	63.2	9.59
Average			55.67	16.78	8.88

3   Nonlinear Global Optimization

3.1   Presentation of the Problem (P)

Problem (P) consists in finding a global minimum of the nonlinear optimization problem $\min_{x \in \mathbb{R}^n} f(x)$, where function $f : \mathbb{R}^n \to \mathbb{R}$ is twice differentiable, but has no special structure. Most of the literature on nonlinear optimization [18–21] is usually dedicated on the global convergence of algorithms toward a local optimum, with a fast local convergence. A point $x^\star$ is a *global* (resp. *local*) minimum of f if $f(x^\star) \leq f(x)$ for all $x \in \mathbb{R}^n$ (resp. if there exists $\varepsilon > 0$ such that $f(x^\star) \leq f(x)$ for each x such that $\|x - x^\star\| \leq \varepsilon$). An algorithm is *globally* (resp. *locally*) convergent if it converges to a (local) minimum from any starting point (resp. when it is converging to a (local) minimum when the starting point x_1 is in a given neighborhood of $x^\star$).

3.2   CVNS for (P)

The employed local search LS is able to prematurely stop its search if the iterates are converging to an already identified local minimum or if they are reaching an area of the solution space where no important improvement can be expected. LS relies on a trust region framework [20]. It is interrupted if one of the following conditions is verified: (1) a maximum number of iterations is reached; (2) LS has converged to a local minimum up to the desired precision; (3) LS seems to converge to an already identified local minimum; (4) the gradient norm is not large enough when the objective function value is far from the value at the best iterate; (5) a significant improvement of the objective function is not encountered. An efficient use of available information on f can strongly impact the design of the neighborhood structures. It was proposed to analyze the curvature of f at x based on the analysis of the eigenstructure of the Hessian matrix H, the approximation of the second derivatives matrix of f at x.

The main loop of CVNS is designed as follows. Let x be the current solution (which is the best visited solution, as in any classical VNS approach). Five neighborhood structures $N_1, \ldots, N_5$ are used (from the smallest N_1 to the largest N_5), and each time a neighborhood structure N_k is used, p candidates $x_1, \ldots, x_p$ (parameter tuned to 5) are generated in it and then improved with LS. If the five so performed LS have been prematurely stopped, a quick option consists in restarting the process with N_{k+1}. Otherwise (i.e., at least one local search application converged to a local minimum), the list Mem of local minima is updated. If the best local minimum of Mem is better (resp. not better) than x, the process is restarted with N_1 (resp. N_{k+1}), which represents a success (resp. a failure). The overall algorithm stops if N_5 has failed.

3.3   Results

CVNS was performed 100 times for each instance, and a run is successful if CVNS finds a global minimum. Two measures of performance are considered: the average percentage of success and the average number of function evaluations among the successful runs. This second criterion is very important when it is computationally cumbersome to evaluate a solution [22]. CVNS is compared with the following methods: (1) Direct Search Simulated Annealing (DSSA) [23]; (2) Continuous Hybrid Algorithm (CHA) [24]; (3) Simulated Annealing Heuristic Pattern Search (SAHPS) [25]; (4) Directed Tabu Search (DTS) [26]. Table 2 provides the number of successes over the 100 runs for 25 problems (left information), and the average number of function evaluations for successful runs on the same 25 problems (right information). Some of the cells associated with competitors are empty if the corresponding information was not available. First, CVNS appears to be the most robust method as it gets a success rate of 100% for almost all instances. Second, CVNS has the lowest average number of function evaluations for most instances. Interestingly, the efficiency of CVNS on Zakharov (Z_n) and Rosenbrock (R_n) functions is improving when the dimension n of the problem augments from 2 to 10. CVNS is also able to significantly reduce the average number of f-evaluations for instances R_{10} and Z_{10}.

Table 2. Results for nonlinear global optimization

Problem	CVNS		CHA		DSSA		DTS		SAHPS	
RC	100	153	100	295	100	118	100	212	100	318
ES	100	167	100	952	93	1442	82	223	96	432
RT	84	246	100	132	100	252			100	346
SH	78	366	100	345	94	457	92	274	86	450
DJ	100	104	100	371	100	273	100	446	100	398
HM	100	335			100	225				
GR_6	100	807			90	1830				
CV	100	854			100	1592				
DX	100	2148			100	6941				
Z_2	100	251	100	215	100	186	100	201	100	276
Z_5	100	837	100	950	100	914	100	1003	100	716
Z_{10}	100	1705	100	4291	100	12501	100	4032	100	2284
Z_{50}	100	17932	100	75520			0	177125		
$H_{3,4}$	100	249	100	492	100	572	100	438	95	517
$H_{6,4}$	100	735	100	930	92	1737	83	1787	72	997
$S_{4,5}$	100	583	85	698	81	993	75	819	48	1073
$S_{4,7}$	100	596	85	620	84	932	65	812	57	1059
$S_{4,10}$	100	590	85	635	77	992	52	828	48	1035
R_2	100	556	100	459	100	306	100	254	100	357
R_5	100	1120	100	3290	100	2685	85	1684	91	1104
R_{10}	100	2363	83	14563	100	16785	85	9037	87	4603
R_{50}	100	11934	79	55356			100	510505		
R_{100}	100	30165	72	124302			0	3202879		

4   Network Design

4.1   Presentation of the Problem (P)

In the context of large-scale production-distribution networks, the considered problem (P) is an extension of the two-echelon multicommodity CFLPSS (capacitated facility location problem with single sourcing) with alternative facility configurations, direct shipments from manufacturing facilities, and inventory holding costs. The design of a supply chain network implies strategic decisions for: (1) opening/closing production and distribution centers; (2) reconfiguring some of these centers; (3) specifying their mission according to (a) the products they have to produce or stock and (b) the customers they should deliver. The related recent literature, usually on simpler problems, includes [27–30].

Consider a network made of sites for potential PDCs (production-distribution centers) $u \in U$ and DCs (distribution centers) $w \in W$. They represent locations where a facility could be opened, or alternatively, existing facilities. The plants are able to manufacture a set of finished products $p \in P$. A product is actually a group of items needing the same type of production capacity. For each p, it may be possible to produce it only on a subset of sites $U_p \subseteq U$. The facilities have to deliver external demand zones (group of ship-to-points located in a specified geographical area) $d \in D$. Only a subset $P_d \subseteq P$ of products might be requested from a demand zone d. Finished products can be stocked in the PDCs, for which the mission consists in supplying the DCs and some demand zones (direct shipments). Each demand zone has to be delivered by a single source (either a PDC or a DC). In addition, in order to satisfy some predefined service criteria (e.g., next day delivery), a facility $s \in S$ could deliver only a subset of demand zones $D_s \subseteq D$ or, conversely, only a subset $S_d \subseteq S = U \cup W$ of the sites are positioned to supply a given demand zone $d \in D$.

The production/storage capacity and the fixed/variable costs characterize the configuration of each existing facility. Alternative configurations can be implemented for each potential site, corresponding to: (a) the addition of new space and/or equipment to augment its capacity; (b) a re-engineering of current equipments/layouts; (c) other facility specifications for the new sites. Therefore, a set J_s of possible configurations can be implemented for each site $s \in S$ of the potential network. For the considered planning horizon, each configuration $j \in J_s$ is characterized by the following information: a production capacity, a flexible storage capacity, a fixed exploitation cost, and a variable throughput cost (covering the relevant procurement/reception/production/handling/shipping expenses). The objective function to minimize is the sum of the following costs: configuration costs for the facilities (fixed + variable), inventory holding costs, and transportation costs. The constraints to satisfy are: the capacity constraints, the flow equilibrium in each node of the network, and the clients' demand satisfaction.

4.2   CVNS for (P)

First, note that only feasible solutions are generated. The following options are considered when performing a move: (1) each demand from zones $d \in D$ is supplied by any of the open center $s \in S_d$ while respecting the service criteria; (2) the capacity constraints (i.e., minimum and maximum) of the used configurations are all satisfied; (3) if there is a demand from a zone d which can only be supplied from a single center (i.e., if $|S_d| = 1$), then the center is always set as open during the search process. Moreover, if for each $p \in P_d$, the demand x_{pd} from a zone $d \in D_w$ is reassigned to a DC $w \in W$, then a new requirement (equal to x_{pd}) is created for the opened PDCs that can ship product p to DC w. The same kind of additional requirements can be designed when an existing PDC is closed. In both cases, the requirements induced at the first echelon are assigned to the second echelon center u with the lowest production and transportation cost, given that a configuration j with sufficient capacity can be employed. If there is not enough capacity, the outstanding requirement is attributed to the next best plant. This implies that the DCs can be delivered by various plants.

Let $W(v) \subseteq W$ (resp. $U(v) \subseteq U$) be the subset of opened DCs (resp. PDCs) associated with solution v. In other words, a pair $(W(v), U(v))$ characterizes each solution v. In the shaking phase of CVNS, the best neighbor solution is chosen, and the stopping condition is a time limit. Five neighborhood structures are used, denoted as N_1 to N_5. (1) $v' \in N_1(v)$ if a PDC is closed but another is opened. (2) $v' \in N_2(v)$ if an additional PDC is opened. (3) $v' \in N_3(v)$ if a PDC is closed. (4) $v' \in N_4(v)$ if an additional DC is opened. (5) $v' \in N_5(v)$ if a DC is closed. As the number of potential DCs is usually far above the number of PDCs, it is appropriate to test many possibilities for $W(v)$. Therefore, the W-shift moves (i.e., a DC is closed but another is opened) will be employed within the local search LS of CVNS.

Two important points related to the design of the above neighborhood structures should be raised: (1) which demand zones should be attributed to a center that is newly available (this is identified with add/shift moves); (2) to which centers must the demands of a closed center (identified with a drop-move or a shift-move) be reassigned? In both cases, the involved costs are the configuration/transportation/production/inventory costs. In order to tackle issue (2), suppose that center s' has to be opened. It is appropriate to assign demand zone $d \in D_{s'}$ to s' instead of its current supplier s if the sum of the costs is decreased, and if the minimum capacity constraint remains satisfied for s. It was however observed that such a reassignment of demands often leads to an infeasible solution s' according to its minimum capacity constraint. To repair it, additional clients are given to s' as follows. While the minimum capacity constraint of s' is violated, a demand zone $d \in D_{s'}$ that is not already delivered by s' is randomly chosen. If there exists an assignment (s'', d) (involving an already open s'') that leads to a solution with superior costs than the assignment (s', d), then d is assigned to s'. If such an assignment does not exist, s' cannot be opened. Issue (1) is tackled as follows. For each demand zone d associated with the investigated center to be closed, d is simply reassigned to the best (according to the costs) possible open center s_b. In the two cases, the tightest center configuration is chosen (i.e., the feasible capacity configuration with the smallest fixed cost).

Let v denote the current solution. The five neighborhood structures are used as follows, starting with $M = \{N_1, \ldots, N_5\}$. In the shaking phase of Algorithm 1, instead of initially choosing $i = 1$, i is randomly picked in $\{1, 2, \ldots, 5\}$, and the best solution v' in $N_i(v)$ is chosen. LS is then applied on v' to get v''. Next, if v'' outperforms v, M is set to $\{N_1, \ldots, N_5\}$ and v is updated (i.e., set $v = v''$). Otherwise: if $|M| > 1$, N_i is removed from M; but if $|M| = 1$, M is set back to $\{N_1, \ldots, N_5\}$. The next neighborhood structure in the shaking phase is then randomly chosen in M.

The employed LS is a tabu search using the W-shift moves (w, w') such that w and w' can supply common demand zones. When a W-shift move (w, w') is performed, it is then forbidden to close (resp. open) w' (resp. w) for a certain number of iterations. LS is stopped when a maximum number I of iterations without improving the best solution encountered so far is reached. Note that the use of filtering techniques [31] might be very helpful to reduce the search space.

4.3   Results

CVNS was tested on a 32-bit 2 GHz Dual Core computer with 1 GB of RAM. An exact method relying on CPLEX was also developed. Random instances with various sizes and cost structures were generated, based on realistic cases documented in [32]. A uniform distribution is used to generate the demand for the different demand zones, with lower/upper bounds based on the total production capacity of the network. It was always assumed that demand zones had to be delivered from facilities located at a distance up to 530 miles from its centroid. Different sizes were obtained by modifying the potential PDCs (4 or 6, with four possible configurations for each PDC), the potential DCs (60 or 100, with two possible configurations for each DC), the demand zones (500 or 1000), and the number of product families (3 or 20).

Average results (with computing times indicated in minutes) are summarized in Table 3, depending on the instances characteristics. The percentage gaps of CVNS are computed with respect to the optimal costs. The focus is put on four components: the number $|P|$ of products (3 or 20), the number $|D|$ of demand

Table 3. Results for a network design problem

Characteristics	CPLEX		CVNS	
	Opt. cost [$]	Time	Gap [%]	Time
$|D| = 500$ demand zones	69,207,275	341.58	0.89	12.5
$|D| = 1000$ demand zones	134,420,183.3	409.17	0.79	14.17
$|P| = 3$ products	25,726,628.25	217.92	1.43	13.33
$|P| = 20$ products	177,900,830	532.83	0.26	13.33
$(|U|, |W|) = (4, 60)$ centers	103,763,688.3	297	0.99	10
$(|U|, |W|) = (6, 100)$ centers	99,863,769.92	453.75	0.7	16.67

zones (500 or 1000), the number of centers ($|U| = 4$ or 6 PDCs, $|W| = 60$ or 100 DCs). Anytime a component is fixed, the three other components vary. One can conclude that on average: (1) CPLEX requires 375 min to find an optimal solution; (2) CVNS is able to find very competitive solutions (as the average gap is 0.84%) in 13 min. Moreover, CVNS appears to be very efficient with a large number of products (indeed, the average gap gets close to 0.30% in such cases). Finally, CVNS is more competitive if more decision variables are involved, which is a good indicator if larger instances have to be tackled.

5   Conclusion

The performance of a metaheuristic can be evaluated according to several criteria [1]: (1) quality (value of the obtained results according to a given objective function); (2) speed (time needed to get competitive results); (3) robustness (sensitivity to variations in problem characteristics and data quality); (4) ease of adaptation; (5) ability to take advantage of problem structure. The CVNS methodology has a good overall behavior according to these criteria. Indeed, for the above presented applications, the solution encoding and the employed moves account for the problem specific features. Next, CVNS is easy to adapt because it only relies on two ingredients (which have to be designed in a collaborative fashion): a local search LS and a collection M of neighborhood structures. In addition, the strategic use of M plays a key role in robustness. The quickness of LS leads to the quickness of CVNS (it is usually the case if an aggressive method is used, such as tabu search). Finally, quality is ensured because of the intensification capability of LS combined with the diversification ability of M. Among the future works on CVNS, we can mention the integration of other learning mechanisms [33] to better guide the search.

References

1. Zufferey, N.: Metaheuristics: some principles for an efficient design. Comput. Technol. Appl. **3**(6), 446–462 (2012)
2. Gendreau, M., Potvin, J.Y.: Handbook of Metaheuristics. International Series in Operations Research & Management Science, vol. 146. Springer, Heidelberg (2010). https://doi.org/10.1007/978-1-4419-1665-5
3. Mladenovic, N., Hansen, P.: Variable neighborhood search. Comput. Oper. Res. **24**, 1097–1100 (1997)
4. Zufferey, N.: Optimization by ant algorithms: possible roles for an individual ant. Optim. Lett. **6**(5), 963–973 (2012)
5. Thevenin, S., Zufferey, N.: Variable neighborhood search for a scheduling problem with time window penalties. In: Proceedings of the 14th International Workshop on Project Management and Scheduling (PMS 2014), Munich, Germany, April 2014
6. Bierlaire, M., Thémans, M., Zufferey, N.: A heuristic for nonlinear global optimization. INFORMS J. Comput. **22**(1), 59–70 (2010)
7. Amrani, H., Martel, A., Zufferey, N., Makeeva, P.: A variable neighborhood search heuristic for the design of multicommodity production-distribution networks with alternative facility configurations. Oper. Res. Spectr. **33**(4), 989–1007 (2011)

8. dos Santos, J.P.Q., de Melo, J.D., Neto, A.D.D., Aloise, D.: Reactive search strategies using reinforcement learning, local search algorithms and Variable Neighborhood Search. Expert Syst. Appl. **41**, 4939–4949 (2014)

9. Li, K., Tian, H.: A two-level self-adaptive variable neighborhood search algorithm for the prize-collecting vehicle routing problem. Appl. Soft Comput. **43**, 469–479 (2016)

10. Stenger, A., Vigo, D., Enz, S., Schwind, M.: An adaptive variable neighborhood search algorithm for a vehicle routing problem arising in small package shipping. Transp. Sci. **47**(1), 64–80 (2013)

11. Mansouri, S.A., Gallear, D., Askariazad, M.H.: Decision support for build-to-order supply chain management through multiobjective optimization. Int. J. Prod. Econ. **135**, 24–36 (2012)

12. Oguz, C., Salman, F.S., Yalcin, Z.B.: Order acceptance and scheduling decisions in make-to-order systems. Int. J. Prod. Econ. **125**, 200–211 (2010)

13. Atan, M.O., Akturk, M.S.: Single CNC machine scheduling with controllable processing times and multiple due dates. Int. J. Prod. Res. **46**, 6087–6111 (2008)

14. Shabtay, D., Gaspar, N., Yedidsion, L.: A bicriteria approach to scheduling a single machine with job rejection and positional penalties. J. Comb. Optim. **23**, 395–424 (2013)

15. Thevenin, S., Zufferey, N., Widmer, M.: Tabu search for a single machine scheduling problem with discretely controllable release dates. In: 12th International Symposium on Operations Research in Slovenia (SOR 2013), pp. 1590–1595 (2013)

16. Liao, C.J., Cheng, C.C.: A variable neighborhood search for minimizing single machine weighted earliness and tardiness with common due date. Comput. Ind. Eng. **52**, 404–413 (2007)

17. Hendel, Y., Sourd, F.: An improved earliness-tardiness timing algorithm. Comput. Oper. Res. **34**, 2931–2938 (2007)

18. Bertsekas, D.P.: Nonlinear Programming, 2nd edn. Athena Scientific, Belmont (1999)

19. Bierlaire, M.: Introduction à l'optimisation différentiable. Presses Polytechniques et Universitaires Romandes, Lausanne, Switzerland (2013)

20. Conn, A.R., Gould, N.I.M., Toint, P.L.: Trust-Region Methods. Series on Optimization. MPS-SIAM, Philadelphia (2000)

21. Nocedal, J., Wright, S.J.: Numerical optimization. Operations Research. Springer, New York (1999). https://doi.org/10.1007/978-0-387-40065-5

22. Silver, E., Zufferey, N.: Inventory control of an item with a probabilistic replenishment lead time and a known supplier shutdown period. Int. J. Prod. Res. **49**, 923–947 (2011)

23. Hedar, A., Fukushima, M.: Hybrid simulated annealing and direct search methods for nonlinear unconstrained global optimization. Optim. Methods Softw. **17**, 891–912 (2002)

24. Chelouah, R., Siarry, P.: Genetic and nelder-mead algorithms hybridized for a more accurate global optimization of continuous multiminima functions. Eur. J. Oper. Res. **148**, 335–348 (2003)

25. Hedar, A., Fukushima, M.: Heuristic pattern search and its hybridization with simulated annealing for nonlinear global optimization. Optim. Methods Softw. **19**, 291–308 (2004)

26. Hedar, A., Fukushima, M.: Tabu search directed by direct search methods for nonlinear global optimization. Eur. J. Oper. Res. **170**, 329–349 (2006)

27. Ahuja, R.K., Orlin, J.B., Pallattino, S., Scaparra, M.P., Scutella, M.G.: A multi-exchange heuristic for the single-source capacitated facility location problem. Manag. Sci. **50**(6), 749–760 (2004)
28. Barahona, F., Chudak, F.A.: Near-optimal solutions to large-scale facility location problems. Discret. Optim. **2**, 35–50 (2005)
29. Michel, L., Hentenryck, P.V.: A simple tabu search for warehouse location. Eur. J. Oper. Res. **157**, 576–591 (2004)
30. Zhang, J., Chen, B., Ye, Y.: A multi-exchange local search algorithm for the capacitated facility location problem. Math. Oper. Res. **30**(2), 389–403 (2005)
31. Hertz, A., Schindl, D., Zufferey, N.: Lower bounding and tabu search procedures for the frequency assignment problem with polarization constraints. 4OR **3**(2), 139–161 (2005)
32. Ballou, R.H.: Business Logistics Management. Prentice Hall, Upper Saddle River (1992)
33. Schindl, D., Zufferey, N.: A learning tabu search for a truck allocation problem with linear and nonlinear cost components. Naval Res. Logist. **62**(1), 32–45 (2015)

Author Index

Printed in the United States
By Bookmasters